Critical Essays on

HERMAN MELVILLE'S
"BENITO CERENO"

CRITICAL ESSAYS
ON
AMERICAN LITERATURE

James Nagel, General Editor
University of Georgia, Athens

Critical Essays on

HERMAN MELVILLE'S *"BENITO CERENO"*

edited by

ROBERT E. BURKHOLDER

G. K. Hall & Co. / New York
Maxwell Macmillan Canada / Toronto
Maxwell Macmillan International / New York Oxford Singapore Sydney

G. K. Hall & Co.　　　　　Maxwell Macmillan Canada, Inc.
Macmillan Publishing Company　　　1200 Eglinton Avenue East
866 Third Avenue　　　　　Suite 200
New York, New York 10022　　Don Mills, Ontario M3C 3N1

Macmillan Publishing Company is part of the Maxwell Communication Group of Companies.

Library of Congress Cataloging-in-Publication Data

Critical essays on Herman Melville's "Benito Cereno" / edited by
　Robert E. Burkholder.
　　p.　　cm — (Critical essays on American literature)
　　ISBN 0-8161-7317-6 (alk. paper)
　　1. Melville, Herman, 1819–1891.　Benito Cereno.　I. Burkholder,
Robert E.　II. Series.
PS2384.B42C75　1992
813′.3—dc20
　　　　　　　　　　　　　　　　　　　　92-10831
　　　　　　　　　　　　　　　　　　　　CIP

The paper used in this publication meets the minimum requirements of American National Standard
for Information Sciences—Permanence of Paper for Printed Library Materials. ANSI Z3948-1984.∞™

10　9　8　7　6　5　4　3　2　1

Printed in the United States of America

For Val,
Adam, and Emily

Contents

◆

General Editor's Note	ix
Publisher's Note	xi
Introduction	1
ROBERT E. BURKHOLDER	

Notices and Essays

[Notice of *The Piazza Tales*] *The Christian Freeman and Family Visiter*	19
[Notice of *The Piazza Tales*] *The Knickerbocker*	20
[Melville's Timonism in "Benito Cereno"] LEWIS MUMFORD	21
["Benito Cereno": "A Masterpiece of Mystery, Suspense and Terror"] STERLING BROWN	24
[The Failure of "Benito Cereno"] NEWTON ARVIN	26
Critical Problems in Melville's "Benito Cereno" JOSEPH SCHIFFMAN	29
Herman Melville and the American National Sin: The Meaning of "Benito Cereno" SIDNEY KAPLAN	37
["Benito Cereno" and the Gothic Horror of Slavery] LESLIE FIEDLER	48

"Apparent Symbol of Despotic Command": Melville's
Benito Cereno   50
   H. BRUCE FRANKLIN

["The Mechanism of Mystification" in "Benito Cereno"]   58
   WARNER BERTHOFF

"Benito Cereno": Melville's Fable of Black Complicity   65
   KERMIT VANDERBILT

Benito Cereno: Slavery and Violence in the Americas   76
   JOYCE SPARER ADLER

The Monastic Slaver: Images and Meaning in "Benito
Cereno"   94
   GLORIA HORSLEY-MEACHAM

"Benito Cereno" and Manifest Destiny   99
   ALLAN MOORE EMERY

The Legal Fictions of Herman Melville and Lemuel Shaw   116
   BROOK THOMAS

Reenvisioning America: Melville's "Benito Cereno"   127
   SANDRA A. ZAGARELL

Benito Cereno and New World Slavery   146
   ERIC J. SUNDQUIST

Benito Cereno: Melville's De(con)struction of the Southern
Reader   168
   CHARLES SWANN

"Follow Your Leader": The Theme of Cannibalism in
Melville's *Benito Cereno*   182
   STERLING STUCKEY

The Riddle of the Sphinx: Melville's "Benito Cereno" and
the *Amistad* Case   196
   CAROLYN L. KARCHER

Past, Present, and Future Seemed One   230
   H. BRUCE FRANKLIN

Index   247

General Editor's Note

◆

This series seeks to anthologize the most important criticism on a wide variety of topics and writers in American literature. Our readers will find in various volumes not only a generous selection of reprinted articles and reviews but original essays, bibliographies, manuscript sections, and other materials brought to public attention for the first time. This volume, *Critical Essays on Herman Melville's "Benito Cereno,"* is the most comprehensive collection of essays ever published on one of the most important works of fiction in the nineteenth century. It contains both a gathering of early reviews and a broad selection of more modern scholarship as well. Among the authors of reprinted articles and reviews are Lewis Mumford, Sterling Brown, Leslie Fiedler, Warner Berthoff, Joyce Sparer Adler, and Sandra A. Zagarell. In addition to a substantial introduction by Robert E. Burkholder, which provides a particularly insightful survey of the history of scholarship on Herman Melville's enigmatic novel, there are also three original essays commissioned specifically for publication in this volume: new studies by Sterling Stuckey on the theme of cannibalism, Carolyn L. Karcher on the *Amistad* case, and H. Bruce Franklin on the historical backgrounds of *Benito Cereno.* We are confident that this book will make a permanent and significant contribution to the study of American literature.

JAMES NAGEL
University of Georgia, Athens

Publisher's Note

◆

Producing a volume that contains both newly commissioned and reprinted material presents the publisher with the challenge of balancing the desire to achieve stylistic consistency with the need to preserve the integrity of works first published elsewhere. In the Critical Essays series, essays commissioned especially for a particular volume are edited to be consistent with G. K. Hall's house style; reprinted essays appear in the style in which they were first published, with only typographical errors corrected. Consequently, shifts in style from one essay to another are the result of our efforts to be faithful to each text as it was originally published.

Introduction

♦

ROBERT E. BURKHOLDER

In the midst of his harrowing day aboard the *San Dominick*, Captain Amasa Delano spies an old man who "looked like an Egyptian priest" fashioning an intricate knot from some tangled strands of rope.[1] When Delano approaches the old man to discover the meaning of the knot, all of his questions are answered with riddles, and the old man finally flings the completed knot at the captain and says, "Undo it, cut it, quick."

This incident has been and continues to be a focal point for the criticism of Melville's "Benito Cereno," a set piece or "tableau," as Melville himself calls it, that, like the shaving scene or the lunch in Cereno's cabin, has become a pivotal cipher for the stratified meanings of the story as a whole. But on a different level of understanding, Delano's encounter with the old man with the knot anticipates the critic's encounter with Melville's text. Certainly on a relatively rudimentary interpretive level, the critic can assign meaning to any given incident in the text, just as Delano does when he observes that "The knot seemed a combination of double-bowline-knot, treble-crown-knot, back-handed-well-knot, knot-in-and-out-knot, and jamming-knot." But to place a name on a given thing or circumstance is not at all to undo it in an interpretive sense, but merely to cast it into familiar terms that may have the effect of demystifying it without yielding up anything like a sense of its complete meaning. If one assumes that it is something approaching complete meaning that critics have attempted to cut to when presented with the knot of Melville's text, then it is also apparent that those same critics, circumscribed, as is Delano, by epistemology or language or historicity, have generally failed to undo the knot that Melville has made in "Benito Cereno."

If this observation of the critical history of "Benito Cereno" seems to devalue critics' efforts to undo Melville's knot, that is not the intention. Rather, it should be understood that the volume and variety of the criticism of this tale serves as fitting testimony both to the complexity of what Melville

1

wrought and the inherent limitations of the practice of criticism itself. "The voyage of the best ships is a zigzag line of a hundred tacks," Emerson says in "Self-Reliance," and the history of the criticism of Melville's text, laden as it is with such explosive potential for interpretation, has been just such a voyage.

"Benito Cereno," the vessel that holds these multiform meanings, was probably composed during the winter of 1854–1855, during the extended period of ill health, financial distress, and professional uncertainty that followed the commercial failures of *Moby-Dick* and *Pierre*.[2] Upon completion of the story, Melville submitted it to *Putnam's Monthly Magazine*, one of the two principal outlets for his magazine fiction (the other being *Harper's Monthly Magazine*) in April 1855. Despite some reluctance on the part of George William Curtis, literary adviser to Dix and Edwards, who had just purchased *Putnam's* in March 1855, the story was accepted for publication, Melville was paid his usual rate of five dollars per printed page for it on 31 July, and it appeared in successive issues of the magazine in October, November, and December 1855. When his financial troubles forced him to propose to Dix and Edwards a volume of collected tales in December 1855, Melville actually considered calling the collection *Benito Cereno & Other Sketches*, but by February he submitted the manuscript for the collection along with the newly composed sketch that would give the volume its title, "The Piazza."

There are at least two important reasons for the dearth of reviews of "Benito Cereno." One is certainly the circumstances of its publication—it was published first in a magazine and, therefore, would under ordinary circumstances have received little attention from reviewers in that form. It was subsequently published as part of a collection of six tales, and in this case it had to vie for the reviewer's attention with the other stories in *The Piazza Tales*. But even these facts do not account for the cursory nature of the reviews of Melville's collection so much as the extraordinary personal and professional debacle of *Pierre*. In fact, Brian Higgins notes that both *Israel Potter* (1855) and *The Piazza Tales* "were not as widely noticed as Melville's books prior to *Pierre*," implying a causal relationship between the public trashing of Melville's novel and a perceived fall-off in the critical attention afforded to his successive work.[3] Harold Bloom has gone even farther in suggesting that after *Pierre* Melville's readership could literally be counted on the fingers of one hand: "What was left of Melville's audience was killed off by the dreadful *Pierre*, a year after *Moby-Dick*, and despite various modern salvage attempts *Pierre* certainly is unreadable, in the old-fashioned sense of that now critically abused word. You just cannot get through it, unless you badly want and need to do so. The best of *The Piazza Tales* show the post-*Pierre* Melville writing for himself, possibly Hawthorne, and a few strangers."[4]

And as one's audience goes, so goes the interest the reviewers take in one's work, or so one might surmise from the notices and reviews that touch on "Benito Cereno." In his bibliography of writings about Melville, Brian Higgins lists only two notices of the publication of "Benito Cereno" in *Putnam's*, one in the 6 October 1855 New York *Citizen*, which notes that the "animated tale" has been commenced in the October issue, and the other in the 25 November New York *Dispatch*, which notes the conclusion of the story in the December 1855 *Putnam's* and predicts that thousands will read with pleasure the resolution of the story's mystery. With the publication of *The Piazza Tales* in May 1856, "Benito Cereno" was once again offered up to the reviewers, but not surprisingly few took the opportunity to deal with the compound mysteries of Melville's tale. Higgins lists thirty-six reviews of the collection that appeared within the year of its publication, and of these no more than five devote some attention to "Benito Cereno." In the wake of the overwhelmingly bad reviews of *Pierre*, *The Piazza Tales* actually received rather positive reviews, perhaps because, as several of the reviewers pointed out, Melville was perceived as having abandoned the linguistic and metaphysical opacity that characterized the former to return to the more accessible style and subject matter of *Typee* and *Omoo*.[5] This view was somewhat modified by an anonymous reviewer in the New York *Churchman* for 5 June 1856, who saw the tales as representing the "just mean" between the stylistic extremes of *Typee* and *Moby-Dick*. Other reviewers sought to explain Melville's new work through comparison with the tales of Charles Brockden Brown, or Irving, or Hawthorne, or Poe.[6] But there were still those reviewers who had seemingly insurmountable problems with Melville's style, like the commentator in *Godey's Lady's Book and Magazine* (53 [September 1856], 277), who complained that "we cannot read his productions with much satisfaction. His style has an affectation of quaintness, which renders it, to us, very confused and wearisome."

Of those reviews that treat "Benito Cereno" specifically, most give it only slight attention, citing it as a great imaginative accomplishment, as does the reviewer in the Boston *Christian Freeman and Family Visiter* for 13 June 1856, or seeing it as melodramatic (New York *Daily Times*, 27 June 1856, 5) or as no real improvement on Melville's earlier romances of the sea (New York *Daily Tribune*, 23 June 1856, 3). Perhaps the most interesting of all the early reviews was that in the Richmond-based *Southern Literary Messenger* for June 1856. One might expect the *Messenger* to be thin-skinned about stories dealing with slave revolts, but its reviewer, without specifically mentioning "Benito Cereno," praised *The Piazza Tales* in general as Melville's return to "his former freshness and vivacity" after the "unfortunate" appearance of *Pierre*.[7]

From the beginning of the Melville revival in the 1920s, "Benito Cereno" has been a text that simultaneously drew the reader into its mystery and directed his attention elsewhere. In the former instance, the text provides interstices that the reader is implicitly asked to fill with his imagination, and in the latter, the reader is implicitly pointed toward an inquiry into the circumstances of Melville's time and the genuine and possible sources for the story that may inform the tensions and gaps that beckon the reader into the text. The first important scholarship published on "Benito Cereno" is a case in point. In "Melville's *Benito Cereno* and Captain Delano's Voyages," Harold H. Scudder discusses, albeit briefly, his discovery that Melville's tale is based on Chapter 18 of Amasa Delano's *Narrative of Voyages and Travels in the Northern and Southern Hemispheres: Comprising Three Voyages Round the World; Together with a Voyage of Survey and Discovery, in the Pacific and Oriental Islands* (Boston: E. G. House, 1817).[8] In fact, Scudder's claim of derivativeness is much stronger than the above characterization of it. He actually says that Melville "merely rewrote this Chapter, including a portion of one of the legal documents there appended, suppressing a few items, and making some small additions" (Scudder, 502). Six decades of critical commentary have shown just how overstated Scudder's claim is, but more to the point, Scudder's reprinting of the pertinent parts of Delano's *Narrative* directed potential critics to Melville's text by offering Delano's actual account as a means of answering the questions raised by Melville.[9] In so doing, Scudder generated new questions that once dictated and continue to influence critical approaches to "Benito Cereno," including the question of what sorts of changes Melville made in his source and why those changes were made. Moreover, in directing potential critics to a source external to Melville's text, Scudder opened the door to those questions of sources, context, history, and politics that have become increasingly important to critical investigations of "Benito Cereno." That is not to say that such questions were entirely unimportant to early critics of Melville's tale, but as the influential comments on the novella by John Freeman and Lewis Mumford suggest, first judgments were just as likely to be made on a general preference for Melville's work as on a serious consideration of the issues raised in the text.[10]

In several extraordinary ways, critical commentary on "Benito Cereno" serves as a sort of gauge to the competing claims of those critical and theoretical schools that have dominated the academy for the past half century. Certainly an important reason for this particular story's ability to produce such an effect is that its subject matter and structure and the complexity of its point of view seem to place it beyond the sorts of assumptions that can be comfortably made about less eccentric works of prose fiction. For example, most of those who have written about "Benito Cereno" would agree that the novella has three distinct parts—the long opening section, apparently from Delano's point of view, that focuses on the American captain's perceptions aboard the *San Dominick*; the "official" deposition of Benito Cereno before the court in Lima; and, finally, the brief "coda" or conclusion that deals with events that occur both before *and* after Cereno's appearance in court. It is a chronology that is certainly less than straightforward, but the interpretive possibilities are clouded by the further mystification of exactly how many points of view are represented in these three sections. Are there three (Delano,

Cereno, and, at least implicitly, Babo), or four (add the authorial point of view that may or may not be the same as the implied narrator's which may, in fact, be a fifth), or should we see Babo's point of view as an absence that is notable principally because, for whatever reason, Melville does not give it to us explicitly? On these questions and many others the criticism of "Benito Cereno" has turned. But these questions seem only to lead us to still larger questions that address the very essence of the ways in which we read and assign meaning to what we read.

Perhaps the largest of these questions is whether a work as fragmented and apparently mystifying as "Benito Cereno" can be considered a self-contained work of literature with an intrinsic "artistic" or literary integrity, or whether there are questions outside the text itself that should be brought to bear on our attempts to locate meaning in it. If one considers Richard Ohmann's characterization of the New Criticism in *English in America*, the reasons for the failure of criticism of the late 1940s through the 1960s adequately to deal with "Benito Cereno" become clear. Ohmann says, "The world is complex, discordant, dazzling. We want desperately to know it as unified and meaningful, but action out in the world fails to reveal or bring about a satisfying order. The order we need *is* available in literature; therefore literature must be a better guide to the truth than are experience and action."[11] Fortunately or unfortunately, the effect of "Benito Cereno" is ultimately not to enfold the reader, either of the 1850s or the 1990s, within the protective embrace of unifying aesthetic experience. Instead, it tends to turn the reader back into the very "complex, discordant, dazzling" world that the reader may well be seeking to escape. For this reason, those critics who have wanted "Benito Cereno" to be other than it is, and especially those who have attempted to locate the unity within it, have met with mixed success.

The earliest of these formalists was not really a formalist at all. In April 1855, George William Curtis, then a literary adviser to Dix and Edwards, responded to the manuscript of "Benito Cereno" in a letter to J. A. Dix that characterized the story as "very good," but added that "It is a great pity [Melville] did not work it up as a connected tale instead of putting in the dreary documents at the end. — They should have made part of the substance of the story. It is a little spun out, —but it is very striking & well done: and I agree with Mr. Law that it ought not to be lost." In a follow-up letter to Dix, Curtis made it clear that he believed that Melville's apparent problems of artistic control were the result of a desperate rush to finish too much. "He does everything too hurriedly now," Curtis reported to Dix on 20 April. And by July, when he was recommending that Dix get Melville's tale into print, Curtis was also advising that he would "alter all the dreadful statistics" at the end of the story, a comment which causes him to lament to Dix, "Oh! dear, why can't Americans write good stories. They tell good lies enough, & plenty of them."[12]

What is most significant about Curtis's judgment of "Benito Cereno" is that he saw the story as effective, but despite his acknowledgment of Melville's success he wished that the story was more ordinary in regard to narrative form. What Curtis did not acknowledge, however, is that throughout his career Melville had been an experimentalist with narrative form, and that especially in his shorter works of the mid-1850s he demonstrates a desire to push past accepted fictional forms into methods of storytelling that redefine the possibilities of the short story or novella.[13] Such at least seems to be the case in works like "The Encantadas" or "The Paradise of Bachelors and The Tartarus of Maids." Perhaps Melville's own apparent desire to challenge contemporaneous social and political assumptions and norms is reflected in analogous challenges to aesthetic norms. In fact, perhaps the indisputable fact of the latter is sufficient evidence to demonstrate the truth of the former. Or perhaps, as Robert Shulman has argued, romantic artists like Poe, Hawthorne, and Melville may have felt intellectually and spiritually pinched by the acquisitive society of Jacksonian America that they "came to see as a prison." Thus each invented a version of "the style of the inmate, the techniques of symbolic indirection and symbolic intensification [that] allowed them to communicate and conceal, to satisfy the demands of their vision and commitments and also to disguise them from unsympathetic readers."[14] Whatever the case might be, it is certain that Curtis, limited perhaps too much by bourgeois taste and a desire for the conventionally fulfilling narrative, was unable to view Melville's experiments as much more than a failure to meet rather commonplace expectations.

What is somewhat surprising is that similar judgments would be brought to bear on "Benito Cereno" a century later by some of the most astute and revered American literary critics of the mid—twentieth century. Chief among these was F. O. Matthiessen. Matthiessen could hardly be accused of lack of interest in social or historical aspects of literature, but according to Giles Gunn, he acquired a New Critical bias from T. S. Eliot that he found confirmed in other critics whom he regarded highly.[15] Therefore, as Russell Reising maintains, Matthiessen "continued to struggle with the social context of both poetry and the poet, but his aesthetic stance in *American Renaissance* contradicts his deep concern with social matters too fundamentally to influence later critics to pursue a balanced line of inquiry" (Reising, 173). Matthiessen's treatment of "Benito Cereno" in *American Renaissance* is a case in point.

While Matthiessen discusses *Pierre* as a product in part of Melville's concern over American social problems,[16] his consideration of "Benito Cereno" seeks aesthetic categories extrinsic to Melville's social milieu as the standard for critical judgment. Matthiessen claims that even though symbolical values are distinct in Melville's tale, "the embodiment of good in the pale Spanish captain and of evil in the mutinied African crew, though pictorially and theatrically effective, was unfortunate in raising unanswered questions. Although the Negroes were savagely vindictive and drove a terror of blackness into Cereno's heart, the fact remains that they were slaves and that evil had thus originally been done to them. Melville's failure to reckon with this fact within the limits of his narrative makes all its prolonged suspense, comparatively superficial" (Matthiessen, 508). It is most interesting to note the tension inherent in Matthiessen's claim. On the one hand, he believes Melville does a much better job of laying the symbolical groundwork for tragedy in "Benito Cereno" than in *Pierre*. However, Melville's supposed ignorance of the Africans' justification for their revolt blurs distinct symbolical or allegorical values, ultimately diffusing the potential power of the tragedy he intended "Benito Cereno" to be, making this finished tale that Melville thought good enough to consider as the title tale for his collection of short fiction a less successfully realized work of art than *Billy Budd*, a work left unfinished at Melville's death and, consequently, a text woven from complex and often arguable editorial choices.[17]

Yet even in his disparagement of Melville's achievement in "Benito Cereno," Matthiessen is straining after something of a balanced view of the work by implying that the extrinsic facts of history can somehow muddle the effect of the author's assumed aesthetic intent. Such, however, is not the case in Newton Arvin's outright dismissal of the story as "an artistic miscarriage, with moments of undeniable power."[18] Whereas Matthiessen was willing to grant Melville credit for the creation of distinct symbolical values that are, nevertheless, compromised by the reader's awareness of the existing crime of slavery or her difficulty in identifying with the weak Captain Cereno, Arvin is unwilling to credit Melville with any such success, arguing that "Of moral meaning, indeed, there is singularly little. This is partly because the two or three leading personages are too simply conceived to be the bearers of any greatly significant burden" (Arvin, 240). To Arvin, then, Delano is "moral simplicity in a form that borders on weak-wittedness," Babo is "a monster out of Gothic fiction at its worst," and Cereno is "not only hopelessly unheroic, as an image of persecuted goodness, but he is not even deeply pathetic" (Arvin, 240). Thus, according to Arvin, the moral structure of the tale is completely undermined, and when this failure is combined with "torpid prose rhythms" and an atmosphere that is "tediously and wastefully" built up, "Benito Cereno" becomes, in Arvin's eyes, not only the most "unduly celebrated" of Melville's fictions but also perhaps his greatest artistic failure.

Because of the unequivocal nature of Arvin's criticism of "Benito Cereno" and the unchallenged professional authority of Arvin and Matthiessen, much of the work done on the story during the 1950s and early 1960s focused on answering perhaps the most basic question of all: Is "Benito Cereno," considered by aesthetic standards, a successful piece of literature? Even Leslie Fiedler, who astutely recognized that black stereotypes were being used by Melville, finds the end of the story unsatisfactory and suggests that Poe was better than Melville at the sort of theatrical gothicism he found at work in

8 ♦ ROBERT E. BURKHOLDER

the tale.[19] Because aesthetic standards remained for many critics the basis of the defense of the story, those who stepped forward to make a case for Melville's brilliance in "Benito Cereno" found that they were arguing in terms first defined by Matthiessen and Arvin. Therefore, one might say that the bases for such defenses were really differences in taste or a sense of loyalty to Melville. For instance, in 1960, Richard Harter Fogle attempted to resolve disagreements over the quality of "Benito Cereno" by arguing that mystery itself is the unifying agent in the tale.[20]

In 1962, Warner Berthoff focused his examination of "Benito Cereno" in his *The Example of Melville* on the inadequacy of the interpretations of those, like Arvin, who saw the tale as the product of Melville's "flagging vitality and depleted inventiveness."[21] Rather than dismissing the tale as a failure because it does not meet extrinsic standards of tragedy or moral allegory, Berthoff, following Fogle, substitutes an intrinsic unifying agent— the irresolvable nature of the story's central mystery. Dubbing this irresolvability "the mechanism of mystification," Berthoff argues that "the story can fairly be seen as composing a paradigm of the secret ambiguity of appearances—an old theme with Melville—and, more particularly, a paradigm of the inward life of ordinary consciousness, with all its mysterious shifts, penetrations, and side-slippings, in a world in which this ambiguity of appearances is the baffling norm" (Berthoff, 153). Curiously, while Berthoff is willing to see Melville's rejection of moral argument, dramatic sensation, and preconceived formality of design as positive choices, in that Melville apparently decided to pursue truth at the expense of meeting the aesthetic and moral expectations of a century of readers and critics, he is also quick to make the argument that "Benito Cereno" does in fact conform to the demands of a subjective formality that Melville himself imposed. Thus, through a strange twist of reasoning, "Benito Cereno" is indeed a formal artistic success because it is the self-contained expression of the artist's defiance of conventional extrinsic demands. Moreover, the terms of its success are exactly those that constituted the story's failure for Matthiessen and Arvin. Perhaps the only way to avoid such ingenious arguments is merely to rest on the general claim that Lawrance Thompson made in a 1972 essay on "Benito Cereno": "Many puzzled critics have insisted that the story, considered as a work of art, is weak and superficial because Melville here failed to take a position against slavery. Such fault-finding seems to be derived, once again, from a failure on the part of critics, to stay with Melville's art long enough to understand the viable subtleties of it."[22]

Positioned against those critics who would view "Benito Cereno" strictly on the basis of its perceived fulfillment of certain formal requirements is that line of investigation that attempts to discover and, in Thompson's words, "to understand the viable subtleties" of Melville's art. Unlike those considerations of the story that focus on its aesthetic success or failure, most or all of the latter group of essays are essentially historicist in approach; focus on particulars rather than universals; deal with possible sources, both historical and literary; explore the matrix of political, social, and personal experiences and attitudes that may be represented in "Benito Cereno"; and ultimately ask larger questions, not only about Melville's personal position on slavery, but also about the way in which that wrenching political, social, and human issue may have affected the culture of the nation. In other words, whereas the formalists wanted to argue whether or not Melville's story was an aesthetic success when measured against formal requirements, historicists implicitly accept the power of the tale to communicate a reality, and, through a variety of concerns, they attempt to discover what that reality might be. There is, then, in this line of criticism a singular aversion to viewing "Benito Cereno" within the frame of tragedy or moral allegory and a refusal to accept moral ambiguity as its final message. Perhaps because of the demonstrated willing-ness of critics working in this vein to continue to push beyond the frontiers of what is accepted and known, this line of criticism has opened new and exciting areas of inquiry about "Benito Cereno," while at the same time raising questions of the limits of historicism as a critical tool.

Among those who deserve some credit for initiating the historicist line of inquiry into interpretive work on "Benito Cereno," is Sterling Brown, whose brief treatment of Melville's tale in his 1937 work, *The Negro in American Fiction*, explicitly argues, on the basis of Melville's perceived opposi-tion to slavery, for a reading which recognizes that "Because Melville was unwilling to look upon men as 'Isolatoes,' wishing instead to discover the 'common continent of man,' he comes nearer the truth in his scattered pictures of a few unusual Negroes than do the other authors of the period."[23] Brown's work was followed by that of Charles I. Glicksberg and Joseph Schiffman, both of whom, in different ways, concentrate on Babo's central importance to the tale.[24] Nearly simultaneously in 1950, Glicksberg and Schiffman published separate considerations of "Benito Cereno," both of which argue for Melville's essentially positive treatment of the African revolu-tionaries in the tale. Most controversially, Schiffman reasoned that "in select-ing a theme of slave rebellion, and in treating Babo and his fellow slaves as able, disciplined people, as capable of evil as the white man, [Melville] treated the Negro as an individual. Both subject and treatment were condi-tioned by the 1850s, and both subject and treatment marked advances for American literature." In Schiffman's view, an elaboration of Brown's earlier assertions, "Babo emerges the moral victor in 'Benito Cereno' " (Schiffman, 323).

Schiffman's claims not only significantly enhanced the development of a line of argument central to the history of interpretation of "Benito Cereno," they also served as a catalyst for one of the most important essays published on Melville's novella—Sidney Kaplan's "Herman Melville and the American National Sin: The Meaning of 'Benito Cereno.' "[25] Kaplan's essay is notable for a number of reasons, not the least of which is that it proposes a strict historicist approach to the novella but also arrives at interpretive conclusions diametrically opposed to Brown, Glicksberg, and Schiffman. Because of this opposition, Kaplan's work represents one pole in the evolving historicist debate about "Benito Cereno," just as the work of Brown and his successors represents the other. Moreover, in taking a position that argues for the affinity of Melville's characterization of blacks with prevailing racist attitudes of his own day, Kaplan's work has served as a lightning rod for much of the left-leaning criticism of the 1970s and 1980s.

Specifically, Kaplan's two-part essay first examines what he dubs "the lineage of *Benito Cereno*"—that is, Melville's depiction of black characters in his novels from *Typee* to *Moby-Dick*. From this survey Kaplan concludes that while Melville's black characters seem to represent "an ascending development" from stock minstrel-show figures to more humanized portraits, in reality Melville's confusion over the problem of slavery and its possible solution was profound; that his political leanings were those of "a liberal democrat in a period when the official Democracy was moving into stronger and stronger alliance with the Southern slavocracy" (Kaplan, 331); and that whatever his feelings for blacks as human beings, Melville consistently depicted the prospect of slave revolt as problematic if not a justification for vigilance or even brutal oppression. For Kaplan, then, the idea of Babo as heroic revolutionary or moral victor is impossible. He is, in fact, "the embodiment of 'malign evil' " that springs in part from Melville's own fears of widespread slave uprisings in the South—the prospect of which, Kaplan believes, serves as a significant element of the historical context that informs "Benito Cereno." Kaplan concludes that "looked at objectively, the tale seems a plummet-like drop from the unconditionally democratic peaks of *White-Jacket* and *Moby-Dick*—an 'artistic sublimation' not, as Schiffman maintains, of anti-slaveryism, but rather of notions of black primitivism dear to the hearts of slavery's apologists, a sublimation in fact of all that was sleazy, patronizing, backward and fearful in the works that preceded it" (Kaplan, 26). Despite the apparent iconoclasm of the particular slant that Kaplan gives his historically based reading, it is interesting to note that his argument anticipates the recent, more theoretically sophisticated work of Wai-Chee Dimock who, in arguing that Melville internalized the logic of Manifest Destiny, imprisons the author in the same deterministic cell that Kaplan's work suggests.[26]

To suggest Kaplan's iconoclasm is also to suggest a tentative critical consensus that began to emerge not long after the appearance of Kaplan's essay. A rough census of bibliographic citations for work on "Benito Cereno" reveals an interesting if not surprising fact.[27] The years 1930 through 1959 saw relatively few essays published that dealt wholly or in part with "Benito Cereno." In the fifties, for instance, only 23 citations appear in standard bibliographies, but the number balloons to 58 in the 1960s, 86 in the 1970s, and 49 in the 1980s. Or, we might say that the number of citations for the years 1970 through 1989 nearly doubles the number for the years 1930 through 1969. There is little doubt that too much can be made of such a census, reflecting, as it surely does, the growth of the academic profession and increased pressures to publish, both to get employed and to stay that way. Nevertheless, it's interesting to speculate about other possible reasons for the astounding growth in the critical attention devoted to "Benito Cereno" in the last twenty years. When one does so, it's impossible to ignore the relationship of interest in the story to the revolutionary social and cultural changes that began in the 1960s, received their most dramatic expression in the 1970s, and were refined under the influence of a growing interest in literary theory in the 1980s. If such speculation has any truth to it at all, then it's not unreasonable to suggest that "Benito Cereno" has attracted so much attention from a generation of critics deeply affected by the Vietnam War and the Civil Rights movement exactly because it is a text that lends itself to the expression of ideas that arise from an awareness of and response to those particular social and political traumas or others of the 1960s and 1970s. Specific considerations of the novella, such as James Matlack's "Attica and Melville's 'Benito Cereno' " or Marvin Fisher's treatment of parallels between Melville's tale and various politically inspired acts of the 1970s in *Going Under*,[28] certainly demonstrate that "Benito Cereno" can be seen as a palimpsest through which the events of recent history can be read. However, to suggest that such is literally the case in much of the recent criticism would be wrong.

The criticism of the last two decades might be seen as taking shape around the generally shared assumption that "Benito Cereno" is a veritable web of history, and that all of the historical associations suggested in the text as well as the historical context of the fiction and its composition deserve exploration. Recent criticism of the novella has thus turned away from the notion that the tale's point is its mystification to locate possible meanings that emerge from the intersection of its history and recent attitudes, events, and movements. But if much of the recent criticism shares in this essentially historicist assumption, there is also such an extraordinary volume of it that it is next to impossible to find a navigable course through it. Therefore, the categories I offer to characterize the critical concerns of the last twenty years are tentative at best and are meant to suggest only one way of ordering the energetic pluralism of approach and response that "Benito Cereno" has inspired most recently.

One prominent line of investigation might best be characterized as that which deals in some way with what Carolyn L. Karcher has identified as "the issue on which critics have deadlocked in interpreting 'Benito Cereno'— whether Melville champions or condemns the rebels."[29] Karcher's own work in *Shadow Over the Promised Land* is unquestionably the most substantial consideration of this question, but it has also figured prominently in the work of Jean Fagin Yellin, Kermit Vanderbilt, and Joyce Sparer Adler, among others.[30] What distinguishes Karcher's work, however, is that she builds a detailed and compelling argument for "Benito Cereno" as an indictment of slavery by examining the story in the context of Melville's career, focusing on how the expression of related social concerns in "The Paradise of Bachelors and The Tartarus of Maids" and "The Bell-Tower" gives us a model for reading Melville's tale of slave revolt.[31]

A related line of investigation that has evolved through the 1980s is that which considers the problem of ideology as a factor in both the composition and interpretation of "Benito Cereno." Much of the work in this vein is based on the assumption that given the story's subject and Melville's approach to it, it's reasonable to assume that it is a critique of the dominant capitalist and expansionist ideology of the time. With the recent exception of Dimock's work, which argues that Melville was co-opted by the very dominant ideology that he sought to undermine,[32] critics writing in this vein have generally testified to the effectiveness of Melville's pointed social criticism. Perhaps the first and one of the most notable examples of such ideological criticism is Michael Paul Rogin's *Subversive Genealogy*, a work that considers "Benito Cereno" against the backdrop of the European revolutions of 1848 and finally argues for viewing the novella as Melville's reproach to Hawthorne for his defense of slavery in his campaign biography of Franklin Pierce.[33] Other work in this vein includes that by Eric Sundquist, James Kavanaugh, Alan Moore Emery, and Sandra A. Zagarell—all of whom attempt to articulate both the true subject of Melville's critique as well as the nature of the rhetorical mechanism for realizing that criticism. Sundquist, for instance, treats the story as a commentary on America's betrayal of its own revolutionary values; Kavanaugh's complex argument demonstrates how the use of what Althusser termed "internal distantiation" (i.e., placing the reader *inside* the text to view and judge the action from an "internal distance") enables Melville to critique the consensus ideology of his day in a marketable form; Emery shifts emphasis away from the question of slavery to examine what he believes to be Melville's real object of criticism—American expansionism; and Zagarell argues that "Benito Cereno" attacks American values and institutions, revising Americans' sense of their own history "by destabilizing a range of cultural conventions from Americans' self-proclaimed benevolence to their unconscious authoritarianism."[34]

A final line of inquiry, closely related to the two discussed above, has also had the effect of broadening the possible areas of interpretive concern in the text of "Benito Cereno." Here work ranges from Gloria Horsley-Meacham's attempt to link the story to Melville's understanding of the connection between New World slavery and the Catholic Church to Brook Thomas's work on the ways in which Melville's fiction reflects his response to legal opinions rendered by his father-in-law, Lemuel Shaw, chief justice of the Massachusetts Supreme Court.[35] This category would also include the iconoclastic work of Charles Swann, who has read "Benito Cereno" as both a mystery story and as Melville's deconstruction of the Southern reader, and that of Sterling Stuckey and Joshua Leslie who, through traditional archival research, have unearthed and published documents that support the reading of "Benito Cereno" as a critique of slavery.[36]

The new work published in this volume is well within the rough consensus just articulated. Sterling Stuckey's consideration of the theme of cannibalism in "Benito Cereno" builds on his own previously published work with Joshua Leslie and adds to considerations of that theme by John Harmon McElroy and Barbara J. Baines, among others.[37] Carolyn L. Karcher's treatment of the link between the *Amistad* case and "Benito Cereno" reinforces her previous work on the novella in *Shadow Over the Promised Land*, but it also adds a wealth of new evidence to Karcher's contention that the story is "an exploration of the white racist mind and how it reacts in the face of a slave insurrection" (Karcher, 128). Finally, special mention must be made of the contribution of H. Bruce Franklin which, in a very real sense, punctuates this collection. In 1961 Franklin published an essay on William Stirling's *Cloister Life of the Emperor Charles the Fifth* as a source for "Benito Cereno."[38] Since then that essay has become pivotal in the history of the criticism of the novella, generally acknowledged as being as important as Scudder's publication of Chapter 18 of Delano's *Narrative*, and cited more frequently than any other work on Melville's tale. In his contribution to this volume, Franklin, now one of our most respected cultural critics, pursues the images of inquisition and empire that he first explored in the 1960s, giving much greater scope to both his own earlier discovery and his evolving sense of the historical contexts of the novella. In that sense, Franklin's essay serves not only to remind us of where the criticism of "Benito Cereno" has been, it also suggests several important directions that readings of the tale may take in the future.

Notes

1. Herman Melville, "Benito Cereno," in *The Piazza Tales and Other Prose Pieces*, ed. Harrison Hayford, Alma A. MacDougall, G. Thomas Tanselle, et al. (Evanston and Chicago: Northwestern University Press and the Newberry Library, 1987), 75–76.

2. Much of my information on the circumstances surrounding the composition and publication of "Benito Cereno" is from Lea Bertani Vozar Newman, *A Reader's Guide to the Short Stories of Herman Melville* (Boston: G. K. Hall, 1986), 95–153; Merton M. Sealts, Jr., "Historical Note," in Melville, *The Piazza Tales*, esp. 476–97; and Sealts, *Pursuing Melville: 1940–1980* (Madison: University of Wisconsin Press, 1982), 230–31.

3. Higgins, *Herman Melville: An Annotated Bibliography, Volume I: 1846–1930* (Boston: G. K. Hall, 1979), iv; for a detailed discussion of the reception of *Pierre*, see Leon Howard and Hershel Parker, "Historical Note," in Melville, *Pierre or The Ambiguities* (Evanston and Chicago: Northwestern University Press and the Newberry Library, 1971), 379–92; and Higgins and Parker, "Introduction," in *Critical Essays on Herman Melville's* Pierre; or, The Ambiguities (Boston: G. K. Hall, 1983), 15–21.

4. Bloom, "Introduction," in *Modern Critical Views: Herman Melville* (New York: Chelsea House, 1986), 1.

5. See the reviews in the *Berkshire County Eagle* (Pittsfield, Mass.), 30 May 1856, and the Newark *Daily Advertiser*, 18 June 1856.

6. See the reviews in the New Bedford *Daily Mercury*, 4 June 1856, 2; the New York *Dispatch*, 8 June 1856; the Springfield (Mass.) *Republican*, 9 July 1856, 1; the London *Athenaeum* no. 1500 (26 July 1856): 929; and the *United States Magazine and Democratic Review* 38 (September 1856): 172.

7. Besides Higgins's admirable summaries of the notices and reviews of "Benito Cereno" one should see Sealts, "Historical Note," in Melville, *The Piazza Tales*, 501–9; Watson G. Branch, ed., *Melville: The Critical Heritage* (London: Routledge & Kegan Paul, 1974), 354–60; and Jay Leyda, ed., *The Melville Log: A Documentary Life of Herman Melville*, 2 vols. (New York: Harcourt Brace, 1951), 2: 510–22.

8. Scudder, "Melville's *Benito Cereno* and Captain Delano's Voyages," *PMLA* 43 (1928): 502–32; hereafter cited in text.

9. For those essays that deal directly with Melville's use of Delano's *Narrative* as a source, see Rosalie Feltenstein, "Melville's 'Benito Cereno,' " *American Literature* 19 (1947): 245–55; Margaret Y. Jackson, "Melville's Use of a Real Slave Mutiny in 'Benito Cereno,' " *College Language Association Journal* 4 (1960): 79–93; Max Putzel, "The Source and Symbols of Melville's 'Benito Cereno,' " *American Literature* 34 (1962): 191–206; Marjorie C. Dew, "*Benito Cereno*: Melville's Vision and Revision of the Source," in Gross, ed., *A Benito Cereno Handbook*, 178–84; David C. Galloway, "Herman Melville's *Benito Cereno*: An Anatomy," *Texas Studies in Literature and Language* 9 (1967): 239–52; and Robert J. Ward, "From Source to Achievement in 'Benito Cereno,' " *Anglo-American Studies* 2 (1982): 233–40.

10. See John Freeman, *Herman Melville* (London: Macmillan, 1926), 145–48, and Lewis Mumford, *Herman Melville* (New York: Harcourt, Brace, 1929), 244–47.

11. Ohmann, *English in America: A Radical View of the Profession* (New York: Oxford University Press, 1976), 75.

12. Leyda, ed., *The Melville Log*, 2: 500–501, 504; also quoted in Newman, *A Reader's Guide*, 95–96.

13. This point of view is effectively developed by Nina Baym in "Melville's Quarrel with Fiction," *PMLA* 94 (October 1979): 909–23.

14. Shulman, *Social Criticism & Nineteenth-Century American Fictions* (Columbia: University of Missouri Press, 1987), 176–77.

15. Gunn, *F. O. Matthiessen: The Critical Achievement* (Seattle: University of Washington Press, 1975), 72; quoted in Russell Reising, *The Unusable Past: Theory and the Study of American Literature* (New York: Methuen, 1986), 173; hereafter cited in text.

16. Matthiessen, *American Renaissance: Art and Expression in the Age of Emerson and Whitman* (New York: Oxford University Press, 1941), 468–69; hereafter cited in text.

17. See Matthiessen's discussion of *Billy Budd* in *American Renaissance*, 500–514. Since the appearance of Matthiessen's views, readers have been supplied with an authoritative text of *Billy Budd*: See *Billy Budd, Sailor*, ed. Harrison Hayford and Merton M. Sealts, Jr. (Chicago: University of Chicago Press, 1962).

18. Arvin, *Herman Melville* (New York: William Sloane, 1950), 238–40; hereafter cited in text.

19. Fiedler, *Love and Death in the American Novel*, revised edition (New York: Stein & Day, 1966), 400–401.

20. Fogle, "*Benito Cereno*," in *Melville's Shorter Tales* (Norman: University of Oklahoma Press, 1960), 147.

21. Berthoff, *The Example of Melville* (Princeton: Princeton University Press, 1962), 150; hereafter cited in text.

22.   Thompson, "Afterword," in Melville, *Benito Cereno* (Barre, Mass.: Imprint Society, 1972), 133.

23.   Brown, *The Negro in American Fiction* (Washington, D.C.: Association of Negro Folk Education, 1937), 13.

24.   Glicksberg, "Melville and the Negro Problem," *Phylon* 2 (1950): 207–15; Schiffman, "Critical Problems in Melville's 'Benito Cereno,' " *Modern Language Quarterly* 11 (1950): 317–24; hereafter cited in text.

25.   Kaplan, "Herman Melville and the American National Sin: The Meaning of 'Benito Cereno,' " *Journal of Negro History* 41 (1956): 311–38; 42 (1957): 11–37; hereafter cited in text. Also see Allen Guttmann's important rebuttal to Kaplan in "The Enduring Innocence of Captain Amasa Delano," *Boston University Studies in English* 5 (1961): 35–45.

26.   See Dimock, *Empire for Liberty: Melville and the Poetics of Individualism* (Princeton: Princeton University Press, 1989).

27.   My census involved collating citations from the following sources: Brian Higgins, *Herman Melville: An Annotated Bibliography, Vol. 1: 1846–1930*; Newman, *A Reader's Guide*, 145–53; Lewis Leary, *Articles in American Literature 1900–1950; 1950–1967; 1968–1975*, 3 vols. (Durham: Duke University Press, 1954, 1970, 1979); and, for those years not covered by Leary, *The MLA International Bibliography of Books and Articles on the Modern Languages and Literatures*.

28.   Matlack, "Attica and Melville's 'Benito Cereno,' " *American Transcendental Quarterly* 26 (1975): 18–23; Fisher, *Going Under: Melville's Short Fiction and the American 1850's* (Baton Rouge: Louisiana State University Press, 1977), 104–17.

29.   Karcher, *Shadow Over the Promised Land: Slavery, Race, and Violence in Melville's America* (Baton Rouge: Louisiana State University Press, 1980), 127–28. Karcher does go on to state that she does not believe that Melville formulated the problem in exactly these terms; nevertheless, this is the issue that seems to command the most attention among recent critics.

30.   See Yellin, "Melville's 'Benito Cereno,' " in *The Intricate Knot: Black Figures in American Literature, 1776–1863* (New York: New York University Press, 1972), 215–27; Vanderbilt, " 'Benito Cereno': Melville's Fable of Black Complicity," *Southern Review* 12 (1976): 311–22; and Adler, "*Benito Cereno*: Slavery and Violence in the Americas," in *War in Melville's Imagination* (New York: New York University Press, 1981), 88–110.

31.   Karcher actually argues that evidence suggests that Melville intended "Benito Cereno" as a companion piece to "The Bell-Tower" in much the same way that he intended "The Two Temples" and "Poor Man's Pudding and Rich Man's Crumbs" to be diptychs. See "Darkening Shadows of Doom in 'The Encantadas,' 'Benito Cereno,' and 'The Bell-Tower,' " in *Shadow Over the Promised Land*, 109–59, esp. 120–22; hereafter cited in text.

32.   For example, Dimock shows how the sort of reform rhetoric Melville employs in *White-Jacket* can also be "exercises in patriotic piety"; see *Empire for Liberty*, 101.

33.   Rogin, *Subversive Genealogy: The Politics and Art of Herman Melville* (New York: Knopf, 1983), 208–20.

34.   The essays to which I refer are Sundquist, "*Benito Cereno* and New World Slavery," in Sacvan Bercovitch, ed., *Reconstructing American Literary History* (Cambridge: Havard University Press, 1986), 93–22; Kavanaugh, " 'That Hive of Subtlety': 'Benito Cereno' as Critique of Ideology," *Bucknell Review* 29 (1984): 127–57, reprinted in Sacvan Bercovitch and Myra Jehlen, eds., *Ideology and Classic American Literature* (Cambridge: Cambridge University Press, 1986), 352–83; Emery, " 'Benito Cereno' and Manifest Destiny," *Nineteenth-Century Fiction* 39 (1984): 48–68; and Zagarell, "Reenvisioning America: Melville's 'Benito Cereno,' " *ESQ: A Journal of the American Renaissance* 30 (1984): 245–59. Sundquist has also contributed two important essays that prefigure his later work, "Suspense and Tautology in *Benito Cereno*," *Glyph* 8 (1981): 103–26; and "Slavery, Revolution, and the American Renaissance," in Walter Benn Michaels and Donald E. Pease, eds., *The American Renaissance Reconsidered (Selected*

Papers from the English Institute, 1982–83) (Baltimore: Johns Hopkins University Press, 1985), 1–33. Similarly, one should note Emery's other important commentary on "Benito Cereno,' " "The Topicality of Depravity in 'Benito Cereno,' " *American Literature* 55 (1983): 316–31.

35. Horsley-Meacham, "The Monastic Slaver: Images and Meaning in 'Benito Cereno,' " *New England Quarterly* 56 (1983): 261–66, and "Melville's Dark Satyr Unmasked," *English Language Notes* 23 (1986): 43–47. Thomas, "The Legal Fictions of Herman Melville and Lemuel Shaw," *Critical Inquiry*, 11 (1984): 24–51; the portion of this essay dealing with "Benito Cereno" was subsequently expanded and published as " 'Benito Cereno': Melville's Narrative of Repression," in Thomas, *Cross-Examinations of Law and Literature: Cooper, Hawthorne, Stowe, and Melville* (Cambridge: Cambridge University Press, 1987), 93–112.

36. I am specifically referring to Swann, *"Benito Cereno*: Melville's De(con)struction of the Southern Reader," *Literature and History* 12 (1986): 3–15; "Whodunnit? Or, Who Did What? *Benito Cereno* and the Politics of Narrative Structure," in David E. Nye and Christen Kold Thomsen, eds., *American Studies in Transition* (Odense: Odense University Press, 1985), 199–234; and Stuckey and Leslie, "Aftermath: Captain Delano's Claim Against Benito Cereno," *Modern Philology* 85 (1988): 265–87. However, Swann has also published "Two Notes on Benito Cereno," *Journal of American Studies* 19 (1985): 111–14. Stuckey and Leslie's other work on "Benito Cereno" includes "The Death of Benito Cereno: A reading of Herman Melville on Slavery," *Journal of Negro History* 67 (1982): 287–301; and "Avoiding the Tragedy of Benito Cereno: The Official Response to Babo's Revolt," *Criminal Justice History* 3 (1982): 125–32.

37. See McElroy, "Cannibalism in Melville's 'Benito Cereno,' " *Essays in Literature* 1 (1974): 206–18; and Baines, "Ritualized Cannibalism in 'Benito Cereno': Melville's 'Black-Letter' Texts," *ESQ: A Journal of the American Renaissance* 30 (1984): 163–69.

38. Franklin, " 'Apparent Symbol of Despotic Command': Melville's 'Benito Cereno,' " *New England Quarterly* 34 (1961): 462–77; reprinted in slightly revised form as "Benito Cereno: The Ascetic's Agony," in *The Wake of the Gods: Melville's Mythology* (Stanford: Stanford University Press, 1963), 136–52. One should also note Hershel Parker's rebuttal to Franklin, " 'Benito Cereno and *Cloister-Life*: A Re-Scrutiny of a 'Source,' " *Studies in Short Fiction* 9 (1972): 221–32.

39. I would specifically like to acknowledge the work on "Benito Cereno" that has been most helpful to me in preparing this volume, notably Seymour L. Gross, ed., *A Benito Cereno Handbook* (Belmont, Cal.: Wadsworth, 1965); John P. Runden, ed., *Melville's* Benito Cereno: *A Text for Guided Research* (Boston: D. C. Heath, 1965); and Newman, "Benito Cereno," in *A Reader's Guide*, 95–98. My sincerest thanks to Kathy Leitzell, L. Layne Neeper, and my research assistant, Robert Myers, and to Carolyn L. Karcher, Sterling Stuckey, and especially H. Bruce Franklin, for their help and advice.

NOTICES AND ESSAYS

◆

[Notice of *The Piazza Tales*]

THE CHRISTIAN FREEMAN AND FAMILY VISITER

Mr. Melville is justly regarded among the first writers of fiction of the present day. He possesses in an eminent degree two indispensable requisites for a successful romance writer—vivid imagination and remarkable descriptive powers. Take, for instance, the story in this volume, entitled "Benito Cereno"—in the descriptive it is unsurpassed by any thing which we ever read, and it keeps the reader's imagination constantly exercised. And "The Encantadas, or Enchanted Islands," another of the tales in this volume, could *not* have been written by a man of ordinary imagination. The publishers have issued this book in an elegant style, and it will become a favorite with the lovers of literature of a high order.

Reprinted from *The Christian Freeman and Family Visiter* [Boston, Mass.] 18 (13 June 1856): 2.

[Notice of *The Piazza Tales*]

THE KNICKERBOCKER

This series of stories, though partaking of the marvellous, are written with the author's usual felicity of expression, and minuteness of detail. The tale entitled 'Benito Cereno,' is most painfully interesting, and in reading it we became nervously anxious for the solution of the mystery it involves. The book will well repay a perusal.

Reprinted from *The Knickerbocker* 48 (September 1856): 330.

[Melville's Timonism in "Benito Cereno"]

Lewis Mumford

In Benito Cereno, published in Putnam's Monthly Magazine in 1855, Melville was again at home. It is such a tale as one might hear, with good luck, during a gam in the South Seas or at a bar in Callao; and Melville himself took it boldly from a book of voyages by Captain Amasa Delano, published in 1816.

A black, ill-kempt ship, commanded by a young Spanish captain and manned by negroes, is in distress, and calls upon Captain Amasa Delano, a bluff, frank American skipper, for aid. Delano, coming aboard with provisions and water, finds the captain almost down with a fever, and by turns confidential and queerly reserved. The Spaniard is attended by a black slave who almost smothers him with watchful endearments; and he has the air of perpetually manoeuvring, in a way that would seem sinister were his plight not so manifestly pathetic. Delano is a little troubled at heart, but he is free from intellectual suspicions. There is something wrong on the Spaniard's ship; but it is hard for Delano to put his hand on it. Don Benito is in command: but he seems helpless, and he tolerates ugly disorder even among the black boys. Promising further aid, Delano finally leaves the vessel and is about to pull for his own ship, still powerfully disturbed by the Spanish captain's pain, trouble, fever, churlishness, courtesy—does it mean some treachery? With a wild leap, the Spaniard throws himself in Delano's boat, followed by his faithful black, dagger in hand; and the black aims his dagger, not at the Americans, but at his Spanish master. When the American crew finally pulls to safety a harrowing story comes out.

I will not spoil Benito Cereno for those who have not read it by revealing its mystery; it is enough to point out that the interplay of character, the cross-motives, the suspense, the central mystery, are all admirably done: in contrast to some of Melville's more prosy sketches, there is not a feeble touch in the whole narrative. The following passage, which sets the key of the whole story, reveals Melville's undiminished ability as an artist:

"Everything was mute and calm; everything gray. The sea, though

Reprinted from *Herman Melville* (New York: Harcourt, Brace, 1929), 244–47.

undulated into long roads of swells, seemed fixed, and was sleeked at the surface like waved lead that has cooled and set in the smelter's mould. The sky seemed a gray surtout. Flights of troubled gray fowl, kith and kin with flights of troubled gray vapors among which they were mixed, skimmed low and fitfully over the waters, as swallows over meadows before storms." As in The Encantadas, the writing itself was distinguished: it had a special office of its own to perform, and did not, as in Typee and Redburn, serve merely as carriage for the story. One can mark Melville's literary powers in the complete transformation of Delano's patent story: he adds a score of details to heighten the mystery and deepen the sinister aspect of the scene; and by sheer virtuosity he transfers the reader's sympathies to the Spanish captain, who in the original story is far more cruel, barbarous, and unprincipled than the forces he contends against. In order to effect this change, Melville deliberately omits the last half of the story, in which the Spanish captain ignobly turns upon his benefactor and seeks to deprive him of the rights of salvage. The moral of the original tale is that ingratitude, stirred by cupidity, may follow the most generous act, and that American captains had better beware of befriending too whole-heartedly a foreign vessel. In Benito Cereno the point is that noble conduct and good will, like that Don Benito felt when his whole inner impulse was to save Delano and his crew, may seem sheer guile; and, further, that there is an inscrutable evil that makes the passage of fine souls through the world an endless Calvary. "Even the best men err, in judging the conduct of one with the recesses of whose condition he is not acquainted." The world is mortified for Don Benito by the remembrance of the human treachery he has encountered: no later benefaction, no radiance of sun and sky, can make him forget it.

Man should offset the malice and evil circumstance one finds in the constitution of the universe: instead, he aggravates it. One does not need to heighten the parallels between Benito Cereno's fate and Melville's own life to catch the semblance to his own dilemma and his own bowed and wounded spirit. "Never," says one of the characters in his next book, "has it been my lot to have been wronged, though but in the smallest degree. Cheating, backbiting, superciliousness, disdain, hard-heartedness, and all that brood, I know but by report. Cold regards tossed over the sinister shoulder of a former friend, ingratitude in a beneficiary, treachery in a confidant—such things may be; but I must take somebody's word for it." The irony of that declaration is obvious: Melville had met these things, and, like a splinter of steel in the eye, they tormented him and during these harassed years the memory of them, the anticipation of them, the helpless attempt to guard against them or remove them, directed his whole life towards this single point of exacerbation. The mighty whale aroused Melville's utmost powers: there was that in man that steaded him manfully for such an encounter: but, like Timon, the spectacle of fair-weather friends and worldly sycophants, turning away from him during his moment of greatest need, unmanned him completely. Moby-Dick might slay one: but the torments of black flies and gnats made life ignoble without bringing death any nearer. Melville did not need to exaggerate these wrongs. It was their very smallness, their unassailableness, that made him desperate.

["Benito Cereno": "A Masterpiece of Mystery, Suspense and Terror"]

STERLING BROWN

Benito Cereno (1855) is a masterpiece of mystery, suspense and terror. Captain Delano of the *Bachelor's Delight*, discovering a vessel in distress along the uninhabited coast of Chile, boards her to render aid. He is interested in the many Negroes he finds on the decks: "like most men of a good blithe heart he took to Negroes not philanthropically, but genially, just as other men to Newfoundland dogs." He is mystified, however, when the gamesome Negroes flare up in momentary rage, and especially by their continual clashing their hatchets together. Only when Don Benito, in desperation, escapes to Delano's ship, does the real truth dawn.

There had been a revolt on board the *San Dominick*; the Negro sailors and the slaves had killed many of the whites, and had kept the others alive only for their skill as navigators in order to reach a Negro country. The mutineers and revolters are overcome in a bloody battle, carried to Lima, and executed. The contrast between the reputed gentleness of Negroes "that makes them the best body-servants in the world," and the fierceness with which they fight for freedom is forcibly driven home. Certain Negroes stand out: Babo who, resembling a "begging friar," engineered the revolt with great skill and is almost fiendish in his manner of breaking down Cereno's morale; Francesco, the mulatto barber; Don José, personal servant of a Spanish Don; and Atufal, an untamed African chieftain, all filled with hatred for whites. Melville graphically pictures the slave mothers, "equally ready to die for their infants or fight for them"; the four old men monotonously polishing their hatchets; and the murderous Ashantees. All bear witness to what Melville recognized as a spirit that it would take years of slavery to break.

Although opposed to slavery, Melville does not make *Benito Cereno* into an abolitionist tract; he is more concerned with a thrilling narrative and character portrayal. But although the mutineers are blood-thirsty and cruel, Melville does not make them into villains; they revolt as mankind has always

Reprinted from *The Negro in American Fiction* (Washington, D.C.: Association of Negro Folk Education, 1937), 12–13. Sincere and repeated efforts to contact a copyright holder have failed.

revolted. Because Melville was unwilling to look upon men as "Isolatoes," wishing instead of discover the "common continent of man," he comes nearer the truth in his scattered pictures of a few unusual Negroes than do the other authors of this period.

[The Failure of "Benito Cereno"]

Newton Arvin

A far more ambitious and superficially more impressive narrative than "The Tartarus of Maids" is of course "Benito Cereno," the longest and most celebrated of the *Piazza Tales*. Unduly celebrated, surely. For neither the conception nor the actual composition and texture of "Benito" are of anything like the brilliance that has been repeatedly attributed to them. The story is an artistic miscarriage, with moments of undeniable power. It was a mistaken impulse this time that led Melville to rewrite another man's narrative; for, as everyone knows, the material of "Benito Cereno" was lifted bodily from a chapter in the *Narrative of Voyages and Travels* of a Yankee ship-captain named Amasa Delano. What Melville could do with the substance of other men's books, at his best, was magical, as we have already seen; but he largely fails to do this with Captain Delano's undecorated tale. Liberties, to be sure, he rather freely takes with his original, but strictly speaking he takes too few, and takes these too half-heartedly; and nothing is more expressive of the low pitch at which "Benito" is written than the fact that with one incident in his original Melville takes no liberties whatever: the scene of the actual mutiny on the *San Dominick*, which might have been transformed into an episode of great and frightful power, Melville was too tired to rewrite at all, and except for a few trifling details, he leaves it all as he found it, in the drearily prosaic prose of a judicial deposition.

Much praise has been lavished on the art with which an atmosphere of sinister foreboding and malign uncertainty is evoked and maintained through all the earlier parts of the tale. It is hard to see why. There are a few fine touches in the very first paragraphs—the "flights of troubled gray fowl," for example, skimming fitfully over the smooth waters like swallows over a meadow before a storm—but even in these first pages the rhythms of the prose are slow, torpid, and stiff-limbed; and they remain so, with a few moments of relief, throughout. Nor is the famous "atmosphere" of "Benito" created swiftly, boldly, and hypnotically, as Melville at his highest pitch might have created it; on the contrary, it is "built up" tediously and wastefully through the accumulation of incident upon incident, detail upon detail,

Reprinted from *Herman Melville* (New York: William Sloane, 1950), 238–41. Copyright © 1950, 1978. Reprinted by permission of William Morrow & Co., Inc.

as if to overwhelm the dullest-witted and most resistant reader. Many of the details, too, are of poor imaginative quality: the hatchet-polishers on the poop are rather comic than genuinely sinister; the symbolism of the key hanging round Don Benito's neck is painfully crude; and it needed only a very commonplace and magazinish inventiveness to conceive the scene in which Benito is shaved by the wily Babo. The traces of contrivance, and fatigued contrivance too, are visible everywhere in the story, and the sprinkling of clichés on every page—"a joyless mien," "the leaden calm," "fiends in human form," "a dark deed"—is only a verbal clue to the absence of strong conviction with which Melville is here writing.

In all the intangible senses, moreover, the substance of "Benito Cereno" is weak and disappointing. A greater portentousness of moral meaning is constantly suggested than is ever actually present. Of moral meaning, indeed, there is singularly little. This is partly because the two or three leading personages are too simply conceived to be the bearers of any greatly significant burden. Captain Delano is moral simplicity in a form that borders upon weak-wittedness, as his perversely misdirected suspicions end by indicating; Babo is a monster out of Gothic fiction at its worst, not at its best; and as for Don Benito, with his husky whisper, his tottering step, and his constant attacks of faintness, he is not only hopelessly unheroic, as an image of persecuted goodness, but he is not even deeply pathetic: in his state of nerveless moral collapse he can only be the object of a half-reluctant compassion. The result would be an undermining of the moral structure of "Benito Cereno" even if the action itself were not so wanting in large significance as it is. It is certainly very credible that a shipload of African slaves should break out into mutiny, and massacre most of the white officers and crew; it is equally credible that the surviving captain should be intimidated and even persecuted by the mutineers, and that their ringleader should be cunning enough to impose upon a simple-minded ship-captain visiting the bedeviled vessel. As a parable of innocence in the toils of pure evil, however, all this is singularly unremarkable, and we are forced to feel that Don Benito has gone very little beyond the rudiments when, at the end, he enforces the lesson his terrible experiences have taught him: "To such degree may malign machinations and deceptions impose. So far may even the best man err, in judging the conduct of one with the recesses of whose condition he is not acquainted." To be sure!

Neither the story nor the images in the real Captain Delano's book had succeeded in rousing Melville from the lethargy into which he was falling: a year or two earlier, when he wrote the long piece called "The Encantadas," he had worked in a much happier and more characteristic vein. It is true that "The Encantadas" is only a loosely organized series of sketches, with no very intense unity among them, rather than a completely fused whole; that one or two of these sketches, the fourth and fifth, are hardly more than pedestrian; and that the eighth sketch, the story of the Chola widow, Hunilla, touching though its subject is, is written in a manner so forcedly and self-consciously pathetic that not even its substance redeems it from the lachrymose. It remains true that nowhere in Melville are there grander images of utter desolation than those evoked, in the first three sketches, of the uninhabited and uninhabitable islands, the Galápagos, solitary, rainless, strewn with volcanic ashes, and overhung by a swirl of gray, haggard mist. "Apples of Sodom, after touching, seem these isles"; and in these first three wonderful sketches Melville's deepest, most despairing sense of abandonment and sterility is expressed. There is a powerful and intended incongruity, later, in the rather wild humor of the seventh sketch, the story of the Dog-King of Charles's Isle, with its Mark Twainish note of the mock heroic; and the ninth sketch, "Hood's Isle and the Hermit Oberlus," is as dismally convincing, in its dramatization of pure deviltry, the delight in degradation for its own sake, as "Benito Cereno" is unconvincing. One touch in this sketch—the spectacle of the hermit Oberlus planting his potatoes, with gestures so malevolent that he seems rather to be dropping poison into wells than potatoes into soil—is worth all the heaped-up horrors of "Benito."

Critical Problems in Melville's "Benito Cereno"

JOSEPH SCHIFFMAN

. . . dreadful insurrections . . . have been made when opportunity offered.
　　　—Absolom Jones and Richard Allen, Negro leaders, 1794.

Herman Melville's ever popular short story, "Benito Cereno," has not yet been sufficiently analyzed. In the first flurries of the Melville revival in the 1920s and 1930s, "Benito Cereno" was hailed as an artful narrative,[1] but it suffered critical neglect since few commentators gave reasons for their judgments. Today, in the full blossom of Melville appreciation,[2] serious appraisal of "Benito Cereno" first appears. However, many problems have been raised but few satisfactorily answered.

Melville found the idea for his story in the journals of a Captain Amasa Delano, and "Benito Cereno" appeared in *Putnam's Monthly Magazine* in 1855. The following year "Benito Cereno" was published in book form, together with several of Melville's other tales, under the title *The Piazza Tales*. Contemporary reviews of the book were brief and did not see fit to single out "Benito Cereno" for special comment. The *United States Democratic Review* of September, 1856, recommended the book as "a companion for the sultry summer months,"[3] and the *Southern Literary Messenger* of June, 1856, spoke of its "freshness and vivacity" without mention of "Benito Cereno."[4] The story did not attract much attention again until Melville's rediscovery in the 1920s and 1930s, when reviews were favorable but slight.[5] Recently Stanley T. Williams[6] and Rosalie Feltenstein[7] have tried to analyze "Benito Cereno." It seems to me that, while both have made important beginnings, they have committed basic critical mistakes, leading them to false conclusions about Melville's short story.

Williams early in his paper reminds us that the meaning of "Benito Cereno" still eludes us, and expresses agreement with Ellery Sedgwick that we "must know all of his [Melville's] books to comprehend his mind, of which each is a 'profile.' " Yet Williams does not take Sedgwick's good advice, for he makes little attempt in his article to cast the mystery of "Benito

Reprinted from *Modern Language Quarterly* 11 (September 1950): 317–24. Reprinted by permission of the author and publisher.

Cereno" against the light that Melville's other books afford us, and so comes to the mistaken conclusion that Babo is evil. Williams says: "[Natural] to Babo . . . is hatred for the happiness of hatred, evil for the sake of evil . . . [his is] a motiveless malignity. . . ."[8]

This is a customary misinterpretation, for Babo's malignity is not motiveless. He was leading a rebellion of slaves in their fight for freedom, and all his acts of cruelty were dictated by this purpose. He ordered the killing of the slave owner, Don Alexandro, "because he and his companions could not otherwise be sure of their liberty." And Don Alexandro's skeleton was nailed to the ship's masthead with the words "Follow Your Leader" under it as a warning to the Spanish captain and crew that, unless the slaves were returned to free Senegal, each Spaniard would follow his leader to death. Babo is evil because of an evil world.

Almost all critics who insist that Babo is evil refuse to discuss the question of slavery. Rosalie Feltenstein, for example, says that Babo's condition of servitude is outside the boundaries of discussion since Melville does not take it into account.[9]

Melville could not felicitously discuss slavery within the framework of the short story, but aside from this problem, Miss Feltenstein's refusal to consider slavery in Babo's case raises other critical problems. The critic is not confined within limits set by the author. If this were so, there would be no true criticism. As Taine said, "It is a mistake to study the document as if it were isolated. This were to treat things like a simple scholar, to fall into the error of the bibliomaniac." Surely a discussion of Melville's attitudes toward slavery and the Negro would throw valuable light on Babo's actions in "Benito Cereno."

What did slavery mean to Melville? In *Mardi* he makes his position clear. In his allegorical trip through the southern part of Vivenza (the United States of America) he is shocked by the sight of slaves in the land of liberty. The travelers cannot believe their eyes when, on close scrutiny of the tribe of Hamo, they discover they are slaves—and yet men![10]

Throughout Melville's books there is warm understanding and sympathy shown for the Negro. In *Redburn* Melville speaks of the freedom Negro sailors enjoy in Liverpool as contrasted with the restrictions on them in their own country.[11] In *Moby-Dick* Melville hits a high-water mark in his presentation of Negro characters as people. The only Negro in the book who betrays any kind of neurosis is young Pip, who shrinks from life after a nightmare experience in chasing a whale. Melville significantly refers to him as "Poor Alabama boy."[12] The other people of color in the book, except Old Fleece, have never lived under slavery, and they show themselves to be the equals of their white mates. It is in keeping with Melville's philosophy that Babo as a human being would desire freedom.

The human desire for freedom is something Melville always understood and admired in men. Gabriel says that for Melville, all positions save two were tentative. The only two absolutes were "the eternal dualism between good and evil, and man's destiny to make war upon wrong."[13] Certainly, to Melville, Babo was warring on wrong.

Thirty years after "Benito Cereno," Melville made clear his attitude towards rebellion. In the Preface to *Billy Budd* he speaks of the French Revolution in these words:

> The opening proposition made by the Spirit of that Age involved rectification of the Old World's hereditary wrongs. In France, to some extent, this was bloodily effected. But what then? Straightway the Revolution itself became a wrongdoer, one more oppressive than the kings. . . . During those years not the wisest could have foreseen that the outcome of all would be what to some thinkers apparently it has since turned out to be—a political advance along nearly the whole line for Europeans.[14]

Melville knew that "the rectification of wrongs" does not always come pleasantly. "Benito Cereno" shows that. This is the answer Melville's whole lifework gives to the riddle of good and evil.

Miss Feltenstein has attempted to discover factual meanings in the rich symbolism of "Benito Cereno." But, like Williams, she comes to the faulty conclusion that Babo signifies evil, and that through him Cereno comes to understand "the blackness at the center of life." Miss Feltenstein says that "blackness and darkness are Melville's predominant symbols of evil, and Babo is blackness, not simply a Negro . . . [hence] he is pure evil. . . ."[15]

It is true that for most people of the Western Hemisphere black symbolizes evil and white symbolizes good. But this does not hold for Melville. He was a rebel against his age and culture,[16] such a deep-going rebel that even his symbolism became unorthodox. To Melville white was evil, harsh, ugly—the unknown. Moby-Dick, the White Whale, had to be killed if the tragic crew of the *Pequod* were to find rest. Ishmael (Melville) speaks of white in these terms:

> It was the whiteness of the whale that above all things appalled me. But how can I hope to explain myself here; and yet, in some dim, random way, explain myself I must, else all these chapters might be naught . . . consider that the mystical cosmetic which produces every one of her hues, the great principle of light, for ever remains white or colorless in itself, and if operating without medium upon matter, would touch all objects, even tulips and roses, with its own blank tinge—pondering all this, the palsied universe lies before us a leper; and like wilful travellers in Lapland, who refuse to wear colored and coloring glasses upon their eyes, so the wretched infidel gazes himself blind at the monumental white shroud that wraps all the prospect around him. And of all these things the Albino Whale was the symbol. Wonder ye then at the fiery hunt?[17]

And at another point in *Moby-Dick* Melville raises his dark and white symbolism to the level of human coloring. The sailors are seated about at ease:

OLD MANX SAILOR

. . . This is the sort of weather when brave hearts snap ashore, and keeled hulls split at sea. Our captain has his birth-mark; look yonder, boys, there's another in the sky—lurid-like, ye see, all else pitch black.

DAGGOO

What of that? Who's afraid of black's afraid of me! I'm quarried out of it!

SPANISH SAILOR

(*Aside.*) He wants to bully, ah!—the old grudge makes me touchy. (*Advancing.*) Aye, harpooneer, thy race is the undeniable dark side of mankind—devilish dark at that. No offence. . . .

5TH NANTUCKET SAILOR

What's that I saw—lightning? Yes.

SPANISH SAILOR

No; Daggoo showing his teeth.

DAGGOO [*Springing*]

Swallow thine, mannikin! White skin, white liver.[18]

Symbolism becomes meaningful only when analyzed in the light of the author's mind, or within the context in which it is used. Williams overlooks this point in attempting to ascribe moral values to the name "Babo." Williams says, "Babo, after all, as perhaps his name suggests, is just an animal, a mutinous baboon."[19] That the name Babo had any special symbolic meaning for Melville is unlikely. He found the name in Delano's *Journals*, the source of his "Benito Cereno." The name Babo can be explained only in the role Babo plays. Though he was mutinous, as Williams says, he was no baboon. Instead he was a forceful, clever, courageous leader of his fellow slaves. If the name Babo connotes evil, what do the names Daggoo and Queequeg connote? These strange names are given to respected harpooneers on the *Pequod*, sworn enemies of Moby-Dick, and the best-paid men in the crew. Only in such terms can "symbolism" in Daggoo and Queequeg be discussed. Similarly, the name Babo, like any other piece of "symbolism," derives its significance from the role the character plays. To attempt to interpret symbols in any fixed, isolated manner is to indulge in mysticism, not criticism.[20]

Within the demands of the short-story form, how does Melville betray his sympathies? It is important to observe that "Benito Cereno" as a story flows from two sources: first, from Don Alexandro's mistaken belief that his slaves were tractable, and, second, from Delano's inability to perceive that a slave rebellion was occurring under his very eyes. Had Don Alexandro not mistakenly advised Cereno that his slaves were content and could be transported without chains, there could have been no slave revolt. And had Delano been able to understand that Negroes could revolt successfully, there would have been no "Benito Cereno." In depicting the short-sightedness of those who thought slavery was acceptable to other people, Melville was condemning slavery.

Practically all of "Benito Cereno" is told through the eyes of one person, Captain Delano. Melville remains carefully in the background. Delano is referred to as "The American" by Melville, and since he is the only American who takes an appreciable part in the story, one can believe that Melville intends Delano perhaps as a microcosm of American attitudes of the time toward Negroes. If this is so, Melville has given us a mind that rings historically true.

Delano suffers a mental block in looking at Negroes. He cannot conceive of them as fully rounded people. To him, they are simple, lovable, sub-human beings, quite happy as slaves and servants. This is the fulcrum on which the whole story is based. Had Delano, the American, been able to understand that here was a shipload of Negroes who had successfully revolted, had he understood that Atufal was really not in chains but that he was periodically reconquering Cereno, had he understood that the "unsophisti-cated" hatchet polishers and "drooling" Negroes were part of an elaborate control system, there could have been no story.[21] So despite a strange atmosphere about the ship, Delano cannot perceive that the slaves are in rebellion. Feeling uneasy, he suspects Cereno. He looks everywhere but in the right place for an answer to the mysterious conduct of Cereno and the whole ship. And so Delano and the reader feel these "currents spin [their] heads around almost as much as they do the ship." A hundred little conflicts lash at Delano and the reader—action and repose, suspicion and reassurance, prickling and balm; and through it all Babo's role mocks the white man's low estimate of the Negro. For Delano "took to negroes . . . genially, just as other men to Newfoundland dogs." A grand hoax is put over on him, to be dispelled only by Cereno's desperate plunge into the rowboat.

In some ways "Benito Cereno" is a fossil relic of the stress and strain that American experienced over the slavery issue in the 1850s. In answer to *Uncle Tom's Cabin*, fourteen pro-slavery novels were published between 1852 and 1854. These novels argued that the Negro "is not fit for freedom, knows himself an inferior, and in the majority of cases prefers to remain a slave." In these ante-bellum tracts, "A thinking Negro is unusual, a Negro expressing himself on slavery is unaccountable. . . ."[22] It was in this climate of controversy that "Benito Cereno" appeared.

Melville did not intend "Benito Cereno" as an abolitionist tract. He wanted primarily to write a "good story," one that would sell. But in selecting a theme of slave rebellion, and in treating Babo and his fellow slaves as able, disciplined people, as capable of evil as the white man, he treated the Negro as an individual. Both subject and treatment were conditioned by the 1850s, and both subject and treatment marked advances for American literature.[23]

Babo emerges the moral victor in "Benito Cereno." Cereno can never return to the slave trade after his experience with Babo. He remains depressed and disconsolate. Delano cannot understand Cereno's depression, since Babo is bound and out of harm's way. Delano asks Cereno: ". . . you are saved; what has cast such a shadow upon you?" To which the beaten Cereno replies, "The negro." And at the trial, Cereno cannot be made to face Babo.

Babo is sentenced to death by the law courts of Lima. His head is stuck upon a pole and his body is burned to ashes:

> . . . for many days, the head [of Babo], that hive of subtelty, fixed on a pole in the Plaza, met, unabashed, the gaze of the whites; and across the Plaza looked . . . toward the monastery, on Mount Agonia without; where, three months [later] . . . Benito Cereno, did, indeed, follow his leader.

Babo's head gazed "unabashed" as Benito Cereno, who would trade in flesh, does "indeed follow his leader." What an indictment of slavery! Melville's thinking, artistically sublimated in form, shines through "Benito Cereno."

Notes

1. Edward J. O'Brien, the American short-story critic, said of "Benito Cereno": "I regard this as the noblest short story in American literature. The balance of forces is complete, the atmosphere one of epic significance, the light cast upon the hero intense to the highest degree, the realization of the human soul profound, and the telling of the story orchestrated like a great symphony. . . ." Unfortunately, O'Brien, like most "Benito Cereno" critics, deals in superlatives but little analysis. Quotation from Edward J. O'Brien, ed., *The Twenty-Five Short Stories* (New York, 1931), p. 507.
2. "In line with the plan to publish the complete Melville, Hendricks House-Farrar, Strauss will do 'Piazza Tales' in late June, 'Pierre' in August and 'Typee' in December." From the New York *Times* Sunday Book Review Section, March 21, 1948.
3. N.S., VII (1856), 172.
4. XXII (1856), 480.
5. Rosalie Feltenstein has outlined the paucity of literary criticism of "Benito Cereno": "Since its first publication . . . 'Benito Cereno' either has been ignored by critics of Melville or has received inadequate treatment. In the *Athenæum* for July 26, 1856, a contemporary reviewer dismissed all of *The Piazza Tales* as something for 'a very young public.'. . . Many of the later critics have really not been much more discerning in their appraisals of the story. Carl Van Vechten says, rather mysteriously, that 'Benito Cereno' is a 'sea story which should be better than it is,' and Van Wyck Brooks catalogues it as a simple, objective tale, merely 'the story of a meeting on a South American ship.' Lewis Mumford thinks it is 'such a tale as one might hear, with good luck, during a gam in the South Seas or at a bar in Callao.'

With an apology for once having called the story 'not markedly original,' Carl Van Doren places Melville's shorter works among 'the most original and distinguished fiction produced on this continent,' but has not much more to say of 'Benito Cereno' than that 'it equals the best of Conrad in the weight of its drama and the skill of its unfolding.' John Freeman shows enthusiasm but tells nothing about the story itself when he calls it 'a flaming instance of the author's pure genius . . . which must have brought tears of pride to Melville's eyes as he looked back upon it.' " Rosalie Feltenstein, "Melville's 'Benito Cereno,' " *American Literature*, XIX (November, 1947), 245.

    6.   Stanley T. Williams, " 'Follow Your Leader': Melville's 'Benito Cereno,' " *Virginia Quarterly Review*, XXIII (Winter, 1947), 61–76.

    7.   Feltenstein, *loc. cit.*, pp. 245–55.

    8.   Williams, *loc. cit.*, p. 75.

    9.   Feltenstein, *loc. cit.*, pp. 254–55. Yvor Winters, like Feltenstein and most other critics, refuses to examine slavery as a cause for Babo's actions. He says: "The morality of slavery is not an issue in this story; the issue is this, that through a series of acts . . . the fundamental evil of a group of men, evil which normally should have been kept in abeyance, was freed to act. The story is a portrait of that evil in action, as shown in the negroes. . . ." See his *In Defense of Reason* (New York, 1947), p. 222.

    10.   *Mardi* in *Works*, IV (London, 1922), 247–52.

    11.   *Redburn* (New York, 1924), p. 228.

    12.   *Moby-Dick*, Modern Library (New York, 1930), p. 174.

    13.   Ralph Henry Gabriel, *The Course of American Democratic Thought: An Intellectual History Since 1815* (New York, 1940), p. 76.

    14.   "Billy Budd, Foretopman," in *Shorter Novels of Herman Melville*, ed. Raymond Weaver (Liveright Publishing Corp., 1928), p. 228.

    15.   Feltenstein, *loc. cit.*, p. 253.

    16.   Melville said " 'No' in an age which demanded that all good citizens should say 'Yes.' " From the *Introduction to Herman Melville: Representative Selections*, by Willard Thorp (New York, 1938), p. xcvii. Note especially the section of the Introduction entitled "Melville's Social Ideas," pp. xcvii–xcix, for a discussion of Melville's attitudes toward slavery, Christian missions, primitive man, etc. Information such as the following is very important to a proper understanding of "Benito Cereno." "He [Melville] seems, indeed, to be unique among his contemporaries in his freedom from zeal and prejudice."

Many modern critics of Melville do not match his tolerant attitudes. For example, Arthur Hobson Quinn speaks of the attraction of "Benito Cereno" in these terms: "It is the picture of one man [Cereno], of our own race, alone amid the hostile strangers who are waiting to strike, that appeals so strongly." See his *American Fiction: An Historical and Critical Survey* (New York, 1936), p. 155.

    17.   *Moby-Dick*, pp. 272–83.

    18.   *Moby-Dick*, pp. 254–55.

    19.   Williams, *loc. cit.*, p. 73.

    20.   "Human life in our age is so . . . diversified that people cannot share a few, historic, 'charged' symbols that have about the same . . . meaning for everybody." From Suzanne K. Langer, *Philosophy in a New Key: A Study in the Symbolism of Reason, Rite and Art* (Cambridge, Mass., 1942), pp. 287–88.

Of Melville's shorter tales, "Benito Cereno" is richest in symbolism. As Delano approaches the *San Dominick*, the boat appears to him like a "white-washed monastery after a thunderstorm" and its inhabitants "a ship-load of monks." Cereno at the end of the tale actually takes refuge in a monastery and "follows his leader" from there. Surely these symbolic references to the Catholic Church are heavy with meaning for the story. Other bits of symbolism that need more analysis are: the giant Negro Atufal in chains when he is actually leading a rebellion; Babo using the flag of Spain for a shaving towel while working on Cereno's face; the oakum pickers; the hatchet polishers and their "barbarous din"; the young African woman lying at ease with her babe; the Spanish sailor's treasured jewel, etc.

21. Delano's inability to comprehend the Negro's reaction to slavery is characteristic of many white American historians. John Fiske, James Schouler, and Ulrich B. Phillips, for example, all believe that the Negro, as an "inferior" being, was docile under slavery. See Herbert Aptheker, *American Negro Slave Revolts* (New York, 1943). Aptheker says: "The data herein presented make necessary the revision of the generally accepted notion that his [the American Negro slave's] response [to slavery] was one of passivity and docility. The evidence, on the contrary, points to the conclusion that discontent and rebelliousness were not only exceedingly common, but, indeed, characteristic of American Negro slaves" (p. 374).

The slave leaders' quote used at the beginning of this paper is taken from Aptheker, p. 14.

22. See Jeannette Reid Tandy, "Pro-Slavery Propaganda in American Fiction of the Fifties," *South Atlantic Quarterly*, XXI (January, April, 1922), 40–50, 170–78.

23. It is interesting to note that one writer, significantly a Negro, comes closest to an understanding of the social implications of "Benito Cereno." Sterling Brown says: "The contrast between the reputed gentleness of Negroes . . . and the fierceness with which they fight for freedom [in "Benito Cereno"] is forcibly driven home. Certain Negroes stand out: Babo who . . . engineered the revolt with great skill . . . ; Francesco, the mulatto barber; Don José, personal servant to a Spanish Don; and Atufal. . . . All bear witness to what Melville recognized as a spirit that it would take years of slavery to break . . . although the mutineers are bloodthirsty and cruel, Melville does not make them into villains; they revolt as mankind has always revolted. . . . [He] comes nearer the truth in his scattered pictures of a few unusual Negroes than do the other authors of this period." See Sterling Brown, *The Negro in American Fiction* (Washington, D.C., 1937), pp. 12–13. While Brown's analysis of "Benito Cereno" is the best I have seen, he misses the point of Babo's moral victory at the end.

Herman Melville and the American National Sin: The Meaning of "Benito Cereno"

SIDNEY KAPLAN

. . . Reluctantly, very reluctantly—for it is with a special sadness that we are forced to repudiate any portion of the "usable past" in the classic figures of our American Renaissance—it must be ventured that the image of Melville as subtle abolitionist in *Benito Cereno* may be a construction of generous wish rather than hard fact. Just as Melville cautioned his readers that they must discriminate between what was indited as Pierre's and what was indited concerning him, so here care must be had to discriminate the thoughts that Melville indites in *Benito Cereno* from what the reader may hope these thoughts to be. The events of a story by themselves do not always clearly reveal the writer's judgment on those events; bare plot does not mechanically provide its interpretation.

As Melville once wrote to Hawthorne, he liked "a skeleton of actual reality to build about with fulness & veins & beauty." Now, Delano's *Narrative* was such "a skeleton of actual reality." Taken as incident, as a news-item reported with horror by a pro-slavery writer in the Southern press, to a John Brown or Ralph Waldo Emerson the revolt of the Negroes against their white masters of the *San Dominick* might seem a healthy and heartening thing (indeed, the *Liberator* is full of such joyful items); conversely, reported by a Frederick Douglass or a Sojourner Truth in the abolitionist press of the North, to a Calhoun, a Simms or a Poe the same revolt would be an illustration of the last evil. Thus, Glicksberg's query—"If they went to extremes of butchery in their desperate bid for freedom, who shall presume to pass final judgment upon them?"—is in a sense a meaningless one; nor is Schiffman to the point when he contends that the anti-slavery intention of *Benito Cereno* is shown by Melville's mere choice of the *subject* of slave-revolt, even at a time when pro-slavery novelists, in order to rebutt Mrs. Stowe, were busy turning out caricatures of contented slaves. The fact is that Melville's intention must be determined mainly by what he did with his plot, how he veined and fleshed it, and in part how he manipulated his source. His mere telling of the story, while it will reveal something about

Reprinted from the *Journal of Negro History* (published by the Association for the Study of Afro-American Life and History) 57 (1957): 12–27. Reprinted by permission of the publisher.

that intention, will not by its bare outline establish Babo as hero or Cereno as villain.

Let us try to clarify this point. To begin with, it seems highly improbable that Melville in writing *Benito Cereno* was not thinking within the framework of the cultural concerns of his time as well as in a timeless region of universal truth. His technique was often to expand a current and concrete context into eternal abstractions, but this technique rarely excluded judgment on the concrete. Now, *Benito Cereno* was written at the mid-point of the hottest decade of the anti-slavery struggle prior to the Civil War, when to many the conflict seemed both irrepressible and impending. Nor was it a struggle fought solely in legislative halls, in the press, in the lyceum circuit, in the pulpit. The threat of a black Spartacus waiting to rise in the South pervaded the decade of the fifties; it was John Brown's idea precisely to raise up such leaders. The names of Gabriel, Vesey, Turner and Douglass were familiar names in American households. One modern historian, Harvey Wish, looking back on the period, has written of what he calls "the slave insurrection panic of 1856"—the year that *The Piazza Tales* came off the press.[1]

Nor were slave revolts on the plantations of the South the only items of Negro unrest that Americans could read about either in their daily press or in the pamphlet literature of the slavery controversy. Black mutiny on the high seas was also a familiar thing. Although by the mid-century, Captain Amasa Delano's original *Narrative* was apparently unknown to contemporary readers of *Benito Cereno*, the mutiny described in it was no antique chronicle either for them or for Melville. Such mutinies, a part of the living tissue of American life, had probably begun not long after Captain John Hawkins had pioneered the slave trade in his good ship, *The Jesus*.[2]

In Melville's young manhood, two famous slave mutinies filled the press—the first on the Spanish blackbird *Amistad* in the summer of 1839, the second on the brig *Creole* two years later. Four nights out of Havana en route to Port Principe the fifty-four slaves on the *Amistad* murdered its captain, sailed the ship north and ultimately surrendered to the authorities at Montauk Point after ascertaining that they were in a "free country." As described in New York and New England newspapers, the appearance of the *Amistad* is strangely reminiscent of the *San Dominick*'s:

> Her sides were covered with barnacles and long tentacles of seaweed streamed from her cable and her sides at the water line. Her jibs were torn and big rents and holes appeared in both foresail and mainsail as they flapped in the gentle breeze. Most of the paint was gone from the gunwails and rail—over which [peered] coal-black African faces.

The *Amistad* case became a *cause célèbre* of the abolitionists, who hired Rufus Choate to defend the Negroes against the claims of the Spaniards.

Kali, one of the mutineers, travelled throughout the North on a speaking tour, while on the New York stage the event was dramatized in *The Black Schooner*, whose protagonist was Joseph Cinquez, leader of the mutiny. Cinquez, reported to be the son of an African prince, "of magnificent physique, commanding presence, forceful manners and commanding oratory," reminds one of Atufal, a prince in his own country.

Every step in the progress of the case was followed by the Northern press. The abolitionist campaign was a strong one, and two years later, as Melville was shipping for the South Seas, Justice Story delivered the opinion of the Supreme Court—a historic decision which stated legally for the first time that black men, carried from their homes as slaves, had the right, when seeking liberty, to kill anyone who tried to deprive them of it. In the North there was great sympathy for the mutineers of the *Amistad* and much hostility against the Spaniards who, claiming indemnity for their lost slaves, called them "pirates who, by revolt, murder, and robbery, had deprived" owners of their property.

The case of the *Creole* received even wider publicity. In the fall of 1841, the brig had set sail from Hampton Roads for New Orleans with a cargo of tobacco and 135 slaves. One Sunday night nineteen of the slaves led by one Madison Washington—a fugitive who had returned from Canada to rescue his wife, had been captured, and was being returned to bondage—rose up, killed a slavedealer on board, wounded the captain, cowed the passengers, and forced the crew to sail the ship to free Nassau. There, although the British authorities held the nineteen on charges of mutiny, the rest, despite the protest of the American consul, were freed. The indignation of Southerners in Congress was violent, and Daniel Webster, then Secretary of State, supported them, for which action Garrison, Channing and Sumner excoriated him. For a dozen years the case was in and out of the papers, and it was only two years before *Benito Cereno* was written that the quarrel between the Americans and the British was finally arbitrated by the Englishman, Joshua Bates, whom Melville had dined with in London in 1849. Some years later, Frederick Douglass wrote a short story, whose hero was Madison Washington.

It was in the atmosphere of the slave insurrection panic of the middle fifties, of the mounting tension of the slavery controversy (in which Melville's relatives and friends took varying positions), of the *Amistad* and *Creole* mutinies, that *Benito Cereno* was conceived and written.

Is it credible, then, that Melville meant *Benito Cereno* to have little or nothing to do with slavery and rebellion, or with the character of the Negro as slave and rebel? Given the Melville we have described and his times, such an opinion seems hardly tenable. Yet to argue thusly, is not, as we shall see, wholly to accept the view of Brown, Schiffman and Glicksberg. Let us turn once more to the text itself.

The most central and completely described character of *Benito Cereno* is

Amasa Delano, through whose temperament filters most, although not all, of the action of the tale. On Delano both schools of interpretation concur in at least one respect: in the Yankee captain Melville meant to paint a satiric portrait. An important question, however, still remains to be answered: What is satirized? What in Delano is the target of Melville's irony? That the duped Delano was meant to be simple, even stupid, both schools agree. It is at the point where agreement stops and divergence begins that we find the crux of the problem of *Benito Cereno*, for whereas one school holds that Delano was naive because he could not discern the motiveless malignity in Babo and his fellows, it is the contention of the other that his stupidity lay in his blindness to the innate and heroic desire of the Negroes for freedom, to their dignity as human beings.

Which side is right? What did Melville mean?

The major premise for the development of Delano's character is given quite clearly in Melville's first assessment of it: Delano was "a person of a singularly undistrustful good-nature, not liable, except on extraordinary and repeated incentives, and hardly then, to indulge in personal alarms, any way involving the imputation of malign evil in man." Thus Melville declares that Delano is blind—not to goodness or courage or the love of freedom in anybody—but to the "malign evil in man." Delano is trusting. Is he intelligent? Not at all. That he is a good-natured fool Melville points up in the ironic sentence that follows: "Whether, in view of what humanity is capable, such a trait implies, along with a benevolent heart, more than ordinary quickness and accuracy of intellectual perception, may be left to the wise to determine." Now, the tale that follows is precisely the parable by which the wise may so determine; by it readers are to be educated; in it Captain Delano is to be educated. Yet, as we shall see, the final truth that Delano will learn is that Babo is the embodiment of "malign evil," Cereno of goodness maligned. For Delano to learn this new truth, he must unlearn the old errors of his period of delusion.

What are these old errors about Negroes in general and about those of the *San Dominick* in particular that Delano must unlearn? He thinks that they are all jolly, debonair, "sight-loving Africans," who invariably love bright colors and fine shows; that their gentleness peculiarly fits them to be good body servants and that they possess the "strange vanity" of faithful slaves; that they sing as they work because they are uniquely musical; that they are generally stupid, the white being the shrewder race; that mulattoes are not made devilish by their white blood and that the hostility between mulattoes and blacks will not allow them to conspire against whites; that yellow pirates could not have committed the cruel acts rumored of them. And of all these beliefs he is disabused. He is a man who has had "an old weakness for negroes"; who has always been "not only benign, but familiarly and humorously so" to them; who has been fond of watching "some free man of color at work or play," and if on a voyage he chanced to have a black

sailor, had inevitably been on "chatty and half-gamesome terms with him."
He is a man who, "like most men of good, blithe heart . . . took to negroes,
not philanthropically, but genially, just as other men to Newfoundland
dogs," and who on the *San Dominick* speaks a "blithe word" to them; who
admires the "royal spirit" of Atufal and pities his chains; who suspects that
Don Benito is a hard master and that slavery breeds ugly passions in men—
and in every item he will be proven blind.

To Delano, in short, Negroes are jolly primitives, uncontaminated
nature, simple hearts, people to be patronized. The "uncivilized" Negro
women aboard the *San Dominick* are "tender of heart"; as the "slumbering
negress" is awakened by her sprawling infant, she catches the child up "with
maternal transports," covering it with kisses. "There's naked nature, now;
pure tenderness and love," thinks Captain Delano, "well pleased." Gazing
at the kindly sea and sky, he is sorry for betraying an atheist doubt about
the goodness of Providence.

All these things Delano has believed—and they are all to be proven
false in fact, masquerades behind which lurk "ferocious pirates," barbarous
sadists, both male and female, shrewd wolves, devilish mulattoes. In the
course of events he must learn what Cereno already knows, and Cereno it is
who rams the lesson home, generalizing what the obtuse Yankee has been
constitutionally unable to comprehend. His last words are, "The negro."
Delano has no answer; it is the silence of agreement. "You were undeceived,"
Cereno had said to him, "would it were so with all men." Delano has been
stripped of his delusions; he is wiser. But wiser in what respect? In that he
now knows that Negroes are courageous lovers of freedom? Not at all; rather
wiser in that he has at last discerned the blacks to be wolves in the wool of
gentle sheep.

The shock of recognition makes brothers of Delano and Cereno; they
now can speak with "fraternal unreserve"; indeed, there was never any real
basic opposition between them. Delano was no philanthropic abolitionist;
he was not even anti-slavery—he offered to buy Babo; for him the *San
Dominick* carries "negro slaves, amongst other valuable freight"; he intends
his sugar, bread and cider for the whites alone, the wilted pumpkins for the
slaves; he orders his men to kill as few Negroes as possible in the attack, for
they are to divide the cargo as a prize; he stops a Spanish sailor from stabbing
a chained slave, but for him the slaves are "ferocious pirates" and he says no
word against their torture and execution, far more cruel than the machinations of Babo. Like Cereno he too has been "a white noddy, a strange bird,
so called from its lethargic, somnambulistic character, being frequently
caught by hand at sea." No more will he be a somnambulist in the presence
of evil. Meeting another *San Dominick* he will not again be duped.

And Cereno? He is the good man, the religious man, whose nobility
may be seen in his hidalgo profile, in health, perhaps, something like the
graceful Spanish gentry who listened to Ishmael tell his Town-Ho story, the

real aristocrat that the superficial democrat, Delano, had wrongly suspected. Everywhere Melville pruned the Cereno of Delano's *Narrative* to vein and flesh him with altruism and goodness. In life, he was a swindler, a liar, the scorn of his friends, the stabber of a helpless Negro slave; as Lewis Mumford justly declares, in the original narrative, Cereno is "far more cruel, barbarous, and unprincipled than the forces he contends against." All this is gone in the tale. Pathetic and beaten he is, done to death by his experience, but only because he has been an altruist and trusted the slaves as tractable; the good man's illusions of goodness have been fatally overthrown. At the last Cereno reminds one of Bartleby the scrivener, who has rejected life as a blank and monstrous wall he cannot pierce. Whereas in *Bartleby* the wall is the enigma of life, in *Cereno* it is Babo.

And what of Babo? Let us forget that objectively he is a maritime Nat Turner. What was he for Melville—for the tale? He is the "malign evil" that Delano at first cannot comprehend—and all his brothers and sisters are that evil too. The fact that for *us*, the heirs of Lincoln, his cunning ruthlessness is worthily motivated is not an issue *within the story*; to Melville "faithful" Babo is an "honest" Iago[3]; to Delano and Cereno he is a ferocious pirate, not a black David. A pirate has motives; his motives are malign—a fact not necessary to discuss.

Babo is more like a minor character of *Omoo*, one Bembo, than like Jackson or Bland. Did Melville, finding Babo in Delano's *Narrative*, remember the "swart" Mowree Bembo, harpooneer of the *Julia*? "Unlike most of his countrymen," Bembo was short and "darker than usual." It was whispered that he was a cannibal, so fearless and blood-thirsty was he in his desire to kill whales. Extremely sensitive to slight, he would not tolerate joshing from Sydney Ben: "Bembo's teeth were at his throat." Thrown down on the deck by Ben's friends, Bembo was "absolutely demoniac; he lay glaring, and writhing on the deck without attempting to rise." In revenge he plots to wreck the ship. Thwarted, Bembo "never spoke one word. . . . His only motive could have been a desire to revenge the contumely heaped upon him the night previous, operating upon a heart irreclaimably savage, and at no time fraternally disposed toward the crew."

True Melville found the name Babo in Delano's *Narrative*, but the Babo of *Benito Cereno* is actually a composite of two characters in the source, Babo and Mure. Melville chose Babo—the baboon, ring-leader of the Negroes who are primitives, beasts.[4] The imagery connected with Babo and the other Negroes throughout the tale is strictly from the bestiary. The *San Dominick*'s headpiece is a dark satyr in a mask, trampling the neck of a writhing figure, likewise masked. It is, of course, Babo trampling on Don Benito: Babo is the satyr, a lecherous sylvan deity, sensual, part beast. He is the "lion rampant" in the white field of the flag of Spain. The four grizzled junk-into-oakum pickers are "sphinx like"—silent, inscrutable, anti-human, part beast; the "ebon flights of naked boys and girls, three or four years old, darting in and out of the den's mouth," are "like a social circle of bats, sheltering in some friendly cave. . . ." Babo "snakishly writhes" to kill Benito—the image is Satanic and is associated with Babo's "central purpose." The Negro women are leopardesses, the nursing mother a doe whose fawn sprawls at its dam's lapped breasts, its paws searching, its mouth and nose rooting for the mark, while it grunts. As the *San Dominick* gives way before the onslaught of the *Bachelor's Delight*, the retreating Negroes are "cawing crows"; during the fight on deck, they are "black-fish" among which sword-fish run amok; their "red tongues drool wolf-like from their black mouths" (while the white sailors fight with pale set faces); to the source account Melville adds a strong hint that Aranda's skeleton has been cannibalistically prepared. Most of these are Melville's direct images—not Delano's. More-over, to show that neither Christianity nor white blood can redeem this beastliness there is the "mulatto, named Francesco, the cabin steward, of a good person and voice, having sung in the Valparaiso churches"—all this added by Melville to Cereno's original deposition. It is Francesco, "just before a repast, in the cabin," who proposes "to the negro Babo, poisoning a dish for the generous Captain Amasa Delano."[5]

Is there anything in the color imagery of *Benito Cereno* to refute this analysis of character and plot? Schiffman maintains that the reversal of con-ventional black-white symbolism in *Moby-Dick* is applied also in *Benito Cereno* and is proof positive that white Cereno is an image of evil. The opposite is the case. In *Moby-Dick*, the traditional equation is rejected so that in the new equation black may equal virtue and white evil. In *Benito Cereno* the traditional equation is merely transposed so that black (delusively virtuous or harmless to early Delano) may equal blacker (incarnate iniquity to later Delano), while white (delusively evil and suspiciously malign to early Delano) may equal whiter (tragically victimized virtue to later Delano). Beyond this, within the color schema of *Benito Cereno* wherever black and white are used for ambiguous or foreboding effects, the aim is simply conventional deception that builds up wrong leads in order to contrive mechanical suspense and a trick finale. Is Cereno's *real* whiteness (conventional) anything like the white-ness of the whale? Is Babo's blackness (conventional) anything like Pip's "lustrous ebony, panelled in King's cabinets"? Again let us go to the text.

As the *San Dominick* swings into view, the opening tone is gray—an appropriate mixture of white and black portending ambiguity, uncertainty, shadows ahead—and the grayness lingers throughout the tale. The *San Dominick* shows "no colors"; what light there is on the ship streams "equivo-cally enough" from the cabin, "much like the sun" (Cereno), which through "low, creeping clouds" (the Negroes) shows like a Lima intriguante's one sinister eye through the Indian loop-hole of her "dusk" saya-y-manta. The flawed bell of the *San Dominick* has a muted gray sound. The ship is "pipe-clayed"—a grayish white; later it is "bleached." And it is wreathed with "dark festoons of sea-grass."

Don Benito himself is "dusked by ill-health." When Delano suspects him most, he is "the dark Spaniard," who sulks in "black vapours," or in "dark spleen." Conventional black-white pairing is seen in Melville's comment: "There was a difference between the idea of Don Benito's darkly preordaining Captain Delano's fate, and Captain Delano's lightly arranging Don Benito's"; again, when Delano suspects Cereno and Atufal of complicity, he thinks of the "Spaniard behind—his creature before." Says Melville: "to rush from darkness to light was his involuntary choice." In assessing a Spanish sailor Delano associates black with evil: "If, indeed, there be any wickedness on board this ship, thought Captain Delano, be sure that man has fouled his hand in it, even as he now fouls in it the pitch." The mahogany chair and settee of Babo's shaving salon are suitably black and Babo follows his nicking of Don Benito's neck with a "dusky comment of silence."

At every opportunity conventional black imagery is worked into the story as symbol, lure and pun. Cereno's "gloomy disdain" is interpreted by Delano: "as if, forced to black bread themselves," he deemed it but equity to make his associates eat the same. Again, Delano, admiring Don Benito's aristocratic profile, reproaches himself for his suspicion: "In short, to the Spaniard's black-letter text, it was best, for awhile, to leave open margin." How hard and consciously Melville worked at this may be seen in a revision of the *Putnam's* printing that he made for *The Piazza Tales*: in *Putnam's* the "cawing crows," as they attempt their flight, hail "the now dusky expanse of ocean"; in the revision, they hail "the now dusky moors of ocean."

The house or ship as symbolic image, so often employed by Poe, Hawthorne, Twain and other writers of the century, is joined to conventional black-white symbolism in the tale. Thus one of the first images of the *San Dominick* is of a "white-washed monastery after a thunder-storm" inhabited by dark-cowled Black Friars who turn out to be black dominies of Dis. Like the House of Usher with its cracked wall, the "strange house" of the *San Dominick* is a ruined mansion, whose rotten balustrade is partly stained with hell's pitch, as is the "purple-black" (Dante's black) "tarred-over panel of its state-cabin door."

Where then *within the story* does Melville use black-white symbolism in the manner of *Moby-Dick*? The reverse-symbolism of *Moby-Dick*, it must be concluded, is simply not present in *Benito Cereno*, nor indeed, will it ever appear again in Melville's fiction, except, perhaps, in a brief interlude on the first page of *Billy Budd*. How different really are seemingly like images in the two works. In *Moby-Dick*, when little Flask is held up by giant Daggoo, Melville tells us—perhaps unnecessarily, but he does not want the point to be missed—that the bearer was nobler than the rider. In *Benito Cereno*: "As master and man stood before him, the black upholding the white, Captain Delano could not but bethink him of the beauty of that relationship which presented such a spectacle of fidelity on the one hand and confidence on the other." The reality, of course, is the negation of fidelity and confidence, and the satire is clear: the true picture is that of satyr trampling on innocence, of black headsman with white head on block, of "Nubian sculptor finishing off a white statue-head." How different the conflict between Daggoo and the Spaniard on the *Pequod* and that between the slave and the Spanish boy on the *San Dominick*.

No, there is no ambiguity about the meaning of black in *Benito Cereno*. "The negro"—Don Benito's last words—whether read as Spanish abstract noun for "blackness" or "darkness," as English concrete noun with abstract connotations, as Swedenborgian emblem, Emersonian correspondence, Bushnellian logos, or simply as synonym for Babo and his fellows,[6] is the wise man's final answer to that question which at the start of the parable was "left to the wise to determine." And the answer of Melville, the wise author, is clear. "I think I understand," says Delano in the conversation that ushers in the close of the tale: "You generalize, Don Benito, and mournfully enough." But Delano does not yet understand, for he thinks the good man's gloom proceeds only from the memory of the time when the American thought him a monster, from the ambiguities of life. Banish that memory, he counsels, "yon bright sun has forgotten it all." When Cereno rejects nature's balm, Delano cannot fathom him: "You are saved: what has cast such a shadow upon you" The question recalls the opening adumbration of the tale: "Shadows present, foreshadowing deeper shadows to come." Don Benito must spell out the full answer; it is—"The negro." Delano, wiser now, has nothing more to say; he knows finally that "malign evil" exists—and where. "There was no more conversation that day." It is the finality of the closing lines of Poe's *Narrative of Arthur Gordon Pym*, where the essential evil of black men in their darkness is written in the black waters and on the ageless rocks. To ignore the Negro in *Benito Cereno*, as some have done,[7] is to do what Wolf Mankowitz has done in his critique of Eliot's *Gerontion*, omitting the Jew in order to praise the piece's "enduring significance."

Is it possible, then, to go along with Schiffman when he says that Melville meant Don Benito's last words to be a villain's final concession of defeat by the heroic will to freedom of the Negro people? Once more it must be said, however regretfully, that such a view is the outcome of generous hope. It is Babo, the prototype of innate depravity, who, like an unrepentant villain, an Iago indeed, gazes "unabashed" from his death's head of unfathomably malign subtlety at the goodness he has murdered. For Melville, in his story, Babo was a victor in the malign sense only.

True it is, of course, that Melville, even in his failures, is almost always an adroit artist, and as many have noted, there are moments of undeniable power in *Benito Cereno*. But looked at objectively, the tale seems a plummet-like drop from the unconditionally democratic peaks of *White-Jacket* and *Moby-Dick*—an "artistic sublimation" not, as Schiffman maintains, of anti-slaveryism, but rather of notions of black primitivism dear to the hearts of slavery's apologists, a sublimation in fact of all that was sleazy, patronizing, backward and fearful in the works that preceded it. It is to put the matter too mildly perhaps to say, as Charles Neider does, that "Melville glosses over extenuating circumstances in his effort to blacken the blacks and whiten the whites, to create poetic images of pure evil and pure virture," so that the result is "sometimes unfortunate in the feelings it arouses against the Negro," or to say, as Matthiessen does, that "the embodiment of good in the pale Spanish captain and of evil in the mutinied African crew, though pictorially and theatrically effective, was unfortunate in raising unanswered questions."[8] When Melville, at a certain point in his development, repudiated his superficial, old notions (which were Delano's too) about the innately jolly, minstrel, religious nature of Negroes, it was, sadly enough, not to perceive the free spirit of the Tawneys and the Daggoos as the reality behind the masks. Instead, in Benito Cereno, the fear and doubt of slave-revolt proclaimed in Mardi and implied in White-Jacket were to be transmuted into hatred of the "ferocious pirates" of the San Dominick—as were demoniac Bembo into demoniac Babo; lordly Daggoo into Atufal, prince of hell; the "poor mulatto," Rose-Water, into the sinister mulatto, Francesco; the good slavemaster—Randolph of Roanoke, the purser of the Neversink, the slaveholder of Vivenza who was not an insensate Nulli—into Don Benito Cereno.[9]

Notes

1. Nor was the panic confined to the United States. Herbert Aptheker [American Negro Slave Revolts (New York: Columbia University Press, 1943), 33] writes: ". . . the American envoys to England, France, and Spain . . . meeting in Ostend in 1854, let the world know that . . . Cuba ought to belong to the United States. An important argument for this, they declared, lay in the possibility that the slaves of the Pearl of the Antilles might emulate their brethren of St. Domingo. [Was Melville thinking of St. Domingo when he changed the real Cereno's Tryal to the San Dominick?] Were that prize within the strong hand of the United States, she would not permit the flames to extend to our neighboring shores, seriously to endanger or actually to consume the fair fabric of our Union."

2. To cite a few: in 1731 and 1747, on Rhode Island slavers returning from the Guinea coast the Negroes killed all the whites in one instance, and spared the captain and his son in the other; in 1732, on a New Hampshire slaver, they murdered captain and crew; in 1735, slaves broke into the powder room of the Dolphin of London and blew her up off the African coast; in 1761, a Boston slaver lost forty of its Negroes in an insurrection. The trials of the conspirators in the Denmark Vesey plot of 1822 revealed that they had sent a letter asking for help to the president of the Republic of San Domingo. The letter was carried by a Negro cook on board a Northern schooner. The press of the 1850s is full of reports of battles between slave-runners and the authorities; such battles were the frequent subjects of popular juvenile and adult literature.

3. Arthur L. Vogelback ("Shakespeare and Melville's Benito Cereno" [Modern Language Notes 67 (1952): 113–16]) has noted the Babo-Iago resemblance in detail.

4. Is there an echo here too of Baubo, obscene leader of the witches in Goethe's Faust, which Melville possibly was reading while writing his story? And was a writer in the issue of Putnam's that carried the final installment of Benito Cereno alluding to Babo when in an article "About Niggers" he had this to say: "But with all this charming jollity and waggishness, the

nigger has terrible capacities for revenge and hatred (which opportunity may develope, as in St. Domingo), and which ought to convince the skeptic that he is a man, not a baboon . . . our Southern partners will learn that they are no joke. The nigger is no joke, and no baboon; he is simply a black man, and I say: Give him fair play and let us see what he will come to."

5.   Note also Dago, another invention, "who had been for many years a grave-digger among the Spaniards. . . ." Was Melville reversing his conception of Daggoo in *Moby-Dick*, who was ready to dig a grave for his Spanish tormenter? As we have pointed out, there is more than a hint in the forecastle tableau of *Moby-Dick* that Melville's choice of the Spanish sailor to quarrel with Daggoo was based on the old conflict between Spaniard and Moor.

6.   That Melville, on the concrete level at least, meant "The negro" to mean Babo, may be seen in a redundant sentence he deleted from the penultimate paragraph of the first printing: "And yet the Spaniard could, upon occasion, verbally refer to the negro, as has been shown; but look upon him he would not, or could not."

7.   Among others, Yvor Winters—and T. E. Sil'man (as John C. Fiske points out) in *Istoria amerikanskoi literatury* (Moscow-Leningrad, 1947).

8.   Matthiessen continues: "Although the Negroes were savagely vindictive and drove a terror of blackness into Cereno's heart, the fact remains that they were slaves and that evil had thus originally been done to them. Melville's failure to reckon with this fact within the limits of his narrative makes its tragedy, for all its prolonged suspense, comparatively superficial." Matthiessen's judgments on *Benito Cereno* are curiously contradictory. Our point, of course, is that Melville did "reckon with this fact within the limits of his narrative." [*American Renaissance: Art and Expression in the Age of Emerson and Whitman* (New York: Oxford University Press, 1941), 508.]

9.   It should be clear by now that although our findings reject the Brown-Schiffman-Glicksberg thesis, we in no manner share the admiration for the allegedly profound "truth" that Feltenstein, et al., discover in the meaning of *Benito Cereno*. Nor do we take part in the praise given the tale by current worshippers of the art of ambiguity. Where *Benito Cereno* is ambiguous—and it is only rarely so—it is the shell-game ambiguity of *The Lady or the Tiger*. Our view of *Benito Cereno* is nearer that of John Howard Lawson, whose brief page of analysis in his *The Hidden Heritage* [New York: Citadel Press, 1950] seems long in insight. For Lawson the tale exhibits a "tragic decline" of Melville's talent, a "cheap melodrama, a distortion of human and moral values . . . a pitiful attempt to accomplish the task which Shelley rejected—to reconcile 'the Champion with the Oppressor of mankind.' "

["Benito Cereno" and the Gothic Horror of Slavery]

LESLIE FIEDLER

Down through the history of the minstrel show, a black-faced Sambo (smeared with burnt cork, whether Negro or white, into the grotesque semblance of the archetypal nigger) tries to exorcise with high-jinks and ritual jokes the threat of the black rebellion and the sense of guilt which secretly demands it as penance and purge. But our more serious writers return again and again to the theme: Melville, for instance, in "Benito Cereno" treating quite explicitly the tragic encounter between certain sentimental and comic stereotypes of the Negro and a historic instance of a slave mutiny. In that story, Captain Amasa Delano fails to recognize the rebellion on a Spanish slave-ship which he encounters, precisely because he is a good American. He is endowed, that is to say, with an "undistrustful good nature" and will not credit "the imputation of malign evil in man." This means in fact that he is quite willing to believe almost any evil of a European aristocrat, like the Don Benito who gives the tale its title; and is prepared to accept the most incredible behavior as the kind of "sullen inefficiency" to be expected of a Latin crew. On the other hand, he is incapable of believing a Negro, particularly a body servant, anything but a "faithful fellow."

It is just this phrase which occurs to Captain Delano as he watches Babo, a black slave who is actually holding his master prisoner, threatening death with the razor he presumably wields to shave him. " 'Faithful fellow!' cried Captain Delano, 'Don Benito, I envy you such a friend, slave I cannot call him.' " But Melville will not let it go, adding on his own behalf—in a tone less ironical than one would expect:

> Most negroes are natural valets and hairdressers. . . . There is . . . a smooth tact about them in this employment. . . . And above all is the great gift of good-humour . . . a certain easy cheerfulness . . . as though God had set the whole negro to some pleasant tune . . . to this is added the docility arising from the unaspiring contentment of a limited mind, and that susceptibility

Reprinted from *Love and Death in the American Novel*, revised edition (New York: Stein & Day, 1966), 400–401. Copyright © 1960, 1966 by Leslie Fiedler. Reprinted by permission of Scarborough House/ Publishers.

of bland attachment sometimes inhering in indisputable inferiors. . . . Like most men of a good, blithe heart, Captain Delano took to negroes . . . just as other men to Newfoundland dogs.

But Babo is, in fact, the leader of a black uprising that has already murdered his master's closest friend and bound his corpse to the prow; and Captain Delano in his unwillingness to imperil his fondness for Negroes, almost kills Don Benito when he makes a last, desperate attempt to escape. Still convinced that the true source of moral infection is to be found only in the decaying institutions of Europe, Captain Delano cannot understand why, even after the exposure of Babo, Benito Cereno continues to pine away and seems to long only for death.

Though the fact of slavery, out of which all the violence and deceit aboard the Spanish ship has been bred, remains a part of his own democratic world as well as Don Benito's aristocratic one, Amasa Delano is undismayed. Though only an incident has been dealt with and its deep causes left untouched, he finds in this no cause for despair, but demands that the Spaniard join with him in recognizing a happy ending. "You are saved . . . ," he cries to Don Benito; "You are saved: what has cast such a shadow upon you?" And he will not understand when the Spanish captain answers, "The negro." Indeed, Melville seems to share the bafflement of his American protagonist; a Northerner like Captain Delano, Melville finds the problem of slavery and the Negro a little exotic, a gothic horror in an almost theatrical sense of the word. Before his story is done, at any rate, he lets it lapse back into the language of the written record when he had to look for it in the first instance—quite unlike Poe who found this particular theme at the very center of his own experience.

"Apparent Symbol of Despotic Command": Melville's *Benito Cereno*

H. Bruce Franklin

When Melville metamorphosed the eighteenth chapter of Amasa Delano's *Narrative of Voyages and Travels* into *Benito Cereno*, he made only one change in Delano's basic plot: he sent his Benito Cereno into monastic retirement, soon followed by death. Shortly after introducing Cereno, Melville hints of his fate: "His manner upon such occasions was, in its degree, not unlike that which might be supposed to have been his imperial countryman's, Charles V., just previous to the anchoritish retirement of that monarch from the throne."[1] This hint leads to a source of more ultimate significance than Delano's *Voyages*—William Stirling's *Cloister Life of the Emperor Charles the Fifth*.

Benito Cereno appeared first in *Putnam's Monthly Magazine* in late 1855. In January of 1855, the *Edinburgh Review* had apologized for quoting from Stirling's *Cloister Life of the Emperor Charles the Fifth*: "We are not sure whether we ought to quote from a book so well known as that of Mr. Stirling" (p. 83). There was some reason to apologize. Stirling's work had first appeared as two articles, entitled "The Cloister Life of the Emperor Charles V," in *Fraser's Magazine* of April and May, 1851. The next year the articles were expanded into a book, and by the year after, the book had run to three editions. The articles themselves were several times reprinted in other magazines, and numerous popular and recondite periodicals continually noticed, reviewed, summarized, and quoted from the book throughout 1853 and 1854.

Many of the same periodicals were at the same time noticing, reviewing, summarizing, and quoting from Melville's work.[2] Melville, busily reading his critics, must have read again of Emperor Charles, to whom he had made five detailed references in *Mardi* and *White-Jacket*. In "I and My Chimney," also submitted to *Putnam's* in 1855, Melville's narrator tries to avoid what he likens to the abdication and monastic retirement of Charles. *Benito Cereno* seems to assume that the readers of *Putnam's* in 1855 were familiar with Stirling's *Cloister Life of Charles*.

Much of the language Melville uses to talk about Cereno is almost

Reprinted from *New England Quarterly* 34 (November 1961); 462–72. Copyright © 1961 by H. Bruce Franklin. Reprinted by permission of the author. This essay has been edited by the author.

identical to the language Stirling uses to talk about Charles; many details of Cereno's physical and social environment have precise correspondents in the environment of Charles; almost every trait of Cereno is a trait of Charles. Benito Cereno is, in more than one sense, the ghost of Charles the Fifth. He is both Charles's supernatural and symbolic ghost, reënacting Charles's abdication and surrender of worldly power, finally becoming, like Charles himself, the symbolic ghost of all power. The meanings of this strange relationship will become clearer as we examine the evidence that defines it.

What Melville calls "the anchoritish retirement" of Charles the Fifth was passed in the mountains of Spain. Benito Cereno's ship seems to be a monastery in the mountains of Spain:

> Upon gaining a less remote view, the ship . . . appeared like a whitewashed monastery after a thunder-storm, seen perched upon some dun cliff among the Pyrenees. But it was no purely fanciful resemblance which now, for a moment, almost led Captain Delano to think that nothing less than a ship-load of monks was before him. Peering over the bulwarks were what really seemed, in the hazy distance, throngs of dark cowls; while, fitfully revealed through the open port-holes, other dark moving figures were dimly described, as of Black Friars pacing the cloisters. (p. 57)

The Black Friars were the Dominicans, who, unbridled by Charles the Fifth, became the principal sponsors of the Inquisition. Melville's Black Friars run a ship which he has rechristened the *San Dominick*, patron saint of the Dominican order. (In Delano's narrative the ship's name is *Tryal*.) The captain of this monastic ship resembles "some hypochondriac abbot" and he lives in monastic quarters. The description of his cuddy relates each object to either monasticism or the Inquisition: the table holds a "thumbed missal"; the bulkhead bears a "meagre crucifix"; cutlasses, a harpoon, and old rigging lie "like a heap of poor friars' girdles"; the settees are as "uncomfortable to look at as inquisitors' racks"; the washstand looks like a "font." Although Cereno's monastic cuddy closely resembles Charles the Fifth's monastic chambers (even the "large, misshapen arm chair" has an exact counterpart in a large, misshapen armchair of much interest to all the emperor's chroniclers), the exteriors of their quarters are even more curiously similar.

Melville reproduces the physical surroundings of Charles's chambers with an incredible exactitude and a strange effect. The emperor lived in the second story of a building attached to the church. On the right side (direction defined as usual by the church) were Charles's bedroom and state cabinet, which led out onto a "gallery" that was cut off from below.[3] Captain Delano stands on this very gallery, "the starboard quarter-gallery," a retreat "cut off from the deck," onto which used to open "the state-cabin door," and senses the presence of royal ghosts:

As his foot pressed the half-damp, half-dry sea mosses matting the place, and a chance *phantom* cats-paw—an islet of breeze, *unheralded, unfollowed* [italics mine]—as this ghostly cats-paw came fanning his cheek; as his glance fell upon the row of small, round dead-lights—all closed like coppered eyes of the coffined—and the state-cabin door, once connecting with the gallery, even as the dead-lights had once looked out upon it, but now calked fast like a sarcophagus lid; and to a purple-black tarred-over panel, threshold and post; and he bethought him of the time, when that state-cabin and this state-balcony had heard the voices of the Spanish king's officers. . . . (p. 88)

The imperial monastic gallery overlooked a grand garden composed of "parterres" on "terraces" and a formal "alley of cypress."[4] Delano fancies he sees just such a garden: "He leaned against the carved balustrade, again looking off toward his boat; but found his eye falling upon the ribbon grass, trailing along the ship's water-line, straight as a border of green box; and parterres of sea-weed, broad ovals and crescents, floating nigh and far, with what seemed long formal alleys between, crossing the terraces of swells, and sweeping round as if leading to the grottoes below." Beyond Charles's garden was the forest, from which the local poachers descended upon his gardens.[5] Delano sees from the balcony a Spanish sailor beckoning from "groves of rigging"; the sailor "as if alarmed by some advancing step along the deck within, vanished into the recesses of the hempen forest, like a poacher." Delano seems to feel the desolation, loneliness, and sense of imprisonment described in the *Cloister Life of Charles*[6]: "Trying to break one charm, he was but charmed anew. Though upon the wide sea, he seemed in some far inland country; prisoner in some deserted chateau, left to stare at empty grounds, and peer out at vague roads, where never wagon or wayfarer passed."

In the emperor's garden was a "summer-house,"[7] which, like the other buildings, was later burnt. Stirling's book ends by describing the ruins of the imperial quarters, garden, and church: "The principal cloister was choked with the rubbish of the fallen upper story. . . . Two sides of the smaller and older cloister were still standing, with blackened walls and rotting floors and ceiling."[8] Delano seems to be among these ruins: "And overhanging all was the balustrade by his arm, which, partly stained with pitch and partly embossed with moss, seemed the charred ruin of some summer-house in a grand garden long running to waste"; "As with some eagerness he bent forward . . . the balustrade gave way before him like charcoal," causing the fall "of the rotten fragments."

At least as similar as the environments of Emperor Charles and Captain Cereno are the men themselves, the things they do, and the language used to describe them. Charles is "broken in health and spirits"[9]; Cereno is "broken in body and mind." Charles, "in the absence of the chief of his household, . . . seems to have fallen in some degree into the hands of the friars"[10]; Cereno, in "the absence of those subordinate deck-officers," has fallen into the hands of the "Black Friars." Charles "almost fell into the arms of his attendants"[11]; Cereno "fell into the ready arms of his attendant." Stirling describes the abdication ceremony with Charles approaching, "supporting himself on the right with a staff, and leaning with his left hand on the shoulder" of his escort.[12] Captain Cereno approaches his abdication from the ship in the same posture: "the better to support him, the servant, placing his master's hand [left hand, as indicated by the context] on his naked shoulder, and gently holding it there, formed himself into a sort of crutch." Charles and Cereno are each described as exceptionally "punctilious"; they are each shaved at a designated hour of the day. Charles's body was so tender that when some of the friars shook his hand, "the pain compelled him to withdraw his hand, and say, 'Pray don't, father; it hurts me' "[13]; Delano wonders about Cereno, "where may one touch him without causing a shrink." They each relay "commands" to a stream of messengers. When Charles landed on the Spanish coast on his passage to the monastery, "being worn with suffering and fatigue, he was carried up from the boat in a chair."[14] As he continued toward the monastery, he was alternately borne in a litter and carried in the arms of his attendants. Benito Cereno is "so reduced as to be carried ashore in arms." He later attends the deposition "in his litter." Charles was "seized with violent vomitings; and . . . lay motionless, with closed eyes"[15]; Cereno's "cough returned and with increased violence; this subsiding, with reddened lips and closed eyes." This description of Charles may have suggested the creation of his supernatural ghost: "He wrapped his emaciated body in hair-cloth, and flogged it with scourges, which were afterwards found in his cell, stained with his blood. Restless and sleepless, he would roam, ghostlike, through the corridors of the convent. . . ."[16] Cereno is called "cadaverous" several times; he is "almost worn to a skeleton"; "he is like one flayed alive"; he is likened to a "somnambulist." And he is nothing if not "ghostlike." Delano "began to feel a ghostly dread of Don Benito"; he thinks of "the dark Spaniard himself, the central hobgoblin of all"; he remarks on "his usual ghastliness."

The ghostly Benito Cereno captains a ship which is continually called unreal and enchanted. The *San Dominick* is in fact a ghost ship, the floating coffin and tomb of the ghost of Charles the Fifth. What Melville calls "a strange craft; a strange history, too, and strange folks on board" float directly from a funeral procession for Charles:

> Its principal feature was a huge galley, large enough for marine service, placed on a cunningly devised sea, which answered the double purpose of supporting some isles, emblematic of the Indies, and of concealing the power which rolled the huge structure along. Faith, Hope, and Charity, were the crew of this enchanted bark.[17]

The sea upon which the *San Dominick* floats also seems devised: "The sea, though undulated into long roods of swells, seemed fixed, and was sleeked at the surface like waved lead that has cooled and set in the smelter's mold"; "the leaden ocean seemed laid out and leaded up." When Delano first boards the ship, he seems to be boarding a ghost ship, an enchanted bark: "The ship seems unreal; these strange costumes, gestures, and faces, but a shadowy tableau just emerged from the deep, which directly must receive back what it gave." The *San Dominick*, that "strange craft" with "enchanted sails" whose bell has a "dreary graveyard toll," links at several points to the strange history of Charles's wandering body and coffins.

In a notorious incident, the emperor performed his own funeral rites before his death, followed his coffin, and perhaps even lay down in it.[18] After his death, his body was guarded by four monks.[19] The *San Dominick* is guarded by the four black oakum-pickers, whose "low, monotonous chant" is likened to a "funeral march." These four are "calkers" who may have some connection with "the state-cabin door . . . now calked fast like a sarcophagus lid." After several years in the monastery, Charles's body was transferred by Philip the Second to a new coffin in the Escorial. "The repose of the emperor was again broken," when, in 1654, Philip the Fourth removed the body to a new sepulchral chamber.[20] At this time the coffin was opened, and Philip saw the mysteriously preserved body of the emperor. (Several months after *Benito Cereno*'s publication, the coffin was again opened and what Philip had seen was seen again.[21])

Just before Philip saw death in the person of his forebear, a long sermon was preached on Ezekiel and the valley of dry bones. Just before the first association between death and the *jefe* of "*Seguid vuestro jefe*," we learn that the *San Dominick*'s "keel seemed laid, her ribs put together, and she launched, from Ezekiel's Valley of Dry Bones":

> Rudely painted or chalked, as in a sailor freak, along the forward side of a sort of pedestal below the canvas, was the sentence, "*Seguid vuestro jefe*," (follow your leader); while upon the tarnished headboards, near by, appeared in stately capitals, once gilt, the ship's name, "SAN DOMINICK," each letter streakingly corroded with tricklings of copper-spike rust; while, like mourning weeds, dark festoons of sea-grass slimily swept to and fro over the name, with every hearse-like roll of the hull. (p. 58)

Philip the Fourth's rites for Charles are climaxed when he confronts his dead forebear: "It became necessary to remove the previous coverings," and Philip came "face to face with his great ancestor."[22] The climax of *Benito Cereno* is also a confrontation, when his previous coverings are removed, with a dead leader: "But by this time the cable of the San Dominick had been cut; and the fag-end, in lashing out, whipped away the canvas shroud about the beak, suddenly revealing, as the bleached hull swung round towards the open ocean, death for the figure-head, in a human skeleton; chalky comment on the chalked words below, *"Follow your leader."*

Stirling last mentions Charles's first coffin in his concluding description of the monastic ruins: "In a vault beneath, approached by a door of which the key could not be found, I was told that the coffin of chestnut wood, in which the emperor's body had lain for sixteen years, was still kept as a relic."[23] While on the *San Dominick*, Captain Delano fancies himself in a "subterranean vault"; later comes that pregnant statement: "If the Deposition have served as the key to fit into the lock of the complications which precede it, then, as a vault whose door has been flung back, the San Dominick's hull lies open today."

The question now is whether we have found a key or a lock, clarification or obscuration of the central meanings of *Benito Cereno*. This question can be answered by turning first to one theme obvious even without the ghost of the emperor—the fading of his empire to a ghost authority:

> Upon a still nigher approach, this appearance was modified, and the true character of the vessel was plain—a Spanish merchantman of the first class, carrying negro slaves, amongst other valuable freight, from one colonial port to another. A very large, and, in its time, a very fine vessel, such as in those days were at intervals encountered along that main; sometimes superseded Acapulco treasure-ships, or retired frigates of the Spanish king's navy, which, like superannuated Italian palaces, still, under a decline of masters, preserved signs of former state. (p. 57)

The emperor's presence vastly extends this comment on empire.

Charles, who in name held absolute rule over more of the earth's surface than any other man in history, ended by exercising in fact almost as little absolute rule as Cereno, whose apparent command is described throughout the story in awesome terms. When Melville describes the sea captain as a being like a land monarch, his simile serves to define not only Cereno's rôle in the story but also the rôle of his counterpart in history. Since in Cereno "was lodged a dictatorship beyond which, while at sea, there was no earthly appeal," he serves as a well-chosen counterpart for the Holy Roman Emperor, who, in turn, functions as a well-chosen symbol of all authority on this earth. Thus, when Delano sees in Cereno the embodiment of supreme earthly power, his imperfect awareness applies just as well to Charles: "Lax as Don Benito's general authority might be, still, whenever he chose to exert it, no man so savage or colossal but must, more or less, bow." When this authority is found to be a sham, "and that silver-mounted sword, apparent symbol of despotic command, was not, indeed, a sword, but the ghost of one," the new awareness applies as well to Charles as it does to Cereno.

But Charles, like the "shield-like stern-piece," is, in this regard, only the "principal relic of faded grandeur." Each historical allusion in the story refers to the overthrow or fading of some particular worldly power. Melville compares Cereno to James the First: "No sword drawn before James the First of England, no assassination in that timid king's presence, could have produced a more terrified aspect than was now presented by Don Benito." Just as Charles's abdication had marked the passing of the Holy Roman Empire, the accession of James (according to a famous account in Melville's possession), "trembling at a drawn sword,"[24] had marked the passing of a British Empire: "On the day of the accession of James the First our country descended from the rank which she hitherto held, and began to be regarded as a power hardly of the second order."[25] Wounds inflicted on the Negroes are likened to "those shaven ones of the English at Preston Pans, made by the poled scythes of the Highlanders." In the battle of Preston Pans (fought, curiously, on September 21, the anniversary of Charles's death) the royalist forces were defeated by those of the Pretender. Delano compares Cereno's "Christian and Chesterfieldian" steward to George the Third, loser of both the American colonies and his own sanity.

A most significant parallel to the successful bloody rebellion of the slaves of the *San Dominick* is the successful bloody rebellion of the slaves of San Domingo, a topic of great antebellum interest. Melville changes the year of Delano's narrative from 1805 to 1799, thus making Babo's rule on the *San Dominick* contemporaneous with Toussaint L'Ouverture's rule over the entire island of San Domingo. Babo substitutes a skeleton for the *San Dominick*'s "proper figure-head—the image of Christopher Colon, the discoverer of the New World." San Domingo, not long after its discovery by Columbus, became the seat of Spanish imperial power in the New World. After the Spaniards had exterminated most of the natives, Charles the Fifth made San Domingo the site of the first large-scale importation of Negro slaves into the Western Hemisphere. Charles's funeral procession, with its "enchanted bark" and "isles emblematic of the Indies," ironically symbolizes the final disintegration of the Spanish New-World empire. Not without reason does Captain Delano think that "past, present, and future seemed one."

Notes

1. Herman Melville, "Benito Cereno," *Piazza Tales* (New York, 1948), 63. Future references are in the text and are by page number to this edition.

2. Since my list of periodicals contemporaneously referring to and quoting Melville and Stirling ran to almost three very dull pages, I have omitted it altogether.

3. William Stirling, *The Cloister Life of the Emperor Charles the Fifth*, 3rd ed. (London, 1853), 103–104, and variant, William Stirling, "The Cloister Life of the Emperor Charles V," *Fraser's Magazine*, XLIII, 372 (1851). These works will be referred to respectively as *Charles* and "Charles."

4. *Charles*, 104–105, 148, 321.

5. *Charles*, 104, 152, and "Charles," 379.

6. *Charles*, 119.

7. *Charles*, 104, and "Charles," 373, 375.

8. *Charles*, 320, and variant, "Charles," 373.

9. *Charles*, 80, and "Charles," 529.

10. *Charles*, 149.

11. *Charles*, 117, and "Charles," 375.

12. *Charles*, 5. The shoulder belongs to William of Orange, soon to be the nemesis of Spanish power. I doubt any relation to Babo.

13. *Charles*, 94.

14. "Charles," 367 and variant, *Charles*, 27.

15. *Charles*, 243.

16. "Charles," 533 and variant, *Charles*, 185.

17. "Charles," 539, and variant, *Charles*, 273.

18. *Charles*, xiii–xvii. 231, and "Charles," 535.

19. *Charles*, 247.

20. *Charles*, 278, and "Charles," 540.

21. For details see "El Emperador, Incorrupto," *ABC: Edicion Semanal Aerea* (Madrid: September 25, 1958).

22. "Charles," 540, and variant, *Charles*, 279.

23. *Charles*, 321.

24. Thomas Babington Macaulay, *The History of England* . . . , 5 vols. (New York, 1849–1861), 1, 69. (Sealts nos. 335–337.)

25. Macaulay, *The History of England* . . . , 1, 64.

["The Mechanism of Mystification" in "Benito Cereno"]

WARNER BERTHOFF

A painstaking casualness of exposition distinguishes all the stories and sketches Melville wrote between 1853 and 1856. Events are reported as they have fallen out, to observation or general hearsay; at the same time there is a continual pressure toward catching them up at once in some summary definition. The rhythm of the recital alternates accordingly between the quick pace of immediate happenings and the slower fluctuations of the teller's progress toward an understanding of them. One or the other rhythm may dominate. So "Bartleby," which runs more to dialogue and an orderly progression of incident, is only a little removed from an essentially dramatic organization; whereas in "Benito Cereno" for nearly a fifth of the text the narrative is wholly superseded by extracts from the record of a court trial that belongs to the story but takes place quite outside its frame of action. These radical shifts of narrative pace and perspective, these interruptions for comment or for validating evidence, are also present in Melville's first several books; but there, where his purposes were descriptive and documentary, they do not seem out of keeping with the general scheme of presentation. For the different purposes of the novella or tale, they are usually felt to be much less suitable. To as sympathetic a reader as Newton Arvin they are simply further indications of Melville's "flagging vitality and depleted inventiveness" in the years after *Moby-Dick*; they are so many obstacles to what was really needed, "a clear and strong perfection of fictional form."[1] My own view of the workmanship in Melville's later stories (and of the standard of "fictional form") is rather different, as must now be fairly clear. In any case it seems only reasonable not to write off so persistent a set of compositional practices as the product of exhaustion or fumbling, but to take them as they come, for the serious virtue that may be in them; for what they positively contribute, that is, to a body of work of which it is scarcely possible not to feel the peculiar originality and expressiveness.

The uneasiness of critics with Melville's narrative procedures has been especially acute in the case of "Benito Cereno."[2] Here, in point of fact, he

Reprinted from *The Example of Melville* (Princeton: Princeton University Press, 1962), 149–58. Reprinted by permission of the publisher.

was retelling an old story, the central situation and many details of which he had come upon in a *Narrative of Voyages and Travels in the Northern and Southern Hemispheres* (1817) by one Amasa Delano—whose name he did not bother to change. What was it that attracted Melville to this story, in which an odd and vaguely ominous succession of incidents is suddenly revealed, in a single instant of action, to mean very terribly the opposite of what it has seemed? If we take Melville's rendering of it as a fable—of innocence and evil, or of spiritual obtuseness and spiritual suffering—we might indeed have to say that the narrative is awkward and negligent in composition, and that it really does not make its point. Surely a competent allegorist could have managed the display more efficiently, and a clear-headed moralist would have devised a less eccentric balance of forces. But is it not reasonably apparent that what primarily caught Melville's practical interest as a writer was just the intense chiaroscuro strangeness of the situation and of its material facts, with their—literally—double meaning? Why else should he stick so closely to the data of his source, and set the additional incidents of his own invention in so nearly the same mold? Melville's leading impulse in working out the sequence of his retelling was to capitalize on just this material ambiguity, and on the delayed double-exposure it results in. That impulse was not greatly different from the conjuror's impulse behind those stories of Poe's (also written for magazines) which are exercises in the fine art of mystification. The appearances put before us in "Benito Cereno" constitute a riddle, and the business of two thirds of the narrative is the elaboration of this riddle and then its sudden clarification (thus the climax is no more a dramatic one than the climax of Poe's "The Gold-Bug").

Of course there is "more" to the story than this—a moral gravity, a psychological intensity, an appropriately shadowy atmosphere, an ironic realization of the stain of human slavery. All these things Melville drew out of his materials, and they have not gone unnoticed. But one way of appreciating his achievement in "Benito Cereno" is to see how all this "more" is built directly upon the central ambiguity, the mechanism of mystification. What we are shown comes largely by way of Captain Delano, through what he notices about the strange Spanish ship and its stranger captain and through what he progressively thinks—or gets almost to the point of thinking. At the end, it is true, the contrast between Captain Delano's awareness and Don Benito's rather displaces the riddle through which we have come to know it. Yet there is no real effort to harden this contrast into a generalized moral figure. It is presented simply as the consistent outcome of the harrowingly different circumstances through which these two lives have come to their strange meeting. "Benito Cereno" does have, I am sure, a seriousness of general implication and a closeness to common reality that reach beyond Poe's capacity as an artist. By its strict narrative fidelity to its particular core of truth, certain features of it are indeed powerfully suggestive of some general order of existence. The states of mind Captain Delano passes through are not, after all, essentially different from the ordinary ways by which we move, more or less blindly, through our works and days. So the story can fairly be seen as composing a paradigm of the secret ambiguity of appearances—an old theme with Melville—and, more particularly, a paradigm of the inward life of ordinary consciousness, with all its mysterious shifts, penetrations, and side-slippings, in a world in which this ambiguity of appearances is the baffling norm. But to say this of "Benito Cereno" is precisely not to lose sight of its form as a story, and of the curious way in which the exposition is actually carried out.

There remains the problem of the ending. The event clearing up the stretched-out riddle—Don Benito's leap, and then Babo's after him, into Captain Delano's whaleboat—takes barely a page and a half to describe; a few more pages quickly close out the main action of the story. But then everything that has happened so far is put before us a second time, and more besides—in the cumbersome style of a judicial exposition (modeled on documents given in the source narrative). Other than that it fills pages, is there anything to be said for this contrivance? Or do we concur in the judgment of the story's first reader, the knowledgeable G. W. Curtis, who told the editor of *Putnam's*: "It is a great pity he did not work it up as a connected tale instead of putting in the dreary documents at the end.—They should have been made part of the substance of the story."

No doubt an argument on the point of form which is involved can be made either way. My own judgment of the matter begins simply with my finding this part of the narrative exactly as interesting as the mystifying incidents which it follows and which it serves to review and explain. If we take "Benito Cereno" as allegory or fable, these court documents must seem a mistake, and a nearly inexplicable mistake. If our measure is dramatic organization, they are scarcely less troublesome. But if we accept it as, in form, an extended narrative riddle, then they are legitimate, or make themselves so. We are not finished with a serious riddle when we hear it solved. It remains to go back over all the significant detail of it from the point of view of the revealed solution. For both the riddler and (if he has been played with fairly) the beriddled, this orderly itemization of data which was first mystifying but now falls into place rounds out the pleasure given by the whole performance. And in this respect the riddle may be seen as a particular, highly stylized variety of the general form of the told story. Hearing a story which holds our attention to its promised end, we are similarly reluctant to let go. We look ahead to retellings. We circle back through the cruxes and important details; perhaps we imagine new details to heighten its special effects. And then we have somewhat to exorcise its charm over us, and our indulgence of that. We must allow the mechanism of our encounter with it to run down, to trail off into "anti-climax"; so we act to contain its disturbing force. The more concentrated the story, the greater the need to relax its hold gradually. For as it has the mettle and integrity of its own purposes, and stands by its own manner of assertion, it will the more compellingly gather to itself (as already in the imagination of its teller) reflections, afterthoughts, analogies, all those gestures of bemusement by which we acknowledge any efficient display of things-in-sequence. For all this to happen, of course, there must be in its readers a free play of curiosity and a willingness to be forcibly entertained. That is, there must be a positive tolerance of story-telling (as of anecdote and gossip) as a main type of the familiar music of civilized discourse—not always useful, not always harmonious. But those capable of this tolerance have their reward.

Actually, in "Benito Cereno," the introduction of explanatory documents is only the most abrupt of a series of shifts and starts in the presentation, roughly corresponding to the developing import of this curious story. The ambiguities of the riddle are acted out by a rapid alternation of moods, at once in the general atmosphere and in Captain Delano's mind. The compositional device that particularly sustains this pattern of alternation is the fragmenting of much of the narrative into very short paragraphs, a great many of which are just a sentence long and barely consecutive. A typical example is this passage following up the episode in which the negro Babo, after shaving Don Benito, whines that he has been punished with a razor cut for inadvertently scratching his master's cheek:

> ". . . Ah, ah, ah," holding his hand to his face.
>
> Is it possible, thought Captain Delano; was it to wreak in private his Spanish spite against this poor friend of his, that Don Benito, by his sullen manner, impelled me to withdraw? Ah, this slavery breeds ugly passions in man.—Poor fellow!
>
> He was about to speak in sympathy to the negro, but with a timid reluctance he now re-entered the cuddy.
>
> Presently master and man came forth; Don Benito leaning on his servant as if nothing had happened.
>
> But a sort of love-quarrel, after all, thought Captain Delano.
>
> He accosted Don Benito, and they walked slowly together. . . .

The very spareness and (emphasized by the paragraphing) brokenness of this kind of exposition are central to the story's massed effect—the sense of tension increasing and diminishing, the irregular measuring out of time, the nervous succession of antithetical feelings and intuitions. But once the riddle is broken open and fairly explained, once our concern can go out at last to the passional outcome of the whole affair, a different tactic is in order. So on the last page of the story we find Melville spinning out the same kind of spare, rapid, matter-of-fact statement into longer paragraphs and a more sustained and concentrated emphasis:

> As for the black—whose brain, not body, had schemed and led the revolt, with the plot—his slight frame, inadequate to that which it held, had at once

yielded to the superior muscular strength of his captor, in the boat. Seeing all was over, he uttered no sound, and could not be forced to. His aspect seemed to say, since I cannot do deeds, I will not speak words. Put in irons in the hold, with the rest, he was carried to Lima. During the passage, Don Benito did not visit him. Nor then, nor at any time after, would he look at him. Before the tribunal he refused. When pressed by the judges he fainted. On the testimony of the sailors alone rested the legal identity of Babo.

Some months after, dragged to the gibbet at the tail of a mule, the black met his voiceless end. The body was burned to ashes; but for many days, the head, that hive of subtlety, fixed on a pole in the Plaza, met, unabashed, the gaze of the whites; and across the Plaza looked towards St. Bartholomew's church, in whose vaults slept then, as now, the recovered bones of Aranda: and across the Rimac bridge looked towards the monastery, on Mount Agonia without; where, three months after being dismissed by the court, Benito Cereno, borne on the bier, did, indeed, follow his leader.

Especially after the teasing oscillations of mood in the long first part and the dry repetitions of the court records that follow, these fine last paragraphs, terse, rapid, taut with detail, seem a particularly impressive instance of Melville's ordinary boldness in fitting his performance to the whole developing occasion. There is no worked-up climax; what is said is shaped strictly to the job of making an end. Other instances, from other work, may be cited. *Moby-Dick* especially is alive with this matching of narrative pace and address to the matter in hand—as in the series of paragraph breaks and openings at the beginning of the splendid chapter, "Brit," coming just after three static expository chapters of whaling lore:

> Steering north-eastward from the Crozetts, we fell in with vast meadows of brit, the minute, yellow substance, upon which the Right Whale largely feeds. For leagues and leagues it undulated round us, so that we seemed to be sailing through boundless fields of ripe and golden wheat.
>
> On the second day, numbers of Right Whales were seen, who, secure from the attack of a Sperm Whaler like the Pequod, with open jaws sluggishly swam through the brit, which, adhering to the fringing fibres of that wondrous Venetian blind in their mouths, was in that manner separated from the water that escaped at the lip.
>
> As morning mowers, who side by side slowly and seethingly advance their scythes through the long wet grass of marshy meads; even so these monsters swam, making a strange, grassy, cutting sound; and leaving behind them endless swaths of blue upon the yellow sea.
>
> But it was only the sound they made as they parted the brit which at all reminded one of mowers. Seen from the mastheads. . . .

—so we keep pace as the *Pequod* is borne deeper and deeper into the marvelous arena of its fated voyage.

Once gained, this sensitivity in handling narrative became for Melville—especially after the drawing-in of his ambition as a declarer of prophetic truths—perhaps the steadiest of his working motives, and the surest source of his unflagging originality. In the closing chapters of *Billy Budd* we find the same deliberate use as in "Benito Cereno" of an interrupted, anticlimactic descent from the main line of action, for the sake of a further climax and consolidation of feeling. At another point in *Billy Budd* a curtain of silence and secrecy is abruptly brought down, in the middle of the thickly circumstantial narration, as a means of setting off the pivotal episode of Vere's last interview with Billy. A similar interruption figures at the center of the eighth "Encantadas" sketch, in the story of the Chola widow ("Against my own purposes a pause descends upon me here"); again, what lies deepest in the story is as if handed back to the imagination of the reader—for whom, of course, the teller's abrupt gesture of reticence is as effective as any dramatic image.

In each case, we see, the effect is managed with a perfect simplicity of means. And it is in this free control of narrative succession, this precise formal response to his story's advancing power of implication, that we find the central compositional tact of Melville's art. It seems to me a creative tact of the very highest order.[3] At his level best he will not force his tales out of their advancing line of truth—not for the sake of a a moral argument, nor for dramatic sensation, nor for any preconceived formality of design. He is indeed, in managing his materials, the least arbitrary of the great American writers—which is one reason, I think, why his work as a writer of stories seems to move the most insistently and yet naturally toward the free suggestiveness, the profounder creativity, of myth.

Notes

1. Newton Arvin, *Herman Melville* (New York, 1950), pp. 231–40.
2. Disagreements about this story tend to be complete, but arise, I think, largely from misconceptions as to the form adopted and the effects proper to it. For various reasons there is a reluctance nowadays to accept Melville as first of all a teller of stories. A work of literature that resists reductive "interpretation," and that primarily intends to rehearse a certain circumstantial course of action, seems somewhat less than wholly serious. The "gray shadows" of those high-minded Puritan forefathers whose dismissal for frivolity Hawthorne pretended to fear are still among us, disguised as interpretive critics, and it is their habit to be ill at ease with imaginative literature until it has been tidied up for value-analysis and tricked out to resemble those decorous humanistic fables or shadow-plays (or paragons of "fictional form") preferred by general-educators and their helpless students.

In any case, consider these two representative views of "Benito Cereno." To Richard Chase it is "masterful," both in building up dramatic suspense and in its resolution of certain unitary "moral ideas." To Newton Arvin, however, it is an "artistic miscarriage," written at too low a pitch to signify much of anything. The difference of opinion seems absolute. Yet both views, we notice as we follow them out, proceed from the assumption that the story is to be understood as a *parable*, a methodically figurative display of, in this instance, the exposure of something called "innocence" to something called "evil" or "the dark side of life."

And by applying to it, arbitrarily it seems to me, the standards of allegorical or of dramatic coherence, both commentators—Chase not less than Arvin—miss the particular logic and fascination of this remarkable narrative. The earlier impressions set down by John Freeman and Yvor Winters seem to me much more responsive to Melville's actual accomplishment— the first finding in the story's "broken and oblique narration" a perfected anticipation of a method dear to Conrad; the second categorizing it as the portrayal of an *action* and its effects, in a style ("the style of a novelist") which is "both classical and austere" in going about its appointed business.

See Richard Chase, "Introduction," *Selected Tales and Poems by Herman Melville* (New York, 1950); Newton Arvin, *Herman Melville* (New York, 1950); John Freeman, *Herman Melville* (New York, 1926); Yvor Winters, *Maule's Curse* (Norfolk, 1938).

3. Is it not what is disturbingly absent, by contrast, at too many critical junctures in Henry James's more intricately designed and (as Gide accurately put it) *dominated* novels and stories? There is too little margin, in James's fiction, for exploiting the purchase gained by the painstaking efficiency of the form and the fluid intelligence of the style.

"Benito Cereno": Melville's Fable of Black Complicity

KERMIT VANDERBILT

I

In spring of 1855, Charles Eliot Norton visited the slave-owning Middletons of South Carolina who in summer were his neighbors at fashionable Newport. The independent son of Andrews Norton (Emerson's Unitarian arch-enemy) could be expected to record the impressions of a not quite orthodox Yankee viewing the plantation system at first hand. In a number of letters home, Norton expressed his moral opposition to slavery in the South. But he based his objection not on the usual moral stance of northern abolitionism—that within this dehumanizing economic and social arrangement the slaves were the principal victims. Instead, Norton argued that the master-slave nexus was devastating not to the slave but to the master. Like certain other antislavery northerners, Norton sensed that present and future evils of human bondage might assume more varied and complex forms than were envisioned in Mrs. Stowe's philosophy. Herman Melville, with Norton, was one of these sensitive and skeptical northerners. In 1855, Melville wrote on the slavery question in "Benito Cereno" and gave the world one of his most perplexing stories. Unfortunately, we do not have a satisfactory record of Melville's private opinions on slavery to 1855 that might aid in unraveling the ambiguities of this fiction. But a brief look at Norton's views will suggest a new way of entering into the meaning of Melville's now-popular story of a slave revolt in the last century.

Norton described to Francis J. Child on March 15, 1855, the salient, though seemingly "indirect symptoms of the curse and blight of slavery, in the conditions of the whites." He termed bondage "deadly" to the masters "on thought, on character, on aim in life, on hope," for it had created a "moral miasma" even within the apparently benign "despotism" of the kindly Middletons. Moreover, the moral blight had visited "the women not less than the men." (This letter and the two that follow are in the Norton collection at Harvard University.) On April 5, to his English friend Arthur Hugh Clough, Norton reiterated his concern over the "blasting effects of

Reprinted from *The Southern Review* 12 (1976): 311–22, by permission of the author.

slavery" upon the masters, who were "bewildered by the perplexities of their position": "The hardest trials and the bitterest results of slavery as it exists here are those which come to the whites not the blacks." And the following day, in a letter to Lowell, Norton rephrased and amplified his main tenet that "one of the worst effects of slavery is to deaden the moral feelings and to obscure the intellects of the masters." He returned to the moral bewilderment of the white women as well. But this time, perhaps because he was writing on Good Friday, he also mused on the seeming impotence of Christianity and human law to eradicate, or even ameliorate, the institution of slavery.

While these brief excerpts do incomplete justice to the complexity of Norton's attitudes during the tension-charged 1850s, they supply the key to an important part of Melville's much-debated "Benito Cereno." Appearing in *Putnam's* later in the same year, the story can be interpreted in Norton's sense that the effects of slavery are deadly—if not deadlier—to the master. Melville's slavemasters Aranda and Benito Cereno, like Norton's Middletons, appear the kindly but overwhelmed victims of black servitude. Also, in his treatment of the vindictive, and largely impotent, white "vice-regal" court hearing in Peru that condemns the black insurrectionist leader, Babo, Melville agrees with Norton's view that the evils of slavery lie beyond any progressive reform through the codes of human law. And lastly, as Norton suggested and Melville confirms in his allusive tale, the sanctions and holy offices of the Church are equally ineffective in arresting these same evils. Melville then, like Norton, denies the moral and legal optimism of the abolitionists and reverses their standard perspective on the black victims of slavery.

Indeed, his conception of oppressive servitude moved Melville farther still from the dominant antislavery voices, and even beyond Norton's moral algebra. Intrigued by Amasa Delano's 1817 *Narrative* of a black mutiny aboard a Spanish slaveship, Melville imagined the moral consequences of a further reversal. If slavery weighs most heavily upon the master class, what happens when the white master and black slave exchange roles? (To turn the elitist white man's burden around, racially and morally, would have been an outrageous fiction beyond the reach of Norton's imagination.) Melville's preliminary conclusion appears to be that when the black slaves become black masters in the shipboard revolt, the effect on their humanity is far more deadly than under their previous black servitude, and upon the black women as well as the men—as Norton, too, had observed of both sexes in the master class. And reciprocally, Benito Cereno, though emotionally ravaged by the mutiny which has reduced him from master to slave, appears to grow in human awareness and tragic wisdom. Melville, in fact, removed the villainous traits from the original Cereno in Delano's historical account. One may conclude then that Melville discovered in slavery more than a contemporary "Negro Question," was even recasting, in Babo and the blacks, the crime of

Hawthorne's Ethan Brand and Chillingworth who commit the "unpardonable sin" of heartless mastery over their brother-man. Looking ahead to the twentieth century, one would observe a significant return of some of these recognitions in the morally awakened southern heroes of Faulkner, Robert Penn Warren, and William Styron, as well as in the writings of Ralph Ellison and the early James Baldwin.

This approach to Melville's meaning through the heartless black mastery by Babo and his followers, however, shares the ultimate defect of many other readings of Melville's story: valid up to a point, it does not quite account for the crucial passages in the text which, together, compose Melville's total vision. And so I must ask the reader's indulgence in advancing with me through one last dark variation which Melville seems to have played on Mrs. Stowe's abolitionism, as well as on Norton's and Hawthorne's sense of the blighting moral consequences of slavery upon the master.

The masters and slaves of Melville's story, in their reversal of roles and duplication of identities, gradually merge in the reader's mind. Oppressive servitude, in short, becomes more than a two-way street in which passage in one direction might be more deadly than in the other. The story takes on not a linear but a spiraling design of intolerance and oppression that will continue throughout human history; and slavery becomes a metaphor of the black complicity of mankind. In dramatizing one instance in these never-ending cycles of persecution and revenge, Melville ranges through obvious contemporary questions of social injustice, through Hawthorne's vision of a dark brotherhood of sin and Ishmael's third view of whiteness—the "heartless void" beyond good or evil—and finally poses a cosmic quarrel with an oppressive God, the Cause of the first cosmic mutiny, the original, heartless Master. So understood, "Benito Cereno" begins to appear the most angry and hopeless of Melville's comments on man's unrelenting search for his humanity and reason for existing. That Melville intended for his contemporary audience some degree of tragic catharsis is problematical. Today, if this ritual-drama of mutual vengeance and righteous massacre seems hideously prophetic to a reader of the 1970s, it may at least return a certain relief in our fuller recognition of the careful, allusive art with which Melville reenacts and illuminates one bloody sequence of crimes in our history. "Benito Cereno" as a Melvillean act of imagination embodies what Nietzsche termed the protection and remedy of art which enables man to tolerate his pained awareness of a bleak universe.

II

Melville conceived "Benito Cereno" in two forward-moving actions, a deputation resumé by Cereno, a brief flashback, and a concluding epilogue. Transparent in outline and, for Melville, remarkably matter-of-fact in style, the tale harbors numerous masks, disguises, and allusive cross-identities, so that a reader's slowly developing sense is of a coiled and knotted inquiry into the slaveship mutiny and the vengeful aftermath. The story opens upon a "gray" dawn, "mute and calm," pointedly ushering in the ominous mood and prevailing theme of the story. In blatantly ironic counterpoint, Melville introduces the American Captain Delano "of a singularly good nature" who reluctantly, if ever, is given "to indulge in personal alarms, any way involving the imputation of malign evil in man." Delano boards Cereno's battered Spanish ship and, during his day-long suspicions, never pierces to the reality that he is the guest at a masked black slave insurrection. Critics of the story have written far too much on the pointed irony of Delano's innocent puzzlements and moral clichés. In the process, such criticism has failed to distinguish between a reader's immediate, and largely shared, experience of Delano's quandary as opposed to one's later understanding of it. Coming to the story as a first-time reader, one will discover Melville's using Delano for two purposes more important than injecting an Emersonian naïveté which one may wish to scoff at in retrospect. First, Delano establishes for the reader the plausible, orthodox view that slavery is a two-way institution that separates men into unyielding masters and dog-like servants. Through Delano's perplexed consciousness, Cereno becomes the felt oppressor. I shall grant that the extent of this response will vary with a reader's quickness to realize some possibility of the black mutiny. Delano speculates on what *kind* of master of this strange foreign slaveship Cereno is. But he never doubts that Cereno is, as black "servant" Babo insistently addresses him, the "master." Or when the imposing black Atufal appears on deck, in chains for the past sixty days because, we are told, he had given Cereno "peculiar cause of offense," the reader recognizes, with Delano, the historical validity of such petty intimidation of master upon slave. Or in a parallel scene, after shaving Cereno, Babo appears on deck, his cheek bleeding from a razor wound inflicted apparently by Cereno because the slave "had given master one little scratch."

Whatever gain the reader has made beyond the perceptions of Delano this late in the day, he can still assent in his own way to Delano's human conclusion: "Ah, this slavery breeds ugly passions in man." And again later, we feel the same truth that Norton had observed, that even the most lenient of plantation gentlemen suffered their own debilitating penalty as slave masters. Delano one last time before departing urges leniency for Atufal and adds, "Ah, Don Benito, for all the license you permit in some things, I fear lest, at bottom, you are a bitter hard master." When Delano believes that Cereno "shrank; and this time . . . from a genuine twinge of conscience," we feel that Delano very well may be observing accurately, may have genuinely awakened Cereno's conscience at last to what it means to be a master—or a slave.

At the same time that he grants the reader a series of orthodox responses to bondage and oppressive mastery, Delano serves a second and more vital function. During his long day of private and open questionings, he creates a webwork of ambiguous facts which Melville can fully exploit in Cereno's deposition for the Lima court. As we shall see, the ultimate effect of Melville's unfolding drama of slavery at that later stage of the tale goes well beyond ironic qualification or reversal of Delano's mistaken conclusions. Instead, we become aware of the intricate complicity of all the actors in the story. To this end, the crucial moments observed by Delano on the opening day are those which suggest or prefigure the merging roles and identities of masters and slaves. Added to those I have already cited, such moments include Delano's fancied observation before boarding Cereno's *San Dominick*, that the ship is like a holy retreat and the blacks like "Black Friars" strolling within the cloisters. (I shall later treat Melville's various allusions to the Church.) Delano soon observes the stern-piece with its central carving of "a dark satyr in a mask, holding his foot on the prostrate neck of a writhing figure, likewise masked."

In addition to these mutually masked oppressor-and-oppressed figures, the ship carries below its canvased bow the words *"Seguid vuestro jefe,"* an injunction to which multiple meanings will accrue. Cereno appears to Delano "like some hypochondriac abbot" and black Babo's "offices" to his "master" seem "filial or fraternal," though appropriate for a "pleasing body-servant . . . whom a master need be on no stiffly superior terms with, but may treat with familiar trust; less a servant than a devoted companion." When Cereno momentarily withdraws from his conversation with Delano, Babo "encircle[s] his master"; Babo appears "a sort of privy-counselor" to his master; or they seem, face to face, to have "the air of conspirators." Delano goes so far as to question if Cereno might in some manner be "in complicity with the blacks," but reassures himself that "they were too stupid." After Babo appears on deck with a cheek bleeding, having previously nicked Cereno during the shaving scene, Delano is relieved to see master and servant reappear closely paired: "But a sort of love-quarrel, after all, thought Captain Delano." The revealing hint here, not unusual in Melville, is that the antagonists have attained a homoerotic closeness.

The same merging intimacy and identity are repeated, with a minor variation, in the case of Atufal—formerly a black master in his native land—whose chains are padlocked at the iron-banded "girdle" which opens, Delano is told, with the key which depends "by a slender silken cord" from the rather effeminate Cereno's neck. Again, the first-time reader shares Delano's uneasy musing upon the nature of the "lordship" here, as well as on the "padlock and key—significant symbols, truly." The steward Francesco, a mulatto, seems to Delano a "good, worthy" product of miscegenation with "us white-skins." The reader may separate himself from the liberal-benevolent racism of Delano's remark; but he is no more aware than Delano that the mulatto servant, now of the master class, is nursing murderous thoughts (later disclosed) against the American. As before, Delano has supplied an observation. With him we shall later know more from Cereno's testimony—and at *that* time with perhaps greater shock than the buoyant Delano regarding the grim discoveries of black-and-white (and mulatto) slave-and-master complicity.

The merging of identities is again the technique that explains the much discussed incident of the knotted rope. Thrown urgently to Delano by one of Cereno's Spanish crewmen ("Undo it, cut it, quick"), the rope, be it noted, is more than a simple two-stranded knot. The old sailor's hands had been "full of ropes" and, aided by several blacks, he had designed a knot that "seemed a combination of double-bowline-knot, treble-crown-knot, back-handed-well-knot, knot-in-and-out-knot, and jamming knot." Delano with "knot in hand, and knot in head" is unable to fathom the black-white reversal of roles, much less the darkly knotted complicity of oppressive bondage aboard the slaveship. But for that matter, at this preliminary stage, neither is the reader capable of knowing what the knotted rope must at last come to imply.

Finally, as he departs in his boat, Delano struggles with the escaped Cereno "while his right foot, on the other side, ground the prostrate negro." Here, perhaps, for the first time, most readers make a clear gain over the analytic, confused, and rather smug Delano who has been their recalcitrant guide through the shadowy world of the *San Dominick*. At the instant when even Delano realizes that Babo is, in fact, the master in pursuit of his enslaved leader, Melville casts Delano, unknowingly, into the role of the new oppressor. For Delano has become, Babo-like, the fierce dark satyr and Babo the writhing victim under his heel—the portentous emblem which Delano had observed on Cereno's stern-piece.

III

The second segment of the story advances too swiftly for Delano, and the reader, to consider as yet the dread implications of the *San Dominick* insurrection and the various forms of "reality" which have lain behind, and coiled within, the appearances which Delano has speculated upon. Fully exposed, however, is the bow of the *San Dominick* bearing the skeleton of slaveowner Aranda above the inscription "Follow your leader" while Babo is lifted aboard Delano's *Bachelor's Delight* and, for Cereno's psychic benefit, taken below deck. The circle of vengeance continues in the dark of the moon without intermission.

The dark-satyr stance of Delano moments before, as we have noticed, announces a new agent of counter-oppression to succeed the Europeans in this brief second stage of the action. Delano now sends his white American crew, greedy for gold and armed with muskets, against the blacks who lack firearms. For the "leader" of this economic aggression, Delano appoints his chief mate. In the battle that follows, nearly a score of blacks are killed and many mangled, whereas the whites suffer no fatalities whatsoever. But Melville evens the score by attaching bestial imagery to the blacks, assuring us that we are witness to a battle of mutual savagery. Of the several wounded among Delano's crew is the chief mate who had echoed the inscription below Aranda's skeleton, "Follow your leader," as he commanded the Americans to invade the *San Dominick*. The obvious equation here links the mission of Delano, his first mate, and the Americans to the career of slaveowner Aranda and the Spanish, as well as to the original author of "Follow your leader," Babo himself, the slave turned master turned slave who now awaits his fate in the hold of Delano's *Bachelor's Delight* at the hands of his previously enslaved whites again become his oppressors. As the reader moves out of this second action, he is more fully prepared for the disclosure at the Lima tribunal and the meaning which Melville has been gradually unfolding: the vicious design of one episode in Western slavery can serve to recapitulate the dark pattern of human history.

IV

Cereno's deposition at the Lima court is ostensibly an account of Babo's mutinous reversal of roles, so that the black servant and his fellow slaves are fully unmasked as the ferocious avengers of their white masters. But there is far more of unmasking than this. In the deceptively flat language of legal depositions, Melville fashions the last touches in the enclosing web of human oppression. A complete cycle of history now stands revealed as Cereno recounts (1) the state of the enslaved blacks before the mutiny; (2) their conducting an elaborately bloody coup in overthrowing the master class aboard the *San Dominick*; (3) their clever role-playing during Delano's visit, climaxed by (4) their being savagely undone by the white sailors. Through all this maze of evidence of white mastery and black mastery, a new agent of vengeance looms. The Lima court now succeeds Delano's crew as the narrowly vindictive and ultimately powerless instrument of white oppression. For the court to execute Babo as the aggressive agent during this characteristic episode in the cyclical history of human bloodletting and intolerance is to reduce justice to an outrageous scapegoat diversion. The court impersonally sanctions the original enslavement of blacks, viewing them but not the whites as defendants in a "criminal cause." In this unruffled acquiescence to one-sided oppression, "the honorable court" at Lima condones Cereno and reinforces the self-righteous myopia of Delano. But more hopelessly, Aranda, Cereno, and the Old World are to be succeeded by Delano and his followers— by a new arrogance of power, that is, dangerously coupled to the myth of American innocence. We realize that one-sided legitimacy of oppression in Europe will be perpetuated in the New World. The original figure on the masthead above Babo's "Follow your leader" was, in fact, Christopher Columbus. Humanity, therefore, does not progress. Moral declarations of independence from the tyranny of ancient law notwithstanding, history inevitably coils back on itself.

Particularly grim in this regard is the evidence in Cereno's deposition concerning the black women's part in the insurrection. Delano as the benevolent racist had observed them in the presumed docility of the benighted sex of a benighted race. "Unsophisticated as leopardesses; loving as doves" is Delano's reassuring verdict on their ignorantly naked and natural motherliness during the opening day's action. The deposition reveals that earlier, during the revolt, the subdued sex of the servant class became, as the master class, more bloodthirsty than the black males. The rising mathematics of enslavement are clear: compensation for the oppressed throughout history has been not merely reparation equal to the degree of oppression, but instead an overcompensation from the oppressor. Hence the self-perpetuating and mounting hopelessness of enslaved mankind continues unabated.

Cereno's deposition also reveals that Aranda had left the black slaves comfortably unfettered upon the deck; so that, momentarily liberated, the blacks in their ingratitude seem far more savage than their white oppressors. But the last page of the deposition reveals that after the white crew again had mastered the black servant-masters, the murdering of the reenslaved slaves, even as they were shackled, at least equaled any of the foregoing black savagery. Indeed, for the final moment in Cereno's testimony which will legalize the uncivilized beheading of Babo, Melville improvised revealingly upon his historical source: "the noble Captain Amasa Delano also wrenched from the hand of Bartholomew Barlo a dagger, secreted at the time of the massacre of the whites, with which he was in the act of stabbing a shackled negro, who, the same day, with another negro, had thrown him down and jumped upon him." In this vivid closing moment of his third act, Melville has prepared the reader in several ways for the concluding flashback and epilogue to follow. First is the posture of Delano who stands as superior American moral referee, presumably outside the tragic history of which he has been, in fact, an accomplice. Second are the endless cycles of vengeance implied within the statement. And clinching the theme is the allusion to "Bartholomew," Melville's own name for this knife-bearing sailor, associating in the reader's mind the fate of the religious martyr who is usually portrayed with a knife as emblem of his death by flaying and beheading. All of this and more will come together in Melville's closing pages.

V

Perhaps obvious now is why Melville chose to climax his tale not with the repressive legal-historical aftermath to the black insurrection but instead with the flashback of Cereno's and Delano's conversations on the voyage from Chile to the Lima court. His detailed account of oppression and counter-oppression now achieved by the deposition of Cereno, Melville can pose implicitly the climactic question of redemptive knowledge. Slavery has emerged as a many-sided universal metaphor of human existence, though the extent of tragic awareness on the part of the various characters is variously and woefully incomplete. One should be wary, for example, of attributing an excess of heroic awakening to Cereno with his moody reference to the cosmic "negro" that now overshadows his life. Delano has failed to experience the degree of dark complicity of Cereno aboard the *San Dominick*. But the effete Old-World aristocrat is scarcely a hopeful figure of redemptive knowledge.

In particular, it is questionable to what degree Cereno has discovered in Babo's suave mastery the "negro" mirror-image of himself. Somewhat like the hero of Hawthorne's "Young Goodman Brown," the tale whose "blackness" Melville had admired several years before, Cereno has accompanied Babo into the universal brotherhood of evil without fully admitting to this moral democracy. At the end, he arms himself with a few weak platitudes of a declining faith to ward off the oncoming shadows. Partly traumatized by "memory," he labors to view himself as "an innocent man" who can piously assure Delano that "God lives" and, with His Son, has "charmed" with "safe-conduct through all ambuscades" the happy-go-lucky American accomplice with the avenging white crew. The more dread possibilities, missed by all of the characters, surface in large part through verbal echoes and thematic allusions at the end.

The palled "melancholy muteness" of Cereno, for example, repeats a persistent motif that first appeared in the gravely "mute" cast of the opening scene looking out to Cereno's slaveship. Cereno later remembers the pervasive "melancholy" with which the black women enveloped the fierce atmosphere of counter-oppression during the earlier slave uprising. The verbal echo links the ineffable perplexity of whites and blacks during the various stages of the action. And Cereno's muteness, like Atufal's earlier ("How like a mute"), is duplicated, in the paragraph to follow, by black Babo's final muteness—recalling, in a neat racial inversion, the silent end of Shakespeare's white Iago after he ensnared his black master Othello. Or if the pallid Cereno has suggested earlier a melancholy Hamlet, Babo in turn resembles a vengeful Hamlet as his late "aspect seemed to say, since I cannot do deeds, I will not speak words." The merging characteristics of Babo and Cereno are again suggested in a religious-historical parallel. Delano's first view of the mutinous *San Dominick* (renamed by Melville from the original *The Tryal*) suggests to him a Spanish "white-washed monastery after a thunderstorm" with "Black Friars pacing the cloisters." The Dominicans were, of course, the leaders of the Inquisition in Spain. Unknown to Delano, the provocative leader these black friars are serving at the time is Babo—surrogate, then, of Charles V, who urged the Dominican friars toward the Inquisition. For his part, Cereno bears an even more sustained resemblance to the historical monarch, as Melville scholar Bruce Franklin has demonstrated.

And there is even more. At the end, with superbly pious presumption, Cereno implicitly likens himself to the risen Christ in describing Delano's earlier doubts: "You were with me all day; stood with me, sat with me, talked with me, ate with me. . . ." And yet ironically, Babo, on the way to court judgment and subsequent martyrdom, is denied more than thrice by his erstwhile disciple: "During the passage, Don Benito did not visit him. Nor then, nor at any time after, would he look at him. Before the tribunal he refused. When pressed by the judges he fainted." The "legal identity of Babo" is never established by Cereno. In Melville's brief epilogue, the mystery of Babo's identity continues, but here with a bizarre religious inversion. Disembodied and impaled, his head appears a "hive of subtlety" which has presumably recognized the pestilence of history. The image also recalls the cosmic rebel Beelzebub (lord of the flies), he who, in the words of Milton's heroic Satan, opposed the original "Tyranny of Heaven." Understandably, then, Babo's face gazes "unabashed" across the square of Lima toward the church of St. Bartholomew, which now harbors the recovered skeleton of the "leader," Aranda, and beyond to the monastery on Mount Agonia. There Cereno, in his imagined Christlike "innoncence," will "indeed, follow his leader." But to which of the several leaders toward death does Melville ambiguously refer?

Most of these knotted cross-allusions, and there are more, become clearer when one realizes that all of the "leaders" in "Benito Cereno" have been St. Bartholomew martyrs, a common equation that ultimately erases the dissimilarity in some of their particular responses. Cereno seems to Delano at first "almost worn to a skeleton" and during the shaving scene with Babo appears like "a man at the block" and later "like one flayed alive." Delano's appointed leader in the next action is his chief mate who is injured by flayings as the blacks and whites on both ships flay each other. In the aftermath, Babo, like St. Bartholomew, is beheaded by order of the court and gazes like an unabashed martyr "towards St. Bartholomew's Church" where lie the bones of the flayed leader Aranda.

Through these religious parallels and inversions, Melville finally teases the reader to undo the knot of a blasphemous, cosmic riddle. For whom have the St. Bartholomews of the world served in downward spiralling and bewildered martyrdom? Or rephrased, who is the ultimate Master, the First "Criminal Cause," Author of the history acted out by the humanity aboard the *San Dominick* in their barbarous exchange of master and martyr roles? In the allusions and motifs of his fable of complicity, Melville has pointed to several possible ways of answering the religious puzzle. The St. Bartholomews of the world have meant to follow their leader, the crucified Master-Servant, and his promise of liberation out of death into a new life; but on the way, they have served in absurd alternation as savaged martyrs and self-justifying headsmen of each other. Or phrased within the initial appearance-and-reality problem which the implicated but morally opaque American Delano cheerily left unsolved at the end: a spiritual brotherhood, "as of Black Friars pacing the cloisters," may appear the shadowy ideal of fallen man, in the hazy foreground; but it is mutual, dark-satyr, inquisitorial persecution (Delano's along with the rest) that coils endlessly in the background to become the bitter, unrelieved experience of the race. Rendered incapable of the redemptive vision of peace and merciful brotherhood, man has followed the lead of Jehovah-like wrath, vengeance, arbitrary justice, and assignations of death. In this light (or dark), "Benito Cereno" finally transcends historical oppression to become one of the bitterest moments in Melville's quarrel with the first vengeful and deadly Master.

Benito Cereno: Slavery and Violence in the Americas

Joyce Sparer Adler

An oracle for the United States before the Civil War, with resonating meaning for all of humanity, *Benito Cereno* (1855)[1] has been, like many a legendary oracle, misconceived by those who expect meaning to be conveyed in conventional ways. The assumption has been that Melville in this work borrowed the old symbolism of black as evil, white as good. Out of this has grown the common interpretation that Babo—leader of the black slave revolt on the *San Dominick*—is symbolic of Evil; that Don Benito Cereno—captain of the ship transporting slaves and friend from youth of the slave-owner— is the good victim of "black" iniquity; that Captain Amasa Delano of Massachusetts—who never seriously questions the enslavement of blacks and unconsciously accepts its rationale, who sees at all times only what is visible on the surface, and who learns nothing from the *San Dominick* experience, which he recommends forgetting—is innocence discovering Evil; and that slavery—without which there could be no *Benito Cereno*—is irrelevant to the story.

But Melville was a poet—maker, not taker, of symbols, methods, and forms. His head, being like Babo's a "hive of subtlety," he transformed the 1817 narrative written by a real Amasa Delano[2] into strange suggestive art through which he explored, more deeply and creatively than ever before, the master-slave relationship and the entanglement of slavery and violence; though he felt here, as everywhere else in his works, that the great iniquity resides in slavery, not in those who fight, no matter how bloodily, against it, he was impelled by the extraordinary situation recounted in the source to probe as profoundly as possible "horrors that happen so."[3]

Far from developing his thought in glaring black and white, Melville beclouded it, challenging American readers to "pierce"[4] in this work, as they needed to in life, the surface and also the upper substratum of slavery in order to arrive at its skeletal reality. In harmony with this purpose, his imagination brought forth entirely original artistic conceptions. The work is a series of palimpsestlike pictures. Layers of irony underlie obvious ironies.

Reprinted from *War in Melville's Imagination* (New York: New York University Press, 1981), 88–110. Copyright © 1981 by New York University Press. Reprinted by permission of the publisher.

Skeletons (human, ship, animal) imply the existence of innermost realities. There are hints of unseen "interiors." Shadows foreshadow; past, present, and future are merged. A fate for the United States akin to that of Spain in the Americas is conveyed through masked symbols. The sun is "screened"; brightness is "eclipsed." And the black and the white figures act as complex dialectical opposites, not unsubtle moral extremes, in a relationship as imprisoning as the "oaken walls" of the *San Dominick*, as contradictory as the situation that puzzles Delano, and as fraught with violence as the seemingly peaceful scene the North American captain fails to understand.

The arrangement of the work, too, implies an interior reality covered over by layers of misconceptions or mere facts. The story is presented in three parts, all objectively narrated. The opening section, read for the first time, seems to present only the facts as they unfold to Delano. The second, the deposition Don Benito gives to the court, provides the background. The third demands that readers think, after the story ends, about what is still missing, go back to the beginning, and try to penetrate to the underlying form and process of which this story is a fascinating instance. What happens in *Benito Cereno* is more a matter of what is hinted than what is told. For that reason a different kind of "plot" summary from the usual review of events alone is needed as the basis for my analysis of this work's fusion of art and thought.

The year is 1799, the place the waters off a small uninhabited island near the southern tip of South America. Captain Delano, whose ship, a combination of sealer and general trader, has anchored at the island for water, sees a "strange sail"—one gets the impression of a phantom ship—showing "no colors." All things are gray; gray fowl skim overhead "as swallows over meadows before storms," and everywhere are "Shadows present, foreshadowing deeper shadows to come." Seeing that the ship is in distress, Captain Delano lowers his whaleboat so that he may board the vessel and help to bring it in. As he approaches, it looks like a "white-washed" monastery. This is the first of a number of strange metaphors that place in juxtaposition the ship carrying masters and slaves and such structures as "superannuated Italian palaces . . . under a decline of masters" (241) and "the charred ruin of some summer-house in a grand garden long running to waste" (269), associations that seem farfetched and arbitrary until one sees that what links them is the idea of pretended value or past power, of social edifices that are skeletons of their "former state" or ghostly indications of their imminent collapse.

When he comes closer, Delano recognizes the ship as a Spanish merchantman carrying Negro slaves "amongst other valuable freight" from one colonial port to another. Once a frigate of the Spanish king's navy, "In the present business in which she was engaged, the ship's general model and rig appeared to have undergone no material change from their original warlike . . . pattern." (Here, as more openly in *White-Jacket* and *Billy Budd*, the ship of war and the ship of enslavement are one.) An oval sternpiece carved with the arms of Castile and León shows a dark satyr in a mask who holds his foot on the "prostrate" neck of a "writhing" figure also masked. Whether the ship has a figurehead is not clear to Captain Delano as he nears the *San Dominick*, for a canvas covers the bow, below which has been rudely painted "Seguid vuestro jefe" (Follow your leader). The name of the ship appears in corroded letters, once gilt.

Delano finds a crowd on board in which blacks, including women, outnumber whites more than is usual on a slave transportation ship. All tell a tale of death by storms and illness. Six black hatchet polishers are seated on an elevated poop and to Delano have "the raw aspect of unsophisticated Africans." Turning to see who is in command, he has his initial view of ill Don Benito and Babo—the first in a long series of tableaux featuring master and slave—and through Delano's early thought about the two, Melville subtly points to the phenomenon his work will explore: "As master and man stood before him, the black upholding the white, Captain Delano could not but bethink him of the beauty of that *relationship* which could present such a spectacle of fidelity on the one hand and confidence on the other. The scene was heightened by the contrast in dress, denoting their *relative* positions" (250; my emphasis).

As the day advances certain things make Delano uneasy: a lack of openness on the part of Don Benito, puzzling aspects of the story he tells, and odd behavior on the part of the crew. Don Benito explains that the slaves are unfettered, since their owner had said that with "his blacks" chains would be unnecessary. But one giant, Atufal, has an iron collar around his neck with a chain thrice wound around his body and a padlock at his waist. Delano is told that until Atufal asks Don Benito's pardon for some unnamed offense the chains must remain, but the Spanish captain has not been able to break down "the entrenched will of the slave." Feelings of security and insecurity ebb and flow in Delano. He feels vaguely that the *San Dominick*, "like a slumbering volcano," may "suddenly let loose energies now hid"—the very image of violence building up because of slavery that will reappear in "The Apparition" in *Battle-Pieces*. He does not suspect the blacks of any plot because he thinks they are by nature "too stupid" (270), but Don Benito's behavior seems at moments to bode ill.

The most significant scene in Part I is the one in which Delano watches Babo shave Don Benito, and the American captain's ideas about black people, which the work as a whole demolishes, flit through his mind. Among other things, he is amused by "an odd instance of the African love of bright colors and fine shows, in the black's informally taking from the flag-locker a great piece of bunting of all hues, and lavishly tucking it under his master's chin for an apron." When Babo chooses the sharpest razor, Don Benito's agitation loosens the bunting that opens up, so that one broad fold sweeps the floor and Delano sees that it is the flag of Spain that Babo has chosen to drape over Don Benito; but Delano smiles, thinking this reflects the black's love of gay colors. Delano presses Don Benito about unusual aspects of the story he has told; Babo somehow cuts his master; and the conversation is cut short. When soon afterward, Babo appears on deck with a bleeding cheek, Delano concludes that Don Benito has wreaked his anger at having been hurt, and he has his one brief feeling about slavery as an institution, a kind of sentimental regret: "Ah, this slavery breeds ugly passions in man." But when he sees Don Benito leaning on Babo as if nothing had happened, the relationship of master and slave again seems good to him. Moreover, it is a picture of the black man in chains that gives him his final reassurance that all is as it should be. The wind has risen, and acting for the sick Spanish captain, he has brought the *San Dominick* close to his own ship. Delano, whom Don Benito has refused to accompany, is about to leave the cabin to get into the small boat to return across a narrow passage of water. He is frightened, for the giant Atufal seems more a sentry guarding Don Benito, whom Delano now suspects of villainy, than a captive. But when he safely passes Atufal and the "screened sun in the quiet camp of the west" lights the scene, with the reassuring, normal "chained figure of the black," he smiles at the "phantoms" that have mocked him. As he takes leave of Don Benito, whom he now trusts again, and seats himself in his whale-boat, Don Benito suddenly springs over the bulwark to land in the boat and is, Delano thinks, about to murder him as a prelude to seizing his ship. Babo on the rail overhead stands "poised, in the act of leaping, as if with desperate fidelity to befriend his master to the last." Delano flings Don Benito aside in order to tackle Babo, who lands with his dagger pointed at Delano's heart. He grasps the weapon and flings Babo down into the bottom of the boat, which begins to speed away from the *San Dominick*. "At this juncture, the left hand of Captain Delano, on one side, again clutched the half-reclining Don Benito . . . while his right foot, on the other side, ground the prostrate negro." Looking down, Delano sees Babo aiming with a second dagger at the heart of Don Benito, his face expressing "the centred purpose of his soul." Then the mask is, for Delano, torn from the relationship of Don Benito and Babo. It is now clear that the slaves have been in control all along after an earlier revolt; all that Delano has seen has been the play of master and slave, the erstwhile slaves performing their expected roles, the erstwhile master playing his role under Babo's direction. Delano looks back at the ship and sees the blacks "with mask torn away" flourishing hatchets, in what to him is "ferocious piratical revolt." He sees also the canvas ripped away from the prow and the skeleton of Don Alexandro Aranda, the owner of most of the slaves, mounted on the bow as the ship's figurehead, in place of its original emblem. Babo, offering no resistance, is bound and hoisted onto Delano's ship. From this point on, he utters no word. Delano's men board the *San Dominick* where, with superior arms, they overwhelm the blacks, who battle to the last possible moment. Sometime later the whole affair is the subject of investigation by the vice-regal courts in Lima, "City of Kings."

Part II is Don Benito's deposition to the court, which many critics accept as a presentation of the full reality beneath the appearance seen by Delano.[5] But Melville's introduction to it, to the effect that the extracts will, "it is hoped" (299), shed light on the preceding narrative, immediately casts doubt on whether it indeed illuminates the most significant realities. It does, however, set the simple facts straight, making it known that on the seventh day of the San Dominick's voyage the slaves had revolted under the leadership of Babo, killing all the crew except those essential to the running of the ship. They then demanded of Don Benito whether there were any Negro countries nearby to which they might go and, discovering that there were none, ordered that they be taken to Senegal no matter how dangerous or difficult the voyage. Don Benito, pretending to consent, headed for the island of Santa María, presumably for water, but actually in the hope that he would there encounter help. Babo informed Don Benito that he had made up his mind to kill Don Alexandro because the slaves could not otherwise be sure of their liberty, and also as a warning to the others that they would follow him if they played the slaves false. On the fourth day thereafter, at sunrise, the negro Babo showed him the skeleton of Don Alexandro, "which had been substituted for the ship's proper figurehead—the image of Christobal Colon, the discoverer of the New World." Babo asked him whose skeleton it was "and whether, from its whiteness, he should not think it was a white's" (304–5). He then asked the same question of each Spaniard in turn, warning them that they would all go "soul and body"[6] the same way as Don Alexandro if he saw them plotting against the Negroes. When, approaching Santa María for water, the rebels saw Delano's ship in the harbor, they covered the skeleton figurehead, and Babo planned how to hide the true state of affairs, warning Don Benito that if he made any attempt to reveal the facts he would be stabbed. Babo made plans "uniting deceit and defense," including the pretense that the Ashantee hatchet carriers were simply at work polishing hatchets, whereas they were actually preparing to use them if necessary, and the pretense that Atufal was chained, whereas the iron collar was part of his costume and he could remove it at any time. Four elderly blacks were placed on high so that they could keep discipline and give orders when necessary. Don Benito was commanded to tell the story Babo invented for him. The rest was theater, the "play" of master and slave, directed by Babo who, at the same time, acted the part of personal slave to Don Benito, the better to control his performance. Benito Cereno is indeed a "juggling play" (282); the roles of master and slave are juggled.

Part III opens: "If the Deposition have served as the key to fit into the lock of the complications which precede it, then, as a vault whose door has been flung back, the San Dominick's hull lies open today" (313). It is an eloquent "If," implying that the deposition is not the key to the reality underlying past events but only to some of the surface perplexities. Part III relates what occurred during and after the voyage to Lima. Delano feels keenly how wrong he was to suspect Don Benito, and Don Benito consoles him. Delano in return tries to console Don Benito, who cannot emerge from the darkness of the voyage: "But the past is passed; why moralize upon it? Forget it. See, yon bright sun has forgotten it all, and the blue sea, and the blue sky; these have turned over new leaves" (314). Don Benito's response is, "Because they have no memory, because they are not human." But the American, who sees only the moment, who has no sense of the influence of the past on both present and future, protests: "You are saved; you are saved: what has cast such a shadow upon you?" Don Benito replies with the most frequently quoted and most misunderstood phrase in the tale: "The negro."

The conclusion again joins Babo and Don Benito:

> Some months after, dragged to the gibbet at the tail of a mule, the black met his voiceless end. The body was burned to ashes; but for many days, the head, that hive of subtlety, fixed on a pole in the Plaza, met, unabashed, the gaze of the whites; and across the Plaza looked towards St. Bartholomew's church, in whose vaults slept then, as now, the recovered bones of Aranda: and across the Rimac bridge looked towards the monastery, on Mount Agonia without; where, three months after being dismissed by the court, Benito Cereno, borne on the bier, did, indeed, follow his leader. (315)

The conclusion does not answer all questions; it gives no final verdict about the men involved. Instead, new questions are suggested. Why does Melville have Babo die "unabashed" while he has Don Benito die at the height of agony? Why does the last sentence end with the idea of following one's leader? And why does the last sentence as a whole leave vague the question of whether Babo or Don Benito died first? Why does Melville show them always together even in death? The gray vapors have not all been blown away. Shadows remain, and no moral judgments have even been hinted— except of slavery.

What lies in the shadows of *Benito Cereno*? Its every page is so rich in implications that the question can never be fully answered, but when one notes fundamental correspondences uniting the artistic methods in the work, and where they point, the main ideas that animate it stand out.

Melville knew that the master-slave relationship does not depend on color, that no race is naturally fit to be either master or slave, that both whites and nonwhites have been slaves at some time in human history: white Oberlus in *The Encantadas* enslaves other whites; Babo reports that Atufal was a king in his country, though he, Babo, was a slave even then. And *Benito Cereno* (as any reader, whatever his other ideas about the work, will agree) refutes ideas like those of Delano that the black person is suited by nature to be the white person's servant and that blacks have innate qualities making them the "indisputable inferiors" of whites.

But Melville knew also that in the Americas, history took a peculiar turn: slavery was given a "racial twist,"[7] and minds were twisted in accordance, *black* becoming almost synonymous with *slave* and *white* with *master*. Even those black Americans who became free continued generally to be viewed in the shadow of slavery, as Delano's "humorous" thinking about free men of color illustrates.

Through this story of black slave and white Spanish master and the reversal of the color situation, Melville seeks out the essential form and nature of slavery, which, like the *San Dominick*, shows "no colors." Seemingly paradoxically, he uses color in his probing for what is colorless.

Black and white in *Benito Cereno* designate the dynamic opposites in the master-slave relationship. Within the context of the system in which they operate, they are *inseparable, irreconcilable* and *interchangeable*: the violent potential of their opposition must build up and eventually break out "whoever be the thrall."[8] This is what Melville makes visible.

The inseparability of master and slave is expressed almost entirely by pictorial means. It is the subject of the whole series of tableaux picturing Don Benito and Babo, which unfolds steadily from the moment of their simultaneous entrance into the story to their virtually simultaneous exit: Babo standing, "like a shepherd's dog," beside Don Benito; Babo offering Don Benito a cordial, his arm encircling him; Babo kneeling to adjust Don Benito's shoe buckle, rubbing out a spot on his sleeve, shaving him, curling and costuming him, placing a cushion behind his back, cooling him with a large feather fan, chafing his brow, smoothing his hair, gazing into his eyes, leading him away when he is overcome, refusing to be separated from him, making himself into a sort of crutch for him, and flinging himself into the whaleboat after him, still the faithful servant, as Delano thinks. In all these scenes, which are like photographic stills, master and slave are bound together, their social connection constituting their chain.

The inseparability is what is apparent in a first reading. Rereading reveals that the irreconcilability of master and slave and the violent potential of the relationship are intimated in the same tableaux. The beautiful, peaceful picture of the relationship as Delano sees it is, on second reading, seen to be superimposed upon the picture of master and slave locked in eternal conflict, as in the shaving scene. After Don Benito's leap for freedom, the irreconcilability of master and slave is expressed openly by Babo's knife aimed at Don Benito's heart in the whaleboat; by Don Benito's turning away from Babo at the trial; and by Babo's confrontation of Don Benito across the Plaza and the Rimac bridge, when the two are seen at opposite poles. But they continue to be seen in indivisible relationship.

The most interesting aspect of the master-slave relationship as Melville envisions it in *Benito Cereno* is the interchangeability of master and slave, indicating that the assignment of black to slave position and white to master role is not immutable or natural; the only natural thing is to try to free oneself when enslaved; the only immutable thing is the fundamental nature of slavery itself, with its destruction of both master and slave. The carefully crafted scenes in which Delano reacts to Don Benito and Babo together show Melville intrigued by the switching of roles, and it may be this that drew him to the story. (One is reminded of the "assailants and assailed reversed" in "Donelson" in *Battle-Pieces*.) How craftily he speaks of Babo dressing Don Benito's hair with the hand of a "master"! And with what less obvious art he early finds "something so incongruous in the Spaniard's apparel, as almost to suggest the image of an invalid courtier tottering about London streets in the time of the plague" (251), since, if we stop to think, not only is the idea suggested that Don Benito's costume is incongruous to his present position as slave, but also the reminder that the plague was a disaster for all, mighty as well as humble.

The four basic aspects of the master-slave relationship—the inseparability, the irreconcilability, the interchangeability, and the violent potential of the combination of parts within the system—are presented as if in black-and-white graphic art. Melville's purpose in the use of black and white is most openly hinted when Delano sees the whites and blacks on deck like pieces on a chessboard, for chess is a game in which white and black are essentially equal. The opposing colors merely represent their opposition; either color may find itself in the better or worse position. The chessboard may be turned around, and black may stand where white has been. But the game itself remains the same, and warfare is its essence. So it is with the black and white men of the *San Dominick*. The positions of black and white may change, but so long as the men are on board the ship of masters and slaves, warfare is inevitable.

This chess image indicates the use Melville makes of black and white throughout. It can best be described in terms of the negative and positive images in black-and-white photography. Melville's technique is to present one image while suggesting the other. In the "positive" and "negative" what is black in one is white in the other, but the basic picture remains the same. In the series of tableaux in which Don Benito and Babo appear, always joined, always opposed, one figure is black and one is white. But their positions, as compared with the ones they occupied before the revolt, have been exchanged; black is now master, white is enslaved. Delano does not know this, so what he sees is what is "normal" to him as a man of the Americas, that is, the "positive" image in which white is master, black is slave. But the reader—or rather the rereader—knows that the "negative" is really accurate here and that the slave figure now has a white face and the master figure's face is black. Were Delano to see the "negatives," the black figure being shaved by the white one, the white figure kneeling before the black one and looking up at him, the white wearing nothing but coarse patched trousers, the black in elegant costume, he would think of the ugliness, not the beauty, of the relationship.

Could the contrast in dress "denoting their relative positions" be eliminated and the figures show "no colors," one would see the form and nature of the relationship without being influenced by social custom. Through the mocking question that Melville has Babo ask, not once but of each Spaniard in succession, about whether from the whiteness of Don Alexandro's skeleton he could not conclude that it was a white man's, he almost openly tells us to look beneath the skin colors in each positive and negative to the x-ray-like picture of slavery-in-essence. If we follow his clue, then beneath each tableau and its opposite we see two skeletons differentiated only in that one stands in the position of master and one in the position of slave. Power, signified by the razor in the shaving scene, may change hands; Melville again hints this when, in the deposition, a Spanish sailor holds a razor seized from the pocket of his own jacket now worn by a "shackled" black and the reader sees him "aiming it at the negro's throat." But whoever at any moment is in power, violence—past, present, and future—is implicit in the relationship. The skeleton of Aranda symbolizes the nature of such a ship as the *San Dominick*, which must of necessity have "death for the figurehead." The skeleton is a great imaginative creation exactly suited to the essential reality Melville prods each reader to arrive at in his own mind.

Beneath the surface of *Benito Cereno* is also its own skeletal structure. Although on first reading the development of the work seems linear, moving from the 1799 present back to the past revolt and forward to events subsequent to the quelling of the revolt, once *Benito Cereno* is reread, it demands to be seen as one triangular form in which the Spaniard, the North American, and the black slave are seen in a historical interrelationship, each representing a point of view, not inborn, but the result of his experience in the Americas in his time.

The first part of the work focuses on the view from Delano's angle. It might be entitled "Delano's Misconceptions," including, in addition to those he forms on the *San Dominick*, those mistaken preconceptions he brings on board with him. The latter are primary. Only because of his failure to see them as fully human beings can the blacks play their deception upon him. Even in the moments when they chafe at playing their role and their masks slip, Delano's notion that serving whites is the natural role of blacks is so fixed that his doubts are stilled; for example, when they act in defense, closing in behind him, he thinks they are acting in deference, "a Kaffir guard of honor." For he has been conditioned to think of blacks, slave or free, as fitted for servitude; that idea is what justifies slavery to him and hence makes it possible for him to see beauty in the Don Benito-Babo relationship. Though he is not himself a slaveowner, he shares the master mentality in regard to the nature and purpose of black people. They are to him at first like delightful animals and then, when the battle is out in the open, like wild beasts; at no time are they men and women. It is important to note, in connection with the triangular structure of the work, that the animal imagery, for which Melville has been criticized, is strictly limited to Part I, which centers on Delano's way of seeing. What Melville has given Delano is the outlook of the average white eighteenth-century American to whom slavery and the slave trade were accepted institutions. That Delano comes from New England (from Duxbury, close to Boston) rather than from the southern states does not make his outlook different from that of the average white American of his day. Many a respected New England fortune was made directly in the slave trade or in the "triangular" voyages that set out from Boston with cargo to be exchanged for slaves in Africa; these slaves, if they survived the middle passage, were exchanged for sugar and molasses in the West Indies, and the molasses was then sold in New England for the manufacture of rum. Moral Christian New Englanders managed to justify slavery by thinking of blacks as inferior by nature. The *Encyclopedia Americana* says of the New England fortunes founded on the slave trade that this was wealth to which "no odium attached in the politest and most moral circles until toward the end of the eighteenth century."

Delano is a man who does not like to dwell upon unpleasant things or puzzle himself about complicated truths. It is he and not Melville who sees things on the *San Dominick* in black-and-white simplicity. Closing his eyes to all hints of complex and unhappy things, he is like one who, "feeling incipient seasickness," strives "by ignoring the symptoms, to get rid of the malady" (271). This is his attitude to the end: "But the past is passed; why moralize upon it?" Like the average American of Melville's day who was also striving, by ignoring the symptoms to avoid the malady, Delano has dismissed from his mind the brief thought that slavery might be the basis for all that has happened on the *San Dominick*, and he will not "moralize" enough about the past to return to that thought and apply it to his own country.

Melville's ironical treatment of Delano's preconceptions and wishful thinking conveys much of the underlying reality of the situation on the *San Dominick* and all that it represents. The simple ironies are easy to perceive. They involve mainly those things that Delano sees in one way and that later turn out to be the opposite: the "docility," the "contentment," the "unsophisticated nature," and the "limited minds" of the blacks. But there is in *Benito Cereno* a duplex irony, exquisitely worked and elaborately hidden. A few examples will illustrate Melville's peculiar method here.

Delano is impressed by the closeness of Don Benito and Babo. Factually they are physically close, mentally hemispheres apart. Below the fact and the simple irony are the realities: the reciprocal enchainment of master and slave; the explosion that must come from their being locked together in the prison of slavery; and the death sentence for master as well as for slave. They are close, but in a way that Delano cannot understand.

Another example involves Delano's amusement at Babo's enjoyment as he uses the Spanish flag as an apron. Delano thinks his use of the flag reflects Babo's love of bright colors. On the factual level it is true that Babo enjoys using the flag, but false that it is because of a love of bright colors. On the level of deeper reality, his enjoyment of the use of the flag as a rag and his draping of the captain of the slave transportation ship in the standard of slavery-sponsoring Spain have historical implications that are lost on Delano who, in contrast to Melville and Babo, is "incapable of satire and irony" (257) and incapable of understanding it.

A third example goes to the heart of the tale. "Ah," Delano thinks on seeing the cut on Babo's cheek, "this slavery breeds ugly passions in man." Although he quickly dismisses the thought when he sees master and slave together again as if nothing has happened, the meaning of the *San Dominick* experience is precisely that the master-slave relationship creates the violent passions. Delano cannot see that ugliness is the nature of the relationship, a direct opposite of the beauty he persists in seeing when he decides the shedding of blood is just part of a "love quarrel." The irony lies in Delano's not seeing the meaning of what he himself has said.

Don Benito stands at the next vertex of the triangle. His membership in "one of the most enterprising and extensive mercantile families in all those provinces" along the Spanish Main (258); his friendship from youth with Don Alexandro, owner of so large a group of slaves; his position as captain— all place him firmly in the ruling group in the South American world. To assume that Melville intended him to represent goodness is to assume that he brings these things into the tale for no reason at all and takes lightly the fact that Cereno is captain of a ship that transports slaves, a role he views with horror everywhere else in his writings; in *Clarel* captains who transported slaves, though they did not do the actual enslaving, are described as guilty of one of the worst "sins refined, crimes of the spirit" and "These, chiefly these, to doom submit" (Pt. II, Canto xxxvi).

The critical interpretation that Don Benito represents goodness is some-times justified by references to his devout Christianity, evidenced by the crucifix on the bulwark of his cabin, the thumbed missal on the table, and his retreat to a monastery. But the evidences of Don Benito's Christianity only highlight the irony of his connection with slaveowning, since Christian values are contradicted by his role. For Melville's general attitude toward Don Benito's kind of piety, we need only refer to any other Melville work in which slavery or oppression are under consideration. One in particular is pertinent in regard to Don Benito—the reference in *Mardi* to the master who may shrive his soul, take every sacrament, give up the ghost on bended knee, and who yet is destined to die despairing. Since this is the very fate that Melville assigns to Don Benito, the earlier passage takes on special significance, as does the later passage in the "Supplement" to *Battle-Pieces*, which speaks of slavery as "an atheistical iniquity."

Don Benito represents no abstract moral quality, good or bad; he is presented as a man imprisoned in a specific social and historical context, a man who has inherited the role of master which must destroy him unless he is able to free himself by freeing the slave. ("The slave there carries the padlock, but master here carries the key," says Babo [256]). History has presented him, "among South Americans of his class" (251), with the black slave taken from Africa, who acts, when the possibility arises, to free himself, as does Don Benito in his turn.

But what does Melville mean when, in answer to Delano's question about what has cast such a shadow upon him, he has Don Benito reply, "The negro"? Yvor Winters presents an example of the classical response: "His reply in Spanish would have signified not only the negro, or the black man, but by metaphorical extension the basic evil in human nature. The morality of slavery is not an issue in this story; the issue is this, that through a series of acts of performance and of negligence, the fundamental evil of a group of men, evil which normally should have been kept in abeyance, was freed to act. The story is a portrait of that evil in action, as shown in the negroes, and of the effect of the action, as shown in Cereno." If Melville does not intend this, what does he mean to convey?

At the time Don Benito says these words, he is a man haunted by his experience. He does not understand it, but he has some realization that it is linked to his role as master of a ship transporting black slaves "amongst other valuable freight." (Since there seems to be no other reason for Delano to speak at the end of the "trades" and for Cereno to reply that they are only wafting him to his tomb, I take the reference to be Melville's pun in connection with the "business" in which the ship was engaged.) Cereno knows his fate has been inseparable from Babo's. The Negro's mind is unknown to him, but he has gone through an experience akin to slavery, and he has a gnawing sense of the slave's condition. He cannot follow Delano's advice to forget the past. Even in the monastery he cannot find sanctuary from it. Like the master in *Mardi*, though he perform every religious rite, he is doomed to die despairing.

When Don Benito answers "The negro" to explain what has cast the great shadow upon him, it is Melville's two-word summary of what he has been developing all along: that while the master-slave relationship exists, neither slave nor master is free of the other. *Each lives in the shadow of the other.* The shadow hanging over Don Benito is imaginatively related to the slavery that "puts out the sun at noon" in *Mardi*, the noon that is like dusk in *Benito Cereno* (272) and the "screened sun" that Delano finds reassuring.

The last part of *Benito Cereno* focuses attention on the fact that whereas the view from the angle of the white North American and of the white Spaniard in South America have been presented, the view from the angle of the third member of the triangle, Babo, the enslaved black man from Africa, remains missing to the end. But Melville does not leave the reader without clues to his thinking, although he presents the tale (as a white sailor presents a knot to the American) as a thing "for someone else to undo."

What do we know of Babo from *Benito Cereno*? His blackness marks him as the man taken by force from Africa to be a slave in the Americas. He has a rich intelligence: he has the qualities of mind of a master psychologist, strategist, general, playwright, impresario, and poet. Melville endows him with his own poetic insight into the symbolic implications that can be found in significant figures and objects: the skeleton, the black giant who may throw off his chains and will not ask pardon, the padlock and key, the Spanish flag used as a rag. We know that Babo has a strong sense of his blackness and an intense resentment of the whites' attitude of superiority, as well as an appreciation of its humor.

We can know, also, that Babo does not act out of innate evil and without motive. Babo's purpose, and that of the other blacks, is a fact clearly stated in Don Benito's deposition to the court. It is to get the black slave group, which fears reenslavement, to a "negro country." The killing of Don Alexandro has a twofold purpose: to ensure the group's newly won freedom and to warn the other whites. Not even Babo's assault on Don Benito in the whaleboat is an expression of pure hatred. The brief but brilliant scene is a reminder of the one in *White-Jacket* in which White-Jacket, swinging to the "instinct" in all living beings, tries to murder Captain Claret, wanting to haul him from an earthly to a heavenly tribunal to decide between him and his oppressor. The justice meted out at the end of *Benito Cereno* is also earthly justice. Specifically, it is the justice of the white European "Christian" colonizers and "civilizers" as determined by the slavery-sanctioning courts acting for the Spanish king in the "City of Kings." There is reason why the head of Babo, fixed on a pole in the Plaza in Lima, can meet "unabashed" the gaze of the whites; their justice is not his justice, their good and evil are not his good and evil; slaveowner and slave do not have the same definition of justice any more than of liberty; what is just and right to the slaveowner is slavery; what is just and right to the slave is freedom. And, Melville implies further, the slaveowner has a double standard of justice. What is criminal when done by the slave is right and just when he himself does it. Babo's actions are considered atrocities by the whites, but the manner of *his* death, dragged alive to the gibbet at the tail of a mule, constitutes justice to them. Don Alexandro's skeleton on the prow proves the slaves barbaric, but Babo's head on a pole in the Plaza is civilized. The enslavement of Don Benito is evil; the enslavement of the blacks is taken for granted. The description of Babo's end, which makes more than questionable the justice of the civilized white Christian rulers in Lima, is Melville's way of dramatizing the ideas presented more journalistically in the *Typee* passage about readers in the colonizing countries who are horrified by the acts of the "diabolical heathens" against the invaders of their lands, but view with equanimity the atrocities committed by their own representatives, and call upon all Christendom to applaud their courage and their justice. In *Benito Cereno* Melville gives his reader an opportunity to test her or his own standard of justice: Will the atrocities inflicted on Babo (and on the shackled blacks by the white sailors) horrify the reader as much as the atrocities inflicted on Don Alexandro and the other whites, killed during and after the revolt against enslavement? Will the reader be aware of the original atrocity, slavery, which gives rise to all the rest? Or will he miss what Melville is saying because he, too, takes the double standard for granted?

So neither Babo nor blackness stands for Evil in this extraordinary work. Indeed, it would have been strange if Melville, in whose work as a whole there is such a large cast of black characters of all kinds, had chosen here to make blackness the sign of any inherent quality. Far from presenting Babo as a clear-cut moral symbol, Melville presents him as a mystery that cannot be easily unraveled and that is not fully explained even at the end of the book, though hints have been given to the reader. "Since I cannot do deeds, I will not speak words," Melville imagines his silence after his capture to say, the likely implication being that Babo feels the only language the whites will understand is action. The slave, Melville seems to be telling America, has yet to be heard from; it would be well to imagine his condition and what is in his mind.

Just as Babo does not represent Evil, changeless and causeless, so *Benito Cereno* is not a fable carrying the moral that the good are powerless unless they recognize that there is Evil in humanity. The evil that the work implies one should recognize is specific and meaningful—the slavery that was introduced into the Western Hemisphere on the heels of its "discovery" by Columbus acting for Spain. To Melville, once widely traveled sailor, South America and North America were closely related. So were slave revolts and wars arising from slavery; the section on the extreme south of Vivenza in *Mardi* foresees violence in the form of both slave uprising and war between North and South, and in *Battle-Pieces* John Brown, whose aim was to touch off a slave insurrection throughout the South, is the heavenly portent of the war. The ship that had carried the figurehead of Columbus conveys three things closely related in Melville's imagination: slavery; Spain in the "New World"; and the United States, once thought of as Columbia. Melville saw Spain as America's predecessor, in that sense her leader, in the hemisphere, and he felt her ultimate fate there, as signified by the *San Dominick*'s, to be a portent for his own country.

At the time of the *San Dominick* events, 1799, Spain was still a great colonial power in whose dominions in South America (awarded to her by a Spanish-born pope), slavery was still firmly planted. But, as the Cuban poet Nicolás Guillén suggests, it was also a time in South America that was so seething with rebellion that only the blind or deaf could fail to perceive the signs or hear the subterranean roar or feel the tremors. Just a few years later independence and emancipation were proclaimed by the South American revolutionaries. By 1825 all the Spanish colonies on the South American continent were free. And by the time *Benito Cereno* was written, the claws of the old Spanish lion had almost all been pulled: the power of Spain in the Americas was over, only Cuba and Puerto Rico remaining to her. Melville was able to look back and see the year 1799 as a time when the sun of Spain was already beginning to set and when the empire that had begun with Columbus's discoveries three hundred years before would soon be no more.

The indications that Melville had the example of Spain in mind in *Benito Cereno* are many. The *San Dominick* bears as its "principal relic of faded grandeur" the sternpiece carved with the arms of Castile and León. The Spanish flag is what Babo chooses to place under Don Benito's chin in the shaving scene, to catch hairs and to trail on the floor. At the end of the shaving scene, the flag is "tumbled up, and tossed back into the flag-locker." The other Spanish symbol the blacks remove from sight is the figurehead of Columbus, symbol for Spain of its expansion and for the blacks of their enslavement. The substitution of the skeleton of the slaveowner is emblematic for Melville of the doom of Spain and of death coming, because of slavery, to the United States. (The ship in Amasa Delano's narrative has no mention of a figurehead or of a skeleton.) The name of the *San Dominick* (selected instead of the name in the original account) also emphasizes the association of the ship with Spain, whose rapid conquest and colonization of the New World began with San Domingo in 1494. The island, originally called Isla Española by Columbus and later Santo Domingo or San Domingo, was the center of Spanish control in the Western Hemisphere.

There are at least a half dozen passages in *Benito Cereno* that hint that the connection should be made between the Spanish experience and the American one. In a work in which no word is wasted, in which almost every descriptive sentence contains a glimmer of deeper meaning, these brief passages should be given their full value. One is the single-sentence paragraph that shows the two ships, the Spanish and the American, anchored together (291). Another is Delano's mental association of Spaniards with the "good folks of Duxbury, Massachusetts," although, as ever, he is unaware of the deeper implications of his thought. A related idea is suggested by mention of the Cereno family as a "mercantile" one with business dealings in all the provinces along the coast; Melville thus makes it a parallel of the equally enterprising and extensive mercantile families of early New England in their relations with the South (families that also had members who were captains of merchant ships that transported slaves and profited from slavery and were on good terms with slaveholders like Don Alexandro). The picture of Don Benito, Babo, and Delano in their last moments together on the *San Dominick* highlights slavery as that which links the Spaniard and the American in a kind of alliance. Babo stands in the middle: "And so still presenting himself as a crutch, and walking between the two captains, he advanced with them towards the gangway; while still, as if full of kindly contrition, Don Benito would not let go the hand of Captain Delano, *but retained it in his, across the black's body*" (293; my emphasis). Tearing his hand loose, the Spanish captain says to the American, "Go, and God guard you better than me." In the light of what Melville says about the United States and slavery in his other works, this prayer can be understood not only as that of the captain who represents Spain for the captain who represents America but also as that of Melville for his own country. In the whaleboat there is a last view of the three together, and here Delano holds the center of the stage: with his left hand he clutches Don Benito; with his right foot he holds down "the prostrate negro"—a fascinating enactment and reminder of the scene depicted on the sternpiece of the Spanish ship at the beginning of the story, even echoing the words "prostrate" and "writhing." In this enactment, the masks are off, and it is Delano, representing America, who has his foot on the prostrate slave. What land, then, has Melville had in mind all along? Remember that Delano is the first and last in the story to read the words "Follow your leader" on the side of the ship. Finally, there is the ship's flawed bell that Delano hears in the *San Dominick*'s narrow corridor, a bell mentioned twice earlier in the tale: "It was the echo of the ship's flawed bell, *striking the hour*, drearily reverberated in this subterranean vault" (my emphasis). Delano's mind is responsive for a moment to the "portent," but the sight of his own American ship "lying peacefully at anchor . . . rising and falling on the short waves by the *San Dominick*'s side" (292) calms him, and he forgets the echo that portends more than the imminent crisis on the ship. The image of the flawed bell suggests the Liberty Bell, flawed, like the *San Dominick*'s, in two ways, the actual crack signifying to Melville the spiritual flaw. Writing of a Spanish ship in the Americas, Melville is thinking of the United States with its tragic flaw. But Delano does not see the portent for the United States of 1799 that was also, seemingly, "lying peacefully at anchor." He is too much a white man of his time to learn much of value from the *San Dominick* experience. The reader, however, can see truths Delano might have seen had he been better able to understand the past. For one thing, Delano might have recognized that the past, present, and future are a continuum, as Melville says in a short paragraph when Babo leaps over the bulwarks: "All this, with what preceded and what followed, occurred with such involutions of rapidity, that past, present, and future seemed one" (294). But to Delano the realization of historical connections is as fleeting as the action. When he tells Don Benito later that it is useless to moralize about the past, he is the typical white American of his time closing his eyes to the catastrophe history is demonstrating will come if slavery continues. Were his eyes open, he would see that all on the surface of a society, as of a ship, may wear an ordinary, even a calm and peaceful aspect, and yet be soon to erupt.

By the time of *Benito Cereno* Melville's artistic methods had moved far from the almost straightforward expression of ideas that characterizes *Mardi*'s section on slavery in Vivenza. His way in *Benito Cereno* is like that of an artist carving a three-dimensional scene in ivory and ebony, working subtle designs that are hidden away in the recesses. Still, the ideas in the tale are not meant to be hidden forever. The clues are there. But preconceptions about black and white, as in the case of Delano, have led to misunderstanding and even to literal misreading. One example of the latter is especially interesting. It reports that Atufal has been appearing before Don Benito periodically to ask his pardon,[9] whereas the plain fact is that Atufal repeatedly refuses to ask pardon. Now, Atufal's appearances and refusals are important to the whole interpretation of the story. The purpose of the scenes—for both Babo and Melville—is twofold. On a "plot" level it is to provide Babo, whose muscular strength is slight, with an aide of great physical might who, since he is apparently chained, will not be feared but will be able to throw off his chains and overpower the American should that become necessary. The poetic purpose is of more profound importance. In Atufal, Babo—like Melville— has a symbol of the enslaved black in revolt, whose powers and will to freedom have been underestimated, a giant who can throw off his chains and, unabashed, will not ask for pardon. That Melville shares with Babo, in the Atufal scenes and elsewhere, his own kind of poetic imagination, his own way of seeing the implications beneath the surface of a situation, and his own way of creating a scene on different levels is the best single clue to Melville's intentions. He is doing in this tale what he has Babo do, create a work of great imagination with a surface appearance and a hidden reality. He would not have made Babo a playwright and poet so like himself in his choice of symbols—above all, the skeleton symbol—had he wanted to portray him as a naturally destructive force. Instead, he depicts a Babo with natural creative gifts who is made destructive by the historical "condition" of black slavery in the Americas, a condition of which Melville speaks indirectly through Don Benito's consolation to Delano: "So far may even the best man err, in judging the conduct of one with the recesses of whose condition he is not acquainted" (314). Of course Melville's purpose is more encompassing than Babo's; he is opposed to slavery whether white or black is enslaved.

Free of preoccupation with black as a symbol of evil and with good and evil as mystic abstractions unrelated to "place and time,"[10] the reader can perceive the inner reality of *Benito Cereno* and can hear the undertone echoing in the "subterranean vault" of the *San Dominick* as it forewarns the United States of a tragic fate to result from its tragic flaw. Penetrating the surface account given by Amasa Delano, Melville saw the "haunted pirate ship" of slavery with "its skeleton gleaming in the horizontal moonlight . . . casting a gigantic ribbed shadow upon the water" (272, 298).

Notes

1.   References are to text in *Great Short Works of Herman Melville*, ed. Warner Berthoff (New York: Harper & Row, 1970).

2.   For text see *Benito Cereno*, ed. John P. Runden (Boston: Heath, 1965). The Yvor Winters passage later quoted also appears in this edition. So does one of the outstanding dissenting views, "The Enduring Innocence of Captain Amasa Delano," by Allen Guttmann.

3.   See *Mardi* (Ch. clxii); "The Swamp Angel" in which the black angel, in the form of the great Parrott gun, is God's messenger bombarding Charleston; and *Clarel* (Pt. II, Canto xxxvi). The quoted words are from "The Apparition" in *Battle-Pieces*.

4.   In *Israel Potter* it is necessary to "pierce" the haze masking the inner reality of the battle of the *Bonhomme Richard* and the *Serapis*.

5.   Warner Berthoff in his introduction to the story says the court documents "unravel its riddling mysteries."

6.   The word *soul* appears twice and only in connection with Babo.

7.   Eric Williams, *Capitalism and Slavery* (London: Andre Deutsch, 1964), p. 7.

8.   *Mardi*, Ch. clxii.

9.   Richard Chase, *Herman Melville* (New York: Macmillan, 1949), p. 158.

10.   From "The Slain Collegians" in *Battle-Pieces*.

The Monastic Slaver: Images and Meaning in "Benito Cereno"

GLORIA HORSLEY-MEACHAM

A number of critics have sought to unravel the meaning of Melville's ecclesiastical imagery in "Benito Cereno," yet none has adequately explained the relationship of these images to the tale of African bondage and revolt. Melville understood that the "roots" of Black servitude "strike deep."[1] The references to monks and monasteries so recurrent in the novella are, in fact, central to the author's treatment of the experience of African enslavement; they link the nascent American slave trade with the church and the crusade for Christian dominion.

Although H. Bruce Franklin does not discuss the connection of monastic imagery to the theme of slavery, he nonetheless touches upon several of Melville's references to the history of racial oppression in the Americas.[2] Franklin avers that Melville altered the date of the actual slave mutiny he recounts (from 1805 to 1799) to suggest the Santo Domingo uprising led by Toussaint L'Ouverture. He also illuminates the meaning of the image of Christopher Colon, the slave ship's figurehead, when he notes that Charles the Fifth "made Santo Domingo the site of the first large-scale importation of Negro slaves into the Western Hemisphere" following Columbus's historic encounter with that island. However, Franklin's discussion does not consider that the decision to export massive numbers of Africans to the New World was greatly influenced by the Catholic clergy during an era when European Christendom was still deeply engaged in its struggle against the Moors. It seems that Melville's various allusions to the life of Charles the Fifth in "Benito Cereno" are not simply a direct link between the Emperor and slavery in the New World, as Franklin suggests, but, interwoven with abundant references to friars, monasteries, and Mohammedans, indicate Melville's perception of a far more complex scenario. This dimension of history—the origins of the African slave trade—is not widely understood.

The New World market for African captives developed during the reign of the Catholic monarchs Ferdinand and Isabella and Charles the Fifth, an era when ecclesiastics were exceedingly influential. The Jeronymite Fathers,

Reprinted from *New England Quarterly* 56 (June 1983); 261–66, by permission of the author and publisher.

who for a time virtually governed Santo Domingo, advocated importing African slaves to replace the rapidly diminishing indigenous peoples compelled to work on the sugar plantations and in the gold mines.[3] Yet, it was the Dominican priest Bartholomew de Las Casas who almost single handedly launched the trade in African men and women. Las Casas, concerned with the brutal exploitation of the indigenous people of Hispaniola, recommended substituting Black slaves for Indian forced labor.[4] Charles the Fifth, acting upon the advice of the Dominican friar, authorized the importation of 15,000 slaves to Santo Domingo in 1517–18, and "thus, through the intercession of God's holy minister, the African slave trade to the new world was begun."[5]

The role of Las Casas in the early slave trade was widely reported in nineteenth-century historical works.[6] Melville may well have been acquainted with Washington Irving's portrait of Las Casas in the appendix of *The Life and Voyages of Christopher Columbus.*[7] Irving cites the Jeronymites' and Las Casas's promotion of African slavery as well as Cardinal Adrian's approval of the "expedient" before he became Pope.[8] Significantly, Irving notes the opposition of the renowned Franciscan Cardinal Ximenes, the "grand inquisitor of Spain" who had enslaved the "refractory Moors of Granada" yet (predicting the Santo Domingo uprisings) believed that Africans were "extremely prolific and enterprising; and that if they had time to multiply in America, they would infallibly revolt, and impose on the Spaniards the same chains which they had compelled them to wear."[9]

More certain is that Melville was familiar with George Bancroft's argument in *History of the United States* that the clergy's lack of sympathy for the Africans' plight in the New World was rooted in the Old World past. Indeed, Melville's perspective on slavery in "Benito Cereno" may have derived principally from his reading of Bancroft's *History*, noted by Charles Robert Anderson as one of the books on "Melville's earliest known reading list."[10] The New England historian maintained that the history of African enslavement in the modern era was inextricably bound to the dynamics of seven hundred years of Islamic-Christian conflict. The traffic in humans of all races that had flourished during the Middle Ages might have been abolished before the discovery of America, according to Bancroft, "but for the hostility between the Christian church and the followers of Mahomet."[11] The Christians' ultimate and fateful triumph over the Moors in Granada, coinciding with Columbus's first voyage to America, was "signalized by a great emigration of the Moors to the coasts of Northern Africa," where religious antagonisms and Christian enslavement persisted. Bancroft asserts that the Christian aversion to Moorish hegemony subsequently extended to the entire continent; all Africans were "doomed" to bondage because "all Africans were esteemed as Moors." Some influential clergy opposed African enslavement, but on the whole, they "felt no sympathy for the unbeliever."[12] Underscoring this connection between African bondage and religious antagonisms, Bancroft calls attention to two contemporaneous events: Charles the Fifth's legal sanction of the slave traffic and his celebrated military expedition against Tunis to combat the Moors and liberate Christian bondsmen in Africa.[13]

In "Benito Cereno," Melville evidently draws upon this history of Islamic-Christian strife—referred to as "the old grudge" by the Spaniard feuding with Daggoo, the African in *Moby-Dick*. To suggest the religious background of African slavery, described by writers like Bancroft and Irving, Melville liberally embellishes his story with ecclesiastical imagery and allusions to Spain's historic experience with the Moors. "Broad ovals" (an apparent reference to the "ample oval of the shield-like stern-piece" featuring the arms of Castile and Leon) are juxtaposed to the image of crescents (the emblem of Islam) as the American captain reflects upon the Spanish past.[14] Equally significant are the description of the longboat "warped as a camel's skeleton in the desert" (p. 38), the portrait of Francisco "approaching with a saalam" (p. 46), the depiction of the other rebel slaves as "dervishes"— Mohammedan friars (p. 57), and the image of "the blacks . . . with upthrown gestures hailing the now dusky moors of ocean" (p. 58). These allusions to Mohammedanism illuminate the meaning of such Christian images as "hypochondriac abbot" (p. 7), the "thumbed missal," "meagre crucifix," "poor friars' girdles," and "inquisitors' racks" (p. 40), as well as references to the monk Infelez (p. 62) and to Charles the Fifth, Holy Roman Emperor. All, including the reference to Babo, the leader of the slave rebellion, as "a begging friar of St. Francis" (p. 13)—seemingly an ironic allusion to the Franciscan cardinal's prophecy—associate the New World conflict with the Old.

In his compelling portrayal of the Spanish slaver, Melville likewise implicates the Church.

> Upon gaining a less remote view, the ship . . . appeared like a whitewashed monastery after a thunder-storm, seen perched upon some dun cliff among the Pyrenees. But it was no purely fanciful resemblance which now, for a moment, almost led Captain Delano to think that nothing less than a ship-load of monks was before him. Peering over the bulwarks were what really seemed, in the hazy distance, throngs of dark cowls; while, fitfully revealed through the open port-holes, other dark moving figures were dimly descried, as of Black Friars pacing the cloisters. [P. 3]

The representation of the *San Dominick* points to sixteenth-century Santo Domingo, where the monastic authorities helped to pave the way for an extensive traffic in Black cargoes.

That Melville had Las Casas particularly in mind as he created the monastic imagery for the novella seems suggested first by the reference to "Black Friars" (the Dominicans), in his rechristening of the original slaveship *Tryal* as the *San Dominick* (which also suggests the religious order), and later in the renaming of the Spaniard (originally Benito Cereno) as Bartholomew

Barlo, whom Delano caught in "the act of stabbing a shackled Negro" (p. 72). Yet the most telling allusion to the Dominican monk is found in Melville's concluding lines of "Benito Cereno," where St. Bartholomew's Church appears amidst the fatal consequences of the *San Dominick* affair— the tragic outcome of priestly counsel to a Catholic king. Las Casas and the Church stand accused as Babo's head, "unabashed," "looked towards St. Bartholomew's church, in whose vaults slept then, as now, the recovered bones of Aranda: and across the Rimac bridge looked towards the monastery, on Mount Agonia without; where, three months after being dismissed by the court, Benito Cereno, borne on the bier, did, indeed, follow his leader" (p. 75). The deaths of Aranda and Cereno are thus linked with Bartholomew de Las Casas, the religious "leader" and advocate of African slavery whom both Spaniards, like Charles the Fifth, surely followed. This final image extends the meaning of Melville's ecclesiastical imagery. The Christian world, Melville suggests, has bequeathed to its progeny a legacy of death and destruction. In fomenting a perilous racial oppression, European Christendom ultimately doomed all "followers" aboard the "monastic slaver."

Notes

1.   Herman Melville, *Mardi, and a Voyage Thither* (Boston: L. C. Page & Co., 1923), p. 468.

2.   H. Bruce Franklin, " 'Apparent Symbol of Despotic Command': Melville's 'Benito Cereno,' " *New England Quarterly* 34 (December 1961): 462–77.

3.   African captives first arrived in the Americas about 1502, but due to concerns with Black rebelliousness, moderate importation was, for brief periods, suspended by Queen Isabella and again by Cardinal Ximenes Cisneros upon the death of Ferdinand. Nevertheless, the demand for Black workers prevailed, and the Jeronymite priets, encouraging the large-scale shipment of Africans to the Indies, requested that "Your Highness should command us to grant licenses to send armed ships from this island to fetch them from the Cape Verde Islands, or Guinea" (Elizabeth Donnan, ed., *Documents Illustrative of the History of the Slave Trade to America*, 4 vols. [Washington, D.C.: Carnegie Institution of Washington, 1930–35], 1:15–16). See also, Leslie B. Rout, Jr., *The African Experience in Spanish America: 1502 to the Present Day* (Cambridge: Cambridge University Press, 1976), pp. 22–24, and Lesley Byrd Simpson, *The Encomienda in New Spain: Forced Native Labor in the Spanish Colonies, 1492–1550* (Berkeley and Los Angeles: University of California Press, 1929), pp. 61–79.

4.   David Brion Davis, *The Problem of Slavery in Western Culture* (Ithaca: Cornell University Press, 1966), pp. 169–70; Daniel P. Mannix and Malcolm Cowley, *Black Cargoes: A History of the Atlantic Slave Trade, 1518–1865* (New York: Viking Press, 1962), p. 3; C. L. R. James, *The Black Jacobins: Toussaint L'Ouverture and the San Domingo Revolution* (1938), 2d ed. rev. (New York: Vintage Books, 1963), p. 4.

5.   Saunders Redding, *They Came in Chains: Americans from Africa* (1950), 2d ed. rev. (Philadelphia: J. B. Lippincott Co., 1973), p. 16.

6.   Las Casas and his proposition were variously censured and defended by nineteenth-century writers. For examples, see George Bancroft, *History of the United States, from the Discovery of the American Continent* (1837), 10th ed., 10 vols. (Boston: Charles C. Little and James Brown, 1844), 1:170; James Bandinel, *Some Account of the Trade in Slaves from Africa*

. . . (1842; reprint ed., London: Frank Cass & Co., 1968), pp. 27–28; Thomas Clarkson, *The History of the Rise, Progress, and Accomplishment of the Abolition of the African Slave-Trade by the British Parliament*, 2 vols. (1808; reprint ed., London: Frank Cass & Co., 1968), 1:34–35; Thomas R. R. Cobb, *An Historical Sketch of Slavery, from the Earliest Periods* (1858; reprint ed., Miami: Mnemosyne Publishing Co., 1969), pp. 138, 140; Esther Copley, *A History of Slavery and Its Abolition* (1839; reprint ed., Detroit: Negro History Press, n.d.), p. 111; Thomas F. Gordon, *The History of America* . . . , 2 vols. (1831; reprint ed., New York: AMS Press, 1970), 2:36–39; Washington Irving, *The Life and Voyages of Christopher Columbus, to Which Are Added Those of His Companions* (1848), rev. ed., 3 vols. (New York: G. P. Putnam's Sons, 1868), 3:490–98.

7. Mary Y. Hallab, "Victims of 'Malign Machinations': Irving's *Christopher Columbus* and Melville's 'Benito Cereno,' " *Journal of Narrative Technique* 9 (Fall 1979): 199–206. This otherwise useful study of parallels between "Benito Cereno" and *Life of Columbus* erroneously assumes that Melville's monastic imagery can be attributed to Irving's treatment of Columbus.

8. Irving, *Life of Columbus*, 3:492, 494.

9. Irving, *Life of Columbus*, 3:495, 365–66.

10. Charles Robert Anderson, *Melville in the South Seas* (New York: Dover Publications, 1966), p. 358.

11. Bancroft, *History of the U.S.*, 1:163.

12. Bancroft, *History of the U.S.*, 1:164. W. E. B. Du Bois in *The World and Africa* (1946), rev. and enl. ed. (New York: International Publishers, 1965), p. 221, notes that "Europe for five centuries described Islamic culture in Spain as a civilization of colored people, 'Moors'-Blackamoors and Tawny Moors; and the whole discussion of human skin color and its social implications in the Middle Ages assumed that Moors and Negroes were identical." Davis, *The Problem of Slavery*, pp. 165–73, contends that Las Casas as well as the Spanish and Portuguese governments adhered to a "double standard in judging the enslavement of Negroes and Indians," which "derived in part from the traditional inclination to associate the Africans with Moors, and thus with a menacing infidelity."

13. Bancroft, *History of the U.S.*, 1:171. Charles Sumner, in *White Slavery in the Barbary States* . . . (Boston: William D. Ticknor and Company, 1847), p. 15, also commenting upon these two events, denounced the "wretched inconsistency" of the emperor who "levied a mighty force to . . . procure the abolition of Christian slavery in Tunis," yet "laid the cornerstone of a new system of slavery in America." William Robertson, in *The History of the Reign of the Emperor Charles V* . . . (1769), 15th ed., 3 vols. (London: T. Cadell, 1821), pp. 420–36, offers an account of the Emperor's expedition against Africa that includes a description of the people of the Barbary States of Morocco, Algiers, and Tunis. They are characterized as "a mixed race, Arabs, Negroes from the southern provinces, and Moors, either natives of Africa, or who had been expelled out of Spain; all zealous professors of the Mahometan religion, and inflamed against Christianity."

14. John P. Runden, ed., *Melville's Benito Cereno: A Text for Guided Research* (Boston: D. C. Heath and Company, 1965), p. 31. Subsequent references will appear in the text.

"Benito Cereno" and Manifest Destiny

ALLAN MOORE EMERY

Like most authors of the first rank, Herman Melville has commonly been considered a devotee of the timeless, one who, especially in *Moby-Dick* (1851), sought ultimate answers to life's eternal questions. Only during the past two decades has Melville's "topicality" come to be recognized, as critics have underlined with increasing frequency his timely interest in racial prejudice and technological progress, in English slums and American naval abuses, in the *Somers* mutiny and the Civil War. Melville's "politics" have received particular attention. Alan Heimert was among the first to suggest that even *Moby-Dick* has its political side—its "symbolic" debt to the Compromise of 1850.[1] Lately, too, Michael Paul Rogin and James Duban have independently read the novel as an elaborate treatment of slavery and Manifest Destiny.[2] All three critics challenge the popular image of Melville as an author so enamored of cosmic generalities as to be essentially unconcerned with political issues. All place Melville's political involvement among his highest literary virtues.

By stressing this involvement, Heimert, Rogin, and Duban provide a valuable corrective to a venerable scholarly overemphasis. Yet one is led, I think, to question their primary piece of evidence—*Moby-Dick*—a work which does perhaps make some political statement, but only in the midst of numerous other statements on nonpolitical subjects ranging from metaphysics to marine biology, from Manichaeanism to monomania. Though unarguably "symbolic," *Moby-Dick* is not, in fact, particularly political: the *Pequod* may be the "Ship of State"[3]—but surely not often, and never for long. Moreover, if Melville's eclectric novel hints at his interest in slavery and Manifest Destiny, it more regularly reveals his preoccupation with nature and human nature and God. Even reinterpreted, then, with its "politics" laid bare, *Moby-Dick* merely reconfirms the stereotype, documenting Melville's relative disregard for politics and his liking for the "large."

The argument for Melville's politicalness should not be abandoned, however; it should simply rest on firmer ground: on "I and My Chimney" (1856), for example, a tale with both a powerful political point and a uniform

Reprinted from *Nineteenth-Century Fiction* 39 (June 1984): 48–68. Copyright © by the Regents of the University of California. Reprinted by permission.

political thrust,[4] and on "Benito Cereno" (1855), a story which not only comments (if rather generally) on the slavery question but also underlines, far more clearly than any other Melville work, the author's serious engagement with Manifest Destiny. If in *Mardi* (1849) and *Moby-Dick* he occasionally alluded to this subject with the air of a promising dabbler in politics,[5] in "Benito Cereno" he became a mature political analyst, devoting much of his authorial energy to portraying the mind-set of those many Americans who fancied themselves citizens of an "elect" nation, destined by Providence to govern the globe. If in *Mardi* and *Moby-Dick* he occasionally descended from the universal masthead to the political deck, in "Benito Cereno" he firmly conjoined the two, producing in his treatment of Manifest Destiny, not, as before, a timeless tale with political asides, but a political tale with timeless implications.

Many critics have read "Benito Cereno" "politically," of course—as an attack, that is, on American slavery.[6] Yet despite the presence of slaves in Melville's story, slavery seems not to have been his primary political concern: he was apparently more interested in American expansionism.[7] The 1850s were years in which the slavery debate loomed large in America, but they were also active years for America's annexationists, who were either too busy glancing abroad to notice local friction or who sensed that a grandly patriotic foreign policy might lure Americans out of their separatist camps. During the 1850s national expansion was, in fact, as "topical" an issue as slavery— or so Melville appears to have believed. For if his tale examines the problem of slavery, it also examines—with considerably more care—the false claims and confidences of Manifest Destiny.[8]

Evidently Melville was particularly concerned by mid-century arguments for American intervention in Latin America, arguments contrasting the "energy," "libertarianism," and "efficiency" of Americans with the "weakness," "despotism," and "disorderliness" of the Spanish. Such arguments were available to Melville in a number of American periodicals, including *Putnam's Monthly Magazine*, to which he probably subscribed and in which "Benito Cereno" eventually appeared.[9] "Cuba," the lead article in the first number of *Putnam's* (January 1853), characterized the sole Spanish dependency left in the New World as suffering under a "despotic and even brutal" administration; annexation would allow America's liberty-loving "Saxons" to "assert political, religious, and commercial freedom" in the island. And though Cuba's recent economic progress seemed a sign of Spanish potency, it had actually stemmed from American "enterprise and energy," Americans being "an enlightened, progressive race; the Spaniards the extreme reverse." Indeed, America was a powerful and prosperous country, while Spain was "a weak nation, tottering toward ruin."[10] One year later another *Putnam's* article preached a similar message. The author of "Annexation" (February 1854) noted that the "weak Mexican and Spanish races" of Latin America were "a prey to anarchy and misrule" and suggested that America could offer these *misérables* the "advantages of stable government, of equal laws, of a flourishing and refined social life." Speaking for all Americans, he declared:

> As the inheritors of whatever is best in modern civilization, possessed of a political and social polity which we deem superior to every other, carrying with us wherever we go the living seeds of freedom, of intelligence, of religion; our advent every where, but particularly among the savage and stationary tribes who are nearest to us, must be a redemption and blessing. South America and the islands of the sea ought to rise up to meet us at our coming, and the desert and the solitary places be glad that the hour for breaking their fatal enchantments, the hour of their emancipation, had arrived.[11]

Among many similar defenses of American expansion, the two *Putnam's* articles were perhaps the most accessible to Melville. Yet, whatever his particular sources may have been, "Benito Cereno" readily reveals his famil- iarity with the case for Latin American "emancipation." Consider first this textual fact: whereas the original Amasa Delano described Cereno's *Tryal* as merely a "Spanish ship," making no mention of her prior history or physical appearance,[12] Melville immediately assigns the *San Dominick* to the class of "superseded Acapulco treasure-ships, or retired frigates of the Spanish king's navy, which, like superannuated Italian palaces, still, under a decline of masters, preserved signs of former state."[13] With its tattered tops, moldering forecastle, and "shield-like stern-piece, intricately carved with the arms of Castile and Leon" (pp. 114–15), the *San Dominick* might well symbolize a "tottering" Spain.[14] Moreover, "the Spanish king's officers" and "Lima vice- roy's daughters" once trod the deck of the *San Dominick*, a vessel whose "proper figure-head" is "the image of Cristopher Colon, the discoverer of the New World" (pp. 176, 254). Thus perhaps that vessel stands, most particularly, for Spain's Western empire, an empire about to dissolve at the time of Delano's adventure (1799).[15]

If this be true, then Amasa Delano's "American" response to the *San Dominick* becomes equally significant. Reminiscent, for example, of American expansionist rhetoric are Delano's complaints regarding the disorderliness of Cereno's vessel—a "noisy confusion" (p. 128) recalling the "anarchy" found by expansionists in Latin America. Moreover, Delano takes a second expan- sionist tack when he attributes the confusion on the *San Dominick* to Cereno's impotence, his strengthless style of command.[16] Though no mention is made of such impotence in Melville's source, Melville's Delano observes at one point: "Had Benito Cereno been a man of greater energy, misrule would hardly have come to the present pass" (p. 122). Yet Delano's response to Cereno is rather complex, for while decrying the weakness of the Spanish captain, he also notes Cereno's tough treatment of Atufal and declares: "Ah, Don Benito, . . . for all the license you permit in some things, I fear lest, at bottom, you are a bitter hard master" (p. 224). Aboard Melville's floating symbol of Spanish empire, Delano finds, then, precisely what his expansionist descendants found in Latin America: a simultaneous pandemonium, enervation, and tyranny.

Incidentally, Delano also experiences "enchantment" aboard the *San Dominick* (pp. 118, 161, 178), a state of dreamy unreality unexperienced by the original Delano—and yet said by the author of "Annexation" to be characteristic of Latin America. Importantly, too, Delano plots to break this enchantment by taking firm control of Cereno's vessel, thus anticipating the interventionism of mid-century Americans. Straying again from his source, Melville unveils Delano's plan to provide Cereno with "three of his best seamen for temporary deck officers," a project that later blossoms into a presumptuous scheme to withdraw command from Cereno (pp. 138, 165). And even after this scheme subsides, Delano jauntily resolves, without being asked, to "remain on board" the *San Dominick* and "play the pilot" (p. 193), a role Melville repeatedly assigns to Delano (pp. 220–22, 228) as the American adjoins the *San Dominick* to the *Bachelor's Delight*, achieving a kind of annexation. "I will get his ship in for him," Delano boldly asserts beforehand, and Melville elaborates: "[Delano] urged his host to remain quietly where he was, since he (Captain Delano) would with pleasure take upon himself the responsibility of making the best use of the wind" (p. 219).[17] The historical reason for Melville's inclusion of such details (all missing from his source) begins to be plain. "With pleasure" would Melville's confident countrymen have similarly taken upon themselves the responsibility for a "spellbound" Spanish America.

Considerable textual evidence exists, then, of Melville's desire to explore the subject of American expansionism in "Benito Cereno." Moreover, other evidence testifies to his negative views on this subject. Near the end of "Benito Cereno," we learn, for example, that the climactic American invasion of the *San Dominick* is prompted not by any wish to "redeem" the oppressed but by a simple desire for material gain: "To encourage the sailors, they were told, that the Spanish captain considered his ship good as lost; that she and her cargo, including some gold and silver, were worth more than a thousand doubloons. Take her, and no small part should be theirs. The sailors replied with a shout." Interestingly, too, the leader of the American expeditionary force, Delano's first mate, is said to have once been "a privateer's-man" (p. 241), a fact unmentioned by Melville's source.[18] Nor should we overlook Melville's renaming of Delano's ship (originally the *Perseverance*) after the ship of an English buccaneer—or his allusion, by way of Delano's boat *Rover* (pp. 184–89), to certain "rovers" of the high seas.[19] The author of "Cuba" insisted that the majority of American expansionists felt merely an "honest, earnest sympathy" for the Cuban people; relatively few had "mercenary motives, than which nothing can be more utterly wicked and contemptible."[20] Aware, however, of America's chief reason for eyeing Cuba (and other lands of agricultural promise), Melville seemingly sought to depict Manifest Destiny as the rhetorical camouflage for a largely "piratical" enterprise.

Delano's embarrassing attempt to buy Babo (p. 168) points rather obviously to another authorial aim. As we have seen, supporters of Manifest Destiny cast America in the role of freedom's standard-bearer: for the prophets of *Putnam's*, America's mission was to "extend" democracy throughout the Western Hemisphere, to spread the "living seeds of freedom" among the subject peoples of the world.[21] Yet as prospective slaveowner, Delano scarcely extends democracy to blacks; indeed, when parrying Babo's final thrust, he physically "[grinds] the prostrate negro" (p. 236). Melville appears to suggest that the continuing allegiance of "emancipating" Americans to a Constitution condoning the ownership of persons was a bit incongruous.[22] Nor is it accidental that when Cereno and Delano finally cement their friendship in the presence of Babo, they do so by clasping hands "across the black's body" (p. 233).[23] Apparently Melville agreed with many abolitionists that the transfer of Cuba from Spanish into American hands would mean only a changing of the guard for Cuban slaves.

Melville's characterization of American expansionism as "mercenary" and nonlibertarian also serves a broader purpose: it invalidates the distinction, recurrent in the periodical literature of Melville's day, between American expansionism and the "corrupt" colonialism of European nations. Sensitive to the charge of imperialism, the author of "Cuba" carefully distinguished America's traditional practice of annexation from "the extension of empire by CONQUEST"; the author of "Annexation" met English objections to American meddling in the Caribbean by pointing to the predatory behavior of England herself and by contrasting the "open, generous, equitable international policy" of the United States with the "overreaching intrigue and secret diplomacy," the "sinister and iniquitous proceedings" of European states.[24] Yet the grim forcefulness of Delano's victorious seamen (pp. 242–46), combined with their rather ignoble motives, suggests that Melville found good reason to doubt the "special" ethics of American expansionism. Likewise troublesome is the imperiousness of Delano himself, who can cheerfully plot to remove Cereno from command of the *San Dominick* because he believes there is a significant "difference" between "the idea of Don Benito's darkly preordaining Captain Delano's fate, and Captain Delano's lightly arranging Don Benito's" (p. 166). In fact, Delano's distinction is suspect. Certainly his own interventionism implies that Melville saw no great "difference" between the blithe scheming of well-meaning Americans and the "dark" machinations of old-style imperialists. To "assert political, religious, and commercial freedom" was still, after all, to assert.

The details of "Benito Cereno" suggest, however, that if Melville discovered similarities between American imperialism and imperialism in general, he was most conscious of America's mimicry of Spain. Though American expansionists emphasized their dissimilarity from the Spanish colonizers they intended to replace in Latin America, they were, of course, taking up precisely where the Spanish had left off, since the colonial ventures of Charles V and Philip II had marked the last serious attempt to impose a moral and political order upon the western hemisphere.[25] Yet another, more complex reason may also exist for Melville's underscoring of the Spanish-American parallel: in 1855 Protestant Americans would have been appalled by any comparison between themselves and a nation of "diabolical" Catholics. In fact, anti-Catholic sentiment peaked in America during the 1850s in conjunction with a rising Anglo-Saxonism and a "nativist" dislike for all things "foreign." Catholicism was condemned for its "totalitarian" church structure, its "authoritarian" methods, its popularity among the "Celtic" races of Southern Europe, and its "imperialistic" commitment to worldwide evangelism. Moreover, Spanish Catholicism, with its famous Inquisition, drew especially heavy fire, since it seemed best to exemplify the "wicked" principles and practices of Popery.[26] Nor were such views limited to the lunatic fringe. Anti-Catholicism demonstrated its fashionableness in 1854 and 1855, when the Know-Nothing Party won a number of state and local elections, including important elections in Melville's home state of Massachusetts.[27]

Melville's awareness of mid-century America's preoccupation with Catholicism is suggested by Amasa Delano's repeated reference to abbots and friars, monks and monasteries—a reference significantly missing from Melville's source.[28] When Delano first approaches the *San Dominick* (a vessel whose name Melville changed, I think, partly in order to invoke a Spanish Inquisition founded by St. Domingo de Guzman and directed by his "Dominican" Order), the spectral ship looms "like a white-washed monastery after a thunder-storm, seen perched upon some dun cliff among the Pyrenees"; meanwhile, those on board recall "monks" in "dark cowls" and "Black Friars pacing the cloisters" (p. 113). Later, too, Cereno becomes for Delano a "hypochondriac abbot," while Babo is said to "look something like a begging friar of St. Francis" (pp. 123, 136). And later still, during Melville's shaving scene, the furnishings of Babo's barber shop also take on a religious significance as Delano's "Catholic" obsession again colors Melville's description:

> On one side was a claw-footed old table lashed to the deck; a thumbed missal on it, and over it a small, meagre crucifix attached to the bulk-head. Under the table lay a dented cutlass or two, with a hacked harpoon, among some melancholy old rigging, like a heap of poor friars' girdles. There were also two long, sharp-ribbed settees of Malacca cane, black with age, and uncomfortable to look at as inquisitors' racks, with a large, misshapen arm-chair, which, furnished with a rude barber's crotch at the back, working with a screw, seemed some grotesque engine of torment. (pp. 197–98)

Neither Melville's shaving scene—nor his inquisitorial similes—appeared in his source. Apparently they too represent a "topical" allusion to Catholicism as envisioned by anxious Americans in 1855.

Yet, to grasp the ironic point of this allusion, we must consider Melville's shaving scene more closely. That scene is puzzling, partly, I suspect, because our stereotypes have gone awry: while Melville's figurative language suggests that an "Inquisition" of sorts is occurring, the Spaniard Cereno is not so much the sponsor as the victim of this inquisition. More importantly, though Babo is a capable torturer, one leading inquisitorial "part" remains to be filled. Where, we might ask, are the inquisitors? I quote from Melville's account of the episode:

> "And now, Don Amasa," [said Babo,] "please go on with your talk about the gale, and all that; master can hear, and, between times, master can answer."
> "Ah yes, these gales," said Captain Delano; "but the more I think of your voyage, Don Benito, the more I wonder, not at the gales . . . but at the disastrous interval following them. For here, by your account, have you been these two months and more getting from Cape Horn to St. Maria, a distance which I myself, with a good wind, have sailed in a few days. True, you had calms, and long ones, but to be becalmed for two months, that is, at least, unusual. Why, Don Benito, had almost any other gentleman told me such a story, I should have been half disposed to a little incredulity."
> Here an involuntary expression came over the Spaniard, . . . and whether it was the start he gave, or a sudden gawky roll of the hull in the calm, or a momentary unsteadiness of the servant's hand, however it was, just then the razor drew blood. (pp. 204–5)

Babo's sadism may obscure the fact that there is but one questioner, one examiner, one true "inquisitor" on hand during Melville's shaving scene—and that is Amasa Delano. Indeed, Delano has been busily "inquiring" all day long, questioning Cereno as to "the particulars of the ship's misfortunes" (pp. 129–35, 142–45), pondering the captain's story (pp. 163–66), and double-checking details, first with a "Barcelona tar" (pp. 172–73), and later with Cereno himself (pp. 194–95). Indefatigably curious, Delano pumps Cereno even after his shave is complete (p. 215). The original Delano asked *no* questions of his host; Melville's protagonist persists in an interrogation which greatly aggravates the anguish of the Spanish captain. After seeing the painful effect of one of his obtuse queries, Delano remarks, "[Cereno] is like one flayed alive . . . ; where may one touch him without causing a shrink?" (p. 224).

As Melville's inquisitor, Delano wants more, however, than historical "particulars": he hopes to discover moral truth.[29] Who on the *San Dominick* is guilty and who is innocent? Who is evil and who is good? Those are Delano's real questions. Yet during his investigation, Delano learns a basic inquisitorial lesson—namely, that moral "answers" are exceedingly difficult to determine. As many critics have observed, Melville places an early emphasis on the ambiguity of the *San Dominick*, describing the "vapors partly mantling the hull, through which the far matin light from her cabin streamed equivocally enough," and noting both the "apparent uncertainty of her movements" and the natural grayness surrounding her arrival in Santa Maria bay (pp. 111, 112, 109–10). Later, too, Melville interprets his own symbolism, underlining the *moral* grayness of the *San Dominick*. A diligent inquisitor, Amasa Delano continually strives to hit moral bedrock. But baffled by contradictory evidences, he quickly loses all track of friend and foe, coming to wonder finally if Cereno, or Cereno's Spaniards, or Cereno and Babo, or Babo and Atufal, or Babo's Ashantees, or the whole amazing mass of humanity on board is most likely to murder him.[30]

To be sure, Delano occasionally abandons his indecision and draws moral conclusions, but then he is badly mistaken, not only in the case of Babo and Cereno (see below) but in other instances as well. Consecutive episodes depict his encounters with a Spanish sailor of haggard face, whose hand is "black with continually thrusting it into [a] tar-pot," and the aforementioned Barcelona tar, whose "weather-beaten visage" ill accords with his "furtive, diffident air."[31] Delano instantly assumes that the tainted hands of the first must be symbolic of vice: "If, indeed, there be any wickedness on board this ship," he thinks, "be sure that man there has fouled his hand in it" (pp. 171–72). And after badgering the Barcelonan, who is nervously unwilling to answer his questions, Delano decides that this man too must be ridden with guilt. Turning away, he declares, "How plainly . . . did that old whiskerando yonder betray a consciousness of ill desert" (pp. 173–74). Later we learn, however, that Delano's confidence was no proof of his perspicacity. Don Joaquin's hands were tarred strictly at the behest of Babo (p. 262); he was wholly innocent of wrongdoing. Moreover, the Barcelonan, subsequently seen at the tiller, was required to alter his expression before Delano in an effort to stay alive (p. 262). When that expression later changes, he is very nearly killed (pp. 221–22, 262).

Why does Delano, as inquisitor, go wrong so often? In part because of misery's effect on the examined. When first speaking of Don Joaquin, Melville, unlike Delano, refuses to make a moral judgment, saying, "Whether [Joaquin's] haggardness had aught to do with criminality, could not be determined; since, as intense heat and cold, though unlike, produce like sensations, so innocence and guilt . . . , through casual association with mental pain, . . . use one seal—a hacked one" (p. 171). In other words, signs of "mental pain" mask all evidence of virtue or depravity. This Delano does not realize; hence he is "operated upon," in the cases of Joaquin and the Barcelonan, "by certain general notions which, while disconnecting pain and abashment from virtue, invariably link them with vice" (p. 171). Problem number one, then: for an erring Delano, "haggardness" and "furtiveness" are always manifestations of guilt.

Yet Delano also has a second, more troubling perceptual difficulty: a tendency to let racial prejudice distort his vision of moral reality. Most obviously, white racism wrongly persuades him that Babo's blacks are too docile (pp. 149, 200, 220) to pose a threat; in addition, a subtle Anglo-Saxonism makes him foolishly suspect Cereno. In Melville's source the latter is everywhere dubbed "the Spanish captain"[32]; in "Benito Cereno" he becomes merely "the Spaniard" (pp. 120, 121, 122, et passim), the type for Delano of a dangerous and disagreeable race. Upon boarding the *San Dominick*, the American is quick to note Cereno's "national formality," his "sour and gloomy disdain" (pp. 121, 125). And later he comes to fear "the secret vindictiveness of the morbidly sensitive Spaniard" (p. 150)—that is, not so much a rancor peculiar to Cereno as a nastiness typical of a nation. Diverging widely from his source,[33] Melville planted in Delano's mind the false fear that he is about to be victimized not by Babo and company but by an exemplary "dark Spaniard" (p. 165), a character drawn no less directly than the "affectionate African" from Delano's capacious bag of moral stereotypes.

Moreover, like many of the elements of "Benito Cereno," Delano's prejudices are historically significant. If his image of blacks recalls the image promoted by certain white liberals during the 1850s,[34] his distrust of Cereno invokes a more traditional bias: Melville's mention of Guy Fawkes (p. 188) reminds us that Delanovian fears of "the Spaniard" had tenanted the minds of Anglo-Saxons since the days of the Gunpowder Plot. Melville may also have had more contemporary precedents in mind when prejudicing his protagonist against Cereno, for he likens Delano's first impression of the *San Dominick* to "that produced by . . . entering a strange house with strange inmates in a strange land," and later records Delano's complaints regarding Cereno's "clumsy seamanship and faulty navigation" (pp. 117, 137–38). In 1854 *Putnam's* printed extracts from a travelogue entitled *Cosas de España*, whose author continually criticized the ways of Spain, objecting, for example, to Spanish rules for courtship, the Spanish custom of pig killing, Spanish stagecoaches, even the Spanish taste for garlic.[35] Like Delano, he found fault too with Spanish seamanship and navigation, citing "the thousand causes of delay incident to all Spanish expeditions," and complaining when his own Spanish vessel sailed eastward toward Italy after leaving Marseilles, while on its way to Barcelona (due west).[36] Most importantly, the author glossed his title as follows: "An explanatory word, at the outset, respecting the *cosas de España*. They are the *strange things of Spain*, which being utterly incomprehensible by foreigners, are never even attempted to be explained to them by the natives."[37] This remark might account for Melville's emphasis on the "strangeness" of the *San Dominick*, an emphasis heightened by a second adjectival barrage: "This is a strange craft; a strange history, too, and strange folks on board," says Delano at one point. "As a nation," he adds, "these Spaniards are all an odd set" (pp. 187, 188).

Yet such allusions, interesting as they are, remain tangential to "Benito Cereno." For whatever specific prejudices Delano may display and whatever prevailing attitudes he may demonstrate, he has the same general failings as moral observer: an overeagerness to condemn the crestfallen and a bigotry that blunts his perception of truth. Nor do these failings lack "larger" significance, being faults as well of a Spanish Inquisition famous for prejudging the innocent and the abashed. Indeed, the fundamental reason for Melville's Catholic imagery, "inquisitorial" plot, and fallible protagonist is now revealed. If Delano is the author's masterful symbol of an American expansionism modeled upon Spain's, he is also Melville's ingenious way of suggesting that at a time when Protestant Americans viewed Spanish Catholicism as an extreme example of dogmatic imperialism, they were becoming involved in a close-minded crusade of their own. While priding themselves on their moral superiority and historical uniqueness, Delano's descendants were taking "immoral" cues from their own worst enemy.

This point leads to another, however, for by recognizing the unoriginality of American expansionism, Melville was not only able to identify its unattractive features but also to predict its nonsuccess. On one occasion Delano encounters a sailor resembling "an Egyptian priest, making Gordian knots for the temple of Ammon"; this individual throws an elaborate knot to Delano, demanding that he "undo it, cut it, quick" (pp. 181, 182).[38] Intricate and perplexing, the knot surely symbolizes the moral tangle of the San Dominick, that tangle which defeats a dim-witted Delano. Yet the knot also reminds us that Alexander the Great visited the temple of Ammon at the beginning of his military career, and finding there the Gordian knot, believed to be unravelable only by one who would conquer Asia, simply cut it with his sword and marched off to his first series of conquests. Offered to Delano, Melville's knot, then, symbolizes more than moral complexity. It suggests that Delano's mid-century successors were commencing not merely a species of "inquisition" but also an "Alexandrian" quest for world dominion. More importantly, it also suggests that this quest was likely to fail, for rather than unraveling or cutting his own Gordian knot, a befuddled Delano simply hands it to an elderly Negro who drops it overboard (p. 183). Delano is obviously no Alexander; nor was America's imperialist future particularly bright.

And why not? Proponents of Manifest Destiny were confident, of course, that Anglo-Saxon "energy" would inevitably triumph where Celtic "feebleness" had failed. So does the "dynamic" Delano patronize the "weak" Cereno. Yet Melville subverts the Anglo-Saxon cause by comparing the Spanish captain to both "an invalid courtier tottering about London streets in the time of the plague" and "that timid King," James the First of England (pp. 137, 206). These similes imply that Anglo-Saxons are as capable of "weakness" as anyone else—simply because weakness is a matter of individual personality and situation rather than a matter of race. Delano eventually learns, for example, that Cereno's "impotence" resulted not from his race but from his life-threatening predicament and the stresses he had undergone for a period of many weeks. Moreover, Delano's discovery is historically important: Melville's reference to the "retiring" Charles V (p. 126) extends his analysis of Cereno to a "decrepit" Spain, suffering, by 1855, not from racial enervation but from a profound fatigue caused by her protracted and ultimately futile attempt to conquer the world for Catholicism. In other words, if Spain, like Cereno, was "tottering" in 1855, that was chiefly because of her historical situation, one that might have "weakened" any nation, and one that might yet "tire" America herself.

For though mid-century Americans felt competent to end the "anarchy and misrule" prevalent in Cuba, Mexico, and other neighboring states, they failed to appreciate the moral and managerial difficulties involved—those very difficulties which had finally "exhausted" Spain. One obstacle to the establishment of "order" was human depravity, a general tendency to wrong-doing that Spanish Catholicism (and the Inquisition in particular) had sought in vain to subdue. Delano assumes that Cereno's ineffectualness has produced the confusion aboard his ship, but from reading Cereno's deposition, we conclude that the barbarity of man was more to blame: an evil (slavery) having been perpetrated on Babo's blacks, they brutally responded in kind. Melville apparently believed that any nation which presumed itself able to "govern" large segments of an unregenerate mankind was hopelessly naive. Apparently he also believed that Americans overlooked certain socioeconomic obstacles standing in the way of Latin American "redemption," for he informs us that physical conditions on the *San Dominick* were another cause of the chaos on board, as thirst, for instance, heightened the restlessness of Babo's blacks (p. 251). Earlier Melville explained that "in armies, navies, cities, or families, in nature herself, nothing more relaxes good order than misery" (p. 122), a truth to be pondered by an America happily planning to "arrange" the affairs of Latin America's "miserable" masses. Summarizing his own case, Cereno eventually insists that "events have not been favorable to much order in my arrangements" (p. 199): the disarray of his vessel is to be blamed, that is, not on his failings as a commander but on the history of that vessel, a direful scenario of savagery and suffering. The related message for Melville's readers? Spain could not be held primarily responsible for the deteriorating condition of her empire. Moreover, a blithe America, determined to "stabilize" the western hemisphere, might be in for a surprise.

American expansionists, however, would have raised one final objection to Melville's dismal forecast, feeling sure that "elect" Americans, whether "energetic" or not, would surely outperform the disciples of the Antichrist. For just as Delano assumes that he is under the protection of "some one above" (p. 184), so did many nineteenth-century Americans feel themselves chosen by a God that had befriended their Puritan forefathers to exert a moral and political hegemony over the other peoples of the earth. Explaining America's election racially, the author of "Annexation" declared that "an instinct in the human soul, deeper than the wisdom of politics, more powerful than the sceptres of states, impels the [Teutonic] people on, to the accomplishment of that high destiny which Providence has plainly reserved for our race."[39]

Yet in "Benito Cereno" Melville challenges the truth of such assertions by again invoking the example of Spain. In particular, he asks his compatriots to recall that Spanish Catholics once had an exceptionally firm faith in *their* heavenly commission—yet that faith was evidently misplaced. Cereno's deposition describes a jewel, unmentioned in Melville's source, which is said to have been found on the body of Don Joaquin after his death at the hands of Delano's myopic Americans. Joaquin intended this jewel "for the shrine of our Lady of Mercy in Lima; a votive offering, beforehand prepared and guarded, to attest his gratitude, when he should have landed in Peru, his last destination, for the safe conclusion of his entire voyage from Spain" (p. 263). However, like the drowned Juan Robles, who dies "making acts of contrition" (p. 254), Joaquin seems a man whose "Popish" divinities have deserted him—in the same way as they seemed to desert those Spanish Catholics who were forced to watch their mighty moral and political edifice crumble into fragments during the eighteenth and nineteenth centuries. Moreover, Melville suggests that what happened once might well happen again—this time to an overly assured America. As the author's final dialogue reveals, Delano's heirs had substituted a favorable "Providence" for Joaquin's "Lady of Mercy" and Cereno's "Prince of Heaven" (p. 266), but the facile assumption of divine patronage was the same; and however blessed Americans might feel in 1855, there would likely come a day when all blessings would end.

While a complacent America saw herself, then, as specially selected to succeed a weak nation cursed with an inferior religion, Melville viewed Spain's troubled history as eminently predictive of America's own. And while Americans saw themselves as riding the wave of history toward a moral and political millennium, Melville noted only their deplorable tendency to reduplicate the past. The author of "Cuba" closed by celebrating "the essential progress of mankind" and America's exemplary role in furthering that progress:

> The extension of empire by CONQUEST will soon be superseded by the irrepressible desire of states to become united to each other by the NEW LAW OF ANNEXATION. This is already inspiring no inconsiderable proportion of the inhabitants of every nation on this continent to become an integral part of our own great Republic. The history of the future will be, in a continually

increasing degree, a detail of the rapid operation of this principle [of ANNEX-ATION], until the world shall be completely united and bound together by the tracks of its intercommunication, the combination of its interests, the sympathies of its intelligence, and the unity and oneness of its hopes; and the last triumph which is ordered by Providence, has realization in the dawn of that period when all the nations of the earth shall be as ONE PEOPLE[40]

For this author, American expansion into the Caribbean was but a phase in man's ineluctable movement toward the establishment of a political utopia; he illustrates the forward-looking optimism of Melville's contemporaries, who chose, with Amasa Delano, to "forget" (p. 267) a problematical past, viewing it as irrelevant to their own glorious future. To Melville, however, the course of human history seemed less pleasantly "progressive," more grimly repetitious; to him, "past, present, and future seemed one" (p. 236). "*Follow your leader*," whisper Aranda's bleached bones to the American invader (p. 239). "Follow your leader!" shouts Delano's mate in reply (p. 244). Melville's countrymen might assert their moral superiority to the Spanish, but to Melville, eyeing American motives and methods, the imperialistic resemblance was clear. And Americans might also propose to evade the Spanish fate; but Melville saw a single destiny as "manifest" for America, and that was to follow the Spanish lead—to join at last the nonselect company of nations gone by.

Six years earlier, in *Mardi*, Melville had likewise lectured an overconfident America, disguising his views as those of an anonymous pamphleteer:

"In these boisterous days, the lessons of history are almost discarded, as superseded by present experiences. And that while all Mardi's Present has grown out of its Past, it is becoming obsolete to refer to what has been. Yet, peradventure, the Past is an apostle.

"The grand error of this age, sovereign-kings! is the general supposition, that the very special Diabolus is abroad; whereas, the very special Diabolus has been abroad ever since Mardi began.

"And the grand error of your nation, sovereign-kings! seems this:—The conceit that Mardi is now in the last scene of the last act of her drama; and that all preceding events were ordained, to bring about the catastrophe you believe to be at hand,—a universal and permanent Republic.

"May it please you, those who hold to these things are fools, and not wise.

"Time is made up of various ages; and each thinks its own a novelty. But imbedded in the walls of the pyramids, which outrun all chronologies, sculptured stones are found, belonging to yet older fabrics."[41]

At the considerable expense of Amasa Delano, "Benito Cereno" advances a similar thesis, eschewing all manner of millennial optimism while exposing both the "grand errors" of the contemporary American mind and the "diabolic" permanences of human history. Intensely topical and deeply political, the tale launches a powerful assault on the principal assumptions of Manifest Destiny. Yet in its profound awareness of past, present, and future, it also shares with the "largest" of Melville's works the merit of tragic timelessness.

Notes

1. See "*Moby-Dick* and American Political Symbolism," *American Quarterly*, 15 (1963), 498–534.

2. See Rogin, *Subversive Genealogy: The Politics and Art of Herman Melville* (New York: Knopf, 1983), pp. 102–51; and Duban, *Melville's Major Fiction: Politics, Theology, and Imagination* (De Kalb: Northern Illinois Univ. Press, 1983), pp. 82–148.

3. See Heimert, "*Moby-Dick* and American Political Symbolism," pp. 499–502.

4. See Allan Moore Emery, "The Political Significance of Melville's Chimney," *New England Quarterly*, 55 (1982), 201–28.

5. For treatments of politics in *Mardi*, see Merrell R. Davis, *Melville's "Mardi": A Chartless Voyage*, Yale Studies in English, Vol. 119 (New Haven: Yale Univ. Press, 1952), pp. 156–59; and Duban, *Melville's Major Fiction*, pp. 11–30.

6. For example, see Rogin, *Subversive Genealogy*, pp. 208–20.

7. The subject of slavery arises "secondarily" in "Benito Cereno" as a result of Melville's concern with expansionism (see pp. 102–3) and his interest in human depravity. See also Allan Moore Emery, "The Topicality of Depravity in 'Benito Cereno,' " *American Literature*, 55 (1983), 316–31.

8. Among the many critics of "Benito Cereno," only Marvin Fisher has noted this emphasis; see his *Going Under: Melville's Short Fiction and the American 1850s* (Baton Rouge: Louisiana State Univ. Press, 1977), pp. 111–13. See also Robert Lowell's stage version of "Benito Cereno" in *The Old Glory*, rev. ed. (New York: Farrar, 1968), pp. 139–214; though Lowell appreciates only a part of Melville's anti-expansionist message, his overall "reading" of "Benito Cereno" is admirably on target.

9. See Merton M. Sealts, Jr., *Melville's Reading: A Check-List of Books Owned and Borrowed* (Madison: Univ. of Wisconsin Press, 1966), p. 87.

10. See "Cuba," *Putnam's Monthly Magazine*, Jan. 1853, pp. 5, 10, 13–16. The author of "What Impression Do We, and Should We, Make Abroad?" *Putnam's*, Oct. 1853, pp. 345–54, similarly contrasted a "young, fresh, and surpassingly vigorous" United States with such "exhausted" nations as Spain (p. 350).

11. "Annexation," *Putnam's*, Feb. 1854, p. 191.

12. See Amasa Delano, *A Narrative of Voyages and Travels, in the Northern and Southern Hemispheres: Comprising Three Voyages Round the World; together with a Voyage of Survey and Discovery, in the Pacific Ocean and Oriental Islands* (1817; rpt. New York: Praeger, 1970), pp. 318, 322–23.

13. "Benito Cereno," in *The Piazza Tales* (New York: Dix and Edwards, 1856), pp. 113–14; hereafter citations in my text are to this edition. Melville's tale originally appeared in the numbers of *Putnam's* for October, November, and December of 1855.

14. For discussion of the *San Dominick* as symbolic of Spain, see Stanley T. Williams, " 'Follow Your Leader': Melville's 'Benito Cereno,' " *Virginia Quarterly Review*, 23 (1947), 61–76; Richard Harter Fogle, "The Monk and the Bachelor: Melville's *Benito Cereno*," *Tulane Studies in English*, 3 (1952), 155–78, rpt. in Fogle's *Melville's Shorter Tales* (Norman: Univ. of Oklahoma Press, 1960), pp. 116–47; H. Bruce Franklin, " 'Apparent Symbol of Despotic Command': Melville's *Benito Cereno*," *New England Quarterly*, 34 (1961), 462–77, rpt. in

Franklin's *The Wake of the Gods: Melville's Mythology* (Stanford: Stanford Univ. Press, 1963), pp. 136–50; and Fisher, *Going Under*.

15.   Melville's use of Lima to typify this empire may have been encouraged by the author of "Lima and the Limanians," *Harper's New Monthly Magazine*, Oct. 1851, pp. 598–609, who viewed Lima's decline as symptomatic of Spain's (p. 598), and who wistfully recalled the glorious days of the viceroys (pp. 599, 608). Melville's early allusion in "Benito Cereno" to "a Lima intriguante's one sinister eye peering across the Plaza from the Indian loop-hole of her dusk *saya-y-manta*" (p. 111) and his later mention of Lima's "Plaza" and "Rimac bridge" (p. 270) further suggest he may have seen the "Lima" article, which contained accounts of both the *saya* and Lima's architectural features (pp. 602–5, 606–8). Melville's first mention of the *saya* (by name) occurs in *Pierre* (1852), which he was writing at the time the "Lima" article appeared; see *Pierre; or, The Ambiguities*, Vol. 7 of *The Writings of Herman Melville*, ed. Harrison Hayford, Hershel Parker, and G. Thomas Tanselle (Evanston and Chicago: Northwestern Univ. Press and Newberry Library, 1970), p. 149. Moreover, Melville's own "Town-Ho's Story" appeared in the same number of *Harper's* as the "Lima" article, making his familiarity with that number more likely. For Melville's acquaintance with *Harper's* (to which he subscribed), see Sealts, *Melville's Reading*, p. 64.

16.   Delano's view may owe something to the author of "Lima and the Limanians," who described Lima's Spanish Creoles as evincing "a look of premature age; as though the powers of nature were exhausted, and insufficient to develop a vigorous manhood" (p. 601). The nearby drawing of an "indolent" Peruvian (p. 600) might almost be a snapshot of Cereno.

17.   Melville was at times a careful stylist. The parenthesis in this sentence slyly underlines Delano's "takeover" of the *San Dominick* while seeming only to clarify pronoun reference.

18.   See Delano, *A Narrative of Voyages and Travels*, pp. 326–27.

19.   The pirate Ambrose Cowley, cited as a Galapagos authority in Melville's "The Encantadas" (1854), was captain of the *Bachelor's Delight*. See *The Piazza Tales*, p. 329; and Robert Albrecht, "The Thematic Unity of Melville's 'The Encantadas,' " *Texas Studies in Literature and Language*, 14 (1972), 465*n*. In *A Narrative of Voyages and Travels* Delano's boat had no name (see pp. 323–25). According to the *Oxford English Dictionary*, "rover" was the standard euphemism for pirate throughout the nineteenth century. See, for example, the use of the term in Fenimore Cooper's *The Red Rover* (1828), which Melville reviewed for the *Literary World* in 1850 (Sealts, *Melville's Reading*, p. 53). The original Delano was accused of being a pirate by an ungrateful Cereno (*A Narrative of Voyages and Travels*, p. 329); this detail may have helped to inspire Melville's christenings.

20.   "Cuba," p. 13.

21.   See "Cuba," p. 15; and "Annexation," p. 191. See also "What Impression Do We, and Should We, Make Abroad?" p. 345.

22.   This suggestion also appears in *Mardi, and a Voyage Thither*, Vol. 3 of *The Writings of Herman Melville*, ed. Harrison Hayford, Hershel Parker, and G. Thomas Tanselle (Evanston and Chicago: Northwestern Univ. Press and Newberry Library, 1970), where hieroglyphics on the archway of Vivenza (an isle representing America) proclaim: "In this republican land all men are born free and equal. . . . except the tribe of Hamo" (pp. 512, 513).

23.   Melville's source reports merely that Cereno gave Delano's hand "a hearty squeeze" (p. 324), no reference being made to Babo.

24.   See "Cuba," p. 16; and "Annexation," pp. 184, 187, 191.

25.   Many critics have opposed Delano as representative of the New World to Cereno as representative of the Old; yet only a handful have sensed that Melville meant an aspiring America and declining Spain to be compared as well as contrasted. See Margaret M. Vanderhaar, "A Re-Examination of 'Benito Cereno,' " *American Literature*, 40 (1968), 179–91; Ray B. Browne, *Melville's Drive to Humanism* (Lafayette, Ind.: Purdue Univ. Studies, 1971), pp. 168–88; Joyce Adler, "Melville's *Benito Cereno*: Slavery and Violence in the Americas," *Science*

and Society, 38 (1974), 19–48, rpt. in Joyce Sparer Adler's *War in Melville's Imagination* (New York: New York Univ. Press, 1981), pp. 88–110; Paul D. Johnson, "American Innocence and Guilt: Black-White Destiny in 'Benito Cereno,' " *Phylon*, 36 (1975), 426–34; and Kermit Vanderbilt, " 'Benito Cereno': Melville's Fable of Black Complicity," *Southern Review*, 12 (1976), 311–22. According to these critics, Melville believed America was following the lead of Spain in refusing to extirpate slavery from the New World. Edgar A. Dryden and Marvin Fisher alone appreciate Melville's emphasis on the more general similarities between American and Spanish imperialism. See Dryden, *Melville's Thematics of Form: The Great Art of Telling the Truth* (Baltimore: Johns Hopkins Press, 1968), pp. 199–209; and Fisher, *Going Under*, pp. 111–13.

26.   The author of "Lima and the Limanians" made special mention of the Inquisition, lamenting the former use made in Lima of "racks, pillories, scourges, gags, thumbscrews, and other instruments of torture" (p. 608). The excesses of the Inquisition were also described in Giacinto Achilli's *Dealings with the Inquisition; or, Papal Rome, her Priests, and her Jesuits, with Important Disclosures* (New York: Harper, 1851), a work briefly reviewed in the *Literary World*, 24 May 1851, p. 417; and in *Harper's*, June 1851, p. 139. Sealts describes Melville's acquaintance with the *Literary World in Melville's Reading*, p. 75. For other evidence of American anti-Catholic feeling, see the jaundiced account of "The Holy Week at Rome" in *Harper's*, June, July, August 1854, pp. 20–32, 158–71, 317–27. See also "Should We Fear the Pope?" *Putnam's*, June 1855, pp. 650–59, though this article could not have influenced "Benito Cereno," since it appeared after Melville's tale was composed; see Sealts, "The Chronology of Melville's Short Fiction, 1853–1856," in *Pursuing Melville, 1940–1980* (Madison: Univ. of Wisconsin Press, 1982), p. 231.

27.   See Ray Allen Billington, *The Protestant Crusade, 1800–1860: A Study of the Origins of American Nativism* (New York: Macmillan, 1938), pp. 380–436. Billington notes that the Massachusetts legislature elected in the fall of 1854 was "almost entirely" composed of Know-Nothings; the governor of the state was also a Party member (pp. 412–15). Melville's familiarity with the Know-Nothings is implied by his reference in "Benito Cereno" to the "silent signs, of some Freemason sort," which pass at one point between Cereno and a Spanish sailor (p. 158); a *Putnam's* article of January 1855 had portrayed the Know-Nothings as the "secretive" heirs of Freemasonry. See "Secret Societies–The Know Nothings," *Putnam's*, Jan. 1855, pp. 88–97.

28.   For discussions of this allusive pattern, see Williams, " 'Follow Your Leader' "; Fogle, "The Monk and the Bachelor"; William Bysshe Stein, "The Moral Axis of 'Benito Cereno,' " *Accent*, 15 (1955), 221–33; Franklin, " 'Apparent Symbol of Despotic Command' "; John Bernstein, "*Benito Cereno* and the Spanish Inquisition," *Nineteenth-Century Fiction*, 16 (1962), 345–50; William T. Pilkington, " 'Benito Cereno' and the American National Character," *Discourse*, 8 (1965), 49–63; David D. Galloway, "Herman Melville's *Benito Cereno*: An Anatomy," *Texas Studies in Literature and Language*, 9 (1967), 239–52; Kingsley Widmer, "The Perplexity of Melville: *Benito Cereno*," *Studies in Short Fiction*, 5 (1968), 225–38, rpt. in Widmer's *The Ways of Nihilism: A Study of Herman Melville's Short Novels* (Los Angeles: California State Colleges, 1970), pp. 59–90; Charles Nicol, "The Iconography of Evil and Ideal in 'Benito Cereno,' " *American Transcendental Quarterly*, No. 7 (1970), pp. 25–31; Charles R. Metzger, "Melville's Saints: Allusion in *Benito Cereno*," *ESQ*, 58 (1970), 88–90; Mason I. Lowance, Jr., "Veils and Illusion in *Benito Cereno*," *Arizona Quarterly*, 26 (1970), 113–26; Bernard Rosenthal, "Melville's Island," *Studies in Short Fiction*, 11 (1974), 1–9; R. Bruce Bickley, Jr., *The Method of Melville's Short Fiction* (Durham: Duke Univ. Press, 1975), pp. 100–108; William B. Dillingham, *Melville's Short Fiction, 1853–1856* (Athens: Univ. of Georgia Press, 1977), pp. 227–70; Thomas D. Zlatic, " 'Benito Cereno': Melville's 'Back-Handed-Well-Knot,' " *Arizona Quarterly*, 34 (1978), 327–43; and Gloria Horsley-Meacham, "The Monastic Slaver: Images and Meaning in 'Benito Cereno,' " *New England Quarterly*, 56 (1983), 261–66. While offering provocative interpretations

of Melville's imagery, these critics fail to consider the "topical" reasons for Melville's concern with Catholicism.

29. An exercise in the "inquisitorial" mode, "Benito Cereno" begins, in fact, with a moral investigation and ends with sworn testimonies, judicial findings, sentencing, and the administering of punishment.

30. For discussions of Melville's emphasis on moral ambiguity, see Rosalie Feltenstein, "Melville's 'Benito Cereno,' " *American Literature*, 19 (1947), 245–55; Fogle, "The Monk and the Bachelor"; Guy A. Cardwell, "Melville's Gray Story: Symbols and Meaning in 'Benito Cereno,' " *Bucknell Review*, 8 (1959), 154–67; Galloway, "Herman Melville's *Benito Cereno*: An Anatomy"; Lowance, "Veils and Illusion in *Benito Cereno*"; Ruth B. Mandel, "The Two Mystery Stories in *Benito Cereno*," *Texas Studies in Literature and Language*, 14 (1973), 631–42; and Zlatic, " 'Benito Cereno': Melville's 'Back-Handed-Well-Knot.' "

31. Neither episode appears in Delano, *A Narrative of Voyages and Travels*.

32. See Delano's *Narrative of Voyages and Travels*, pp. 318, 319, 320, 323, et passim.

33. The original Delano was merely shocked by the Spaniard's lack of authority and miffed at his coldness; see *A Narrative of Voyages and Travels*, pp. 323–24.

34. See Emery's discussion of this subject in "The Topicality of Depravity in 'Benito Cereno,' " pp. 318–19.

35. See *Cosas de España; or, Going to Madrid via Barcelona* (New York: Redfield, 1855); and "Cosas de España," *Putnam's*, May 1854, pp. 482–93; June 1854, pp. 583–93; July 1854, pp. 14–21; and Nov. 1854, pp. 518–24. The author of both the articles and the book was John Milton Mackie, who remained anonymous to his readers. The first *Putnam's* excerpt appeared in a number of the magazine containing a portion of Melville's "Encantadas"; the final two excerpts shared *Putnam's* numbers with segments of *Israel Potter*. In his "Chronology of Melville's Short Fiction, 1853–1856," Sealts suggests that "Benito Cereno" was "probably composed during the winter of 1854–1855" (p. 401); thus Melville could have seen the *Putnam's* articles, but not Mackie's book, prior to the writing of his tale.

36. See "Cosas de España," *Putnam's*, May 1854, pp. 482–84.

37. "Cosas de España," *Putnam's*, May 1854, p. 483; the italics are Mackie's own.

38. The episode does not appear in Delano's *Narrative of Voyages and Travels*.

39. "Annexation," p. 191.

40. "Cuba," p. 16.

41. *Mardi*, pp. 524–25. In *White-Jacket* (1850), on the other hand, Melville attacked the American navy's practice of flogging by insisting that a depraved past need furnish no precedent for an elect America. "The Past is dead," he wrote, "and has no resurrection; but the Future is endowed with such a life, that it lives to us even in anticipation. . . . We Americans are driven to a rejection of the maxims of the Past, seeing that, ere long, the van of the nations must, of right, belong to ourselves." Melville then waxed Hebraic: "We Americans are the peculiar, chosen people—the Israel of our time; we bear the ark of the liberties of the world. Seventy years ago we escaped from thrall; and, besides our first birthright—embracing one continent of earth—God has given to us, for a future inheritance, the broad domains of the political pagans, that shall yet come and lie down under the shade of our ark, without bloody hands being lifted. God has predestinated, mankind expects, great things from our race; and great things we feel in our souls." See *White-Jacket; or, The World in a Man-of-War*, Vol. 5 of *The Writings of Herman Melville*, ed. Harrison Hayford, Hershel Parker, and G. Thomas Tanselle (Evanston and Chicago: Northwestern Univ. Press and Newberry Library, 1970), pp. 150–51. Apparently, however, such views—eminently characteristic of Delano and his expansionist heirs—were a passing product of Melville's polemical urge, his revulsion at flogging and fervent desire for its abolition, rather than a symptom of his continuing confidence in American "specialness"; for both *Mardi* and "Benito Cereno" carefully contradict the thesis of the *White-Jacket* passage.

The Legal Fictions of Herman Melville and Lemuel Shaw

BROOK THOMAS

I have three aims in this essay. (1) I want to offer an example of an interdisciplinary historical inquiry combining literary criticism with the relatively new field of critical legal studies. (2) I intend to use this historical inquiry to argue that the ambiguity of literary texts might better be understood in terms of an era's social contradictions rather than in terms of the inherent qualities of literary language or rhetoric and, conversely, that a text's ambiguity can help us expose the contradictions masked by an era's dominant ideology. (3) I try to prove my assertion by applying my method to Herman Melville's "Benito Cereno," a work that deals with the law and lawyers and is widely acknowledged as ambiguous.[1] I will base my critical inquiry into this story on Melville's relationship with his father-in-law, Lemuel Shaw, who, while sitting as the chief justice of the Supreme Judicial Court of Massachusetts from 1830 to 1860, wrote some of the most important opinions in what Roscoe Pound has called "the formative era of American law."[2]

Before I get started, I should clarify what this study does not entail. By using Shaw and his legal decisions in conjunction with Melville's fiction, I am not conducting a positivistic influence study. My method will not depend on the positivist assumption that Shaw's legal opinions can be used to illuminate Melville's texts only when his direct knowledge of Shaw's opinions can be proved. Nor will I limit myself to a traditional psychoanalytic reading: my emphasis is on political and social issues, and too often these issues are deflected by translating them into psychological ones. At the same time, I recognize that critics concerned with political and social issues too often neglect questions raised by a writer's individual situation. I compare Shaw to Melville not to reduce Melville's politics to psychology but to prevent a political study from neglecting the political implications of psychology, to remind us—as the title of Fredric Jameson's book *The Political Unconscious* reminds us—that psychological questions always have political implications.

If, for instance, psychological critics refer to the early death of his father

Reprinted from *Critical Inquiry* 11 (1984): 24–34. Reprinted by permission of the University of Chicago Press and the author.

to explain Melville's fascination with paternal authority figures who abandon their "children," I would argue that given the patriarchal structure of authority in both his family and society, Melville's fascination inevitably has political implications. That Melville, fatherless for years, finally acquired a father-in-law who was the most important figure upholding the law in the Commonwealth of Massachusetts presents almost too neat a coincidence for anyone interested in studying the politics of their relationship, for it suggests that part of the power of Melville's works can be explained by his unique personal situation. It is, after all, important that it was Melville's father-in-law who made such important legal decisions. When Melville wrote stories about the law, he was no doubt influenced by the fact that his father-in-law was a famous judge. Even so, that personal relationship is significant for me because of what it reveals about the dominant ideology of Melville's times, an ideology that his father-in-law's court decisions both reflected and helped to shape.

This emphasis on ideology is what moves my study beyond a positivistic influence study. When I cite Shaw's legal opinions, I usually do so not to imply that Melville had direct knowledge of them; I cite them because they are the best evidence we have of Shaw's way of thinking about political matters, a way of thinking shared by many people in power during the antebellum period. It is not so important to prove that Melville had detailed knowledge of any one of Shaw's opinions as it is to demonstrate that he had some sense of the opinions behind the opinions. What my interdisciplinary method offers, therefore, is not so much a new interpretation that extracts a long-hidden meaning from Melville's stories, as a demonstration of their relationship to the dominant ideology of their times, especially their capacity to allow us to see the contradictions in that ideology, contradictions that they themselves cannot avoid.

As such, my investigation into the ideological implications of Melville's stories agrees basically, if not totally, with Louis Althusser's understanding of literature's relation to ideology. Althusser rejects the view that submission to the laws of art made a writer like Balzac abandon his own political convictions and generate telling social criticism despite his conservative beliefs. "On the contrary," Althusser argues, *"only because he retained them could he produce his work*, only because he stuck to his political ideology could he produce *in it* this internal 'distance' which gives us a critical 'view' of it." Art does not escape ideology, for Althusser, but what it "makes us *see* . . . is the *ideology* from which it is born, in which it bathes, from which it detaches itself as art, and to which it *alludes*."[3]

I will start by reading "Benito Cereno" in conjunction with Shaw's fugitive slave decisions, for if there was one issue which dramatically revealed contradictions in the American legal system, it was slavery. Shaw's decisions will help us better understand Melville's only direct treatment of slavery, at the same time that Melville's fictional account of a slave uprising will help us expose the inconsistencies within Shaw's decisions.

Prior to the Fugitive Slave Act of 1850, Shaw went out of his way (with one exception) to find loopholes in the existing Fugitive Slave Act of 1793. Shaw's desire to help runaway blacks achieve their freedom whenever possible grew out of his personal abhorrence of slavery. Shaw's reputation as an opponent of slavery was so strong that in an 1845 decision, Judge Nevius of New Jersey questioned whether Shaw's personal beliefs might have biased his opinions on slavery: "It is no matter of surprise that Chief Justice Shaw, entertaining the opinions he did upon this question of slavery, should have found it repugnant to the spirit of [the] Constitution" (*JA*, p. 58 n.*). Given Shaw's antislavery reputation, it was a matter of considerable surprise to some that he reversed himself and supported the new 1850 fugitive slave law.

The new fugitive slave law was part of Daniel Webster's compromise to hold the country together. Yet it was widely known that prior to 1850 no fugitive slave had been returned from Boston, the seat of much of Webster's support. Thus strong political pressure was exerted on Webster's friends (Shaw was one) to enforce the new law, in order to counter Southern charges that Massachusetts was ruled by abolitionists. Their first chance to prove their loyalty to the union came in February 1851, when a black named Shadrach was apprehended in Boston. But to the dismay of Southerners and Webster supporters, Shadrach escaped from the courthouse, aided by an unruly crowd of antislavery forces. Thus, on 3 April 1851, when Thomas Sims was taken into custody, officials made certain that he was brought to "justice." Curtailed by a state law from holding an accused runaway slave in a state jail, officials locked Sims in the federal courthouse and barricaded the door with chains. As abolitionists were quick to point out, the chains produced a highly symbolic scene the next day when Judge Shaw had to bow beneath them in order to enter a court of justice. In his decision Shaw himself felt fettered by the existing law of the land. When asked to rule on the constitutionality of the 1850 law, Shaw upheld it in a decision that for a decade was regarded as the highest authority on the issue. Free to proceed, the federal commissioner ordered the return of Sims to slavery, and, guarded by three hundred armed men, Sims was delivered to a ship and sent on his way south.

Shaw's decisions in the 1850s were not necessarily inconsistent with his earlier stand against slavery. In his pre-1850 decisions, Shaw never transgressed what he deemed the letter of the law. When the 1850 law tightened the loopholes which had allowed him to decide in favor of blacks, he saw no recourse but to decide as he did. Equally important, his decisions revealed principles he stated as early as 1820. Discussing the Missouri Compromise, Shaw had used abolitionist language to denounce slavery, but he added that immediate emancipation might cause misery. Furthermore, he felt the most important consideration was the "moral" necessity to hold the union together.

That Shaw saw maintaining the union in moral terms helps clarify a common misunderstanding about the conflict between antislavery forces and their opponents. Persuaded by powerful antislavery rhetoric, we often see the conflict as one between defenders of rule by secular authority—man-made law manifested in positive law—and proponents of rule by sacred authority—divine law manifested in private conscience. To a certain extent this statement of the conflict is accurate, but it is important to recognize that Shaw and many members of the legal profession also saw their secular responsibility in sacred terms. Preserving the union was a moral imperative because the United States was not merely one government among many but the hope of mankind: it, above all others, guaranteed the absolute and entire supremacy of the law. If abolitionists claimed that the country was not worth saving because its passage of laws like the Fugitive Slave Act violated its sacred mission, Shaw felt that unless the union *was* saved its sacred mission could never be fulfilled. To obey the act of 1850 would not only reaffirm the sacred principle of rule by law, which made the union worth preserving, it would also support a law that everyone knew was designed specifically to keep the country united. Thus, those who praised Shaw's *Sims* decision praised it because it declared that rule by law would prevail over the violence threatening to tear the country apart. Associated with blackness, that violence could easily be linked with satanic forces.

Those in power feared a violent slave uprising that might threaten the peace of the country and the sanctity of the law; this is evinced by the response to the Shadrach escape. The escape was reported as an example of "negro insurrection"; Secretary of State Webster labeled it "a case of treason"; President Fillmore called a special cabinet meeting to discuss the crisis; on the Senate floor Henry Clay asked whether "a government of white men was to be yielded to by a government of blacks."[4] For those so threatened, Shaw's decision in the *Sims* case signaled a victory for the forces of light over the forces of violence and darkness. The problem that the slavery issue posed for people who saw America's mission as furthering the cause of enlightenment—which, as I have argued, included both Shaw *and* antislavery factions—was that it was not always clear which were the forces of light and which of darkness.

This is, of course, precisely the dilemma facing readers of "Benito Cereno." Melville confronts us with a story which starts as a world full of grays only to transform into a world divided between blacks and whites, where the whites who seem to be in power are not and where a violent slave uprising, masterminded by a black man described in satanic terms, is squelched by an American captain who, because he is oblivious, appears innocent. A history of conflicting interpretations has arisen because the story provides no authoritative point of view to help us determine whether the blacks, the whites, or neither fight for an enlightened cause. This is not to say that Melville does not offer points of view which can traditionally be considered authoritative. To be sure, the two points of view through which the events of the story are filtered would conventionally be accepted as authoritative: first, the personal authority of a ship's captain; second, the impersonal authority of a legal deposition. But the authority of both of these points of view is undercut. The deficiencies of the legal deposition prompt us to examine the nature of justice guaranteed by the rule by law held so sacred by Justice Shaw. But first we need to review the limitations of Captain Delano's personal point of view.

Despite the many conflicting interpretations of the story, almost all readers agree that it exposes the narrowness of Captain Delano's innocent point of view. His innocent, straightforward reading of the events aboard the *San Dominick* turns out to be a complete misreading, a misreading that ironically saves him. As Don Benito Cereno, the *San Dominick*'s captain, tells him toward the end of the tale, if he had accurately interpreted the state of affairs aboard ship, he would have faced instant death. As a result, both he and Don Benito attribute his salvation to Providence; the reader, however, can see that Captain Delano's salvation results as much from his prejudice as from a providential concern for the innocent. Or put another way, his innocence is riddled with prejudice. As kind as Captain Delano seems to the Africans, he is unable to decipher the bizarre events on board ship because the possibility that Africans rather than Europeans could be in power is incomprehensible to him. When he sees blacks and whites, he immediately relegates blacks to a subservient role. He can think of blacks as only valets, hairdressers, or body servants. The true extent of Captain Delano's kindness to blacks is apparent when we learn that "like most men of good, blithe heart, Captain Delano took to negroes, not philanthropically, but genially, just as other men to Newfoundland dogs" (p. 265).

If the reader has not realized the limitations of Captain Delano's point of view, they are further emphasized in the story's second half, when the events are recounted from the point of view of the legal deposition. As opposed to Captain Delano's partial account of events, the legal point of view purports to offer an impartial account. But there are hints in the text that even the legal point of view might be partial, although in a much more subtle manner than Captain Delano's "innocent" prejudice.[5] First, the "document" Melville includes from the proceedings is "selected, from among many others, for partial translation" (p. 289). We do not receive all of the documents or even a complete translation of the one we do receive. Second, the selected document contains Don Benito's deposition, including testimony originally "held dubious" because of his "not undisturbed" state of mind (p. 289). Third, the final decision on what evidence is accepted as authoritative is made by a tribunal none of whose members witnessed any of the events under litigation. Rather than bringing us closer to the actual events, the legal point of view in one sense removes us even further from them. Finally, nowhere is the Africans' position voiced, a point I will return to later.

Despite the questionable accuracy of the legal point of view, many readers accept its authority. What the authority of the law legitimates becomes poignantly clear in the story's final paragraph. Certainly, one of the most heinous acts that Babo, the leader of the slave uprising, commits is using the decaying body of the slaveowner Don Alexandro Aranda as the *San Dominick*'s figurehead. But that act of violence is no worse than the one committed against Babo during his execution. "Dragged to the gibbet at the tail of a mule, the black met his voiceless end. The body was burned to ashes; but for many days, the head, that hive of subtlety, fixed on a pole in the Plaza, met, unabashed, the gaze of the whites" (p. 307). Babo's bleached skull, like the bleached bones of Don Alexandro, had been put on display to ensure obedience. The law, however, has the power to sanction an act that outside the law is censured as inhumane. Violence is justified when backed by the authority of the law, condemned as brutal and satanic when not. Rule by law, supposedly the only safeguard against the irrationality of violence, depends upon violence or the threat of violence to maintain itself, whether it be the suppression of the African's revolt or the armed enforcement, by three hundred men, of Sims' return to slavery.

Of course, it could be objected that Melville's story is a fictional account of the proceedings of a legal tribune in Peru, with no bearing on American law and its treatment of the slavery issue. But the *Amistad* case, a case sometimes cited as a source for "Benito Cereno," suggests otherwise. In 1839 forty-nine Africans bloodily seized control of the Spanish ship *Amistad* and tried to return to Africa. The ship was captured off Long Island by the American Navy. The lawsuit that followed involved two Americans filing for salvage; the Spanish owners demanding the ship's cargo, including the Africans; and the Africans claiming their freedom. The United States Government intervened on behalf of the Spaniards, citing a treaty between Spain and the United States promising to restore merchandise rescued from the hands of robbers or pirates. Justice Joseph Story, a Massachusetts judge similar in ideology to Shaw, wrote the opinion of the United States Supreme Court which granted the Africans their freedom. Arguing that the treaty did not apply since under Spanish law the Africans had been unlawfully enslaved and hence were not property, this notably conservative judge went so far as to concede the right of the Africans to rebel in their circumstances. "We may lament the dreadful acts by which they asserted their liberty, and took possession of the Amistad, but they cannot be deemed pirates or robbers in the sense of the law of nations" (*JA*, p. 112).[6]

In granting the Africans their freedom, the *Amistad* decision seems to manifest the concern the American legal system had for slaves. But Story was careful to point out that the Africans' rebellion was justified only on the high seas. If it had occurred within the United States, under American law, the legal questions would have been different. It was, for instance, the same Justice Story—an antislavery man himself—who ruled a year later in *Prigg* v. *The State of Pennsylvania* that according to United States law the Fugitive Slave Act of 1793 was constitutional and that state laws conflicting with it were unconstitutional. Story's decision was the one that Shaw cited to send Sims back to slavery. These cases indicate that, as far as slavery was concerned, American law was more repressive than "the law of nations." The action of "Benito Cereno" would seem to bear this out.

For anyone who considers the United States a progressive country, there is a certain irony in a plot in which a representative of the democratic United States (Captain Delano) returns Africans to slavery after they have achieved their freedom from a representative of the decaying, feudal power of Spain (Don Benito). Read as a political allegory, the story marks the ascendancy of the United States to its role as a new, more effective, imperialist power. The moment of ascendancy occurs in the boat departing from the *San Dominick*, when Captain Delano uses his hand to hold down Don Benito while simultaneously, with his foot, holding down Babo, who is "snakishly writhing up from the boat's bottom" (p. 283)—which recalls the symbolic sternpiece described at the beginning of the story, often cited as an emblem for exploitation.[7]

Melville's story even suggests one motive generating the rise of the United States to power. Boarding the *San Dominick* to put down the black insurrection, the sailors of Captain Delano's ship, the *Bachelor's Delight*, are spurred on by a promise that they will be economically rewarded, since Don Benito has declared the cargo lost and for their taking. One of the most valuable cargoes on the *San Dominick* is, of course, human beings. Thus, while mistakenly killing two of the remaining Spanish crew members, the Americans take great care not "to kill or maim the negroes" (p. 286).

The economic interest impelling the American sailors is paralleled by the economic interest which promoted the passage of the Fugitive Slave Act of 1850. That act was the product of an affiliation of the cotton spinners of the North and the cotton producers of the South, or as Charles Sumner put it, "the lords of the loom and the lords of the lash" (*LC*, p. 86). In the name of national unity and loyalty to the Constitution, Boston "Cotton Whigs" protected their Financial interests. Indeed, parts of the Boston merchant class were outright supporters of the South and its peculiar institution. That Shaw's decisions upholding the return of fugitive slaves aided the commercial interests of Boston merchants was readily noticed by his critics. One abolitionist accused Shaw of being as morally reprehensible as a "slave pirate on the African coast" (*LC*, p. 82). Probably more accurate, Richard Henry Dana wrote in his journal after the *Shadrach* case that Shaw's conduct "shows how deeply seated, so as to affect, unconsciously I doubt not, good men like him, is this selfish hunkerism of the property interest on the slave question" (*LC*, p. 91). Similarly, Captain Delano, a good, honest man serving on a merchant ship, aids in the exploitation of human beings for commercial interests, unconsciously I doubt not, helping to make the new United States' democracy as exploitative as the feudal system it replaced. The exploitive power of the United States promises to be more difficult to unmask than even that of the cunning Babo, since it is disguised by the benevolence, goodwill, and spirit of equality that both Captain Delano and Justice Shaw embody.

While it would be too crude to identify Shaw with Captain Delano, it is important to point out that these two good, fair-minded men from Massachusetts reenslave blacks who had achieved freedom. Furthermore, we can discover in Shaw the same sort of prejudice masked by condescending kindness toward blacks that we found in Captain Delano. The case providing the best evidence is not a slave decision but one which endorsed segregation in Boston public schools. In *Roberts* v. *The City of Boston* (1849), Shaw proclaimed the famous separate-but-equal doctrine that was adopted by the federal courts until it was overruled in 1954. Arguing that the prejudice which existed "is not created by law, and probably cannot be changed by law," Shaw went on to reveal his own prejudice in deciding the law, stating that while all were equal under the law, some were more equal than others.[8]

Commenting on Shaw's stand on the Fugitive Slave Act, Judge Benjamin Thomas remarked that Shaw "was so simple, honest, upright, and straightforward, it never occurred to him there was any way around, over, under, or through the barrier of the Constitution" (*LC*, p. 102). But Shaw's hidden prejudice toward blacks suggests another reason why he saw no way around the Constitution. Just as Captain Delano's prejudiced point of view gives way to a legalistic point of view which legitimates the repression of the black revolt, so Shaw's prejudiced attitude becomes embodied in the law and therefore legitimated.

As I have argued, however, the thrust of Melville's story undercuts the authority of both the personal and the legal points of view. I could go on to claim that this undercutting invites us to read the story from a point of view not overtly contained within its pages. That alternative perspective, it could be argued, of necessity goes beyond and challenges the two presented in the story. But the problem with this argument is that not all readers construct an alternative perspective. Because Melville formulates no alternative himself, he allows readers either sharing Captain Delano's prejudices or believing in the objectivity of legal documents to accept the version of the story closest to their own perspective. Even readers holding neither view can argue that because the alternative, antislavery point of view is not explicitly supplied in the story, it cannot be attributed to it. In fact, if a reader insists on locating a point of view *within* the story, he can only conclude that Melville presented a story from a proslavery perspective. While one reader can argue that it is precisely through presenting proslavery prejudices that Melville undercuts them, another can argue that Melville's technique reinforces them. Ultimately, then, "Benito Cereno" subverts its own power of subversion. Readers who see the text undercutting the proslavery perspectives within it cannot propose their own antislavery perspective as an impartial and complete account of the text, because their perspective is based solely on an absence.

A number of liberal and radical critics have tried to fill this absence by propounding the point of view most obviously missing: Babo's.[9] Indeed, when they tell the story from Babo's viewpoint, they eliminate the ambiguity of the story by turning it into an antislavery tract. But it is precisely Babo's point of view that Melville does not offer. Instead, we are confronted by Babo's mysterious silence. That silence makes Babo the most difficult character to assess, a difficulty compounded because Babo's power is so great that he also silences Don Benito, the only character seemingly capable of understanding him. Rather than deciding whether Melville is sympathetic or not toward Babo, I would agree with those critics who consider silence as Melville's comment on him. But unlike those who conclude from Melville's silence that the story is about indeterminacy, I contend that the text's silences and ambiguities can be explained in terms of the historical contradictions which slavery posed to "enlightened" whites such as Melville and Shaw.

The most simple explanation of Babo's silence is to see it in terms of the silencing of blacks throughout antebellum America. Not only were blacks generally repressed; specifically, the Fugitive Slave Act of 1850 refused to accept testimony of accused slaves in proceedings against them. But to consider Babo's silence merely as Melville's comment on the silencing of blacks in American society would be far too simple. Psychological critics who see Babo as a frightening product of Melville's psyche, a character whose Iago-like silence indicates Melville's inability to comprehend him, are not irresponsibly imposing their own reading onto the text. Babo is indeed frightening to a white audience; he is not at all sympathetic like Harriet Beecher Stowe's Uncle Tom. And Babo is indeed a creature of Melville's imagination, an essential part of his imaginary narrative treating the complexity of the slavery issue.

In *The Political Unconscious*, Jameson has argued that most writers, when confronted with a historical issue as complex as slavery, adopt a "strategy of containment" whereby their imagined narrative gives historical contradictions an illusory resolution.[10] Babo has often been read as a vital part of Melville's strategy of containment. Sidney Kaplan, for instance, sees Babo's portrayal as a retreat from Melville's "democratic" treatment of blacks in *Moby-Dick* because Babo reinforces every antiblack fear of his 1855 audience. That audience could read the story as a warning against indulging in lax discipline and naive trust in blacks, since such indulgence encourages a rebellion producing violence worse than that maintaining slavery.[11] The story's conclusion would indicate, accordingly, that Melville supports Shaw's rule by law, no matter how flawed, as a necessary defense against the violence threatened by Babo.

But if Babo is part of Melville's imagined resolution, Melville's resolution does not actually resolve anything. While rule by law seems to have settled all questions about the events aboard the *San Dominick* and transformed its violent chaos into rational order by eliminating Babo, Babo continues to cast a shadow over the world of the book. As a true representative of the repressed, Babo cannot be contained. He marks the return of the repressed not only in Freud's psychological sense but also in the political sense. At the same time that he is the embodiment of the dark, irrational forces repressed by Melville's psyche, forces which in the culture at large only the legal system seems able to control, he is also the repressed black, who, denied voice by that very legal system, has no way to speak but through violence. He is a figure whom Melville, in examining slavery, must represent, but for whom, as the alien other, Melville can provide no voice.

Another factor complicates Melville's treatment of slavery: Melville does not share the secure confidence of most critics of slavery that the Northern alternative is unambiguously better. Southerners countered Northern attacks on slavery by arguing that their system was only a more explicit version of the exploitation occurring daily in the Northern "wage-slave" system. Melville, while opposed to all forms of exploitation, seems to have recognized a limited truth to the Southern response. In *White-Jacket*, for instance, Melville is not unequivocally sympathetic to Guinea's plight as a slave. Instead, he uses Guinea's slavery to comment on the slavery of the "free" men enlisted in the navy. It is in "Bartleby, the Scrivener," however, that we find Melville's most poignant account of how the lords of the loom and their commercial friends on Wall Street held their workers in bondage much as the lords of the lash held their slaves.

Like "Benito Cereno," "Bartleby" is haunted by a figure whose silence—although different from Babo's—has produced endless critical controversies. Once again that silence can help us discover contradictions in Shaw's legal ideology, while his legal ideology can help us understand the causes of that silence. If in "Benito Cereno" we saw how a general belief in the paramount necessity of rule by law could have led whites theoretically sympathetic to blacks to support the slave economy of the South, in "Bartleby" we will see how the specific individualist basis of Shaw's legal system could have led those full of benevolence and charity to support the wage-slave economy of the North. We will also see the dilemma of a writer who senses the injustice of that system but does not feel capable of offering alternative, affirmative visions to combat its injustice.

Notes

1. See Herman Melville, "Benito Cereno," *"Billy Budd, Sailor" and Other Stories*, ed. Harold Beaver (Harmondsworth, 1967); all further references to this work will be included in the text.

2. See Roscoe Pound, *The Formative Era of American Law* (Boston, 1938). For discussions of Melville and Lemuel Shaw, see Charles Roberts Anderson, *Melville in the South Seas*, Columbia University Studies in English and Comparative Literature, no. 138 (New York, 1966), pp. 432–33; Charles H. Foster, "Something in Emblems: A Reinterpretation of *Moby-Dick*," *New England Quarterly* 34 (Mar. 1961): 3–35; Robert L. Gale, "Bartleby—Melville's Father-in-Law," *Annali sezione germanica, Istituto Universitario Orientale di Napoli* 5 (Dec. 1962): 57–72; Keith Huntress, " 'Guinea' of *White-Jacket* and Chief Justice Shaw," *American Literature* 43 (Jan. 1972): 639–41; Carolyn L. Karcher, *Shadow over the Promised Land: Slavery, Race, and Violence in Melville's America* (Baton Rouge, La., 1980), pp. 9–11 and 40; John Stark, "Melville, Lemuel Shaw, and 'Bartleby,' " in *Bartleby, the Inscrutable: A Collection of Commentary on Herman Melville's Tale "Bartleby the Scrivener,"* ed. M. Thomas Inge (Hamden, Conn., 1979), pp. 166–73; and Robert M. Cover, *Justice Accused: Antislavery and the Judicial Process* (New Haven, Conn., 1975), all further references to this work, abbreviated *JA*, will be included in the text.

3. Louis Althusser, "A Letter on Art in Reply to André Daspre," *"Lenin and Philosophy" and Other Essays*, trans. Ben Brewster (New York, 1971), pp. 225, 222.

4. *New York Journal of Commerce*, Daniel Webster, Henry Clay, quoted in Leonard W. Levy, *The Law of the Commonwealth and Chief Justice Shaw: The Evolution of American Law, 1830–1860* (Cambridge, Mass., 1957), pp. 89, 90; all further references to this work, abbreviated *LC*, will be included in the text.

5. See Allen Guttmann, "The Enduring Innocence of Captain Amasa Delano," *Boston University Studies in English* 5 (Spring 1961): "The official and attested view of the matter, the view put forth by Don Benito and ingenuously accepted by Captain Delano, is *the very thing which Melville is subverting*. With its legalistic pretensions of objectivity, the deposition misses the truth as widely as did Delano in his completest innocence" (p. 42). See also Edgar A. Dryden, *Melville's Thematics of Form: The Great Art of Telling the Truth* (Baltimore, 1968).

6. See *The "Amistad" Case* (New York, 1968). Sidney Kaplan discusses the *Amistad* affair and also another important case, the *Creole* affair, in relationship to "Benito Cereno" (see "Herman Melville and the American National Sin: The Meaning of 'Benito Cereno,' " *Journal of Negro History* 42 [Jan. 1957]: 14–16).

7. There is not space here to enter into the long critical debate about the meaning of this emblem. For points of view with which I share sympathy, see Joyce Sparer Adler, *War in Melville's Imagination* (New York, 1981), p. 108, and Edward S. Grejda, *The Common Continent of Men: Racial Equality in the Writings of Herman Melville* (Port Washington, N.Y., 1974), p. 144.

8. Shaw, quoted in *Jim Crow in Boston: The Origin of the Separate but Equal Doctrine*, ed. Levy and Douglas L. Jones (New York, 1974), p. 230. Edwin Haviland Miller notes a similarity between Captain Delano and Shaw in passing (see *Melville* [New York, 1975], p. 299).

9. Karcher argues throughout *Shadow over the Promised Land* that Melville's strategy in the 1850s was to adopt a proslavery point of view in order to undercut it. The most radical Melville is the working-class Melville proposed by H. Bruce Franklin (see "Herman Melville: Artist of the Worker's World," in *Weapons of Criticism: Marxism in America and the Literary Tradition*, ed. Norman Rudich [Palo Alto, Calif., 1976], pp. 287–310).

10. See Fredric Jameson, *The Political Unconscious: Narrative as a Socially Symbolic Act* (Ithaca, N.Y., 1981).

11. See Kaplan, "Herman Melville and the American National Sin."

Reenvisioning America: Melville's "Benito Cereno"

Sandra A. Zagarell

"How unlike we are made!" thinks Amasa Delano, the American captain of Herman Melville's "Benito Cereno," about the weak and sickly Spanish captain Benito Cereno.[1] Through national and racial appellations, Delano constantly marks differences between himself and others. He perceives the black slaves aboard the Spanish ship the *San Dominick* as animals; he so frequently labels Cereno "the Spaniard" that the epithet comes to imply indelible and tainted national characteristics; he thinks himself possessed of superior energy and decisiveness that emanate from his privileged nationality. Delano's smugness is characteristic of the prevailing American political and cultural climate of the 1850s, for Melville was writing at a time when many Americans insisted on their country's superiority and saw its destiny as historically unique. In 1854–55, when he composed "Benito Cereno,"[2] such feelings were taking political expression in the doctrine of Manifest Destiny and the Young America movement, which had just had their heyday, in the American Party and Know-Nothingism, which were at their peak, and in the glorification of the revolutionary fathers, who were viewed as having freed America from a decadent Europe.[3]

In "Benito Cereno," Melville challenges his countrymen's Delano-like sense of superiority by showing how very like other nations America was. In fact, he turns inside out some of nineteenth-century America's most cherished visions of itself by portraying the country not as an historical clean slate but as the unwitting perpetuator of forms of commercialism, colonialism, and slavery that began centuries earlier in the Old World from which Delano holds himself disdainfully aloof. In a painstaking anatomy of the mind of the American captain, he lays bare the elaborate ideology by means of which Americans denied the historical implications of such practices, and he presents slavery and the rationalizations that justified it not simply as discrete phenomena but as powerful synecdoches for economic activities and cultural disjunctions that threatened the country's stability at every level. In short, "Benito Cereno" implicitly portrays the United States as a nation—to borrow

Reprinted from *ESQ: A Journal of the American Renaissance* 30 (1984): 245–59. Reprinted by permission of the journal.

from a description of the *San Dominick*—whose "every inch of ground" was "mined into honey-combs" (p. 138). Like *Pierre*, it attacks American values and institutions; like *Israel Potter* it revises Americans' sense of their own history; and it does so, this essay argues, by destabilizing a range of cultural conventions from Americans' self-proclaimed benevolence to their unconscious authoritarianism.

Critics have long been interested in the historicity of "Benito Cereno," many of them focusing on issues connected with slavery in the Old World and the New.[4] Recent studies have expanded the scope of that interest, seeing the novella as comprising a broad reenvisioning of antebellum America. Michael Paul Rogin's *Subversive Genealogy: The Politics and Art of Herman Melville*, while interpreting the novella in terms of slavery, sees it as a sort of meditation on contemporary political theory, a realization that neither prevalent model of race relations, not the natural rights argument of Abolitionists nor the paternalism favored by slaveholders and their apologists, provided a safe and peaceful way out of the violent conflict that, as Melville saw, slavery would soon produce. While Rogin demonstrates Melville's concern with both the character of American society and with the ways Americans conceptualized that character, Allan Moore Emery in " 'Benito Cereno' and Manifest Destiny" establishes a hitherto unrecognized historical frame of reference, American expansionism, and demonstrates how "Benito Cereno" exposes with almost allegorical precision both the expansionist, anti-Catholic, Anglo-Saxonist mentality of America in the 1850s and the ironic fact that this expansionism mirrored the earlier colonialism of the very country—Spain—whose New World presence was being contested.[5] The fruitfulness of each of these very different readings attests to how stubbornly "Benito Cereno" resists being keyed to any single historical referent.[6] The present study—which is indebted to the many critics who have demonstrated the extent and historicity of Melville's indictment of slavery—profits especially from Emery's renewed attention to historical context and Rogin's focus on Melville as a kind of social theorist, and it attempts to extend these arguments by showing that the novella contains a keen analysis of the *cultural* dimensions of the ways social systems are interpreted.

In particular, this paper maintains that in "Benito Cereno" Melville subjects a panoply of American cultural codes and assumptions to intense critical pressure in order to expose gaps in his countrymen's knowledge and characteristic modes of thought. If his vision is radical, his approach is wide-ranging. The portrayal of Amasa Delano, to be considered in the first section, is, as most readers assume, that of a representative northerner, but it is at once denser and more dynamic than has been realized. Elaborating a complex ideology, it also dramatizes the epistemological fancy footwork Delano must perform in order *not* to understand what is amiss on the *San Dominick*, and it ominously doubles Delano's ideology with that of the Spanish captain, Benito Cereno. In elucidating the means by which Melville structures his portrait of Delano, this section explores one level on which "Benito Cereno" discloses what Americans did not know, why they did not know it, and the potential consequences of that ignorance.

The second section examines a more theoretical aspect of Melville's critique in "Benito Cereno," its presentation of the extensive cultural discontinuities that prevail under an unstable social order. In presenting Delano's ideology with a situation it cannot explain—the slaves' revolt and subsequent pretense of enslavement—Melville reveals that the conventions whose fixity men like Delano take for granted are actually exceedingly fluid. In social orders built on inequity, disempowered groups like the black slaves convert such conventions into unspoken languages of dissent and, when possible, insurrection. This section focuses on Melville's explication of the multivalent indeterminacy of these conventions. The last section addresses Melville's indirect but powerful effort to destabilize the existing social order by undermining the sort of authority on which it rests. This section attempts, first, to establish how Melville links accession to social-cultural authority with incapacity for independent, clear-sighted interpretation.[7] For different reasons, none of the characters, black or white, can genuinely resist the hierarchical social system that circumscribes him, and therefore none can achieve the kind of disinterested analysis that "Benito Cereno" itself accomplishes. Finally, a comparison of "Benito Cereno" with its source, the eleventh chapter of the historical Amasa Delano's *Narrative of Voyages and Travels in the Northern and Southern Hemispheres*, illustrates how Melville's composition of the novella itself amounted to a symbolic dismantling of the kind of authority which perpetuates hierarchical social systems. Melville revises the *Narrative* to put Delano, and America, in a context that damns the American system; he also reverses the real Delano's portrait of himself as moral innocent, recasting him as a minor originator of the self-celebrating hypocrisy that allowed Americans to think themselves historically unique.

I

Through the thought processes of Amasa Delano, Melville critiques northern antebellum thought by letting it speak for itself. Delano's sentimental racism, which prevents him from perceiving the blacks' hatred of slavery, and his expansionist mentality and chauvinism[8] are only two of his ideology's many components: the code of gentility, debased romanticism, and sensational melodrama are developed with equal care. In fact, Delano's ideology is meticulously keyed to Melville's America, each aspect being drawn from specific motifs and linguistic registers prominent in contemporary culture.

Charity and courtesy, predominant among Delano's values, were central to Victorian America's emphasis on gentility. From first to last, and in sharp contrast to Melville's other captains, Delano judges acts and gestures in accordance with how they measure on a scale of politeness. This code is conspicuously irrelevant to the situation he actually faces, and his persistent faith in it obscures the real problem by preventing him from seeing clues as clues. Critical though Delano is of Cereno's apparent indifference to all the routines of ship life and to the arrival of an American rescuer, he labels such behavior "unfriendly," quickly ascribes Cereno's attitude "in charity" to ill health, and soon thereafter castigates himself for not exercising "charity enough" in making allowances for the Spanish captain (p. 63). After being subjected to a highly suspicious cross-examination about security measures on his own ship, he leaves the suddenly taciturn Cereno alone because he is "unwilling to appear uncivil even to incivility itself" (p. 80). Because he values gentility, he is fooled by the crude parody enacted by the steward Francesco, whose excessive shuffling and bowing cause Babo to look "askance" (p. 105), and declares himself pleased with the man's "nods, and bows, and smiles; a king indeed—the king of kind hearts and polite fellows" (p. 106). Even at the end of a day filled with doubts about Cereno's motives, Delano is gratified to discover the Spanish captain recovering from an anguished silence, which the American thinks merely a "recent discourtesy," and to hear his own name "courteously sounded" as Cereno advances toward him; in consequence, he "self-reproachfully" dismisses his suspicions on the grounds that Cereno had not "meant to offend" (p. 116).

Like the code of gentility, Delano's chauvinism undercuts his ability to discover what is amiss on the *San Dominick* and to analyze his suspicions about Cereno. Embroidering upon the epithet "Spaniard" to explain the captain on the basis of national characteristics, he thinks Cereno afflicted with "Spanish spite" when he appears to have mistreated Babo (p. 105). When Delano's suspicions about a plot against him multiply, he comforts himself with the chauvinistic thought that "as a nation . . . these Spaniards are all an odd set; the very word Spaniard has a curious, conspirator, Guy-Fawkish twang to it" (p. 94). Likewise, his racism, identified by most critics as a northern variety,[9] usually surfaces when he is confronted by something unsettling. It too functions as an epistemological smoke screen, dispelling his suspicions by reaffirming his comfortable ideology about the blacks' docile inferiority. He assuages his anxieties by envisioning all blacks as "odd-looking" and sees the oakum pickers, who are disguised figures of authority, as "bed-ridden old knitting women" (p. 82); he perceives a black mother as a "dam" nursing her "wide-awake faun" (p. 87). When Babo shaves Cereno, Delano has what he terms an "antic conceit" (p. 101) that the black is an executioner, then quickly takes refuge in the platitudes of racism. Attributing the black's seditious use of the Spanish flag as a barber's cloth to his love of color, Delano lays his own fears to rest once more (p. 102).

Delano also sometimes indulges in a debased romanticism, the closest he comes to a conscious philosophy. This romanticism—reminiscent of Melville's double parody of Wordsworth's "Resolution and Independence" and of American Transcendentalism in "Cock-A-Doodle-Doo!"[10]—is linked to Delano's racism, enabling him also to view blacks as noble savages. Delano revises the romantic view of the child as the father of the man: he thinks the (white) man enjoys heavenly protection because he was once a child. When his fears of being murdered mount, he calms himself with the thought that because he was formerly a boy, "little Jack of the Beach," "some one above" will shield him from harm (p. 92). Such complacency culminates in his late declaration to Cereno about the uselessness of drawing conclusions from their experiences, because "the past is passed . . . yon bright sun has forgotten it all, and the blue sea, and the blue sky; these have turned over new leaves."[11] Whereas Emerson invokes nature partly as a medium through which the individual is transported beyond personal and social mediocrity, Delano does so to avoid the responsibility of understanding human experience. Emerson's "liv[ing] in nature in the present, above time" degenerates into an escape from time, history, and inquiry.[12]

Despite its multiple components, Delano's ideology finally fails him, forcing him, however reluctantly, to modify his complacent interpretation of the *San Dominick* as a ship in distress with the darker view of it as a pirate ship with Cereno masquerading as a legitimate captain.[13] The theme of piracy, which dominated antebellum sea fiction in such an influential novel as Cooper's *The Red Rover*, had become popularized and sentimentalized by the 1840s.[14] It is a sensationalist tale that Delano produces; he "had heard of [tales of pirates]—and now, as stories, they recurred" (p. 81). He imagines a lurid scenario in which, "[o]n heart-broken pretense of entreating a cup of cold water, fiends in human form had got into lonely dwellings, nor retired until a dark deed has been done," and recalls tales of Malay pirates who lure unsuspecting seamen aboard ships that look empty, while beneath the decks "prowled a hundred spears with yellow arms ready to upthrust them through the mats" (p. 81). These fantasies relieve him of the need to think inductively, for personally threatening though they are, they do not admit of any significant threat to the social order. Moreover, Delano's sensationalist explanation of the *San Dominick* as a pirate ship complements his sentimental racism: not only are both informed by cliché, but the two are also interchangeable. When Delano finally discovers the true nature of the blacks' position, he shifts effortlessly from sentimentalizing them to brutalizing them as monsters, "flourishing hatchets and knives, in ferocious piratical revolt" (p. 119).

Because they filter out information which could challenge his ideology, Delano's modes of perception keep his faith in the social order intact. The content of his ideology, moreover, actively supports that order. All its parts have a common denominator, a belief in that unequal distribution of power which "Benito Cereno" shows as perilously unstable. Thus genteel regard for proper conduct, the racist justification of the subordination of blacks to whites, chauvinistic assumptions about the inferiority of other nations, the pseudo-romantic insistence on the natural order of present arrangements, and even the melodramatic scenario in which a sickly white captain controls a crew composed of a few renegade whites and an enormous supporting cast of blacks, all depend on a stable social hierarchy. Delano quite openly advocates such hierarchy. He assumes that "good order" should prevail in "armies, navies, cities, families, in nature herself" (p. 61) and defines that order in terms of the absolute authority of those at the top. As in so many of Melville's works, "the top" is symbolized by the ship's captain, in whom, as Delano thinks approvingly, is "lodged a dictatorship beyond which, while at sea, there is no earthly appeal" (p. 63).

The American's complacent piety and smug compassion, then, overlie a vigorous dedication to the personal exercise of authority: he tells Cereno by way of example how, in order to maintain discipline, he relentlessly kept his crew busy "thrumming mats for my cabin" during a three-day storm when survival seemed impossible (p. 71). As Rogin points out, the rhetoric of paternal relations characterized nineteenth-century American public discourse about the organizations of institutions like the navy, the asylum, and the educational system[15]; along these lines, Delano thinks of his ship, with its "quiet orderliness," as a "comfortable family of a crew" (p. 64). The authoritarianism underlying this family model becomes apparent when he observes the contrasting "noisy confusion" of the *San Dominick*. Noting the troublesome character of "living freight," he attributes the blacks' unruliness to the absence of "the unfriendly arm of the mate, . . . [of] stern superior officers" (pp. 64–65). His plan to reestablish order by withdrawing Cereno's command and placing his own surrogate, his second mate, in charge until Cereno is well enough to be "restored to authority" (p. 83) indicates just how important the hierarchy of command is to him: to depose another captain, however gently and temporarily, is to assume that the proper wielding of authority takes precedence over considerations of national sovereignty or private ownership of a vessel. Uppermost for Delano is a strong-minded devotion to preserving a highly vertical institutional organization.

If "Benito Cereno" lays American ideological limitations bare in Amasa Delano, it also undermines notions of American uniqueness by depicting Delano as parallel to the foreigner Cereno in many regards. Each man is a cultural type—the hearty Yankee Delano is balanced by the effete Spaniard.[16] "[B]rother captain[s]" (p. 61), both are merchants, engaging in free trade in economies dependent on slavery.[17] Each is also an established representative of the social order: Cereno belongs to "one of the most enterprising and extensive mercantile families" in South America (p. 77), while the historical Delano is from a prominent New England family whose descendants would eventually include Franklin Delano Roosevelt. Most important, placed in a situation which could throw their beliefs into disarray, they exhibit equal fervor in preserving their ideologies and their commitments to social order.

Cereno's "foreign" ideology has clear parallels in Delano's American beliefs; their values are strikingly similar. When the Spaniard finally speaks in his own voice, in the deposition and in the third section of the novella, he echoes Delano's racism and morality. The American articulates racial differences as a matter of "species" (p. 90); Cereno divides the *San Dominick*'s population into "men" and "negroes" (p. 124). Each man embraces a rigid, absolutist morality, Delano operating according to "certain general notions which, while disconnecting pain and abashment from virtue, invariably link them with vice" (p. 86) and Cereno making a similarly fixed distinction between the blacks, with their "malign machinations and deceptions" and his own position as "an innocent . . . the most pitiable of all men" (p. 139). Even more fundamentally, by juxtaposing Cereno's deposition, the second section of "Benito Cereno," with Delano's interpretations of events in the first, Melville emphasizes that for each captain, the "story" of "Benito Cereno" is an interpretation shaped and structured by ideology.

Cereno's narrative is more obviously ideological than is Delano's interpretation. Cereno's voice is almost never personal: primarily expressed through his deposition, it is a voice sanctioned by, and sanctioning, the Spanish legal system. His narrative, a declaration "against the negroes of the ship San Dominick" (p. 124), serves the express purpose of perpetuating slavery. Despite its seeming neutrality of tone and its apparent factuality, it is a sharply limited account of what Cereno has witnessed, and its limits are set by unquestioned assumptions. The deposition accepts as synonymous the legality and the moral rightness of the whites' ownership of and trade in blacks. Thus it presents the statistics of the case—names, ages, status of whites and blacks—in scrupulous detail, as though the facts speak for themselves, and speak for the innocence of the white owner, Aranda, and his entourage of clerks and cousins, and against the large group of slaves whose labor supports them. Although the narrative fails to connect its stated facts about the slaves with their revolt, it shows that Aranda's slaves epitomize the atrocities their race has suffered since the commencement of black slavery, for this group includes "raw" blacks and mulattos, old men, young men, a black chieftan, mothers and children, all uprooted, all massed together. Nor does Cereno ever question how this miscellany developed the resources to forge itself into a disciplined, purposeful organization. Even the deposition's ennumerative syntax, which Melville preserved from the original, discourages the recognition of causal connections among the events it details and thus serves to preserve the social order, not to inquire why it has failed.

The human results of this repression are manifested in Cereno's final mystification of the figure of Babo. Placing Babo in a metaphysical category, "the negro," which conflates racial and moral connotations, Cereno haunts himself with the slave. When he faints under the court's pressure to confront the black, his swoon is a double avoidance: fainting in fear, he is also fainting to escape having to explain "the negro" institutionally or historically, as "Benito Cereno" itself does. Because he chooses to mystify rather than clarify, Cereno exemplifies the price of this self-elected incapacity. Retreating further, first into silence, then into death, he becomes the victim of his ideology by remaining its spokesman.

II

In contrast to the whites, the blacks have no ideology; they are simply opposed to the social order. "Benito Cereno" incorporates their stance into the stunning depiction of the instability of any culture emanating from a fluctuating social order. The novella demonstrates that the hierarchy and the characteristics of both race and gender, thought to be natural by antebellum Americans, are merely conventions; it also implies that all culture is a human creation, subject to change and frequently unstable.[18] The novella pivots upon a major reversal in racial relations, the blacks' inversion of the usual master-slave conditions. Presenting blacks as enslavers, whites as slaves, it goes beyond challenging the slave system's literal hegemony, as an actual slave revolt like the Nat Turner rebellion did, to show racial characteristics as cultural constructs. Not only does the intelligence of the blacks turn prevalent white supremacy on its head, as Karcher and others have noted, but the doublings between Cereno and Babo demonstrate that racial dominance is a matter of circumstance. Approximately the same age, one the former captain of the ship, the other former captain of the slaves turned leader of the ship, Babo and Cereno encircle each other in a perpetual embrace in which ruler plays ruled, ruled plays ruler, and from which racial authority emerges as a question of context only.

By playing on the intense physical contact between Babo and Cereno, Melville also dramatizes gender as a cultural convention. Readers have sometimes detected a homoerotic coloring to Delano's perceptions of the two men,[19] but grounded as it is in a reversal of power, the relationship actually reveals the literal instability of gender. In cultures where the status of women is low, subordinated people are often feminized in order to perpetuate and to justify their inferiority. "Benito Cereno" frequently refers to nineteenth-century America's version of this practice, which blended feminization and domestication, as in the observation, made from Delano's perspective, that "most negroes" are peculiarly fitted for "vocations about one's person" because they are "natural valets and hair-dressers" (pp. 100–101). When the blacks reverse power relations, forcing the whites into captivity, they impose on the white leader, Cereno, feminine attributes like those conventionally imposed on them. They emasculate the former master, forcing him to wear an empty scabbard, "artificially stiffened" (p. 140), and feminize him by casting him in a powerless role which often renders him speechless, sickened, and swooning—a parody of the fragile, genteel lady. Cereno evinces the consequences of his emasculation by responding as though he has been raped.

Indeed, his inability to face Babo after the normal order has been restored resembles many rape victims' inability to name or confront their assailants.

Melville goes beyond portraying race and gender as cultural constructs, moreover, to suggest that *all* meaning in his readers' world derives from convention, and that meaning itself is therefore unfixed. In the blacks' revolt, Melville may represent his increasing sense of the fluidity of meaning which, as Nina Baym has pointed out, was a ground for profound despair.[20] He may also have seen this fluidity to result from the essential instability of a social order based on a highly unequal distribution of power. "Benito Cereno" suggests that even under normal circumstances, at least in a slave society, conventional ideologies like Delano's remain coherent only at the price of vast oversimplification. In reality, mutability prevails. Even artifacts are cultural markers lacking inherent properties. This contingency is half-apparent to Delano, who muses that the *San Dominick*'s rusty main-chains are "more fit for the ship's present business," transporting slaves, than for its original purposes as a war vessel (p. 89). Once the slaves' revolt has demonstrated the instability of the social order, many other artifacts also acquire new functions. Tar is no longer just a preservative but a medium by which the blacks degrade and punish recalcitrant white sailors (pp. 85, 136). Hatchets—presumably to have been used by slaves in clearing land for cultivation—become weapons against the whites; the whites' sealing-spears are also transformed into weapons.

Even more dramatically, unexceptional parts of the cultural fabric emerge as unspoken languages which encode mutually exclusive meanings, some of them seditious. Babo's properly slave-like ministrations to Cereno appear solicitous to Delano but communicate veiled threats to Cereno; Cereno's moments of faintness betoken ill health to Delano, passive resistance to Babo.[21] Clothing is a particularly mutable form of visual language. Babo's near-nakedness projects the image of a submissive, powerless servant, but it also potently signifies his power and intelligence in appropriating the connotations of the rags which inscribe his former subjugation. Cereno's elaborate apparel is a traditional sign of status and the intricacy of protocol in Spain's colonial government—Delano thinks his "toilette . . . not beyond the style of the day among South Americans of his class" (pp. 68–69)—as well as a token of the wealth derived from an economy dependent on slavery. In his present circumstances, however, his adornment also bespeaks the blacks' ability to convert these traditional signs into the means of deceiving one white while degrading another.

Meaning within a culture ultimately rests on a consensus. When basic opposition to the social order prevails, as it is bound to in a slave society, the lack of such consensus produces radically divergent assumptions about meaning and communication. Those who are privileged, like Delano, will simply assume—as Delano does—that their culture is stable and determinate; disempowered groups such as black slaves will be alert to and intent on exploiting every ambiguity. "Benito Cereno" not only reveals cultural markers such as gestures and clothes to be heavily laden codes of communication, but it shows the blacks' genius in disrupting the meaning of such markers. They so increase the normal ambiguity of gestures, for example, that they seem on the verge of reversing commonly accepted meanings altogether. Thus Francesco's smiles and bows appeal to Delano, mock Cereno, and signal pleasure in their shared masquerade to Babo; Atufal appears strategically as a shackled slave to calm Delano, alarm Cereno, and support Babo. And Babo's every smile threatens Cereno while reassuring Delano on one level and the other blacks on quite another. After he cuts Cereno while shaving him, Babo's body language becomes strikingly multivalent. As he directs the Spaniard to answer questions about the *San Dominick*'s difficulties, "his face was turned half round, so as to be alike visible to the Spaniard and the American, and seemed, by its expression, to hint, that he was desirous, by getting his master to go on with the conversation, considerately to withdraw his attention from the recent annoying accident" (p. 103). Babo's single gesture conveys consideration to Delano, menace and malice to Cereno; on another level, it communicates to the reader Babo's extraordinary skill at appropriating and subverting all the nuances of the traditional role of the black body servant. More generally, his practices also cast new light on the double signification frequently employed by American slaves, "puttin' on ole Massa." Being in a position of unusual power, Babo can pitch his gestures to three different readings at once. If this slave's silent communication comprises a richer language than Delano's spoken platitudes, it also implies that a slaveholding society is a minefield of reversed meanings and unuttered languages.

III

The assumption in "Benito Cereno" that culture and ideology are imperiled human creations extends with equally destabilizing results to Americans' attitudes toward authority. Not only laying bare the authoritarianism of a Delano, the novella also implies that Americans accede to authority on all levels, from the literal authority of public officials and public records to the more abstract, even more powerfully culture-shaping authority which inheres in standard versions of the country's origins and values. Such accession bears heavily on the country's present and future, for unquestioning acceptance of authority discourages disinterested interpretation. Interpretation is part of the process of producing a literal or metaphoric text, and these texts— Cereno's deposition, the blacks' masquerade, the real Delano's *Narrative*, Melville's novella—are instrumental in perpetuating or modifying social structures. This conception of authority anticipates twentieth-century associations between authority and authorship; it is also distinctly political. The white captains accept all institutionalized authority because of their privileged status; though the blacks contest such authority, taking advantage of the instability of existing cultural codes, the literal power of the social order denies them the possibility of true creative achievement.

The backbone of the ideologies which limit the white captains' interpretations is the equation of authority with meaning. For both men, the official truth is the complete truth. When Delano boards the *San Dominick*, he encounters a "shadowy tableau" that seems "unreal" (p. 59) and in need of interpretation, but he sees only the need to get the facts, "details" (p. 65). Taking for granted that "the best account would, doubtless, be given by the captain" (p. 65)—the proper authority—he seeks out Cereno. When Cereno finally gives all the details that Delano seeks, he does so in as authoritative a mode as the American could possibly desire, speaking under oath and before the Spanish king's councilor. "Benito Cereno," of course, repudiates such modes of interpretation: after Cereno's testimony is given, the narrator even asserts that "If the Deposition have served as the key to fit into the lock of the complications which precede it, then . . . the *San Dominick*'s hull lies open today" (p. 138). By allying themselves with the authority they serve, embody, and perpetuate, Delano and Cereno have ceded to that authority control of their own capacity to interpret. Rather than unlock the complications of the actual events on the *San Dominick*, rather than face the multivalent meanings of the symbols of lock and key to which the narrator also alludes here, they will turn out documents like Cereno's deposition—and Delano's *Narrative*—which dutifully enshrine the status quo.

So heavy is the weight of social authority that conscious interpreters must also always take it into account. They, however, can question the authority which upholds the existing order, turning it against itself through illicit acts of creative rewriting. In one sense, as commentators have suggested, both Melville and Babo perform these acts,[22] Melville rewriting Chapter Eleven of Delano's *Narrative*, Babo attempting to refashion a sociocultural script which embodies the social order. Indeed, Babo's consummate artistry appears to grant him stunning success. Readers have often remarked on how the novella's theatricality reproduces the slave system in order to destroy it. With its tableaux, its stark images, the ominous symmetry of the four oakum pickers and the six hatchet-sharpeners, "Benito Cereno" looks forward uncannily to the subversive metamorphoses of Black Arts agitation-propaganda dramas such as Amiri Baraka's "Slave Ship." Babo is brilliant as the impressario of the *San Dominick*'s drama because he can read through the white authorities and therefore thwart their objective of sustaining slavery. Yet he can achieve no authority on his own terms. As a social actor, he essentially perpetuates the slave system; he destroys the authority of the whites only to claim the same authority for himself, unleashing terror and murder likened to those of the Inquisition, while his later plan to pirate

Delano's ship would entangle him in an economic web which ties free enterprise to slavery. His script, too, duplicates rather than goes beyond the old order—it is, for all its grandeur, only a masquerade. Melville makes clear that Babo can produce no genuinely new rewritings of the old script because he is completely circumscribed by the slave system. Slavery prevails so thoroughly in South America that the blacks are afraid to venture on shore for desperately needed water; moreover, though they recognize that their only chance for freedom lies in getting to a "negro country" (p. 126), their choice, Senegal is—in a detail Melville added to his source—a country where blacks enslave blacks.

All of the novella's characters are, then, claustrally restricted by preexisting authority. Discourse within "Benito Cereno," with its echoes and tautologies, reflects this entrapment,[23] as do the images of chains and knots, the recurring motifs of becalmed ships and becalmed minds, the many types of doubling. The central symbol of the stern-piece explicates the levels of this confinement. The "shield-like" "oval," "intricately carved with the arms of Castile and Leon," is decorated with mythological figures, the central pair consisting of a masked figure whose foot grinds the "prostrate neck of a writhing figure, likewise masked" (p. 58). The stern-piece distills the essence of the social structure. All the characters literally or figuratively play the roles of both victors and victims. No other roles are structurally possible. The antiquity of the stern-piece, moreover, bespeaks the longevity of the social relations it depicts, for though the might of Castile and Leon had diminished by 1799, when "Benito Cereno" takes place, its characters continue to enact the traditional historic parts. That Delano finally and most conspicuously assumes the posture of victor, clutching the unconscious Cereno and grinding the "prostrate" Babo with his foot (p. 118), suggests that Americans are the latest to inherit this social structure. Finally, the medallion's status as a heraldic device reflects on the functions of official art: as a synecdoche of the social order which predates the characters, it prescribes the roles they must play. The social system becomes, in effect, a text which writes the characters. All of them are inside it, imprisoned within its oval. No one, not even Babo, can rewrite it.

In contrast, Melville himself, as an author, inherits a tangible, literal document, not a social script. Delano's *Narrative* purports to be a representation of certain historical events, but it is, as Melville recognizes, an interpretation, open to reinterpretation. While he must reckon with its authority, he can transform such reckoning into recreation. Taking off from *Moby-Dick*'s playful spoofing of its authorities, he enters into a subversive dialogue with Delano's *Narrative* which furthers the project he had undertaken in *Israel Potter*: he turns an historical document reflective of America's sense of identity on its head. In both pieces he also specifically undermines the authority of American forefathers, though "Benito Cereno" attacks a minor progenitor rather than such luminaries as Benjamin Franklin and John Paul Jones; Delano's ancestor, Phillipe de la Noye, came to America in 1621, and both Delano and his father fought in the Revolutionary War.[24] Highlighting the gaps in Delano's *Narrative* and playing on its unacknowledged inconsistencies, Melville indicts Delano as a minor author of the Americanism which was straightjacketing his contemporaries.

The major hiatus in the original Delano's *Narrative* is its lack of historical consciousness; its author was given instead to reflecting on the transcultural, transhistorical traits common to all humanity.[25] This same lack was implicit in the assumption of many of the country's founders that America's connection with Europe had been contractual, not organically historical. It was also shared by Melville's contemporaries, whose sense of history was consonant with their belief that they were superior to the rest of the Western world; as George B. Forgie and others have suggested, they were inclined to foreshorten American's past by imagining the founding fathers as their first ancestors.[26] For many, their greatest tie to Europe consisted in freeing themselves from it. Melville rebukes the ahistoricism of his source and of his contemporaries by weaving into his text a rich tapestry of historical allusion and analogy which challenges the idea of America's uniqueness. It specifies unsettling similarities between the Old and New Worlds and locates America's history within a general expansionist trend among Western nations that began with the first great European marriage between commerce and the sea in Venice.

Melville's framework far exceeds the Spanish-American connection critics have reconstructed.[27] Embellishing Delano's *Narrative* by blending expansive analogies with compressed symbols, Melville fuses mercantilism, free enterprise, and the slave trade. The novella's comparisons range throughout modern Western history, often pivoting, as if in warning, on the rebelliousness of subordinated populations.[28] At the same time, the Spanish slave ship—rechristened the *San Dominick* to allude to the slaves' revolts in Santo Domingo—becomes a condensation of this revisionary history. A "Spanish merchantman," the *San Dominick* is a "very large, and, in its time, a very fine vessel, such as in those days were at intervals encountered along that main; sometimes superseded Acapulco treasure-ships, or retired frigates of the Spanish king's navy, which, like superannuated Italian palaces, still, under a decline of masters, preserved signs of former state" (p. 57). The reference to Acapulco treasure calls attention to the raiding parties transported by the Spanish ships that followed on Columbus' discovery of the New World; the paralleling of the Conquistadores' ships with the vessels of a naval fleet famous for its bellicosity connects Spain's aggressive posture in the Old and New Worlds. Generalizing the example of Spain, the capping comparison to superannuated Italian palaces, later expanded through a reference to the ship's "Venetian-looking balustrade," specifically links the Spanish empire with the Italian city-state where early modern mercantilism flourished, while the *San Dominick*'s concealed slave revolt warns of a continuing cycle of violent enmity.

By reconstructing Delano's *Narrative* to accommodate this historical vision, Melville implicitly indicts Delano as an ironically fit ancestor for a country which preferred to regard slavery within its borders as an ahistorical institution peculiar to one of its regions. He also mines inconsistencies in Delano's text to subject Delano to a witty, historically resonant character assassination.[29] The historical Delano had been stung by the "misery and ingratitude" he had suffered at the hands of the "very persons to whom [he] had rendered the greatest services"—particularly the real Cereno, who, by besmirching his character, had treacherously tried to avoid recompensing him for saving the Spanish ship.[30] Chapter Eleven of Delano's *Narrative* is in a sense its author's character reference for himself: he carefully presents himself as an honorable and blameless man. At pains to establish his rectitude, he corroborates his version of events by including numerous testimonies to his disinterested goodness, among them his own letters to the Spanish king's emissaries insisting that "the services rendered off the island of St. Maria were from pure motives of humanity" (p. 528, repeated in substance, p. 529) and two versions of the Chilean Tribunal's official recommendation that the king be informed of his "generous and benevolent conduct" in succoring Cereno (pp. 526, 527). In his own deposition, which he also includes, Delano reports himself to have woven humanitarian appeals into the monetary pitch he made to his crew when encouraging them to retake the Spanish ship: he told them, he says, that they could return half the value of the ship to Cereno "as a present" and reminded them of the suffering of the Spaniards still on board (pp. 509–510).

Melville reformulates the terms of this presentation so as to expose Delano's self-interest. Eliminating all documents praising Delano except Cereno's ideologically biased deposition, Melville also discredits Delano's claims to disinterest and subtly reduces his motives to the sheer, unacknowledged drive for profit. In "Benito Cereno," the sailors are urged to recapture the *San Dominick* by being told only that they stand to gain a good part of the "ship and her cargo, including some gold and silver . . . worth more than a thousand doubloons" (p. 120). Taking off on the real Delano's protestations that he is an innocent, Melville's Delano holds himself above slavery—"Ah, this slavery breeds ugly passions in man," he thinks (p. 105)—while his drive for profit actually implicates him in the slave trade. The "cargo" his crew is to liberate includes one hundred and sixty slaves—Melville doubled his source's figures—and the American stands to gain from their sale.[31]

Far beyond this reversal of Delano's character, Melville reinterprets the *Narrative* to show that Delano's pursuit of profit implicates him in illegitimate as well as legitimate economic activities. Without acknowledging it, the historical Delano revealed a significant blurring of such boundaries. He reported that he had trouble with his crew because many were escaped convicts. The real Cereno exploited Delano's use—however unwilling—of sailors who were outlaws: Cereno got testimony from some of them "to injure [Delano's] character," including, an offended Delano reports, their affirmation that "I was a pirate" (p. 511). Melville plays with this accusation of piracy most adroitly. Aside from being one of the ideological categories Delano uses to stereotype others, it becomes emblematic of his economic activities. Although Melville ironically makes his Delano fear that Cereno may be a pirate, the novella strongly hints that it is Delano himself who is a pirate, or very like one—just as the real Cereno claimed. Changing Delano's ship from the Yankee-sounding *Perseverance* to the *Bachelor's Delight*, the name of the ship of buccaneer William Ambrose Cowley,[32] is only the most obvious aspect of Melville's indictment. In order to flesh out the accusation, he plays on the real Delano's failure fully to separate legitimate free enterprise from illegal activities. Persuaded by his men not to go after the *San Dominick* himself, Melville's Delano has the attack headed by a surrogate, his chief mate. This man, we are told, "had been a privateer's-man" (p. 120). Melville may be referring obliquely to the fact that Delano himself served on the privateer *Mars* during the Revolutionary War. In any case, since privateering is legalized piracy in time of war, Melville suggests guilt by association to establish a definite tie between the American captain and the practice of piracy. He also expands this association between the honest trader and his ex-privateer mate to show that the boundaries separating national histories are as indistinct as the boundaries supposedly separating types of illegal activity. Leading Delano's men in their attack on the *San Dominick*, Melville's mate cries, "Follow your leader." Literally, the cry is in response to seeing the ship's hull, with this epithet chalked beneath Aranda's bleached skeleton. Contextually, its echoes connect the New World conclusively with the Old. "Leader" refers to Aranda, whose death will be avenged, but also to Columbus, whose figure his skeleton replaces, to Babo, who led the slaves' revolt and caused the words to be chalked, to the mate himself, who leads the American crew, and to the captain he represents. In the traditions Melville's Delano carries forward, exploration is inseparable from colonization, free enterprise from slavery, profit from plunder.

Because Melville's reversals of Delano's *Narrative* are apparent only through close study of a fairly obscure source, it may seem that he deliberately concealed his reenvisionment rather than offering it as an instance of creative reinterpretation. Yet "Benito Cereno" is more deliberately accessible than many of Melville's other tales, for even without knowing Delano's text, those who read Melville as closely as Melville read Delano could profit from his challenge. Indeed, Melville explicitly proffers his reinterpretation to his contemporaries in the final passage of "Benito Cereno": Babo's severed head looks out over a plaza toward the church "in whose vaults slept *then, as now,* the recovered bones of Aranda" and toward the monastery where Benito Cereno, in dying, "did indeed follow his leader" (p. 140, emphasis added). By echoing the earlier appearances of this resonant phrase, this last sentence once more connects Old and New Worlds, blacks and whites; the reference to the present, the only reference in the entire novella, openly includes antebellum America in the novella's vision. Focusing on three characters who have all been victors and victims in the social structure framed by the stern-piece, "Benito Cereno" also faintly but clearly sounds the possibility for change. The grim fates of these three characters are given some closure by being past, while the conspicuous absence of Amasa Delano raises the possibility that his descendants might still avoid the fate of blindly following the lead of the Old World. If, like Melville rather than his characters, they queried their culture-bound encoding of texts of social and racial roles, if they queried their inadequate histories and hierarchical ideologies, they might at last sever the chains that bind their interpretations of their world to the authority of an old, unjust, unstable order. Only by seeing how like the Old World they had made their own, "Benito Cereno" suggests, could they genuinely begin to ask how the New World could, indeed, be made "new."

Notes

1. Herman Melville, *Piazza Tales*, ed. Egbert S. Oliver (New York: Hendricks House, Farrar Straus, 1948), p. 73; hereafter cited parenthetically in the text.
2. Merton M. Sealts, Jr., *Pursuing Melville, 1940–1980* (Madison: Univ. of Wisconsin Press, 1982), pp. 230–231, documents the probable composition of "Benito Cereno" during the winter of 1854–55.
3. Allan Moore Emery, " 'Benito Cereno' and Manifest Destiny," *Nineteenth-Century Fiction*, 39 (1984), 48–68, addresses the issues of Manifest Destiny and Know-Nothingism but places the novella exclusively in the context of the United States' expansionist desires with regard to Latin America. I am indebted to this discussion, but I maintain that "Benito Cereno" refers to a much broader political and cultural climate; moreover, I find that, directly and indirectly, slavery is, as earlier critics recognized, central to the novella.
4. Among the many critics who have seen "Benito Cereno" as a cautionary work, I have found the following particularly useful: Jean Fagin Yellin, "Black Masks: Melville's *Benito Cereno*," *American Quarterly*, 22 (1970), 678–689; Joyce Adler, "Melville's *Benito Cereno*: Slavery and Violence in the Americas," *Science and Society*, 38 (1974), 19–48; and Carolyn L. Karcher, *Shadow over the Promised Land: Slavery, Race, and Violence in Melville's America* (Baton Rouge and London: Louisiana State Univ. Press, 1980). More generally, Eric J. Sundquist, "Suspense and Tautology in *Benito Cereno*," *Glyph 8*, Johns Hopkins Textual Studies (Baltimore: Johns Hopkins Univ. Press, 1981), pp. 101–126, connects the novella's context, a social order poised on the verge of conflict yet keeping conflict at bay, with its pattern of suspense and tautology. Allan Moore Emery, "The Topicality of Depravity in 'Benito Cereno,' " *American Literature*, 55 (1983), 316–331, summarizes earlier work on the novella's references to slavery and reads it as the portrayal of universal human depravity, black and

white. Barbara J. Baines, "Ritualized Cannibalism in 'Benito Cereno,' " *ESQ*, 30 (1984), 163–169, interprets cannibalism as a "central event and metaphor" by means of which Melville portrays slavery as an institution that consumes white master and black slave, body and soul. Marianne DeKoven, "History as Suppressed Referent in Modernist Fiction," *ELH*, 15 (1984), 137–152, sees "Benito Cereno" as a work which, though making little explicit reference to the historical reality of slavery, contains powerfully oblique historical political referents. Ann Douglas, *The Feminization of American Culture* (New York: Alfred A. Knopf, 1977), pp. 292–320, gives an excellent account of Melville's general opposition to contemporary American culture.

5.   Rogin, *Subversive Genealogy: The Politics and Art of Herman Melville* (New York: Alfred A. Knopf, 1983); Emery, " 'Benito Cereno' and Manifest Destiny."

6.   DeKoven makes the important point that the novella's historical referents are indirect. While DeKoven links the novella solely to slavery, her method—elucidating how "Benito Cereno" inscribes its historical framework through allusion, imagery, and diction—underscores the fact that many readers have reduced its figures of speech, which are not usually one-dimensional, to markers for colonial Spain and/or the slaveholding United States.

7.   For an important discussion of other aspects of authority, including its connection with authorship, see Edward W. Said, *Beginnings: Intention and Method* (New York: Basic Books, 1975), especially Chapter Three, "The Novel as Beginning Intention." Said argues that in novels authority, or invention, is inseparable from molestation, or constraint, that texts always both assert and usurp their own authority.

8.   Karcher, for instance reads the novella primarily as "an exploration of the white racist mind and how it reacts in the face of a slave insurrection" (p. 128). Emery, " 'Benito Cereno' and Manifest Destiny," sees Delano as Melville's exemplification of American expansionist attitudes toward Latin America. He points out that Delano's "Anglo-Saxonism" causes him to stereotype Cereno as a certain kind of Spaniard but finds Delano's prejudices tangential to Melville's purpose of indicting Americans for following Spain in becoming dogmatically imperialist (pp. 61–63).

9.   Karcher, however, feels that Delano often exhibits the language of the southern apologist for slavery (p. 132).

10.   See, for example, Edward H. Rosenberry, *Melville and the Comic Spirit* (Cambridge, Mass: Harvard Univ. Press, 1955), p. 163; and R. Bruce Bickley, Jr., *The Method of Melville's Short Fiction* (Durham, N.C.: Duke Univ. Press, 1975), pp. 58–59 and 62–66.

11.   P. 139. Compare pp. 113, 115, where Delano finds solace in a parodic conversion of romanticism into cliché. Cereno's black spirits become a natural phenomenon: the "foul mood was now at its depths, as the fair wind was at its heights" (p. 113).

12.   "Self-Reliance" in *The Collected Works of Ralph Waldo Emerson*, ed. Alfred R. Ferguson *et al.* (Cambridge, Mass. and London: Belknap of Harvard Univ. Press, 1971), II, 39.

13.   See p. 77 for the first instance, pp. 81, 90, 92, 115, 117 for later ones.

14.   Thomas Philbrick, *James Fenimore Cooper and the Development of American Sea Fiction* (Cambridge, Mass: Harvard Univ. Press, 1961), especially pp. 116–203. Rogin, pp. 3–11, discusses connections between piracy and slavery and analyzes Melville's references to Cooper's novel in Delano's piracy fantasies; his focus, however, is on antebellum distinctions between (illegitimate) piracy and (legitimate) slavery.

15.   Rogin, p. 22. In an interesting alternative reading, Emery, " 'Benito Cereno' and Manifest Destiny," pp. 52–54, sees the American's plan to take over the Spanish ship as a mirroring of Americans' conviction that their Anglo-Saxon energy would succeed in bringing order to Latin America where Spain's enervation had brought only disaster.

16.   H. Bruce Franklin, *The Wake of the Gods: Melville's Mythology* (California: Stanford Univ. Press, 1963), examines the parallels between Cereno and William Stirling's portrayal of the Spanish monarch Charles V in *Cloister Life of the Emperor Charles the Fifth* (pp. 136–152);

Karcher identifies in Cereno the stereotype of the effete southern plantation owner (p. 136).

17.   Adler notes the economic similarity between the two (p. 45); Karcher identifies the ideological, unanalytic nature of Cereno's deposition (p. 135).

18.   I am indebted here to Rogin's view that in portraying the master-slave relation in terms of a charade, "Benito Cereno" reveals that the bond between the two, regarded as "natural" by apologists for slavery, is a social construct (pp. 208–220). Emery, "The Topicality of Depravity in 'Benito Cereno,' " argues that Melville challenges cultural assumptions about blacks and whites, men and women, for the moral purpose of exposing universal human depravity.

19.   See, for instance, Harold Beaver's comment in his edition of *Billy Budd, Sailor, and Other Stories*, (Middlesex and New York: Penguin Books, 1970), pp. 33–34. While Delano may feminize the blacks, as Beaver, Karcher (p. 134), and others have suggested, Melville also shows that the blacks likewise deny Cereno status. I am indebted to Lauren Shohet, "Discovering Oppression in Melville's *Benito Cereno*," unpublished paper written for American Romanticism, Oberlin College, 1983, for noticing that the blacks emasculate Cereno, whose response is similar to a rape victim's.

20.   Baym, "Melville's Quarrel with Fiction," *PMLA*, 94 (1979), 910, maintains that "Melville's Emerson-derived notion of language [proceeded] from a divine Author or Namer," and his "loss of belief in an Absolute entailed the loss not only of truth in the universe but also of coherence and meaning in language."

21.   In an interesting reading, DeKoven sees the "false appearances" of the blacks' masquerading as proper slaves to contain "the actual truth of the social order": its despotism and irrationality, and its destructiveness of whites as well as blacks (see pp. 139–143).

22.   Adler associates the playwright Babo with the poet Melville (p. 48); Sundquist sees Babo and the narrator as silent figures who carry out "plots" and express their authority over Cereno and Delano, respectively, with razor-sharp rituals (pp. 111, 119).

23.   See Sundquist, especially p. 116, on this discourse.

24.   John D. Wade, "Delano, Amasa," *DAB* (1934).

25.   Delano reflected that "virtue and vice, happiness and misery, are much more similarly distributed to nations than those are permitted to suppose who have never been from home . . ." (quoted in Wade, p. 217).

26.   Forgie, *Patricide in the House Divided: A Psychological Interpretation of Lincoln and His America* (New York: W. W. Norton, 1979), especially pp. 3–54; Rogin, pp. 33–41.

27.   Franklin was among the first to establish Melville's careful evocation of Spanish history. Among more recent researchers, Gloria Horsley-Meacham, "The Monastic Slaver: Image and Meaning in 'Benito Cereno,' " *New England Quarterly*, 56 (1983), 262–266, develops connections between the American slave trade, the Church, and the campaign for Christian dominion.

28.   The novella's first extended simile establishes a resemblance between the half-shadowed slave ship and a "Lima intriguante's one sinister eye peering across the Plaza from the Indian loop-hole of her dusk *saya-y-manta*" (p. 56); the last comparison suggests that the wounds the whites inflict on the blacks as they retake the slave ship are like "those shaven ones of the English at Preston Pans, made by the poled scythes of the Highlanders" (p. 122). In between, comparisons are made between Cereno and the tyrannical James I of England (p. 103); North Americans forcing slave women to bear their children and Spanish planters' similar treatment of enslaved Indians (p. 106); Delano's sailors, as they fight the blacks, and "troopers in the saddle" (p. 122); the blacks' hatchets and the weapons of Indians and woodsmen (p. 121); the *San Dominick* and a decaying Italian palace (pp. 58, 88).

29.   Despite a confusion between Ledyard and Mungo Park, Melville similarly discredits the authority of both as sources of information about Africa. In a passage adapted by Park, Ledyard, in his *Proceedings of the Association for Promoting the Discovery of the Interior Parts of Africa*, described the generosity of African women; Melville indicates Ledyard's inaccuracy by

stressing how fiercely the women oppose the whites. He also exposes Ledyard's celebration of the black women's hospitality as a useful rationalization for their enslavement, for Delano takes special pleasure in thinking that the female slaves on the *San Dominick* might be the same women who were so gracious to Ledyard. See Emery, "The Topicality of Depravity in 'Benito Cereno,' " for a discussion that summarizes earlier work on Melville's emendation of these sources and contains new information on his adaptations of material in *Harper's* and *Putnam's*.

30. All citations are to Amasa Delano, *Narrative of Voyages and Travels in the Northern and Southern Hemispheres* (Boston, 1817), Chapter Eleven, reprinted in Horace Scudder, "Melville's *Benito Cereno* and Captain Delano's Voyages," *PMLA*, 43 (1928), 502–532; here 513.

31. These textual associations between New England merchants and Spanish slave traders are rooted in facts of which Adler gives a concise account (p. 38).

32. Beaver, p. 435.

Benito Cereno and New World Slavery

Eric J. Sundquist

In the climactic scene of *Benito Cereno*, after the terrified Spanish captain has flung himself threateningly into Captain Delano's boat, followed by his servant Babo, dagger in hand, Melville writes: "All this, with what preceded, and what followed, occurred with such involutions of rapidity, that past, present, and future seemed one." The revelation of Babo's true design, as his disguise of dutiful slave falls away to reveal a "countenance lividly vindictive, expressing the centered purpose of his soul," is mirrored in the countenance of Delano himself, who, as if "scales dropped from his eyes," sees the whole host of slaves "with mask torn away, flourishing hatchets, and knives, in ferocious piratical revolt."[1] The masquerade staged by Babo and Benito Cereno to beguile the benevolent Delano probes the limits of the American's innocence at the same time it eloquently enacts the haltingly realized potential for slave rebellion in the New World and, in larger configuration, the final drama of one stage in New World history.

The American, the European, and the African, yoked together in the last crisis as they are throughout the pantomime of interrupted revolution that constitutes Melville's story, play parts defined by the climactic phase slavery in the Americas had entered when Melville composed his politically volatile tale during the winter and spring of 1854–55. The American Civil War reduced New World slavery to Cuba and Brazil; it brought to an end the threatened extension of slavery throughout new territories of the United States and Caribbean and Latin American countries coveted by the South. In the 1850s, however, the fever for such expansion was at a pitch, and Melville's tale brings into view the convulsive history of the entire region and epoch—from the Columbian discovery of the Americas, through the democratic revolutions in the United States, Haiti, and Latin America, to the contemporary crisis over the expansion of the "Slave Power" in the United States. "In 1860 pressures, past, present, and future, blasted the Union apart," writes Frederick Merk in his study of manifest destiny.[2] Unable to see the future but nonetheless intimating its revolutionary shape, Melville adds to these recent national pressures an international structure of exceptional scope and

Reprinted from *Reconstructing American Literary History*, ed. Sacvan Bercovitch (Cambridge: Harvard University Press, 1986), 93–122. Reprinted by permission of the publisher.

power, such that past, present, and future do indeed seem one aboard the *San Dominick*.

Benito Cereno's general significance in the debates over slavery in the 1850s is readily apparent; moreover, Melville's exploitation of the theme of balked revolution through an elaborate pattern of suppressed mystery and ironic revelation has helped draw attention to the wealth of symbolic meanings the slave revolt in San Domingo in the 1790s would have for an alert contemporary audience. Even so, the full implications of Melville's invocation of Caribbean revolution have not been appreciated, nor the historical dimensions of his masquerade of rebellion completely recognized.

In changing the name of Benito Cereno's ship from the *Tryal* to the *San Dominick*, Melville gave to the slave revolt a specific character that has often been identified. Haiti, known as San Domingo (Saint-Domingue) before declaring its final independence from France in 1804 and adopting a native name,[3] remained a strategic point of reference in debates over slavery in the United States. Abolitionists claimed that Haitian slaves, exploiting the upheaval of the French Revolution, had successfully seized the same Rights of Man as Americans two decades earlier; whereas proslavery forces claimed that the black revolution led to wholesale carnage, moral and economic degradation, and a political system that was (in the words of the British minister to Haiti in the 1860s) "but a series of plots and revolutions, followed by barbarous military executions." The outbreak of revolution in 1790 produced a flood of white planter refugees to the United States, some 10,000 in 1793 alone, most of them carrying both slaves and tales of terror to the South. Thereafter, especially in the wake of Nat Turner's bloody uprising in 1831 and the emancipation of slaves in British Jamaica in the same year, Haiti came to seem the fearful precursor of black rebellion throughout the New World. When Melville altered the date of Amasa Delano's encounter with Benito Cereno from 1805 to 1799, he accentuated the fact that his tale belonged to the age of democratic revolution, in particular the period of violent struggle leading to Haitian independence presided over by the heroic black general Toussaint L'Ouverture.[4]

After Napoleon's plans to retake San Domingo (in order to retrieve in the Gulf of Mexico glory he had lost in the Mediterranean) were undercut by the demise of Leclerc's army in 1802, he lost the main reason to retain and occupy Louisiana. "Without that island," Henry Adams wrote, the colonial system "had hands, feet, and even a head, but no body. Of what use was Louisiana, when France had clearly lost the main colony which Louisiana was meant to feed and fortify?" The ruin and seeming barbarism of the island, and the excessive expense and loss of lives it would require to retrieve and rebuild, made San Domingo a lost cause of large dimensions to France and at the same time the key to the most important territorial expansion of the United States—an expansion that would soon make the Caribbean appear as vital to American slave interests as it had to France and prepare the way for the crisis question of slavery's expansion into new territories. In making their country "the graveyard of Napoleon's magnificent army as well as his imperial ambitions in the New World," Eugene Genovese has written, the slaves of San Domingo thus cleared the way for a different expression of New World colonial power destined to have more decisive and lasting effect on the stage of world history.[5]

Were the noble and humane Toussaint the only representative figure of the Haitian revolution, fears of slave insurrection in the United States might not have taken on such a vicious coloring. The black activist William Wells Brown compared him in an 1854 lecture not only to Nat Turner ("the Spartacus of the Southampton revolt") but also to Napoleon and Washington—though with the withering irony that whereas Washington's government "enacted laws by which chains were fastened upon the limbs of millions of people," Toussaint's "made liberty its watchword, incorporated it in its constitution, abolished the slave trade, and made freedom universal amongst the people." Brown's lecture on San Domingo, subtitled "Its Revolutions and Its Patriots," adopted the familiar antislavery strategy of declaring the San Domingo uprising the model for an American slave rebellion that would bring to completion the stymied revolution of 1776. When Americans contemplated what would happen if the San Domingo revolt were "reenacted in South Carolina and Louisiana" and American slaves wiped out "their wrongs in the blood of their oppressors," however, not Toussaint but his successor as general-in-chief, Dessalines, sprang to mind. Whatever ambivalent gratitude might have existed toward Haiti for its mediating role in the United States' acquisition of Louisiana was diluted by the nightmarish achievement of independence under Dessalines, whose tactics of deceitful assurance of safety to white landowners, followed by outright butchery, enhanced his own claim that his rule would be initiated by vengeance against the French "cannibals" who have "taken pleasure in bathing their hands in the blood of the sons of Haiti." When he made himself emperor in 1804 Dessalines wore a crown presented by Philadelphia merchants and coronation robes from British Jamaica; but in the histories of San Domingo available in the early nineteenth century, both these ironies and unofficial economic ties to the island tended to be forgotten amid condescending accounts of his pompous reign and the frightful bloodshed that accompanied it. Although a sympathetic writer could claim in 1869 that the independence of Haiti constituted "the first great shock to this gigantic evil [slavery] in modern times," what Southerners in particular remembered were accounts of drownings, burnings, rapes, limbs chopped off, eyes gouged out, disembowelments—the sorts of Gothic violence typified by an episode in Mary Hassal's so-called *Secret History; or, The Horrors of St. Domingo* (1808), in which a young white woman refuses the proposal of one of Dessalines' chiefs: "The monster gave her to his guard, who hung her by the throat on an iron hook in the market place, where the lovely, innocent, unfortunate victim slowly expired."[6]

While Hassal's "history" both in form and substance more resembles such epistolary novels as *Wieland*, its account of the Haitian trauma is hardly more sensational than the standard histories and polemics of the day. Antislavery forces for good reason hesitated to invoke Haiti as a model of black rule; even those sympathetic with its revolution considered its subsequent history violent and ruinous. Until the 1850s, moreover, most Americans agreed with assessments holding "that specious and intriguing body, the society of the *Amis des Noirs*," responsible for the rebellion and subsequent descent of the island "into the lowest state of poverty and degradation." What Bryan Edwards asserted of the British West Indies in 1801 remained persuasive in the United States for decades: if encouragement is given to those "hot-brained fanaticks and detestable incendiaries, who, under the vile pretense of philanthropy and zeal for the interests of suffering humanity, preach up rebellion and murder to the contented and orderly negroes," the same "carnage and destruction" now found in San Domingo will be renewed throughout the colonial world. Precisely the same fears permeated the South, even in exaggerated form after Jamaica itself was added to the list of revolutionized colonies in 1831. Lasting paranoia among shareholders about abolitionist responsibility for slave unrest thus continually referred back to San Domingo and became, according to David Brion Davis, "an entrenched part of master class ideology, in Latin America as well as the United States." Implicit in the assumption of abolitionist conspiracy, of course, is a doubt of the slaves' own ability to organize and carry out a revolt, a doubt contradicted by any of the slave revolutionaries Melville might have had in mind—by Toussaint, by Dessalines, by Nat Turner, by Cinque (the notorious leader of the revolt aboard the slave ship *Amistad*), and by Mure, the original of his own Babo.[7]

When the sixty-three slaves aboard Benito Cereno's ship revolted, killing twenty-five men, some out of simple vengeance, they especially determined to murder their master, Don Alexandro Aranda, "because they said they could not otherwise obtain their liberty." To this Melville's version adds that the death would serve as a warning to the other seamen; not only that, but a warning that takes the form of deliberate terror. Aranda's body, instead of being thrown overboard, as in reality it was, is apparently cannibalized and the skeleton then *"substituted for the ship's proper figure-head—the image of Cristobal Colon, the discoverer of the New World,"* from whose first contact with the New World in Hispaniola—that is, San Domingo—flowed untold prosperity and human slavery on an extraordinary scale. The thirty-nine men from the *Santa Maria* Columbus left at the north coast base of Navidad on Hispaniola in 1492 were massacred by the natives after quarreling over gold and Indian women; on his second voyage in 1494 Columbus himself took command, suppressed an Indian uprising, and authorized an enslavement of Indians to work in the gold fields that was destined to destroy—by some estimates—close to one million natives within fifteen years.[8]

Responding to pleas of the Dominican priests, led by Bartholomew de Las Casas, that the Indian population would not survive slavery, Charles V, Holy Roman Emperor, in 1517 authorized the first official transport of African slaves to San Domingo: the New World slave trade, destined to carry some 15 million slaves across the Atlantic by 1865, had begun. The substitution of Negroes for Indians was justified by Las Casas on the humanitarian grounds that the blacks, unlike the Indians, were hardy and suited to such labors in a tropical climate. "Like oranges," wrote Antonio de Herrera in 1601, "they found their proper soil in Hispaniola, and it seemed even more natural than Guinea." Just so, added the American author who quoted Herrera in 1836: "The one race was annihilated by slavery, while the other has ever since continued to thrive and fatten upon it." Only the master class of their sympathizers made such an argument. Their antagonists, such as black abolitionist Henry Highland Garnett, especially stigmatized Charles V and his "evil genius," Las Casas; "clouds of infamy will thicken around them as the world moves on toward God."[9]

Alongside the paradoxical outcome of the Columbian discovery and settlements, the forms of debate in the antebellum period over the Christian justification of slavery are compressed by Melville into a structure of monastic symbolism meant to evoke the role of the Catholic Church, the Dominicans in particular, in the initiation of New World slavery. The comparison of Benito Cereno to Charles V, who became a virtual tool of the Dominicans in the end of his reign, and Delano's momentary vision of the *San Dominick* as "a whitewashed monastery" or a shipload of Dominican "Black Friars pacing the cloisters," are only the most central of the ecclesiastical scenes and metaphors that animate the tale. The aura of ruin and decay that links Benito Cereno and his ship to Charles V and his empire point forward in addition to the contemporary demise of Spanish power in the New World and the role of slave unrest in its revolutionary decline. The less apparent Islamic symbolism in *Benito Cereno* indicates Melville borrowed from several contemporary sources—Irving's portrait of Las Casas in his *Life* of Columbus, Bancroft's *History of the United States*, and Charles Sumner's *White Slavery in the Barbary States*—in order to invoke an Islamic-Christian conflict predating by some seven hundred years the introduction of African slaves into America. Bancroft in particular remarked the hypocritical coincidence of Charles V's military liberation of white Christian slaves in Tunis and his enslavement of Africans bound for the Americas, and emphasized the further coincidence, its irony commonplace by Melville's day, that "Hayti, the first spot in America that received African slaves, was the first to set the example of African liberty."[10]

It is this coincidence and its ironic origins that are illuminated by Babo's symbolic display of the skeleton of a modern slave-holder in place of the image of Columbus. Along with the chalked admonition, *"Follow your leader,"* it too appears to Delano at the climactic moment when Benito Cereno and Babo plunge into his boat and the piratical revolt is unveiled; but the benevolent American, self-satisfied and of good conscience, remains oblivious to the end to the meaning of Babo's terror and to the murderous irony summoned up in Melville's symbolic gesture. Like those of Aranda, the sacred bones of Columbus, rumored still in 1830 to have been lodged in the cathedral of Santo Domingo before being transferred to Havana upon the Treaty of Basle in 1795, might well join those of the millions of slaves bound for death in the New World. Of them is built Benito Cereno's decaying ship as it drifts into the harbor of the Chilean island of Santa Maria: "Her keel seem laid, her ribs put together, and she launched, from Ezekiel's Valley of Dry Bones."[11]

Delano, as Jean Fagan Yellin suggests, may portray the stock Yankee traveler in plantation fiction, delighted by the warm patriarchal bond between the loyal, minstrel-like slave and his languid master; he may even, like Thomas Gray, who recorded and published Nat Turner's *Confessions*, penetrate the violent center of that relationship and yet prefer to ignore its meaning. Recognizing that "slavery breeds ugly passions in man" but banishing from mind the significance of that realization, Delano is a virtual embodiment of repression, not simply in the sense that he puts down the revolt aboard the *San Dominick* and thereby restores authority that has been overturned, but also in the sense that his refusal to understand the "shadow" of the Negro that has descended upon Benito Cereno is itself a psychologically and politically repressive act.[12]

Melville borrows Amasa Delano's trusting disposition and generosity directly from the captain's own account, which records that the *"generous captain Amasa Delano"* much aided Benito Cereno (and was poorly treated in return when he tried to claim his just salvage rights), and was saved from certain slaughter by his own "kindness," "sympathy," and "unusually pleasant" temperament. A passage earlier in Delano's *Narrative* might also have caught Melville's eye: "A man, who finds it hard to conceive of real benevolence in the motives of his fellow creatures, gives no very favourable testimony to the public in regard to the state of his own heart, or the elevation of his moral sentiments." The self-serving nature of Delano's remarks aside, what is notable is the manner in which Melville may be said to have rendered perversely ironic the entire virtue of "benevolence," the central sentiment of abolitionist rhetoric and action since the mid-eighteenth century. Delano's response is not "philanthropic" but "genial," it is true—but genial in the way one responds to Newfoundland dogs, natural valets and hairdressers, and minstrels set "to some pleasant tune." Delano's "old weakness for negroes," surging forth precisely at Melville's greatest moment of terrifying invention, the shaving scene, is the revolutionary mind at odds with itself, energized by the ideals of fatherly humanitarianism but, confounded by racialism, blind to the recriminating violence they hold tenuously in check. Like that most eloquent advocate of benevolence, Harriet Beecher Stowe, for whom "the San Domingo hour" would be ushered in only by slaves with "Anglo Saxon blood . . . burning in their veins," Delano himself is emblematic of the paralyzed American revolution, at once idealistic and paternalistic, impassioned for freedom but fearful of continuing revolution.[13]

The brutal course of the San Domingo revolution led Jefferson, himself a reputed father of slave children, to remark in 1797 that "the revolutionary storm, now sweeping the globe," would soon be upon us; we shall be, if nothing prevents it, "the murderers of our own children." The fear of allowing the spread of revolutionary violence defines both Melville's tale and the course of slavery after the age of Revolution. The character of Delano speaks both for the founding fathers, who sanctioned slavery even as they recognized its contradiction to the Rights of Man, and the contemporary northern accommodationists, who too much feared sectional strife and economic turmoil to bring to the surface of consciousness a full recognition of slavery's ugliness in fact and in principle. The repressing "bright sun" and "blue sky" that have "forgotten it all," which Delano invokes at the tale's conclusion, echo Daniel Webster's praise of the Union and the founding fathers in the wake of the nearly insurrectionary struggle over the Compromise of 1850: "A long and violent convulsion of the elements has just passed away," Webster remarked, "and the heavens, the skies, smile upon us." Benito Cereno's reply?—"Because they have no memory . . . because they are not human."[14]

Webster's memory, longer and more fraught with complications than Delano's, repressed the true meanings of the revolutionary traditions his own career had celebrated, but not so much or so easily as his opponents thought. In the 1843 case of the American slave ship *Creole*, whose cargo mutinied off the coast of Virginia and sailed to Nassau, where they were freed by British authorities, Webster's seemingly hypocritical protest was spurred by his suspicions about British intentions in the Caribbean, coupled with a more specific concern that would reach a new height by the time Melville was writing *Benito Cereno*. To the American consul in Havana Webster wrote in 1843 to beware a British plot to invade Cuba and put in power "a *black Military Republic* under British *protection*." With 600,000 blacks in Cuba and 800,000 in her West Indian islands, Britain could "strike a death blow at the existence of slavery in the United States" and seize control of the Gulf of Mexico.[15] Webster's concern anticipated by ten years the climate of opinion about the Caribbean to which Melville's tale responds, but it throws into relief the split between revolutionary ideals and revolutionary sentiment that perennially compromised and postponed the question of slavery in the United States until it exploded in civil war—the "war of the rebellion." Although contention over the Gulf did not ultimately play a large role in the Civil War, it seemed a vital issue throughout the 1850s—all the more so because, like Melville's tale, it represented the shadow play, one might say, of America's own balked Revolution and its ensuing domestic turmoil.

As it happened, American hegemony in the New World was increased rather than retarded by the Civil War. From Melville's perspective, however, the nature and extent of future American power remained a function of the unfolding pattern of anticolonial and slave revolutions in the Americas. Even though slaves fought at different times on opposing sides, the national revolutions of South and Central America in the early part of the century helped undermine slavery throughout the region (in most cases, slaves were not freed immediately upon independence but legislation abolishing slavery was at least initiated—in Mexico, Uruguay, Chile, Argentina, and Bolivia in the 1820s; in Venezuela and Peru in the 1850s). The end of slavery in the British West Indies in 1833 and in the Dutch and French Islands in 1848 left the United States more and more an anomaly, its own revolutionary drama absurdly immobilized. Thus, when extremists of Southern slavery later sought to tie an extension of the peculiar institution to new revolutions in a policy of manifest destiny in Latin America, they ignored the decline of colonial rule on the one hand and on the other the trepidations expressed by one of the best known of South American revolutionaries, Francisco Miranda, who wrote as early as 1798:

> as much as I desire the liberty and independence of the New World, I fear the anarchy of a revolutionary system. God forbid that these beautiful countries become, as did St. Dominque, a theatre of blood and of crime under the pretext of establishing liberty. Let them rather remain if necessary one century more under the barbarous and imbecile oppression of Spain.

Miranda's plea expresses well the paradox of New World liberation and of the United States' continued, expanding enslavement of Africans between 1776 and 1860. Drawn by the territorial dreams opened by Louisiana, the post-Revolutionary generation advocated expansion through a conscious policy of America's manifest destiny to revolutionize the continent—eventually the entire hemisphere—spreading Anglo-Saxon free institutions, as one writer put it, from the Atlantic to the Pacific and "from the icy wilderness of the North to . . . the smiling and prolific South." That dreams of a global millennium ever exceeded reality is less relevant here than the fact that the harsh conflict between dream and reality was anchored in the wrenching paradox that had come to define New World revolution itself: would it advance freedom or increase slavery? At the time of *Benito Cereno*'s publication, the question was concentrated in the Caribbean, where the energy of manifest destiny had been redirected after its initial efforts had failed to bring "All Mexico" into the United States orbit.[16] The region offered in miniature an emblem of the hemisphere in its historical revolutionary moment, with the remnants of Spain's great empire, free blacks who had revolutionized their own nation, and American expansionist interest all in contention. Melville's tale does not prophecy a civil war but rather anticipates, as at the time it might well have, an explosive resolution of the conflict between American democracy, Old World despotism, and Caribbean New World revolution.

Readers of *Benito Cereno* who take any account at all of Melville's use of the San Domingo revolution focus for the most part on its extension of the French Revolution and the heroism of Toussaint. Yet the island's continuing turmoil in subsequent years not only kept it alive in the Southern imagination of racial violence but also made it of strategic significance in counter-arguments to Caribbean filibustering. For example, an 1850 pamphlet by Benjamin C. Clark, though sympathetic to Haitian freedom, condemned the "condition worse than that of slavery" into which he thought the island had been plunged by Great Britain's political maneuvering in the Caribbean; Haiti's failure to develop its resources and its continued threat of revolution to Cuba and the Dominican Republic thus made it a barrier both to the United States interests in the region and to the emancipation of American slaves. On a different note, an essay "About Niggers," appearing in one of the same 1855 issues of *Putnam's Monthly* that carried the serialization of *Benito Cereno*, argued that Haiti, unlike the United States, demonstrated that liberty and slavery cannot coexist and that the "terrible capacity for revenge" unleashed in the San Domingo revolution proves that the "nigger" is "a man, not a baboon." The sarcastic article, in line with the general antislavery tone of *Putnam's*, anticipated black colonialists in voicing the novel hope that the black West Indies would one day develop "a rich sensuous civilization which will bring a new force into thin-blooded intellectualism, and save our noble animal nature from extreme emasculation and contempt."[17] Melville's tale, antislavery though it may be, contains no invocation of noble savagery and no such hope about the fruitful merging of cultures.

While Haiti had its defenders, the common opinion among those who studied it was that its record, like that of emancipated Jamaica, was largely one of economic sloth and political barbarism. *De Bow's Review*, the influential organ of Southern interests, carried an essay in 1854 typical in its critique of Haitian commerce and government. For over thirty years, the essay claims, the "march of civilization" has been dead in Haiti, its social condition one of sustained indolence and immorality:

> From its discovery by Columbus to the present reign of Solouque, the olive branch has withered under its pestilential breath; and when the atheistical philosophy of revolutionary France added fuel to the volcano of hellish passions which raged in its bosom, the horrors of the island became a narrative which frightened our childhood, and still curdles our blood to read. The triumphant negroes refined upon the tortures of the Inquisition in their treatment of

prisoners taken in battle. They tore them with red-hot pincers—sawed them asunder between planks—roasted them by a slow fire—or tore out their eyes with red-hot corkscrews.

Here, then, are the central ingredients that Melville's tale adds to Delano's own *Narrative*. The conflation of Spanish and French rule, coupled with the allusion to the Inquisition, yokes anti-Catholic and anti-Jacobin sentiment; indeed, the rhetoric of manifest destiny in the Caribbean was often a mix of the two, though with the submerged irony—one Melville treats with complex care—that Northern critics of Slave Power expansion liked as well to employ the analogies of European despotism and Catholic subversion in attacking the South. For the North, National expansion would morally entail the eradication of slavery, not its extension. It would illuminate the world in such a way, Lyman Beecher had already argued in *A Plea for the West* (1835), that "nation after nation, cheered by our example, will follow in our footsteps till the whole earth is free . . . delivered from feudal ignorance and servitude." The only danger, according to Beecher's anti-Catholic tract, lay in the Roman Church's attempt to salvage its dying power by subversion of liberty in the New World, notably in South America, Canada, and San Domingo, which were "destined to feel the quickening powers of Europe, as the only means remaining to them of combating the march of liberal institutions . . . and perpetuating for a season her political and ecclesiastical dominion." The slave power of the South, said the generation of Beecher's children, would behave in precisely the same way in order to rescue and extend their dying institution.[18]

The antislavery imagination, no less than the proslavery, tended to collapse history into timeless images of terror and damnation. Theodore Parker, for instance, comparing the strength of Anglo-Saxon free institutions to the decay of Spain and her colonies in "The Nebraska Question" (1854), had no trouble linking together the early butchery and plunder of Indians in Hispaniola and greater Latin America in the name of the Virgin Mary, and the contemporary confluence of Slave Power and Catholicism. Spain "rolled the Inquisition as a sweet morsel under her tongue . . . butchered the Moors and banished the plundered Jews," Parker wrote; in San Domingo she "reinvented Negro Slavery" six thousand years after it had vanished in Egypt and "therewith stained the soil of America." With what legacy? Spain's two resulting American empires, Haiti and Brazil, so Parker saw it, were "despotism throned on bayonets"; over Cuba, France and England "still hold up the feeble hands of Spain"; most of South and Central America takes the form of a republic "whose only permanent constitution is a Cartridgebox"; and Mexico goes swiftly back to despotism, a rotting carcass about which "every raven in the hungry flock of American politicians . . . wipes his greedy beak, prunes his wings, and screams 'Manifest Destiny.' " Parker attacked the North for conciliating slave interests time after time (most recently in the Compromise of 1850) and predicted the Slave Power's attempted acquisition of Cuba, the Mesilla Valley, Nebraska, Mexico, Puerto Rico, Haiti, Jamaica and other Caribbean islands, the Sandwich Islands, and so on. Despotic, Catholic tyranny was at work, which so far the Puritan, Anglo-Saxon spirit of liberty and religious freedom had been unable to contain. "I never knew a Catholic Priest who favored freedom in America," Parker admonished; "a Slave himself, the medieval theocracy eats the heart out from the celibate Monk."[19]

Benito Cereno, as he delivers his halting, incoherent narrative to Delano, seems to be "eating of his own words, even as he ever seemed eating his own heart." This coincidence in phrasing need do no more than remind us that Don Benito, who resembles a monk or a "hypochondriac abbott" and in the end retires to a monastery to die, is made by Melville a symbol of American paranoia about Spanish, Catholic, slaveholding despotism. To the extent that he also represents the Southern planter, the dissipated cavalier spiritually wasted by his own terrifying enslavement, Benito Cereno requires the reader to see the tale in Parker's terms: North and South, like Delano and Cereno, play the parts of Anglo-Saxon and Roman-European currently working out the destiny of colonial territories in the New World. Benito Cereno, at once a genteel courtier ("a sort of Castilian Rothschild") and an impotent, sick master painfully supported by the constant "half embrace of his servant," virtually *is* the Spanish New World, undermined by slave and nationalist revolutions and adrift aboard a deteriorated ghost ship on the revolutionary waters of history, which are now "like waved lead that has cooled and set in the smelter's mold." For his part, Delano, like the nation he represents, vacillates between dark suspicion and paternalistic disdain of the Spaniard. What the tale cannily keeps hidden, of course, is that it is Babo who stages the events Delano witnesses aboard the *San Dominick*, artistically fashioning his former master like "a Nubian sculptor finishing off a white statue-head."[20] Melville's scenario—driving between the example of *De Bow's Review*, which saw Haiti as a volcano of Jacobin horrors, and that of Theodore Parker, who saw the Slave Power itself as a manifestation of Old World despotism and popish insurgency—makes the Negro slave the subversive, the terrorist, and, in the tale's central imaginary scene, the inquisitor.

Melville's portrayal of Babo would have aroused memories of notorious American slave rebels like Gabriel Prosser, Denmark Vesey, and Nat Turner, all of them in one faction of the public mind artful and vicious men prompted to their deeds by madness, dreams of San Domingo, or—what was much the same thing—abolitionist propaganda. Turner in particular was perceived to be deranged, the victim of apocalyptic hallucinations. In contrast, Babo is a heroic figure—though full of that "art and cunning" the real Delano attributed to all African slaves. Melville's depiction of his ferocity and cruelty, his comparison of Babo to a snake and his followers to wolves, and most of all his attribution to him of great powers of deception—these characteristics make Babo fearsome and commanding at the same time. His masquerade of devotion to Benito Cereno concisely portrays the complexly layered qualities of rebellion and submission—of "Nat" and "Sambo" roles—that historians have detected among the accounts of slave behavior, and it is a virtual parody of Thomas Wentworth Higginson's observation in an 1861 essay on Turner: "In all insurrections, the standing wonder seems to be that the slaves most trusted and best used should be the most deeply involved." Higginson goes on to quote James McDowell, member of the Virginia House of Delegates, who remarked in the historic 1832 debates over emancipation and colonization that Southern paranoia was prompted by the "suspicion that a Nat Turner might be in every family; that the same bloody deed might be acted over at any time and in any place; that the materials for it were spread through the land, and were always ready for a like explosion."[21]

The same debates produced Thomas Dew's famous "Abolition of Negro Slavery" (expanded as *Review of the Debate in the Virginia Legislature of 1831–2*), which characteristically called the Haitian revolution a failure, productive only of disorder and poverty; which predicted that emancipation would lead to the South's "relapse into darkness, thick and full of horrors"; and which asserted that black rebels, unlike contemporary revolutionaries in Poland and France, were "unfit for freedom" and should be considered "*parricides* instead of *patriots*." Dew's mixing of the rhetoric of slave paternalism with that of revolution is entirely to the point. Insurrection destroyed the cherished southern fiction of the tranquil plantation "family," revealed it as a charade. This, as Michael Rogin argues, is what Melville himself does in *Benito Cereno*: "By overthrowing slavery and then staging it as a play, Babo has conventionalized the supposedly natural relations of master and slave." Melville's tale "recontains a slave revolt inside a masquerade," just as it contains the American Revolution itself inside its own masquerade and the paternalistic fiction inside a fiction that Delano himself continues in his naivete to empower and authorize.[22]

No one saw the irony of slaveholding paternalism more clearly than Frederick Douglass, whose revised autobiography, *My Bondage and My Freedom*, appearing the same year as *Benito Cereno*, advised that "a person of some consequence here in the north, sometimes designated *father*, is literally abolished in slave law and practice." This is all the more true when the slaveholder has the arrogance to invoke the "inalienable rights of man": "He never lisps a syllable in condemnation of the fathers of this republic, nor denounces any attempted oppression of himself, without inviting the knife to his own throat, and asserting the rights of rebellion for his own slaves." Or, as Higginson said in an 1858 address to the American Anti-Slavery Society: "I have wondered in times past, when I have been so weak-minded as to submit my chin to the razor of a coloured brother, as his sharp steel grazed my skin, at the patience of the negro shaving the white man for many years, yet [keeping] the razor outside of the throat." The American slave might soon act on his own, Higginson warned. "We forget the heroes of San Domingo."[23]

Melville's most significant moment of invention in *Benito Cereno*, the shaving scene, brings to a climax of terror the "juggling play" that Babo and Benito Cereno have been "acting out, both in word and deed," before him. The "play of the barber" compresses Delano's blind innocence, Cereno's spiritual fright, and Babo's extraordinary mastery of the scene's props and actors into a nightmare pantomime symbolic of the revenge of New World slaves upon their debilitated masters. The cuddy, with its "meagre crucifix" and "thumbed missal," its settees like an "inquisitor's rack" and its barbering chair that seems "some grotesque engine of torment," is a scene defined by symbols of Spain's violent Catholic history. Babo's use of the Spanish flag as a barber's apron, which through his agitation unfolds "curtain-like" about his master, heightens Delano's playful affection for "the negro" and coordinates the personal and historical dramas of vengeance that are acted out—dramas that Delano, as he often does, unwittingly or unconsciously glimpses but fails fully to comprehend:

> Setting down his basin, the negro searched among the razors, as for the sharpest, and having found it, gave it an additional edge by expertly stropping it on the firm, smooth, oily skin of his open palm; he then made a gesture as if to begin, but midway stood suspended for an instant, one hand elevating the razor, the other professionally dabbling among the bubbling suds on the Spaniard's lank neck. Not unaffected by the close sight of the gleaming steel, Don Benito nervously shuddered; his usual ghastliness was heightened by the lather, which lather, again, was intensified in its hue by the contrasting sootiness of the negro's body. Altogether the scene was somewhat peculiar, at least to Captain Delano, nor, as he saw the two thus postured, could he resist the vagary, that in the black he saw a headsman, and in the white a man at the block. But this was one of those antic conceits, appearing and vanishing in a breath, from which, perhaps, the best regulated mind is not always free.

The conceit of decapitation—uniting Jacobin terror, the Inquisition, and slave vengeance—has here more actuality than the literal barbering that is taking place. It epitomizes Melville's masterful employment throughout the tale of metaphors whose submerged meaning momentarily exceeds in truth their literal contexts, only to be forced—repressed—once again beneath the conscious surface of Delano's mind and the story's narrative.[24] The entire tale, most of all its revolutionary import, is similarly repressed by the legalistic documents and the executions of the slave rebels that codify Delano's putting down of the piratical revolt. Yet in that very act the fullest rebellious power, like the energy of the unconscious, is released in Melville's questioning of the moral authority of such documents and tribunals.

Melville's fascination with revolt and mutiny, as the cases of *White Jacket* and *Billy Budd* remind us, was tempered always by his equal fascination with the mechanics of repression. Captain Vere's combined paternalism and rigid justice refine qualities found in both the fictional and the actual Captain Delano. Even for the good captain, like the good master, benevolence may be no barrier either to rebellion or to its consequences. "I have a great horror of the crime of mutiny," wrote Delano in a discussion of the case of the *Bounty* in his *Narrative*, for it leads only to greater abuses against the mutineers. "Vengeance will not always sleep, but wakes to pursue and overtake them." A virtual "reign of terror" against blacks followed Turner's insurrection; likewise, Delano had to prevent the Spanish crew and Benito Cereno himself from "cutting to pieces and killing" the Negroes after the *Tryal* had been retaken. But as Joshua Leslie and Sterling Stuckey have shown, legal retribution followed the same instinct. At Conception, as graphically as in Melville's tale, five of the rebels are sentenced to hanging and decapitation, their heads then "fixed on a pole, in the square of the port of Talcahuano, and the corpses of all . . . burnt to ashes." Justice here echoes revolution: among more gruesome brutalities, both sides in the San Domingo revolution displayed the severed heads of their opponents; the heads of defeated black insurrectionists in New Orleans in 1811 and Tennessee in 1856 were fixed on poles or carried in parades. Babo's head, "that hive of subtlety," gazes across the Plaza towards St. Bartholomew's Church, where the recovered bones of Aranda lie, and beyond that the monastery where Benito Cereno lies dying, soon to "follow his leader."[25]

The repressive mechanisms of justice—legal or not—worked swiftly to contain slave insurrection in the United States when it occurred. And aside from the revolt of Turner, the instances that most drew public attention in the late antebellum period took place aboard ships and involved international rights entailing long court disputes. The case of the *Creole*, which prompted Webster's warning about black military rule in Cuba, was the subject of Frederick Douglass's short story, "The Heroic Slave," which appeared in Julia Griffiths' 1853 collection *Autographs for Freedom* and played ironically on the name of the revolt's leader, Madison Washington, to highlight the shadowed vision of the founding fathers. But the more famous case of the *Amistad*, whose slaves revolted in 1839 and eventually came ashore on Long Island after an abortive attempt to sail to Africa, is even more likely to have been on Melville's mind, not least because the enactment of the revolt resembled that aboard the *Tryal–San Dominick* and because the slave leader, Cinque, was viewed as an intriguing combination of guile and humanity whose "moral sentiments and intellectual faculties predominate considerably over his animal propensities," but who "killed the Captain and crew with his own hand, cutting their throats." Garnett and other abolitionists celebrated Cinque's heroism, even considered him an American patriot; and when John Quincy Adams won freedom for the slaves before the Supreme Court (much to the embarrassment of President Van Buren and the outrage of the Spanish authorities who had demanded their return to Cuba), he appealed to "the law of Nature and Nature's God on which our fathers placed our own national existence."[26]

What, though, was the "law of Nature" and what evidence was there that it was synonymous with the law of the fathers? Webster celebrated the *Amistad* decision but refused to recognize the same rights in American slaves aboard the *Creole*: the perceived threat of the spread of black rebellion was one difference, enduring contention with England another. Although Babo acts according to the laws both of Nature and of the Revolutionary fathers, Delano cannot conceive of such action in black slaves. Like the "naked nature" of the slave mothers aboard the *San Dominick*, which turns out to conceal in them a rage for torture and brutality surpassing that of the men (a feminine brutality corroborated, it might be added, by accounts of the San Domingo rebellion), the "natural" relationship of master and slave defined by the fathers, despite their inclusive dream of freedom, remained a disguise and a delusion.[27]

Webster's warning about Cuba, a symptom of his own ambivalence about the tortured relationship between union and slavery, sheds a different light as well on Babo's symbolic role. Not only might Babo evoke Toussaint, Dessalines, Nat Turner, or Cinque, he surely brought to mind in Melville's audience the current ruler of Haiti, Faustin Soulouque, who came to power in 1847 and had himself made emperor on the model of Dessalines in 1849. His empire was renowned for its gaudy displays of pomp and feared for its brutality. He employed voodoo, priests, assassination, torture, and massacre to put down any threat of revolt; in 1849 he mounted the first of several attacks on Santo Domingo (that is, the Dominican Republic, independent since 1844) that were perceived as a campaign to exterminate the white race. An article in the *Democratic Review* in 1853 declared Solouque "the dark image of Louis Napoleon" and ridiculed the reluctance of the United States, France, and England to join together in putting down this "despot of a horde of black savages, whose grandfathers murdered their masters, and whose fathers murdered their brothers . . . and [who] would as readily exterminate every white man, as would their ancestors in the jungle of Africa."[28] The fear that a black empire would spread throughout the Caribbean was in turn countered by (or acted as a cover for) Southern calls for American intervention that were spurred on by the arrival of Pierce's expansionist administration.

Among the constellation of historical and contemporary issues Melville invoked in the drama of the *San Dominick*, present concern over the sporadic war between Haiti and the Dominican Republic is central for several reasons. From the mid-1840s on, claims had been made by Frederick Douglass and others that Haiti would be annexed to protect American (slave) interests. Now threats to the Dominican Republic—another Texas—seemed to offer a suitable excuse. The significance of the whole island was heightened by the simultaneous crisis over the Kansas-Nebraska Act and the "Africanization of Cuba," a purported plot by Spain and Britain to free slaves and put blacks in power. In retrospect, the fact that the South spent energy on the battle for Kansas that it might otherwise have directed toward Cuba, a territory of greater value to it, does not contradict the fact that at the time *both* seemed possible. Franklin Pierce's May 1854 interdiction against filibustering in Cuba was based on his reports that Cuba was too well protected and on the great Northern pressure brought to bear on him as a result of his conciliation of Slave Power in signing the Kansas-Nebraska Act the day before. Cuba, in addition, would have been too much. If the South, in David Potter's words, "sacrificed the Cuban substance for the Kansas shadow," it did not do so intentionally. Besides, the fears of endless slave expansion that Theodore Parker voiced in "The Nebraska Question" were still echoed a year later in an essay on "The Kansas Question" appearing in the October 1855 issue of *Putnam's* in which *Benito Cereno*'s serialization began. Kansas, the essay maintained, was still but the next step, in the spread of slavery to Mexico, the Amazon, and eventually back to Africa. In the long run, the conjunction of Kansas and Cuba devastated both the Democratic Party and the idea of popular sovereignty; crushed the South's dream of a Caribbean empire; lost a territory destined to be of strategic importance to the United States in later years; rekindled fears about the spread of Haitian terror and counterbalancing proslavery plots against that republic; and at the same time sparked premonitions of the greater domestic convulsion to come. "The storm clouds of [war over] slavery were gathering so fast in the South," wrote John Bigelow to Charles Sumner after an 1854 visit to Haiti, "that writing letters about Hayti seemed like fiddling while the country was burning."[29]

Melville's tale circles continually around a plot against himself that Delano vaguely suspects Benito Cereno to be meditating, perhaps with the aid of Babo and the slaves. But Delano's own blindness and its psychological significance should not overshadow the secondary effects Melville surely counted on. Purported plots of slaves against their masters were outstripped at the time by fears of the two other "plots" we have touched on—that of the South to expand its power and that of Cuba to be Africanized. The supposed conspiracy of 1853 between Spain and Britain to end slavery and the slave trade in Cuba and promote armed black rule produced calls from Cuban and American slaveholders for American intervention. New Spanish policies liberalizing slave laws, combined with the seizure in February 1854 of the American steamer *Black Warrior* on a violation of port regulations, accelerated both legal and extra-legal maneuvering to obtain Cuba before it became, as a State Department agent, Charles W. Davis, wrote in March 1854, another "Black Empire" like Haiti, "whose example they would be proud to imitate" in destroying the wealth of the island and launching "a disastrous bloody war of the races." The height of imperialistic rhetoric came after the crisis had passed and attempts to force a purchase of Cuba had failed, in the notorious Ostend Manifesto of October 1854, which declared that Cuba belonged "naturally to that great family of States of which the Union is the providential nursery" and that the United States would be justified "in wresting it from Spain . . . upon the very same principle that would justify an individual in tearing down the burning house of his neighbor if there were no other means of preventing the flames from destroying his own home." The issue of Cuba, that is to say, was couched in the familiar rhetoric that Lincoln would exploit, combining the domestic language of the revolutionary fathers and that of slaveholding paternalism. And it brought together just those threats Delano perceives aboard the *San Dominick*: Spanish misrule and deterioration, and threatened black insurrection and liberation.[30]

The South's—and the Pierce administration's—plan to "rescue" Cuba from black rule presupposed the decay of the Spanish empire and its replacement by an Anglo-Saxon empire in the western hemisphere. Peculiar to the South's version of manifest destiny, of course, was the extension of slavery and the shift of national power geographically to the south. This, perhaps, more than any single point of reference such as Haiti or Cuba, alerts us to the complex dimensions of the actions dramatized in *Benito Cereno*. The Southern dream of a Caribbean empire reached its most extreme formulations in somewhat later documents such as Henry Timrod's "Ethnogenesis," William Walker's *The War in Nicaragua*, and Edward Pollard's *Black Diamonds Gathered in the Darkey Homes of the South*, published in 1861, 1860, and 1859, respectively, but based on sentiments common throughout the decade. Pollard, for example, claimed southern expansion was not a sectional issue but one involving "the world's progress, and who shall be the founders of its greatest empire of industry." Eventually, he maintained, the seat of the Southern Empire would be in Central America; control of the West Indies, the isthmuses of Central America, and the production of the world's cotton and sugar would complete America's destiny:

> What a splendid vision of empire! How sublime in its associations! How noble and inspiriting the idea, that upon the strange theater of tropical America, once, if we may believe the dimmer facts of history, crowned with magnificent empires and flashing cities and great temples, now covered with mute ruins, and trampled over by half-savages, the destiny of Southern civilization is to be consummated in a glory brighter even than that of old, the glory of an

empire, controlling the commerce of the world, impregnable in its position, and representing in its internal structure the most harmonious of all systems of modern civilization.

Walker, too, in one chapter of the account of his filibustering career in Sonora and Nicaragua, celebrated the destined rejuvenation of Central and South America. The effort the South wasted on the "shadow" of Kansas, Walker wrote, could have brought her the "substance" of Central America, a territory necessary to protect slavery, to raise the African from darkness and teach him the "arts of life," and to forestall the spread of degeneracy that has occurred in Haiti and Jamaica.[31]

Walker among others adopted in his rhetoric a new ideology of progress that paternalized the remnants of Spain's American empire. He believed too that popular sovereignty could be applied as effectively to the Caribbean and Central America as to Kansas, and that expansion was necessary to complete the republican defeat of dying European monarchism. (So extreme did this idea become in the early 1850s that at one point Louis Kossuth, the enthusiastically courted hero of the 1848 Hungarian revolution, became embroiled in a southern plot to invade Haiti on the pretext that Soulouque was a czarist agent.) "Empire" became a common word in discourse about the region— not only among such slave interests as the Knights of the Golden Circle, which promoted a Gulf circle of power drawing together New Orleans, Havana, Yucatan, and Central America, but remarkably also among black American colonizationists such as J. Dennis Harris, who proposed to build an "Anglo-African Empire" in Haiti, a mulatto utopia, and James T. Holly, who imagined a similar regeneration originating in Haiti, "the Eden of America," and overspreading the whole world.[32]

Although such visions counted for little against the South's need to stabilize its economic and political power, they accentuate from a different angle the paradisial dream that the Americas continued to represent. California gold, the dream's great symbol in this period, would soon so enrich the nation, claimed *De Bow's Review* in 1854, that no possible investment would be equal to it but the cultivation of the entire western hemisphere. Lying between two of the great valleys of the world, the Mississippi and the Amazon, the Gulf would link the most productive regions of the earth, and by unlocking trading access to the wealth of the Pacific Basin (China, Australia, California) make the Atlantic in the modern world what the Mediterranean was "under the reign of the Antonies in Rome." Given the continued dissolution of European political power and possession of Cuba, Santo Domingo, and Haiti, the United States might control the Gulf and through it the world: "Guided by our genius and enterprise, a new world would rise there, as it did before under the genius of Columbus." This new Columbian vision had a price, however, one which the circular argument of the writer for *De Bow's* did little to hide:

Heretofore, the great difficulty in civilizing the barbarian races of the world has been to procure cheap and abundant clothing for them. A naked race must necessarily be a wild one. To Christianize or civilize a man, you must first clothe his nakedness. In the three millions of bags of cotton the slave labor annually throws upon the world for the poor and the naked, we are doing more to advance civilization and the refinement of life than all the canting philanthropists of New and Old England will do in centuries.

As the author noted, "slavery and war have [always] been the two great forerunners of civilization."[33]

Of course the utopian schemes of the South now seem precisely that; but as the possibilities of renewed Caribbean revolution and civil conflict in the United States unfolded in the 1850s, they too served to focus with critical symbolic significance the historical and contemporary role of San Domingo in the question of slavery. Lincoln's diplomatic recognition of Haiti in 1862 ensured the island's harassment of Confederate privateers, and black rule was hardly an issue between the two governments once the South seceded; moreover, the Caribbean and Latin America ceased for the time being to be of pressing national interest once the issue of slavery was resolved and a transcontinental railroad completed later in the decade.[34] The disappearance from view of the region until conflicts fifty and a hundred years later brought it back into the public mind has contributed to the general disregard of its critical role in *Benito Cereno*. Still, there can be little doubt as to Melville's richness of allusion and dramatic enactment, his masterful exploitation of the revolutionary spirit locked in the heart of the American New World, in this most troubled and explosive tale of America's antebellum destiny.

Notes

    1.   *Benito Cereno, Great Short Works of Herman Melville*, ed. Warner Berthoff (New York: Harper and Row, 1969), pp. 294–295.
    2.   Leon Howard, *Herman Melville: A Biography* (Berkeley: University of California Press, 1951), pp. 218–222; Frederick Merk, *Manifest Destiny and American Mission in American History* (1963; rpt. New York: Vintage-Random, 1966), p. 214.
    3.   In English and American usage of the nineteenth century the entire island at times and even after the revolution the western half (a French possession since the seventeenth century) was often designated San Domingo or St. Domingo. The Spanish, eastern half (the Dominican Republic after 1844) was usually designated Santo Domingo, as was the principal city founded by Columbian expeditions and named in memory of Columbus's father, Dominick.
    4.   Spenser St. John, *Hayti, or the Black Republic* (London: Smith, Elder, 1884), p. x; C. L. R. James, *The Black Jacobins: Toussaint L'Ouverture and the San Domingo Revolution*, rev. ed. (New York: Vintage Books, Random House, 1963), p. 127; Clement Eaton, *The Freedom-of-Thought Struggle in the Old South*, rev. ed. (New York: Harper and Row, 1964), pp. 89–90; Eugene D. Genovese, *From Rebellion to Revolution: Afro-American Slave Revolts in the Making of*

the New World (1979; rpt. New York: Vintage Books, Random House, 1981), pp. 35–37, 94–96; Winthrop D. Jordan, *White Over Black: American Attitudes toward the Negro, 1550–1812* (1968; rpt. New York: Norton, 1977), pp. 375–402.

5. Ludwell Lee Montague, *Haiti and the United States 1714–1938* (Durham: Duke University Press, 1940), pp. 35–46; Rayford W. Logan, *The Diplomatic Relations of the United States with Haiti, 1776–1891* (Chapel Hill: University of North Carolina Press, 1941), pp. 112–151; Henry Adams, *History of the United States during the Administrations of Jefferson and Madison*, quoted in Logan. *Diplomatic Relations*, p. 142; Genovese, *From Rebellion to Revolution*, p. 85.

6. William Wells Brown, *St. Domingo: Its Revolutions and Its Patriots* (Boston: Bela Marsh, 1855), pp. 23, 36–38, 32–33; James, *Black Jacobins*, pp. 370–374; Charles MacKenzie, *Notes on Haiti, Made During a Residence in that Republic*, 2 vols. (London: Colburn and Bentley, 1830), II, 61; Jonathan Brown, *The History and Present Condition of St. Domingo*, 2 vols. (Philadelphia: William Marshall, 1836), II, 152–154, 147–148; Mark B. Bird, *The Black Man; Or, Haytian Independence* (New York: American News Co., 1869), pp. 60–61; Mary Hassal, *Secret History; or, The Horrors of St. Domingo* (Philadelphia: Bradford and Inskeep, 1808), pp. 151–153.

7. James Franklin, *The Present State of Hayti* (London: John Murray, 1828). pp. 90–96, 409–410; Bryan Edwards, *An Historical Survey of the Island of Saint Domingo* (London: John Stockdale, 1801), p. 226; David Brion Davis, *The Slave Power Conspiracy and the Paranoid Style* (Baton Rouge: Louisiana State University Press, 1969), p. 35.

8. Amasa Delano, *Narrative of Voyages and Travels in the Northern and Southern Hemispheres* (Boston: E. G. House, 1817), p. 336; see also Harold H. Scudder, "Melville's *Benito Cereno* and Captain Delano's Voyages," *PMLA*, 43 (1928), 502–532; Melville, *Benito Cereno*, p. 310; John Edwin Fagg, *Cuba, Haiti, and the Dominican Republic* (Englewood Cliffs, N.J.: Prentice-Hall, 1965), pp. 114–115; Brown, *History and Present Condition of St. Domingo*, I, 22–23; Edwards, *Historical Survey of the Island of Saint Domingo*, p. 208; Samuel Eliot Morison, *Admiral of the Ocean: A Life of Christopher Columbus* (Boston: Little, Brown. 1942), pp. 297–313, 423–438.

9. Daniel P. Mannix and Malcolm Cowley, *Black Cargoes: A History of the Atlantic Slave Trade, 1518–1865* (1962; rpt. New York: Viking/Compass, 1965), pp. viii, 1–5; Brown, *History and Present Condition of St. Domingo*, I, 36–37: Henry Highland Garnett, *The Past and Present Condition and Destiny of the Colored Race* (1848; rpt. Miami: Mnemosyne Publishing, 1969), pp. 12–13.

10. Melville, *Benito Cereno*, pp. 246, 240; H. Bruce Franklin, *The Wake of the Gods: Melville's Mythology* (Stanford: Stanford University Press, 1963), pp. 136–150: Gloria Horsley-Meacham. "The Monastic Slaver: Images and Meaning in *Benito Cereno,*" *New England Quarterly*, 55, no. 2 (June 1983), 261–266; George Bancroft, *History of the United States of America*, 10 vols. (New York: Appleton and Co., 1885), I, 121–125.

11. MacKenzie, *Notes on Haiti*, pp. 263–266; Melville, *Benito Cereno*, pp. 296, 241.

12. Jean Fagan Yellin, *The Intricate Knot: Black Figures in American Literature, 1776–1863* (New York: New York University Press, 1972), pp. 215–227; Melville, *Benito Cereno*, pp. 283, 314.

13. Delano, *Narrative of Voyages*, pp. 337, 323, 73; David Brion Davis, *The Problem of Slavery in Western Culture* (Ithaca: Cornell University Press, 1966), pp. 333–390; Melville, *Benito Cereno*, pp. 278–279; Harriet Beecher Stowe, *Uncle Tom's Cabin* (New York: Penguin, 1981), p. 392; cf. George Fredrickson, *The Black Image in the White Mind: The Debate on Afro-American Character and Destiny, 1817–1914* (New York: Harper and Row, 1971), pp. 97–129.

14. Jefferson, letter of 1797, quoted in Jordan, *White over Black*, p. 387; Melville *Benito Cereno*. p. 314; Daniel Webster, *The Writings and Speeches of Daniel Webster*, 18 vols. (Boston: Little Brown, 1903), XIII, 405–407; cf. Michael Paul Rogin, *Subversive Genealogy: The Politics and Art of Herman Melville* (New York: Alfred A. Knopf, 1983), pp. 142–146.

15. Webster quoted in Mary Cable, *Black Odyssey: The Case of the Slave Ship Amistad* (1971; rpt. New York: Penguin, 1977), p. 152.

16. Genovese, *From Rebellion to Revolution*, pp. 119–121; C. Duncan Rice. *The Rise and Fall of Black Slavery* (1975; rpt. Baton Rouge: Louisiana State University Press, 1976), pp. 262–263; Miranda quoted in Salvador de Madariaga, *The Fall of the Spanish American Empire* (London: Hollis, Carter, 1947), pp. 322–323; James Bennett, quoted in Merk, *Manifest Destiny and Mission*, p. 46; Merk, pp. 180–214.

17. Benjamin C. Clark, *A Geographical Sketch of St. Domingo, Cuba, and Nicaragua* (Boston: Eastburn's Press, 1850), p. 7; "About Niggers," *Putnam's Monthly*, 6 (December 1855), 608–612.

18. "Hayti and the Haytiens," *De Bow's Review*, 16, no. 1 (January 1854), 35; Davis, *The Slave Power Conspiracy*, pp. 72–78; Lyman Beecher, *A Plea for the West* (Cincinnati: Truman and Smith, 1835), pp. 37, 109, 144.

19. Theodore Parker, "The Nebraska Question," *Additional Speeches, Addresses, and Occasional Sermons*, 2 vols. (Boston: Little, Brown, 1855), I, 301–303, 352, 367, 378.

20. Melville, *Benito Cereno*, pp. 276, 245, 250–251, 258, 241, 239, 283; cf. Carolyn Karcher, *Shadow over the Promised Land: Slavery, Race, and Violence in Melville's America* (Baton Rouge: Louisiana State University Press, 1980), pp. 136–139.

21. Seymour L. Gross and Eileen Bender, "History, Politics, and Literature: The Myth of Nat Turner," *American Quarterly*, 23, no. 4 (October 1971), 487–518; Delano, *Narrative of Voyages*, p. 550; Melville, *Benito Cereno*, pp. 295, 299; John W. Blassingame, *The Slave Community: Plantation Life in the Antebellum South*, rev. ed. (New York: Oxford University Press, 1979), pp. 192–248; Thomas Wentworth Higginson, "Nat Turner's Insurrection," *Travellers and Outlaws: Episodes in American History* (Boston: Lee and Shepard, 1889), pp. 322–325; cf. Genovese, *From Rebellion to Revolution*, pp. 116–117, and Herbert Aptheker, *American Negro Slave Revolts* (New York: International Publishers, 1952), pp. 293–324.

22. Thomas R. Dew, "Abolition of Negro Slavery," in Drew Gilpin Faust, ed., *The Ideology of Slavery: Proslavery Thought in the Antebellum South, 1830–1860* (Baton Rouge: Louisiana State University Press, 1981), pp. 56–59; Rogin, *Subversive Genealogy*, pp. 215, 210.

23. Frederick Douglass, *My Bondage and My Freedom*, ed. Philip S. Foner. (New York: Dover, 1969), pp. 35, 269–270; Higginson quoted in Tilden G. Edelstein, *Strange Enthusiasm: A Life of Thomas Wentworth Higginson* (New Haven: Yale University Press, 1968), p. 211.

24. Melville, *Benito Cereno*, pp. 277–283; cf. Eric J. Sundquist, "Suspense and Tautology in *Benito Cereno*," *Glyph 8: Johns Hopkins Textual Studies* (Baltimore: Johns Hopkins University Press, 1981), pp. 103–126.

25. Delano, *Narrative of Voyages*, pp. 146–147, 347; Aptheker, *American Negro Slave Revolts*, pp. 300–310; C. L. R. James, *Black Jacobins*, pp. 95–96; Genovese, *From Rebellion to Revolution*, pp. 43, 106; Melville, *Benito Cereno*, p. 315; Joshua Leslie and Sterling Stuckey, "Avoiding the Tragedy of Benito Cereno: The Official Response to Babo's Revolt," *Criminal Justice History*, vol. 3 (1982), 125–132.

26. *New London Gazette*, August 26, 1839, quoted in John W. Barber, *A History of the Amistad Captives* (New Haven: E. L. and J. W. Barber, 1840), p. 4; Henry Highland Garnett, *Present Condition and Destiny*, p. 16; Adams, *Argument in the Case of the United States vs. Cinque* (1841; rpt. New York: Arno Press, 1969), p. 9; cf. Mary Cable, *Black Odyssey*, pp. 76–108, and Sidney Kaplan, "Herman Melville and the American National Sin," *Journal of Negro History*, 41 (October 1956), 311–338.

27. Melville, *Benito Cereno*, pp. 268, 310; Delano, *Narrative of Voyages*, p. 341; James, *Black Jacobins*, p. 117; Franklin, *Present State of Hayti*, p. 62.

28. Robert I. Rotberg, *The Politics of Squalor* (Boston: Houghton Mifflin, 1971), pp. 76–90; Bird, *The Black Man*, pp. 288–306; St. John, *Hayti, or the Black Republic*, pp. 90–99;

"On the Rumored Occupation of San Domingo by the Emperor of France," *United States Democratic Review*, 32, no. 2 (February 1853), 181–183.

29. Dexter Perkins, *The Monroe Doctrine, 1826–1867* (Baltimore: Johns Hopkins University Press, 1933), pp. 253–317; Charles Callan Tansill, *The United States and Santo Domingo, 1798–1873: A Chapter in Caribbean Diplomacy* (Baltimore: Johns Hopkins University Press, 1938), pp. 137–212; Logan, *Diplomatic Relations*, pp. 238–292; Basil Rauch, *American Interest in Cuba, 1848–1855* (New York: Columbia University Press, 1948), pp. 280–294; David M. Potter, *The Impending Crisis, 1848–1861* (New York: Harper and Row, 1976), pp. 177–198, quote at p. 198; Robert E. May, *The Southern Dream of a Caribbean Empire, 1854–1861* (Baton Rouge: Louisiana State University Press, 1973), pp. 21–75; "The Kansas Question," *Putnam's Monthly*, 6 (October 1855), 425–433; John Bigelow, quoted in Logan, *Diplomatic Relations*, p. 281.

30. Rauch, *American Interest in Cuba*, pp. 275–277; Philip S. Foner, *A History of Cuba and Its Relations with the United States*, 2 vols. (New York: International, 1963), II, 75–85; Charles W. Davis quoted in Foner, II, 81–82; "Ostend Manifesto," *Documents of American History*, 2 vols. in 1, ed. Henry Steele Commager (New York: F.S. Croft, 1934), I, 333–335.

31. A. Curtis Wilgus, "Official Expression of Manifest Destiny Sentiment Concerning Hispanic America, 1848–1871," *Louisiana Historical Quarterly*, 15, no. 3 (July 1932), 486–506; Edward A. Pollard, *Black Diamonds Gathered in the Darkey Homes of the South* (New York: Pudney and Russell, 1859), pp. 106–115; William Walker, *The War in Nicaragua* (Mobile: S.H. Goetzel, 1860), pp. 251–280.

32. C. Stanley Urban, "The Ideology of Southern Imperialism: New Orleans and the Caribbean, 1845–1860," *Louisiana Historical Quarterly*, 39, no. 1 (January 1956), 48–73; Donald S. Spencer, *Louis Kossuth and Young America: A Study of Sectionalism and Foreign Policy, 1848–1852* (Columbia: University of Missouri Press, 1977), pp. 166–169; May, *Southern Dream*, pp. 148–150; Mannix and Cowley, *Black Cargoes*, pp. 266–274; J. Dennis Harris, "A Summer on the Borders of the Caribbean Sea," (1860) in Howard H. Bell, *Black Separatism and the Caribbean, 1860* (Ann Arbor: University of Michigan Press, 1970), p. 172; James T. Holly, "A Vindication of the Capacity of the Negro Race Demonstrated by Historical Events of the Haytian Revolution," in Bell, *Black Separatism*, p. 64.

33. "Destiny of the Slave States," *De Bow's Review*, 17, no. 3 (September 1854), 280–284; cf. Eugene Genovese, *The Political Economy of Slavery: Studies in the Economy and Society of the Slave South* (New York: Vintage Books. Random House, 1967), pp. 243–274.

34. Logan, *Diplomatic Relations*, pp. 293–314; Montague, *Haiti and the United States*, pp. 85–88.

Benito Cereno: Melville's De(con)struction of the Southern Reader

CHARLES SWANN

I remember when Dr Keitt was murdered by his negroes. Mr Miles met me and told the dreadful story.

"Very awkward indeed, this sort of thing. There goes Keitt, in the house always declaiming about the 'beneficent institution.' How now?"

Horrible beyond words.

Babo came to the place where the deponent was, and told him that he had determined to kill his master, Don Alexandro Aranda, . . . because he and his companions could not otherwise be sure of their liberty.

His [Babo's] aspect seemed to say, since I cannot do deeds, I will not speak words. . . . On the testimony of the sailors alone rested the legal identity of Babo.[1]

Some thirty years ago, Sidney Kaplan at length indicted Melville in an article entitled "Herman Melville and the American National Sin: the Meaning of *Benito Cereno*":

Reluctantly, very reluctantly—for it is with a special sadness that we are forced to repudiate any portion of the 'usable past' in the classic figures of our American Renaissance—it must be ventured that the image of Melville as subtle abolitionist in *Benito Cereno* may be a construction of generous wish than hard fact.

The hesitant tone of Kaplan's prose is evidence of his troubled regret at losing a much-needed democratic author rather than of any uncertainty about his verdict on the meaning of *Benito Cereno* for he makes it quite clear that it is, for him, alas, a racist pro-slavery tale—one which locates "innate depravity" in the blacks. Among the reasons he gives for bringing in the "guilty" verdict are that there were no hostile Southern responses to the story and that there is nothing in the text to stop a supporter of the slavocracy reading it as an anti-abolitionist tale, having his or her prejudices confirmed rather than challenged:

Reprinted from *Literature and History* 12 (1986): 3–15, by permission of the journal.

there must have been some common readers in the brutal-chivalric south of 1855, who like Arthur Hobson Quinn, our own contemporary, felt its appeal as "the picture of one man of our own race, alone amid the hostile strangers, who are waiting to strike."[2]

These are points that must be answered if any Melville-as-radical argument is to stand—for if Kaplan is right in his facts and inferences, then (to put it mildly) that position has some problems. (That he is right as far as he goes seems to me to be unquestionable: his failure, I shall argue, lies in not going further into history and the problems of interpretation.) Yet supporters of that political reading of Melville have simply not met this part of Kaplan's comprehensive case as can be seen if we look at two of the best of the recent proponents of this view—Marvin Fisher in *Going Under* and Carolyn Karcher in *Shadow Over the Promised Land*. They have not even claimed that Melville had just given up on the South—and was willing to let Southern readers make of *Benito Cereno* what they would. This would not, in any case, be an easy argument to make—as one would have to explain away Melville's invention of a Southern persona for "Hawthorne and His Mosses" (1850)— by "A Virginian Spending July in Vermont." Nor does Melville leave this Southerner as merely an alliterative attraction: he provides himself with a fictive hot-headed Carolina cousin (1163, 1165) and insists that Hawthorne can inform and inspire the South:

> I feel that this Hawthorne has dropped germinous seeds into my soul. He expands and deepens down, the more I contemplate him; and, further, shoots his strong New-England roots into the hot soil of my Southern soul. (1167)

Marvin Fisher (who, very sensibly, begins his study of Melville's short fiction of the 1850s with a reading of "Hawthorne and His Mosses") is so keen to claim that we, as products of the Civil Rights movement, as witnesses to the emergence of the Third World, are historically advantaged in our reading that he feels no need to consider the historical situation in which the story was produced—and, crucially for Kaplan's case, consumed. Karcher, at once more conscientious and less cavalier, acknowledges the existence of Kaplan's case but does not answer it, suppressing and supplanting it with her own (admittedly intelligent) reading. In effect, she gives Kaplan decent burial in a scholarly footnote—but fails to give the causes of death.[3] Yet this failure to confront a challenging case simply will not do. If the story is as threatening and as explosive as they claim, it should have seemed doubly so to a South engaged in developing an elaborate rhetoric of self-defence against the North, and riven by fears (however irrational) of slave insurrection. The reception of *Uncle Tom's Cabin* (1852), for example, shows that the South was not insensitive nor likely to suffer at least one kind of criticism in silence. Not only were there numerous editorials, there was also a flood of books with titles like *Aunt Phillis's Cabin, Uncle Robin in His Cabin and Tom without One in Boston,* and *The Cabin and Parlor; or, Slaves and Masters.*[4] (But perhaps that response was so massive and so visible because Stowe's criticism was not threatening on anything but the moral level: she does not present insurrection as either desirable or possible. Her whites are merely immoral: it is their souls, not their bodies that are in danger.)

Benito Cereno comes from the 1850s and, at least in the first instance, was addressed to 1850s audiences. These are facts that cannot be ducked— and I do not think we can get off Kaplan's hook by claiming that our interpretations are privileged by our historical position (however true that may be). If one believes that *Benito Cereno* is (and was) a politically radical tale (and I do), then Kaplan's point must be confronted directly. What is there to stop a Southern reader from having his or her prejudices and fears confirmed? I have to agree with Kaplan: Nothing. If the story is as anti-slavery and anti-racist as Fisher and Karcher claim, this is (on the face of it) surprising. Any explanation I can provide has to risk speculations about intention and reception—both hazardous tasks. To reconstruct the possible or probable responses of a section of that 1850s readership may be (at least as I attempt it here) to speculate, as much to construct or even create as to re-create. Yet if the text is to be historicized, some such considerations must take place.

II

The argument from silence, it may be felt, gives too much space and freedom to the interpreter. There may, of course, be a very simple explanation—that nobody read it. *The Piazza Tales* (1856) sold notoriously badly. Yet *Benito Cereno* had been serialized in *Putnam's* the year before, and though the magazine was denounced in the South as a tool of "the Black Republican Party," that is at least evidence that it was known there and that it was felt to be important enough to be worth denouncing. And William Gilmore Simms was still published by *Putnam's* even though he was a victim of "the narrowing isolation into which political developments were thrusting" him, even though the magazine became "more and more anti-slavery." Since Simms still took enough interest to complain that "Putnam seems a blockhead in his choice of management" and since he had not shown himself slow to detect (or discover) slurs on the South in Melville's earlier work, his silence is suggestively revealing. It certainly seems unlikely that it was the product of ignorance, nor, given his willingness to see himself as the literary voice and conscience of the South, is it likely to be the product of benign neglect.

Simms was virtually alone in praising *Mardi* for its "many glowing rhapsodies, much epigrammatic thought, and many sweet and attractive fancies." But he ended his review by complaining that Melville "spoils everything to the Southern reader" with his "loathsome picture of Mr. Calhoun, in the character of slave driver, drawing mixed blood and tears from the victim at every stroke of the whip." Even more revealing of his Southern touchiness was his response to *White-Jacket*. Unsoftened by the reference to the "chivalric Virginian, John Randolph" (Ch. XXXIV), unsoftened too by the description of the purser as a "Southern gentleman" with "a pleasant, kind, indulgent manner toward his slave" which made White-Jacket think he had "a generous heart" and made him cherish "an involuntary friendliness toward him," a phrase is enough to set him off. A seaman "whose demeanour shows some dignity within" is, Melville tells us, as unendurable to a naval officer "as an erect lofty-minded African would be to some slave-driving planter" (Ch. XC). For Sims "It is somewhat strange that a writer who can think so shrewdly and observe so well should . . . reflect upon the Southern slaveholder, as one necessarily more tyrannical than any other class of persons." Melville has given "a most unjust and wanton fling at the South, in compliance with the stereotyped prejudices of his own region."[5] Given this kind of sensitivity to the South's King Charles's head, Simms' Southern silence seems suggestive when *Benito Cereno* with its tale of a slave revolt is considered. Of course there is the silence of ignorance: there is also, however, the silence of suppression and repression. As de Tocqueville wrote

> The more or less distant but inevitable danger of a conflict between the blacks and whites of the South of the Union is a nightmare constantly haunting the American imagination. The northerners make it a common topic of conversation, though they have nothing directly to fear from it. . . . In the southern states there is silence; one does not speak of the future before strangers; one avoids discussing it with one's friends; each man, so to say, hides it from himself. There is something more frightening about the silence of the South than about the North's noisy fears. (*Democracy in America*, Vol. I, Ch. X)

There is also the assertion which implies its own negation—as Russell of *The Times* noted a quarter of a century later:

> There is something suspicious in the constant never ending statement that "we are not afraid of our slaves." The curfew and the night patrol in the streets, the prisons and the watch-houses, and the police regulations, prove that strict supervision, at all events, is needed and necessary.[6]

The fear may not be spoken to the stranger—but it is articulated and inscribed in the institutions of the state and thus available for interpretation by the perceptive outsider.

III

I speculate that Southern silence here implies assent to the picture that Melville among others draws of smiling black masks behind which revolt lurks (either potentially or in actuality)—and that Melville permits and even intends such a reading. Melville names the slave ship San Dominick. To read San Dominick → Santo Domingo → slave revolt is a clue that the South would have no trouble in deciphering. I add one example to the already large amount of evidence but that from a particularly authoritative source: Mary Chesnut's Civil War diary—authoritative largely because it *is* a diary, a private voice which can confess to itself that which cannot always be publicly said. She interpolates the following comment in her more general commentary on the "representative" murder of Betsy Witherspoon by her slaves: "Mrs Chesnut [her insufferably saintly mother-in-law], who is [the slaves'] good angel, is and always has been afraid of negroes. In her youth the St. Domingo stories were indelibly printed on her mind" (211).[7] Nor would the South as Karcher shows in drawing on Taylor's work in *Cavalier and Yankee*, have had any trouble in reading Cereno as a variant of the cavalier: the Southern Hamlet figure. I insist that we must agree with Kaplan that there is nothing to forbid and everything to encourage a Southern planter of the 1850s from reading *Benito Cereno* with one hand even if—especially if—there is a pistol in the other and from having his fears not merely confirmed but reinforced. As James Stirling wrote of the insurrection panic of 1856: "Even at this moment the planter lays himself to bed with pistols under his pillow, never knowing when the wild whoop of insurrection may awaken him to a bloody fight."[8] The only serious omission from the repertory are rape fantasies—perhaps as a concession to the large female audience for the magazines though *Benito Cereno* is equally if differently discomforting for the Southern woman. As so often, Mary Chesnut puts her finger on the sore spot:

Mrs Witherspoon was a saint on this earth. And this is her reward.

Kate's maid came in—a strongly built mulatto woman. She was dragging in a mattress. "Missis, I have brought my bed to sleep in your room while Mars David is at Society Hill. You ought not to stay in a room by yourself *these times*." . . .

"For the life of me," said Kate gravely, "I cannot make up my mind. Does she mean to take care of me—or to murder me?" I do not think she heard, but when she came back she said, "Missis, as I have a soul to be saved, I will keep you safe. I will guard you."

We know Betsy well. Has she soul enough to swear by? She is a great, stout, jolly, irresponsible, *unreliable*, pleasant-tempered, bad-behaved woman with ever so many good points. Among others, she is so clever she can do anything. And she never loses her temper—but she has no moral sense whatever.

That night Kate came into my room. She could not sleep. Those black hands strangling and smothering Mrs Witherspoon's gray head under the counterpane haunted her. (199).

Cereno, of course, thought of himself if not as a saint then as not only "innocent" but as "the most pitiable of all men"—yet (perhaps correctly!) Delano's "last act was to clutch" at him "for a monster" (754). It is precisely in his appeal to this set of Southern fears of definition by others as well as the fear of violence that Melville is at his most perceptive and subtly subversive. The story that Mary Chesnut broods over has representative significance for her and helps us to see that *Benito Cereno* is more than a narrative of a unique, odd occurrence. It is not just the threat of death—but that Betsy Witherspoon's death was, however clumsily, designed to make it look as though she had died naturally. And

> How about Mrs Cunningham? He was an old bachelor, and the negroes had it all their own way till he married. And then they hated her. They took her from her room, just over one in which her son-in-law and her daughter slept. They smothered her, dressed her, and carried her out—all without the slightest noise—and hung her by the neck to an apple tree, as if she had committed suicide. Waked nobody in the house by all this. If they want to kill us, they can do it when they please—they are as noiseless as panthers. (211)

That murder made her feel "that the ground is cut away from under my feet. Why would they treat me any better than Betsy Witherspoon?" (198). Why indeed? Yet I'd hazard that a woman would not read *Benito Cereno* as a Southern patriarch would: the more she identifies herself as a slave, as a powerless possession, the less likely she is to conceive of a *general* insurrection but the more likely to think in terms of individual acts of (however violent) domestic rebellion. And there is always the comfort of "it wouldn't happen to *me*":

> We ought to be grateful that any one of us is alive. But nobody is afraid of their own negroes. These are horrid brutes—savages, monsters—but I find everyone like myself, ready to trust their own yard. I would go down on the plantation tomorrow and stay there, if there were no white person in twenty miles. My Molly and half a dozen others that *I know*—and all the rest I believe—would keep me as safe as I should be in the Tower of London. (211–212)

Of course it is traitors (often under a sentence of death) who are kept in the Tower . . . But one takes (doesn't one?) Mrs Chesnut's point.

IV

The lapidary formulation of the contradictions within the ideology of slavery in the passage that serves as my first epigraph (spoken, significantly, in an almost amused tone by a man with Mary Chesnut responding in a more extreme manner) points very nicely to its lack of intellectual coherence. As much as anything, its parts seem to be held together by an act of the will— an act made easier by reaction to external pressure. Overtly to attack such a mentality may be self-defeating. We usually have excellent defences against our open and constant opponents—especially if the ways we get our money are attacked. (And if attack is among the best forms of defence, the South deployed that strategy too in its critique of laissez-faire capitalism and wage-slavery). Stanley Elkins (whatever criticisms can be made of his Sambo thesis) makes the points well:

> What the abolitionist blasts of Garrison and the others could then do, and did with peculiar effectiveness, was to bring . . . consensus to an acute pitch of self-awareness . . . [T]he fact that the abolitionists were virtually all North-erners—could hardly have been better suited for a general mobilization of sectional patriotism . . . And so it would be with the most humane and sensitive planter . . . ; such a man was just as much Garrison's target as was the most brutal slave-beater in Mississippi. Be he ever so ridden with doubts about the morality and justice of slavery, the fanatics of New England seemed to leave him little choice . . . [H]e might simply discharge his sense of guilt by turning upon his tormentors.

> Only in such a setting of nightmare does its seem plausible . . . that one of the most non-intellectual of paradoxes should have developed in men's writing and talk regarding the Negro slave and his present and hypothetical behaviour. On the one hand, the ideal picture of Southern life was one of contentment, of plantations teeming with faithful and happy black children young and old—helpless, purposeless children incapable of sustained and unsupervised initiative. On the other hand was the picture of doom; the hint of freedom, whispered by designing abolitionists, would galvanize the sleeping monster in every slave, arouse bloody revolts, and bring hordes of black primitives bent on murder and destruction.[9]

That mass insurrection was unlikely makes its imagining the more insignificant: the *fear* was real—even if it was a way of externalizing guilt and justifying oppression. *Benito Cereno* speaks to these fears—and plays on them. Fear of poison was a common Southern fantasy. Mary Chesnut's mother-in-law responded to Betsy Witherspoon's murder by suspecting that her soup was poisoned: Dr. Keitt had his throat cut by his slaves because he accused them of poisoning his when they were without his knowledge giving him medicine—or so the story went (218). The mulatto was a constant reproach, taking the image of the patriarch and the extended family a little too far, a little too literally. Mary Chesnut suspected her patriarchal father-in-law of only being able to number his legitimate issue. Melville put it this way: "the mulatto steward . . . was of the first band of revolters . . . [H]e, just before a repast . . . proposed . . . poisoning a dish for the generous Captain

Amasa Delano" (749). Fear of the literate black slave was such that Fanny Kemble could write as follows:

> I must tell you that I have been delighted, surprised, and at the very least perplexed, by the sudden petition on the part of our young waiter, Aleck, that I will teach him to read . . . I told him I would think about it. I mean to do it. I will do it; and yet, it is simply breaking the laws of the government under which I am living. Unrighteous laws are made to be broken—*perhaps*—but then, you see, I am a woman, and Mr. [Butler] stands between me and the penalty. If I were a man, I would do that and many a thing besides, and doubtless should be shot some fine day from behind a tree by some good neighbor, who would do the community a service by quietly getting rid of a mischievous incendiary; and I promise you, in such a case, no questions would be asked, and my lessons would come to a speedy and silent end; but teaching slaves to read is a finable offense, and I am *femme couverte*, and my fines must be paid by my legal owner, and the first offense of the sort is heavily fined, and the second more heavily fined, and for the third, one is sent to prison. What a pity it is I can't begin with Aleck's third lesson, because going to prison can't be done by proxy, and that penalty would light upon the right shoulders! I certainly won't tell Mr. [Butler] anything about it. I'll leave him to find it out, as slaves, and servants, and children, and all oppressed, and ignorant, and uneducated, and unprincipled people do; then, if he forbids me, I can stop—perhaps before then the lad may have learned his letters.[10]

Babo does not only "understand well the Spanish." He writes it well enough too: "the negro Babo was he who traced the inscription below" the skeleton of Aranda—"chalky comment on the chalked words below, '*Follow your leader*' " (749, 734).

Whether it was cannibalism or not that produces Aranda's whiter than white bones in a mere three days, the reader has to speculate on what horror would reduce Cereno to silence: "Yau was the man who . . . willingly prepared the skeleton of Don Alexandro, in a way the negroes afterwards told the deponent, but which he, so long as reason is left him, can never divulge" (749). What the Southern reader has to *exclude* if he accepts such a narrative is the illusion of paternalism, of the happy stupid blacks sincerely singing as they joyfully toil on board ship or in the cotton fields. The fuller the assent to this reading, the heavier is the price. The fantasy of the Southerner's virtue may be sustainable (as Cereno continues to believe in his own innocence) but his—or her—confidence in his (or her) black slaves' assent to that self-definition, in their own security cannot be. (Before the news of the sainted Betsy Witherspoon's death, Mrs. Chesnut "had never thought of being afraid of negroes. I had never injured any of them. Why should they want to hurt me?" (199). Babo loses any chance for his own freedom because of his hatred of his white master: "Captain Delano saw the *freed* hand" of the slave "aiming with a . . . dagger at the heart of his master, his countenance lividly vindictive, expressing the centred *purpose of his soul"* (734; my emphases). If hatred even to the point of self-destruction is more important to the blacks than freedom, then the whites are in deep trouble. To agree with this reading of the Negro is to limit belief in the usefulness of one's benevolence, in the existence of loyalty or gratitude, and thus increases oppression, unmasks by unbalancing the ideology—and thus makes conflict and rebellion more likely.

V

Melville repeatedly rages in his letters against the multiple constraints on full, sincere, public utterance. "What a madness and anguish it is, that an author can never—under no conceivable circumstances—be at all frank with his readers" is a typical cry. And in a letter to Hawthorne in which he speaks of his "ruthless democracy" which leads him "boldly" to declare "that a thief in jail is as honorable a personage as Gen. George Washington," he makes the famous statement: "Dollars damn me . . . What I feel most moved to write, that is damned." Connected with this is his sense of the *powerlessness* of (his) writing: "what influence have authors to bring upon any question whose settlement must necessarily have a political form?—They can bring scarcely any influence whatever."[11] (Perhaps it is partly this sense that accounts for Melville's fascination with the legal language of Cereno's evidence: here is a language that does, frighteningly, have effect, that can speak—and enact—"capital sentences" [739]). When, with *Pierre*, Melville did risk an (ambiguous) direct challenge, the response was recognition of the threat— followed by rejection, repression and repudiation:

> Mr Melville has done a very serious thing, a thing which even unsoundness of intellect could not excuse. He might have been mad to the very pinnacle of insanity; he might have torn our poor language into tatters, and made from the shreds a harlequin suit in which to play his tricks; . . . he might have done all this and a great deal more and we should not have complained. But when he dares to outrage every principle of virtue; when he strikes with an impious, though, happily, weak hand at the very foundation of society, we feel it our duty to tear off the veil with which he has thought to soften the hideous features of the idea, and warn the public against the reception of such atrocious doctrines. If Mr Melville had reflected at all . . . when he was writing this book, his better sense would perhaps have informed him that there are certain ideas so repulsive to the general mind that they themselves are not alone kept out of sight, but by a fit ordination of society, everything that might be supposed to even collaterally suggest them is carefully shrouded in a decorous darkness. Nor has any man the right, in his morbid craving after originality, to strip these horrors of their decent mystery. But the subject which Mr Melville has taken upon himself to handle is one of no ordinary

depravity; and however he may endeavour to gloss the idea over with a platonic polish, no matter how energetically he strives to wrap the mystery in a cloud of high-sounding but meaningless words, the main conception remains unaltered in all its moral deformity. We trust we have said enough on this topic.

The reviewer has set himself a nice problem: how is one to discuss a subject one insists is not supposed to be discussed? What, of course, the reviewer is succeeding in not saying at great length is—INCEST (though this must have all been rather bewildering if intriguing for someone who had not read the book). And, of course, he had not said enough on the topic. He could not resist giving the cultured a clue: "We have already dismissed the immorality of Mr. Melville's book, which is as horrible in its tendency as Shelley's *Cenci.*" (Perhaps fortunately he did not remember Shelley writing "Incest, though a very improper, is a very poetical subject"). He was not alone in using that radical atheistical Shelley or those suspicious Italians as ways of saying the unsayable:

> We wish we could close here, but we regret to add that in several places the ambiguities are still further thickened by hints at that fearfullest of all human crimes, which one shrinks from naming, but to which the narrative alludes when it brings some of its personages face to face with a copy of the Cenci portrait.[12]

How is a society to be attacked or even analyzed when it is so defensive and so fiercely defended—and how is the writer to continue to get published and paid? This is so often the problem for the radical but professional writer in a market economy. One mark of his or her "success" in challenging the dominant mores may be, ironically, precisely the failure to market one's goods successfully:

> my only desire for [*Redburn*'s and *White-Jacket*'s] "success" (as it is called) springs from my pocket, and not from my heart. So far as I am individually concerned, and independent of my pocket, it is my earnest desire to write those sort of books which are said to fail. (L.92)

This was written to his father-in-law, Judge Lemuel Shaw, in 1849 with some amount of wordly success behind Melville. After *Moby-Dick* and *Pierre*, he certainly had his wish fulfilled—and had to reconsider whether he really meant what he had told that enforcer of the fugitive slave law.

The short fiction of the 1850s shows Melville trying out different tactics by giving a critical perspective on many of the central institutions of power of the day (the law, the church, industrialism, the home, etc.)—but that criticism is there mediated through indirection and irony. When Melville's protective irony slipped as it did in "The Two Temples," the story was rejected by the editor, Briggs: "My editorial experience compels me to be very cautious in offending the religious sensibilities of the public, and the moral of the Two Temples would array against us the whole power of the pulpit."[13] The destruction of confidence in these institutions is attempted through a series of confidence tricks. The strategy that informs these stories—and especially *Benito Cereno*—is, I suggest that of the consciously weak. And here it is useful to look at the work of Ralph Waldo Ellison (who took one of his epigraphs for *Invisible Man* from *Benito Cereno*) and who writes so perceptively about the defences and weapons of the powerless. In "Change the Joke and Slip the Yoke," an essay which has some profoundly interesting things to say about masks, the national identity, history and race, he comments on the grandfather of the narrator who is the *Invisible Man*, that he was

> a weak man who knows the nature of the oppressor's weakness. There is a good deal of spite in the old man . . . and the strategy he advises is a kind of jiujitsu . . . , a denial and rejection through agreement . . . Thus his mask of meekness conceals the wisdom of saying the "yes" which accomplishes the "no."[14]

If, in *Benito Cereno*, Melville does not say of slavery "NO! in thunder," as he claimed Hawthorne spoke in *The House of the Seven Gables* of life in general, he subversively allows "the Devil himself" to make himself say a slave's lying "*yes*"—and uses jiujitsu to allow the white supporter of the slavocracy to pull himself off balance in his agreement. Here is the answer to Kaplan: Melville has, as he said himself of *Moby-Dick*, "written a wicked book" and can legitimately feel as "spotless as the lamb" (L. 125, 142).[15]

The more the Southern reader accepts Melville's picture of the blacks— that the smiles of servitude are or may be masks and that one cannot tell the difference—the more unstable his world picture becomes and the more destabilizing Melville's seeming assent to the dark part of that divided world picture. The more convincing, the more "realistic" *Benito Cereno* is felt to be, I'd suggest, the more the Southerner has to abandon his reassuring if illusory vision of a happy, stable patriarchy. Does not Melville's strategy correspond to the grandfather's advice to "agree 'em to death and destruction"? Of course this story can only be a nudge in the direction the South was moving. "Hell," as the invisible man says late on in the novel, musing on the enigmatic words of the ex-slave, self-declared spy and traitor (unrecognized as such even by his own family), "weren't they their own death and destruction?"[16] As Melville recognized in the prose supplement to *Battle-Pieces*, that strange body of work by a poetic war-correspondent who never saw a battle, "emancipation was accomplished not through deliberate legislation; only through agonized violence could so mighty a result be effected."[17] But it was a nudge in the right direction—or at least in the direction that some perceptive observers felt history to be moving. Stirling's comments on the white fears of black insurrection are relevant:

> The remedy proposed for this state of things is repression, severity; ever more severity. This will not do. Statesmen have yet to learn the law of social dynamics, that compression only increases the explosive force of disaffection. Terrorism does not pacify a people. It only changes complaint into conspiracy.

He points (optimistically?) to a nice irony: "the slave-owner is himself the prime agent in arousing slave insubordination." By a "striking retribution, the passions of men are made to recoil upon themselves: the slave-owner is made the chief of the Abolitionists" (301, 297, 298). The slave-owner's increasing repression—increased by his fear of insurrection—may, then, be a hopeful sign—whether because repression (as Stirling argues) produces ever more forceful opposition or because that oppression will generate external (Northern) insistence that this "national sin" be extinguished. This argument may seem unhappily close to that of some radicals in the 1960s—that one must force the state to unmask, to declare its naked power—and if a few people get their heads bashed in by the pigs, that's just too bad: they will have been radicalized and the state will have declared its real, violent nature. However, "repressive tolerance" is hardly a relevant concept for the South of the 1850s. The various violences of slavery were only too apparent.

To refrain from denouncing an iniquity is difficult: moral indignation is so satisfying and irony makes one liable to be misunderstood. My argument is that Kaplan has misunderstood Melville, that Melville has, in *Benito Cereno*, put into brilliant practice advice he gave himself in *White-Jacket* (Ch. XXXV): "It is next to idle, at the present day, merely to denounce an iniquity. Be ours, then, a different task." And if he had consulted his *Webster's Dictionary* with its "accurate and discriminating definitions" (title page), Melville would have been reminded that iniquity derives from in-equity (and wickedness thus connected to inequality)—and that the first definition reads like this: "Injustice, unrighteousness; a deviation from rectitude; as, . . . the iniquity of the slave trade."

POSTSCRIPT

Isn't this then to exclude the Northern liberal?—it may be asked. By no means—though that is not another story but rather the subject for another, expanded, reading which would begin by suggesting that *Benito Cereno* asks the Northern liberal to stop his or her knee-jerk liberalism and to consider just how and why slavery is wrong—an argument which might begin from consideration of this passage from *White-Jacket* (Ch. XXXVI).

> It is to no purpose that you apologetically appeal to . . . general depravity . . . Depravity in the oppressed is no apology for the oppressor; but rather an additional stigma to him, as being, in a large degree, the effect and not the cause and justification of oppression.

Equiano's deeply felt perception: "When you make men slaves you deprive them of half their virtue, you set them in your own conduct an example of fraud, rapine, and cruelty, and compel them to live with you in a state of war." It might note the authority that Equiano fascinatingly attaches to writing and literacy:

> I had often seen my master and Dick employed in reading, and I had a great curiosity to talk to the books as I thought they did, and so to learn how all things had a beginning: for that purpose I have often taken up a book and have talked to it and then put my ears to it, when alone, in hopes it would answer me; and I have been very much concerned when I found it remained silent.

And it might continue by suggesting that *Benito Cereno* is a dramatization of the perception enunciated by T.W. Higginson—about the dangers of one way of writing about black slaves:

> It bewilders all the relations of human responsibility, if we expect the insurrectionary slave to commit no outrages; if slavery has not depraved him, it has done him little harm. If it be the normal tendency of bondage to produce saints like Uncle Tom, let us all offer ourselves at auction immediately.[18]

Notes

1. C. Van Woodward (ed.), *Mary Chesnut's Civil War*, New Haven and London: Yale University Press, 1981, p. 198.

Herman Melville, *Pierre, Israel Potter, The Piazza Tales, The Confidence-Man, Uncollected Prose, Billy Budd, Sailor*, New York: Library of America, 1984, pp. 742, 755.

All subsequent references to both editions will be placed parenthetically in the text. I am grateful to Ian Bell and Martin Crawford of the Keele American Studies Department for their help.

2. Sidney Kaplan, "Herman Melville and the American National Sin: The Meaning of *Benito Cereno*," *Journal of Negro History*, XLI, October 1956, pp. 311–338, and XLII, January, 1957, pp. 11–37, pp. 12, 24, 28.

3. Marvin Fisher, *Going Under: Melville's Short Fiction and the American 1850s*, Baton Rouge and London: Louisiana State University Press, 1977, pp. 104–117.

Carolyn L. Karcher, *Shadow Over The Promised Land: Slavery, Race, and Violence in Melville's America*, Same publisher, 1980, *passim*.

4. William R. Taylor, *Cavalier and Yankee: The Old South and American National Character*, New York: George Braziller, 1961, p. 307.

5. Perry Miller, *The Raven and the Whale: The War of Words and Wits in the Era of Poe*

and Melville, New York: Harcourt Brace and World, 1956, pp. 319, 322. C. Karcher, *op. cit.*, pp. 18, 45–46.

6. William Howard Russell, *My Diary North and South*, London: 1863, 2 Vols.

7. I know that Mary Chesnut revised her diary heavily and may well have had plans for publication. But the fact that she did not publish it—even though 20 years had elapsed—is suggestive.

8. James Stirling, *Letters from the Slaves States*, London: John W. Parker and Son, 1857, p. 59. Subsequent references will appear parenthetically in the text.

9. Stanley M. Elkins, *Slavery: A Problem in American Institutional and Intellectual Life*, Chicago: Chicago University Press, 1959, pp. 217, 221.

10. Frances Anne Kemble, *Journal of a Residence on a Georgian Plantation in 1838–1839*, London: Jonathan Cape, 1961, pp. 271–2. Edited and with the Introduction by John A. Scott and first published in 1863. Perhaps a later statement is also relevant: "I know that the Southern men are apt to deny the fact that they do live under an habitual sense of danger; but a slave population, coerced into obedience, though unarmed and half-fed, *is* a threatening source of constant insecurity, and every Southern *woman* to who I have spoken on the subject has admitted to me that they live in terror of their slaves," p. 342.

11. Merrell R. Davis and William H. Gilman, eds., *The Letters of Herman Melville*, New Haven: Yale University Press, 1960, pp. 96, 128, 134. Subsequent references will appear parenthetically in the text.

12. Watson G. Branch, ed., *Melville: The Critical Heritage*, London and Boston: Routledge and Kegan Paul, 1974, pp. 317, 299. It is only fair to note that at least one critic did have the courage to use That Word: "We cannot pass without remark, the supersensuousness with which the holy relations of the family are described. Mother and son, brother and sister are sacred facts not to be disturbed by any sacrilegious speculations. Mrs Glendenning and Pierre, mother and son, call each other brother and sister, and are described with all the coquetry of a lover and mistress. And again, in what we have termed the supersensuousness of description, the horrors of an incestuous relation between Pierre and Isabel seem to be vaguely hinted at." This was, however, by Evert or George Duyckinck—self-defined "Rabelaisians": nice to know how respectable those "Rabelaisian" friends are—at bottom.

13. Perry Miller, *op. cit.*, p. 319.

14. R. W. Ellison, *Shadow and Act*, New York: Vintage Books, 1972, p. 56.

15. The letters to Hawthorne are justly famous. Melville clearly felt that (for however short a time) here was someone to whom he could fully open his mind and heart. But what is odd about them is Melville's frequent use of a very public tone of voice in what are very clearly very private letters. The letter on *The House of the Seven Gables* is a good example (pp. 123–5). That tension between public statement and private context is a fascinating example of the problems of voice and audience. He ends the letter "What's the reason, Mr. Hawthorne, that in the last stages of metaphysics a fellow always falls to *swearing* so? I could rip an hour. You see, I began with a little criticism extracted for your benefit from the 'Pittsfield Secret Review,' and here I have landed in Africa." It is hard to believe that Melville could not have found public space for this private utterance—if he had been willing to delete two or three sentences. His reluctance to speak in his own voice in his published writings is striking. As we have seen, even "Hawthorne and His Mosses" is by "A Virginian"—a Virginian who tells us that "the names of all fine authors are fictitious ones."

16. R. W. Ellison, *Invisible Man*, Harmondsworth, Middlesex: Penguin, 1965, pp. 17, 463.

17. Howard P. Vincent, ed., *Collected Poems of Herman Melville*, Chicago: Hendricks House, 1947, p. 465.

18. I have tried to do something along these lines in "Whodunnit? Or Who did What? *Benito Cereno* and the politics of Narrative Structures" in *American Studies in Transition*, edited by David Nye & Christen Thomsen, Odense University Press, 1985, pp. 199–234.

"Follow Your Leader": The Theme of Cannibalism in Melville's "Benito Cereno"

STERLING STUCKEY

"Master told me never mind where he was or how engaged, always to remind him, to a minute, when shaving time comes. Miguel has gone to strike the half-hour afternoon. It is *now* master. Will master go into the cuddy?"

Melville, "Benito Cereno"

The solution to the problem of cannibalism in "Benito Cereno" involves concerns that are at the heart of the novella. Since that problem, represented by Alexandro Aranda's skeleton, shadows the work as a whole, it is not surprising that its solution has implications for aspects of the work that have received little or no critical attention to date. In other words, aspects of the novella that once seemed essential to the brilliance of its crafting but with little or no relationship to Melville criticism will be shown to be deeply related to that criticism.

Though final resolutions are difficult to argue in a work of such complexity, one can argue that of all problems before "Benito Cereno" critics none quite compares—as an artistic construct—with that of Aranda's skeleton. It is a great mystery to be unraveled and only a few scholars have attempted to begin the process. This overall reluctance probably has much to do with critics, until recently, having overwhelmingly viewed blacks in "Benito Cereno" as so evil and savage that it was enough merely to conclude that Aranda's body was cannibalized. Carolyn Karcher is incisive in this regard, arguing that Melville offers "innuendo which we are left to flesh out in accordance with our most primitive fears and fantasies."[1] Considering the place of Africans in the American mind, those fears and fantasies, as Melville must surely have anticipated, would encourage most readers to conclude that Africans cannibalized Aranda. But given the fiercely ironic nature of "Benito Cereno," in which Melville continually reveals new means of ensnaring us with his magic, we should be suspicious of our tendency to confuse our conclusions with his. In addition, he was at home in cultures radically different from our own, the provincial as distasteful to him as assumptions

This essay was written specifically for this volume and is published here for the first time by permission of the author.

of white superiority: "I walk a world that is mine; and enter many nations, as Mungo Park rested in African cots."[2]

That Africans practiced cannibalism on the *San Dominick* has been suggested by Sidney Kaplan, a distinguished critic especially noted for his enlightened stance on matters of race. More than forty years ago, Kaplan wrote that Melville adds "a strong hint that Aranda's body has been cannibalistically prepared," that the hint of cannibalism is additional evidence of Melville's being anti-black in the novella.[3] To be sure, it is largely due to Kaplan that, over the past fifteen years, critics finally began to address this problem in Melville criticism.

John Harmon McElroy's "Cannibalism in Melville's Benito Cereno" affirms Kaplan's thesis regarding Aranda's body having been cannibalized without affirming Kaplan's conclusion that Melville is anti-black in the novella. He argues that Babo ordered a ritualistic act of cannibalism on board the *San Dominick*, an act that is "passed over silently within the narrative but is hinted at consistently. This feature of controlled omission makes "Benito Cereno" one of Melville's most unusual and most brilliant performances."[4] But cannibalism is not silently passed over in the narrative. It is expressed so subtly that, as is so often the case with "Benito Cereno," one can easily miss it, which is an even greater measure of Melville's skill.

In a more recent attempt to demonstrate ritualized cannibalism in the novella, Barbara J. Baines argues that Babo ordered an unsuspecting Don Benito Cereno, thinking he is eating food, to cannibalize Aranda. Thus, the Spanish captain, she writes, joined the blacks in malevolent communion. For Baines, Babo is evil personified, more intent on revenge than on being free of enslavement. Her whole elaborate case stands or falls on her certitude that the Africans prepared Aranda's body as a symbol of terror by cannibalizing it, and she advances this thesis despite her conclusion, in line with McElroy, that there is no "concrete evidence for [cannibalism] in the text."[5]

The symbol of Aranda's skeleton is so consistently and dramatically invoked that an analysis of the means by which Melville created it should lead to reconsideration of the work as a whole. This is so because the skeleton fuses past, present, and future for whites on the ship, darkly insinuating its influence as it hovers above the action from beginning to end. Moreover, the cultural matrix with which Melville associates it leads him to ingenious artistic experimentation in the novella.

The skeleton's relationship to epochal oppression is suggested by its substitution for the figurehead of Christopher Colon, discoverer of the New World. In addition, the ship itself is emblematic of declining spiritual and political authority, its eerie sounds and scenes creating a mood appropriate to what has transpired and, with Amasa Delano's presence, what will occur. Within view, as Delano boarded the slave ship, beneath the canvassed figurehead of Aranda, "was the sentence, '*Sequid vuestro jefe*' (follow your leader);"

while upon the tarnished headboards, nearby, appeared, in stately capitals, once gilt, the ship's name, SAN DOMINICK, each letter streakingly corroded with tricklings of copper-spike rust; while, like mourning weeds, dark festoons of sea-grass slimily swept to and fro over the name, with every hearse-like roll of the hull.[6]

If Delano saw the legend beneath the canvassed covering, he does not indicate as much—another instance of Babo's having calculated correctly in risking the presence of the American on the ship.

Aranda, the slaveowner, was killed because otherwise the slaves would not be free, also because the whites needed

a warning of what road they should be made to take did they or any of them oppose [Babo]; and . . . by means of the death of Don Alexandro, that warning would best be given. . . . (293)

It will be recalled that Babo assigns the task of dispatching and handling the body of Aranda to Ashantee men on the ship, Melville writing that "Babo commanded the Ashantee Martinique and the Ashantee Lecbe to go to commit the murder. . . . [T]hose two went down with hatchets to the berth of Don Alexandro." Aranda, brought half-dead to the deck, was finished off on orders from Babo but was not thrown overboard. Rather, on orders from Babo, "the body was carried below . . . nothing more was seen of it by the deponent for three days" (293). It was, naturally, a matter of concern to Benito Cereno that Aranda's remains were taken below, concern that was heightened since others killed by the Africans were thrown overboard. Over the three-day period Don Benito, on numerous occasions, asked Babo "where they were, and, if still on board, whether they were to be preserved for interment ashore, entreating him so to order it" (294). But Babo, on the fourth day, as Benito Cereno came on deck at sunrise,

showed him a skeleton, which had been substituted for the ship's proper figure-head—the image of Christopher Colon, the discoverer of the New World; that the negro Babo asked him whose skeleton that was, and whether, from its whiteness, he should not think it was a white's; that upon discovering his face, the negro Babo, coming close, said words to this effect: "Keep faith with the blacks from here to Senegal, or you shall in spirit, as now in body, follow your leader," pointing to the prow. (294–95)

By succession Babo took each Spaniard forward and asked "whose skeleton that was, and whether, from its whiteness," it was not that of a white. And each of the Spaniards, on seeing Aranda's remains, "covered his face." And each was warned that if an attempt were made to plot against the Africans, "they should, soul and body, go the way of Don Alexandro . . . a torment which was repeated everyday" (295). To reinforce the threat, Babo left Aranda's skeleton uncovered on the bow until Amasa Delano, the American captain, was spotted in the distance and it was thought strangers might board, at which point canvas was placed over it, as for repairs. It was then that the unsettling inscription was written beneath it.

On hearing of the departed Aranda, Delano was led to conjecture what gave "the keener edge" to the Spaniard's grief, explaining that it was once his sad fortune to lose his brother at sea. He then vowed never to voyage again with one he loved "unless, unbeknown to him, I had provided every requisite, in case of a fatality, for embalming his mortal part for interment on shore" (235). The following exchange then took place:

> "Were your friend's remains now on board this ship, Don Benito, not thus strangely would the mention of his name affect you."
> "On board this ship?" echoed the Spaniard. Then, with horrified gestures, as directed against some specter, he unconsciously fell into the ready arms of his attendant, who, with a silent appeal toward Captain Delano, seemed beseeching him not again to broach a theme so unspeakably distressing to his master. (235–36)

Delano missed his one opportunity to discover that the canvas over the bow had concealed Aranda's remains. A stark unveiling of the figurehead occurred after he hailed the *Bachelor's Delight* and ordered the ports up and the guns run out to fire on the fleeing *San Dominick*. By this time, the cable of the fugitive vessel had been cut "and the fag-end, in lashing out, whipped away the canvas shroud about the beak, suddenly revealing, as the bleached hull swung round toward the open ocean, death for the figure-head in a human skeleton; chalky comment on the chalked words below, 'Follow Your Leader.' " This sight caused Benito Cereno to cover his face and to wail out "Tis he, Aranda! My murdered, unburied friend!" (284).

The last view of the figurehead, an eerie one, is offered just before crewmen from the *Bachelor's Delight*, after long pursuit of the *San Dominick*, board the ship for the final battle with the Africans.

> With creaking masts, [the *San Dominick*] came heavily round to the wind; the prow slowly swinging into view of the boats, its skeleton gleaming in the horizontal moonlight, and casting a gigantic ribbed shadow upon the water. One extended arm of the ghost seemed beckoning the whites to avenge it. (287)

The reader will note that a single African, an Ashantee, "prepared the skeleton of Don Alexandro," that at no time other than when the skeleton was substituted for the figurehead of Christopher Colon does Melville associate more than one African with it. Only Ashantees, one alone and two together, are mentioned in relation to handling the skeleton. This must be kept in mind in weighing the significance of the following passage from the novella:

> Yau and Lecbe were the two who, in a calm by night, riveted the skeleton to the bow. . . . Yau was the man who, by Babo's command, willingly prepared the skeleton of Don Alexandro, in a way the negroes afterwards told the deponent, but which he, so long as reason is left him, can never divulge. (300–301)

Though there were many things that Benito Cereno could never divulge, what he was told about the preparation of Aranda's remains must in due course be seriously considered.

In his treatment of the women on board the *San Dominick*, Melville draws on Mungo Park. In a famous passage in the novella, he has Delano observe a group of them—they outnumbered slave men on the vessel—and think to himself that, "like most uncivilized women, they seem at once tender of heart and tough of constitution. . . . Ah! thought Captain Delano, these, perhaps, are some of the very women whom Ledyard saw in Africa, and gave such a noble account of." While it is not clear if these women are meant to be Ashantees, there is less doubt about the ethnicity of the women in the following passage: "Why see," reflects Delano, "the very women pull and sing, too. These must be some of those Ashantee negresses that make such capital soldiers, I've heard" (251, 275).

Interestingly, there is no mention of Ashantees in Delano's account of the revolt, nor are they mentioned in the depositions attached to Chapter XVIII of *Voyages*. It is likely that Melville detected an Ashantee presence on the *Tryal* from a single passage in the deposition submitted by Benito Cereno, though explicit reference to them is not made: "[T]he negresses of age, were knowing to the revolt, and influenced the death of their master. . . . They also used their influence to kill the deponent; that in the act of murder, and before that of the engagement of the ships they began to sing, and were singing a very melancholy song during the action, to excite the courage of the negroes" (341).[7]

It is likely that the reading of travel accounts about Africa led Melville to develop interest in Ashantee culture and customs. Without a grasp of Ashantee culture, it is doubtful that the reference to melancholy songs spurring Africans to greater valor could have been identified by Melville as an Ashantee practice, unless of course Melville had contact with Ashantees in the New World, which is certainly a possibility. In any event, his grasp of Ashantee culture led him to place Ashantees in key roles in the novella, as we know from the prominence of the hatchet polishers.[8]

There is reason to believe that an Ashantee king, who reigned in the early nineteenth century, was a source of inspiration for Melville's creation of important and related dimensions of "Benito Cereno" that are tied to the primary concern of this essay. Certain features of Benito Cereno's attire, though clearly South American, owed much to somewhat analogous ones worn by the king in question. The Spaniard, Melville writes, was dressed in "a loose Chili jacket of dark velvet"; moreover, he wore

> white small clothes and stockings, with silver buckles at the knee and instep; a high-crowned sombrero, of fine grass; a slender sword, silver mounted, hung from a knot in his sash—the last being an almost invariable adjunct of a South American gentlemen's dress to this hour. . . . [T]here was a certain precision in his attire curiously at variance with the unsightly disorder around. . . . (231)

Though the toilette of Don Benito was consonant with the fashion of the day for South Americans of his station, it was unusual for the setting—indeed, to the point of Don Benito's having the appearance of something of a buffoon. This Melville makes clear by remarking that, considering the nature of the voyage, "there seemed something so incongruous in the Spaniard's apparel, as almost to suggest the image of an invalid courtier tottering about London streets in the time of the plague" (232).

The Ashantee king about whom Melville read in T. Edward Bowdich's *Mission From Cape Coast Castle to Ashantee* was dressed as incongruously, considering his surroundings, as Don Benito Cereno, and therefore was said to have "walked abroad in great state one day, an irresistible caricature."[9] The description of the cloth from which his main outfit was made suggests that of Benito Cereno, as do certain other features of his attire and possession, for

> he had on an old fashioned court suit of General Daendels' of brown velveteen, richly embroidered with silver thistles, with an English epaulette sewn on each shoulder, the coat coming close to round the knees, from which the flaps of the waistcoat were not very distant, a cocked hat bound with gold lace, in shape just like that of a coachman's, white shoes, the long silver headed cane we presented to him, mounted with a crown, as a walking staff, and a small dirk around his waist. (Bowdich, 122)

That the dress of the king sparked Melville's imagination, leading him to have Babo dress Don Benito on that fateful day at sea, is the more evident when considering the remarkable shaving scene in the cuddy of the ship. At that time, Delano is so moved observing Babo, "napkin on arm, so debonair about his master, in a business so familiar as that of shaving, too," that "all his old weakness for negroes returned," a weakness retained despite a fleeting sense that Babo, "one hand elevating the razor, the other professionally dabbling among the bubbling suds on the Spaniard's lank neck"—might be a headsman, "the white man at the block" (265–66).

Shortly before that Delano was amused by a peculiar instance of African love of fine shows and bright colors—"in the black's informally taking from the flag-locker a great piece of bunting of all hues, and lavishly tucking it under his master's chin for an apron" (265). But when the agitation of the Spaniard so loosened the bunting around him, causing a broad fold to sweep like a curtain over the arm of the chair to the floor, there was revealed, "amid a profusion of armorial bars and ground-colors—black, blue, and yellow— a closed castle in a blood-red field diagonal with a lion rampant in a white." At this point Delano exclaimed: "The castle and the lion, why Don Benito, this is the flag of Spain you use here." True to form, he added: "It's well it's only I, and not the king, that sees this. . . . It's all one, I suppose, so the colors be gay," which playful remark "did not fail somewhat to tickle the Negro" (266).

Immediately thereafter, Babo remarked, "Now master . . . now master," as "the steel glanced nigh his throat." When Don Benito shuddered, Babo suggested that Delano resume his discussion "about the gale, and all that; master can hear, and between times, master can answer." But Delano focused on the period of alleged calm that followed the gales, noting that "had almost any other gentleman told me such a story I should have been half disposed to a little incredulity" (266–67). This remark brought over the Spaniard "an involuntary expression," and either the start Don Benito gave, or the sudden and gawky roll of the hull in the calm, or any unsteadiness of Babo's hand, "however it was, just then the razor drew blood. . . . No sword drawn before James the First of England, no assassination in that timid King's presence, could have produced a more terrified aspect than was now presented by Don Benito" (267).[10] Within seconds, however, Babo, with napkin in hand, encouraged Don Benito to answer Delano's question about the *San Dominick* being becalmed for two months, then proceeded to wipe the blood from the razor before stropping it again.

Almost finished, he worked with scissors, comb and brush. Clipping a wayward whisker, smoothing first one and then another curl, he gave "a graceful sweep to the temple-lock, with other impromptu touches evincing the hand of a master." As Don Benito sat "so pale and rigid . . . the negro seemed a Nubian sculptor finishing off a white statue-head." He then removed the Spanish flag from round the Spaniard and tossed it into the locker from which it was taken. And with his usual attention to detail, surveying Don Benito, he whisked a bit of lint from his velvet lapel. Delano's congratulations deepened Don Benito's distress, and "neither sweet waters, nor shampooing, nor fidelity, nor sociality, delighted the Spaniard," who relapsed into gloom (269).

Now that the barber chair scene has been called to mind, we can appreciate a passage from Bowdich's *Mission to Ashantee* that resonates remarkably with that scene. Bowdich writes of the Ashantee king:

The king sent a handsome procession of flags, guns, and music to conduct us to the palace on the occasion; and meeting us in the outer square, preceded us to the inmost, where about 300 females were seated, in all the magnificence which a profusion of gold and silk could furnish. The splendor of this coup d'oeil made our surprise almost equal to theirs. We were seated with the King and the deputies, under large umbrellas in the centre, and I was desired to declare the objects of the Embassy and the Treaty, to an old linguist, peculiar to the women. The King displayed the presents to them; the flags were all sewn together, and wrapped around him as a cloth. (Bowdich, 124)

Melville was under Ashantee influence in having Babo, in one of the great moments in world literature, use the flag of Spain as an apron, in the process lending a highly charged aura to Babo's interaction with whites around him. Indeed, the transfer of a custom from one culture to another to achieve a different objective is masterfully employed in "Benito Cereno." When he uses African culture as the source of such inspiration, Melville poses special problems for the critic because the deeper irony comes with knowledge of African cultural realities beneath surface appearances.

A variation on that theme occurs when Melville takes a European-made object, the walking staff that was used by the Ashantee king, out of an African setting and places it—more precisely, an object strikingly similar to it—on the *San Dominick*. Such a nuance refines highly ironic play, the means required to place the object on an oceangoing vessel constituting a further refinement. It is one that deflects the reader's thought away from Africa even as the Ashantee king and Benito Cereno are linked once more in the cuddy, a portion of which "had formerly been the quarters of officers; but since their death all the partitionings had been thrown down, and the whole interior converted into one spacious and airy marine hall. . . ." Then Melville's elegant solution to the problem of how to get the object on the ship, a solution that involves the suggestion of its presence without it actually being there, the ship's

absence of fine furniture and picturesque disarray of odd appurtenances, somewhat answering to the wide, cluttered hall of some eccentric bachelor-squire in the country, who hangs his shooting-jacquet and tobacco-pouch on deer antlers, and keeps his fishing-rod, tongs, and walking-stick in the same corner. (262)

"The similitude," Melville writes, "was heightened; if not originally suggested, by glimpses of the surrounding sea; since in one aspect, the country and the ocean seem cousins-german" (263).

In an extremely subtle stroke, Melville underscores the link between Benito Cereno and the Ashantee king. During the shaving scene in the cuddy, Delano noticed, as Babo brandished the razor, that there was something hollow in Don Benito's manner, that he and Babo, in view of their "whispered conferences," might be acting in collusion, but abandons the possibility "as a whimsy, insensibly, suggested, perhaps, by the theatrical aspect of Don Benito in his Harlequin ensign. . . ." Harlequin recalls King Herle, "the mythical figure, Harlequin ensign, *the king's flag* (268)."

But Don Benito was no king, except in the sense that, as Aranda's successor, he was a kind of king of slaveholders. As such, his was no mantle of authority but a cloth of shame—a means by which Babo insulted him and Delano, the former to further terrorize and strengthen control over him, the latter because he knew Delano would not understand. Babo's final touch seems to have been inspired, at least in part, but only in part, by the attire of the King, who wore a dirk round the waist. Melville writes that Benito Cereno's dress included a "silver-mounted sword, apparent symbol of despotic command," which "was not, indeed, a sword, but the ghost of one. The scabbard, artificially stiffened, was empty" (306).

After the blacks were subdued in a desperate struggle, a number of developments occurred that are related to the barber chair scene and, like it, to Aranda's skeleton. In fact, part of the reason Melville had Aranda's body shaved down was from consideration of them, especially from one that triggered others as in a chain reaction. In *Voyages*, Delano reports that when he boarded the *Tryal* "the next morning with handcuffs, leg-irons, and shackled bolts, to secure the hands and feet of the negroes," the sight presented to his view "was truly horrid."

> They had got all the men who were living made fast, hands and feet, to the ring bolts in the deck; some of them had part of their bowels hanging out, and some with half their backs and thighs shaved off. This was done with our boarding lances which were always kept exceedingly sharp, and as bright as a gentleman's sword.[12]

A development that contributed to Melville's creation of the shaving scene in the cuddy concerns Benito Cereno's behavior during this bloodletting. Don Benito, according to Delano's account in *Voyages*, "had a dirk, which he had secreted at the time the negroes were massacreing [sic] the Spaniards." But Delano did not notice Don Benito's attempt to use it until one of his sailors gave him "a twitch by the elbow," to draw his attention to what was occurring. It was then that he saw Don Benito in the act of stabbing one of the slaves." Such shavings were occurring elsewhere on the ship, one that brings to mind Babo, razor extended while dabbling at the suds on Benito Cereno's neck: A Spanish sailor, according to Delano, opened a razor and made a cut on a Negro's head, then "seemed to aim at his throat, and it bled shockingly." After exercising "great authority" over the Spanish crew to prevent them from cutting "these unfortunate beings . . . all to pieces," Delano writes that he put the mangled blacks "in irons" (Delano, 328).

On discovering what happened following the battle, Melville was reminded of the Battle of Preston Pans:

> Nearly a score of the Negroes were killed. Exclusive of those by the balls, many were mangled; their wounds—mostly inflicted by the long-edged sealing-spears, resembling those shaven ones of the English at Preston Pans, made by the poled scythes of the Highlanders. (288).

It can be argued that the shaving of Aranda's body down to its skeleton was a symbolic reflection of a white historical act, for Melville knew, through *Voyages*, of the shaving of Africans by the Spanish crew, just as he knew, through other sources, of the shaving of the English at Preston Pans by the Highlanders,[13] instances of shaving that he explicitly links. Both dovetailed with his decision to introduce the theme of cannibalism into the tale, and, as we shall see, he had good reason to raise it as an issue throughout the story.

Thus far it has been demonstrated, especially in Don Benito's attire and in the shaving scene in the cuddy, that Ashantee cultural influences figure significantly in *Benito Cereno*, but there is even more striking evidence of that presence in the novella. Just as Melville was able to link Benito Cereno to an Ashantee king, he was able to do the same for Aranda: Bowdich writes, astonishingly enough, that "The Kings, and Kings only, are buried in the cemetery at Batama, and the sacred gold with them . . . their bones are afterwards deposited in a building there." Moreover, when the Ashantee king dies, others must die: "Here human sacrifices are frequent and ordinary, to water the graves of kings" (Bowdich, 289).

Therein lies the key to the solution of the problem of cannibalism in "Benito Cereno," at least with respect to whether Africans were involved in such an act. The manner in which they prepared the bodies of their kings for burial involved the removal of the flesh from their remains until, in the end, only the skeleton was left. From this knowledge alone, that is, from what is revealed of the burial of kings by Bowdich, Melville had the essential elements of Ashantee burial practices with which to work, enough to fire his imagination.

It should be noted that the sacrifices were for the purpose of providing the King with attendants after death. In a reference to "such Funerals as those," Willem Bosman writes, in 1704, that "Slaves of the Deceased are killed and sacrificed on [the king's] account in order to serve him in the other world."[14] Melville almost certainly read Bosman, who is referred to by Bowdich.

It is reasonable to conclude, therefore, that Melville, in treating the preparation of Aranda's skeleton, based himself mainly on such sources together with the earlier instances of shaving to which reference was made. But he may well have, in addition, talked to Ashantees in the New World and discovered details of the preparation that, like those found in R. S. Rattray's *Religion and Art in Ashanti*, would seem so alien to the European mind that Benito Cereno might not want to recall or to divulge anything at all of the process. We know, for example, from Rattray, that before the king's body was stripped of its flesh and taken to the sacred mausoleum at Batama, referred to by Bowdich:

> The royal corpse was carried to "the place of drippings" by the court officer. . . . Here for eighty days and nights the body lay in a coffin, which rested on supports and was placed above a pit. The bottom of the coffin was perforated with holes. As decomposition set in, the liquids "dripped" through the holes into the pit. Attendants sat beside it day and night, fanning away flies, and sprinkling earth into the pit. On the eightieth day the corpse was removed, and the process of disintegration hastened by scraping the remaining flesh from the bones. . . .[15]

The evidence argues that Yau greatly telescoped this ancient rite, over three days shaving and scraping the flesh from Aranda, violating the usual procedure for preparing the bodies of kings for burial. A quite rich slaveholder, sort of a king without honor in Ashantee eyes, it was only natural that Aranda's body be used in carrying through the terror thought essential to the success of the revolt. Aranda's skeleton, therefore, is at once symbolic of white oppression and the desire of blacks to be free of it, an object of mockery and an instrument of terror.

Though Bowdich asserted that the grave of the king was watered by human sacrifices, what that means in Ashantee terms is treated in more detail by Rattray, who states, echoing Bosman, that "It was incumbent upon those left on earth to see that the king entered the spirit-world with a retinue befitting his high station" (Rattray, 106). The retinue included a certain number of the king's wives and servants, which probably accounts for the presence of "Follow Your Leader" beneath Aranda's skeleton.

The last chapter of *Voyages* reveals how cannibalism became a difficult source of inspiration for Melville. The passage in question concerns the family of Amasa Delano:

> His father, Samuel Delano, was, with his brother Amasa, in the military service, under George II. . . . Amasa was an officer in Roger's Rangers, a corps well known in those days. Though very young, he was much esteemed for his bravery and good conduct; and at the age of twenty was honored with a lieutenancy. He was with a party of rangers on an expedition near the Canada lines; which being led astray their guide was lost in the wilderness. They were obliged to separate and to hunt for food; and were compelled to eat an Indian

child which they met in the woods. They soon came to an Indian settlement, and they were massacred in a most horrid manner. The writer of this journal was named for this unfortunate uncle. (Delano, 580)

Delano appears to have had a happy childhood in Duxbury, Massachusetts. At no time were his memories of that period more reassuringly present than when his boat, *Rover*, was sighted shortly after an African elder had gotten him to yield the intricate knot that was thrown to him by a Spaniard. Though the African proceeded to jettison the knot without permission, seconds later, the sight of *Rover* "evoked a thousand trustful associations, which, contrasted with previous suspicions filled him not only with lightsome confidence, but somehow with half humorous self-reproaches at his former lack of it" (256).

Rover brought back reminders of his boyhood, including his reputation as an expert swimmer—"Jack of the Beach"—who could "dive into the water like a sea fowl sporting in its natural element," an image that brings to mind an important symbol of the novella, that of the white noddy (Delano, 580–81).[16] As Delano contemplates *Rover's* return, his thoughts waver between the trustful and the suspicious:

> I, little Jack of the Beach, that used to go berrying with Cousin Nat and the rest; I to be murdered here at the ends of the earth, onboard a haunted pirate ship by a horrible Spaniard? Too nonsensical to think of! Who would murder Amasa Delano? His conscience is clear. There is someone above, Fie, fie, Jack of the Beach! You are a child indeed; a child of the second childhood, old boy; you are beginning to dote and drule, I'm afraid. (256)

Thus, Delano moved, in a matter of minutes, from imagining Benito Cereno, lantern in hand, dodging around a grindstone below deck, sharpening a hatchet to use against him to reproving himself for such a thought: "Well, well, these long calms have a morbid effect on the mind I've often heard, though I never believed it before." And soon thereafter: "Ha! glancing towards the boat; there's *Rover*; a white bone in her mouth. A pretty big bone though, it seems to me.—What? Yes, she has fallen afoul of the tide-rip there" (256–57).

The only evidence of cannibalism in "Benito Cereno" is in that passage, and is drawn from the experience of Delano's uncle, Amasa Delano. His act of cannibalism was recalled in extraordinary form as Delano awaited his return to the *Bachelor's Delight*.

Though no Ashantee, Babo, in his genius, was at ease with Ashantee values and applied them skillfully as Africans on board the *San Dominick*, as they did on the *Tryal*, worked in concert in an attempt to free themselves. His ability to draw on the values of non-Senegalese Africans, in reality as in the novella, was not the least remarkable of his achievements. Ironically,

Melville has revealed, through the almost tangible presence of Babo in the novella—as distinct from his remote, Olympian stance in reality—the power of African culture and the degree to which it influenced him in shaping the novella. An indication of that power and influence is evident in the last scene:

> Some months after, dragged to the gibbet at the tail of a mule, the black met his voiceless end. The body was burned to ashes; but for many days, the head, that hive of subtlety, fixed on a pole in the Plaza, met, unabashed, the gaze of the whites; and across the Plaza looked towards St. Bartholomew's church, in whose vaults slept then, as now, the recovered bones of Aranda: and across the Rimac bridge looked towards the monastery, on Mount Agonia without; where, three months after being dismissed by the court, Benito Cereno, borne on the bier, did, indeed, follow his leader. (307)

Notes

1. Carolyn Karcher, *Shadow over The Promised Land: Slavery, Race and Violence in Melville's America* (Baton Rouge: Louisiana State University Press, 1980), 142. I thank the eminent Africanist Ray Kea for assisting me in locating Ashantee sources published prior to the appearance of "Benito Cereno." This essay is dedicated to the memory of my mother, the poet Elma Stuckey.

2. Herman Melville, *Mardi* (Evanston and Chicago: Northwestern University Press, and Newberry Library, 1970), 368. Originally published in 1849.

3. Sidney Kaplan, "Herman Melville and the American National Sin: The Meaning of *Benito Cereno*," *Journal of Negro History* 41 (1956): 287–301.

4. John Harmon McElroy, "Cannibalism in Melville's *Benito Cereno*," *Essays in Literature* (Spring 1974): 206–14.

5. Barbara J. Baines, "Ritualized Cannibalism in *Benito Cereno*: Melville's 'Black Letter' Texts," *ESQ* 30 (1984): 163, 166.

6. Herman Melville, "Benito Cereno," in *Billy Budd and Other Stories* (New York: Penguin, 1981), 220–21; hereafter cited in text.

7. The Ashantee nature of such singing is treated by Joshua Leslie and Sterling Stuckey in "The Death of Benito Cereno: A Reading of Herman Melville on Slavery," *The Journal of Negro History* (Winter 1982): 290.

8. The role of the hatchet polishers, in relation to the revolutionary order maintained on the *San Dominick* by the Africans, is explored by Leslie and Stuckey in "Benito Cereno," 287–301.

9. T. Edward Bowdich, *Mission From Cape Coast Castle to Ashantee* (London: Frank Cass & Co., 1966), 122. Originally published in 1819; hereafter cited in text.

10. When this occurred, Delano thought: "Poor fellow . . . so nervous he can't even bear the sight of barber's blood; and this unstrung, sick man, is it credible that I should have imagined he meant to spill all my blood, who can't endure the sight of one little drop of his own? Surely, you have been beside yourself this day. Tell it not when you get home, sappy Amasa" (267).

11. See *Webster's Third New International Dictionary* (Springfield, Massachusetts: Merriam-Webster, Inc., 1986), 755, 1034.

12. Amasa Delano, *A Narrative of Voyages and Travels in the Northern and Southern*

Hemispheres (New York: Praeger, 1970), 328. Originally published in 1817; hereafter cited in text. The leader of the men who suppressed the revolt acted in perfect solidarity with the slaveholder Aranda, in a sense becoming a poor man's successor to him. Melville writes: " 'Follow Your Leader!' cried the mate; and, one on each bow, the boats boarded. . . . Huddled upon the long-boat amid ships, the negresses raised a wailing chant, whose chorus was the clash of steel" (207).

13.   Leslie and Stuckey have written of the relationship between Delano's account of such butchery and the battle of Preston Pans. Their conclusions fit perfectly with those found in this essay. See Leslie and Stuckey, "Benito Cereno," 297.

14.   Willem Bosman, *A New and Accurate Description of the Coast of Guinea* (London: Frank Cass & Co., 1967), 231. Originally published in 1704.

15.   R.S. Rattray, *Religion and Art in Ashanti* (Oxford: Clarendon Press, 1927), 106; hereafter cited in text.

16.   It appears that Melville was so struck by Delano's slowness in grasping the obvious that the symbol of that slowness takes the form of a "white noddy, a strange fowl, so called from its lethargic, somnambulistic character, being caught by hand at sea." The reference in *Voyages* to Delano's diving like "a sea fowl" very likely led Melville, bearing in mind the quality of the captain's intellect, to introduce, at the beginning of the novella, the "strange fowl." The white noddy together with the satyr figure and Aranda's skeleton wrapped in canvas are treated in succession and constitute a truly rich concentration of metaphors. See "Benito Cereno," 220.

The Riddle of the Sphinx: Melville's "Benito Cereno" and the *Amistad* Case

CAROLYN L. KARCHER

I

Melville's "Benito Cereno" opens with the Yankee captain Amasa Delano trying to discern the "true character" of a strange vessel entering the harbor where his own ship lies at anchor "with a valuable cargo."[1] Because the newcomer shows "no colors," Delano at first fears she might be a pirate craft. Her clumsy sailing and manifest unfamiliarity with the locale soon convince him that she must be "no wonted freebooter on that ocean," however, and he instead supposes her to be a "ship in distress." As he rows toward her with the intention of piloting her in, the ship appears to him "like a white-washed monastery" inhabited by cowled Black Friars. Approaching nearer, he finally identifies her as a former treasure-ship or "retired" frigate of war, now serving as a slaver. Immediately afterward, Melville introduces the culminating metaphor of this extraordinary series: "Her keel seemed laid, her ribs put together, and she launched, from Ezekiel's Valley of Dry Bones" (48). Through it, he offers the reader a clue to the mystery Delano will never fully resolve, and an alternative frame of reference for interpreting the evidence Delano habitually filters through the racist ideology he shares with most white Americans of his time.

As we will learn, the ship Melville christens the *San Dominick* is indeed "no *wonted* freebooter," for the aim of her crew is not booty, but freedom; she is not, "*at present*, . . . of a piratical character," though in her former role as treasure-ship she was engaged in despoiling newly conquered lands of their riches (47, 68). Only in the sense that her Spanish captain and his royal masters have always invoked religious sanction for their greed can such a ship be taken for a "white-washed monastery." The slaves who have revolted on board the *San Dominick* in 1799—the very year their peers under Toussaint L'Ouverture were consolidating their revolution in San Domingo—resemble "Black Friars," or Dominicans, only by association.[2]

This essay was written specifically for this volume and is published here for the first time by permission of the author.

In contrast to the preceding metaphors, the allusion to Ezekiel's Valley of Dry Bones does reveal the actual errand that has turned a slave ship into a death craft with a skeleton for its figurehead. Like the Israelites carried into Babylonian captivity, the Africans aboard the *San Dominick* have been forcibly transported to a strange land as slaves. They, too, can say, in the words through which God interprets to Ezekiel the meaning of his vision: "Our bones are dried, and our hope is lost: we are cut off for our parts." They, too, are seeking restoration to their homeland; and God's promise to Ezekiel applies to them as well: "Thus saith the Lord GOD unto these bones; Behold, I will cause breath to enter into you, and ye shall live. . . . Behold, O my people, I will open your graves, and cause you to come up out of your graves, and bring you into the land of Israel" (Ezek. 37.1–14). Nor is the analogy merely the product of an erudite Anglo-American imagination. Given the close contact Melville had with African-American sailors, he probably knew that at least in the Protestant colonies, generations of enslaved Africans had made the saga of the Israelites their own, weaving the sufferings of the Chosen People and the visions of the Hebrew prophets into such spirituals as "Go Down Moses," "Joshua Fit de Battle ob Jericho," and "Dry Bones." If we ponder the analogy Melville invites us to draw between these ancient and modern captive peoples—both subjected to enslavement, exile, and dispersion into a "diaspora," and both impelled by the dream of returning to their native shores—we will find ourselves reading the story of the *San Dominick* from the perspective no longer of the masters, but of the slaves.[3]

To do so may seem perverse, since Melville deliberately narrates the story from the viewpoints of the Yankee and Spanish captains representing the ruling classes of their respective societies. Yet I will argue that through a multitude of clues like the allusion to Ezekiel's Valley of Dry Bones, Melville repeatedly directs attention to the suppressed viewpoint of the slaves. His narrative technique does not merely obscure the truth by confining readers to Delano's myopic perception. It also allows readers to see the evidence Delano sees and to draw different conclusions from it. While a rhetoric simulating Delano's mental processes continually translates straightforward observations into racist stereotypes, a complex of metaphors emanating from Melville's poetic imagination simultaneously recreates an alternative reality, rooted in a very different understanding of African culture.

A particularly illuminating example occurs in the scene depicting Delano's arrival on board the *San Dominick*. As his "one eager glance" sweeps across the deck, the first sight it takes in is "the conspicuous figures of four elderly grizzled negroes, their heads like black, doddered willow tops, who, in venerable contrast to the tumult below them, [are] couched sphinx-like, one on the starboard cat-head, another on the larboard, and the remaining pair face to face on the opposite bulwarks above the main-chains" (49–50). They are picking oakum, Delano notices, "with a sort of stoical self-content" and "accompan[ying] the task with a continuous, low, monotonous chant; droning and druling away like so many gray-headed bag-pipers playing a funeral march."

Initially, this passage presents readers with vital objective information: the four black men, whose age and "venerable" appearance signal their authority, are occupying "conspicuous" and strategically chosen positions, dominating the crowd below them. Readers familiar, as Melville was, with Mungo Park's widely known *Travels in the Interior Districts of Africa* (1799) might also realize that the men are engaged in a traditional African activity of structuring their labor with song, or possibly even of "reciting the great actions of their ancestors, to awaken . . . a spirit of glorious emulation"— the specific function of the *"singing men"* who accompanied soldiers into battle. An especially sensitive and knowledgeable reader, familiar with some abolitionist literature, might guess that the men's "low, monotonous chant" conveys some hidden meaning in their own language.[4]

Embedded in the factual indications Melville furnishes of the four elderly Africans' role on the *San Dominick* and of its cultural context is a simile characteristic of his own wide-ranging intellect. The men, he tells us, are "couched sphynx-like" (50). The allusion hints at a riddle of life-and-death importance to be solved, like the one posed by the sphinx in the Greek legend of Oedipus, who dashed to pieces or devoured everyone unable to answer her question: "What creature walks on four legs in the morning, two at noon, and three in the evening?" Melville's simile hints, too, at the solution to the sphinx's riddle—"man"—in that the key to unlocking the riddle of American slavery and to disburdening the nation of its incubus lies in recognizing Africans as fellow human beings. On a still deeper level, the Africans' "sphynx-like" posture calls to mind the stone sphinxes guarding the tombs of the Pharoahs, and hence the Egyptian origin of Greek (and European) civilization.[5] The first of many allusions to Egypt in the story, it identifies the enslaved Africans of the *San Dominick* as heirs of the race credited with diffusing knowledge throughout the ancient world.[6]

Having given readers access to the means of explaining the enigma that confronts Delano as he climbs aboard the *San Dominick*, Melville takes them into the consciousness of a man blinded by racism. The white supremacist ideology to which Delano subscribes defines Africans as an inferior race, consigned by nature to subordinate status.[7] Thus Delano perpetually reinterprets what he sees to conform with his racist stereotypes. Ignoring the oakumpickers' prominent stations and dismissing their chanting as meaningless jargon, he reduces them to stupid menials performing their task with "stoical self-content" and comically "droning and druling away like so many gray-headed bag-pipers playing a funeral march" (50). Once again, however, Melville embeds a clue to an alternative viewpoint in the very midst of a racist stereotype. Scottish bag-pipers, like African "singing men," traditionally accompanied soldiers into war. Melville's cross-cultural analogy runs counter to the racist mind's practice of dividing human beings into separate categories. Furthermore, his imagery registers the message Delano senses but represses from consciousness—that the Africans are indeed "playing a funeral march" for their white oppressors.

A close analysis of Melville's narrative technique uncovers countless examples of the ways he challenges readers to resist Delano's dangerous distortions and to reexamine Africans in the light of their native culture, as described in contemporary travel accounts and abolitionist tracts. At the same time the dominance he accords to Delano and Benito Cereno as witnesses of the events on board the *San Dominick* reflects Melville's understanding of a problem with which all who have sought to recapture the slaves' reality have wrestled—that the slaves' "tyrants have been their historians," as the abolitionist Lydia Maria Child put it.[8] Reacting to a newspaper report of "hellish" acts committed by slaves in the Red River Valley, Child had commented: "We never read such accounts, either of Indians or negroes, without asking ourselves, 'What was *their* side of the story? What long-continued, insupportable wrongs drove human nature to such frightful atrocity, such reckless desperation?' "[9] Abolitionists, like the social historians of our own day, learned to seek the slaves' "side of the story" between the lines of fugitive slave advertisements, law codes, court cases, legislative records, and other documents of the master class. Melville, I submit, similarly read between the lines of the documents on which he based "Benito Cereno"— Amasa Delano's account of the revolt he helped put down on the Spanish ship *Tryal* and the appended court Deposition by Benito Cereno, captain and partial owner of the *Tryal* and its slave cargo.[10] The narrative strategy Melville devised in "Benito Cereno" prompts readers to follow the same procedure in reconstructing the motives and aims of the slaves denigrated by their white oppressors as mindless savages.

II

Although Melville re-envisioned the story he found in Delano's reminiscences, he took his primary inspiration for "Benito Cereno" from another source: the slave uprising on board the Spanish schooner *Amistad*, which broke out in July 1839, just as he was experiencing his first taste of the sailor life he would repeatedly compare to slavery.[11] It is this source and its convergence with Melville's initiation into oppression that lies behind his imaginative engagement with the subject of slave revolt. If we are to understand the transmutations the story underwent in his mind before acquiring its final shape in 1855, we must look more closely at the historical event that left such a deep impression on his consciousness.

The earliest reports of the 1839 *Amistad* revolt appeared in American newspapers at the end of August, while Melville was homeward bound on the *St. Lawrence* after six weeks in Liverpool. When he docked in New York on 1 October, the trial of the rebels was dominating headlines all over the country, particularly in the Northeast. It would recapture public attention again and again during the fifteen months that intervened before Melville went back to sea aboard the *Acushnet* in January 1841.

The very stuff of exotic adventure fiction, the *Amistad* case riveted Melville's contemporaries, from the earliest sightings off the coast near Long Island of a "suspicious looking schooner" rumored to be a pirate vessel, to the latest missionary bulletins from Africa several years later, after the ex-slaves' repatriation to their native Mendi.[12] Initially, the press reacted much as Delano does to the plight of the *San Dominick*. So close are the parallels, in fact, that Melville seems to have borrowed almost as extensively from news accounts of the *Amistad* as from Delano's *Narrative*.

Reporting on the capture of the alleged "pirate" ship by the Delano-like Captain Gedney of the Brig *Washington*, the *New London Gazette*, for example, described the Africans as "bucaniers" and the Spanish owners, Jose Ruiz and Pedro Montez, as "gentlemanly" and "martyr-like"[13]—motifs that reverberate through Delano's ruminations about Benito Cereno and his slave Babo. The Spaniards' sufferings had been "truly deplorable," claimed the *Gazette*, based on an interview with them the day after their rescue. "[T]heir lives being threatened every instant," they had been "treated with the greatest severity" by the rebels, who had murdered the captain and three crew members shortly after leaving Havana and ordered Montez, a former shipmaster, to steer them to Africa.[14] They had survived only by trickery. Forced by the Africans to sail east during the day, Montez had secretly altered the ship's course at night to the north and west, "always in hopes of falling in with some vessel of war, or being enabled to run into some port" where the Spaniards might be "relieved from their horrid situation." He had thus succeeded in prolonging the voyage for two months, remaining near the North American coast, and necessitating a landing to replenish the ship's water supply—the maneuver that had led to the capture of both the *Amistad* and the *San Dominick*. As in the case of the *San Dominick*, the captain's stalling had aroused the Africans' suspicions and prompted them to terrorize him into compliance. Hours before the Americans' arrival, Ruiz—the preponderant owner, like Aranda in "Benito Cereno," of the slaves on board—had been condemned to death "by the chief of the bucaniers, and his death song chanted by the grim crew, who gathered with uplifted sabres around his devoted head," still bearing the scars of the wounds inflicted at the time of the murders. The vignette may have suggested one of the most chilling incidents Melville invented in reshaping Delano's *Narrative* into "Benito Cereno": the episode in which Babo orders the murder of Aranda and the display of his skeleton (105–7). More demonstrative than Benito Cereno, Montez, when finally "assured . . . of his safety," had thrown his arms around the neck of the prize master, "while gushing tears coursing down his furrowed cheek, bespoke the overflowing transport of his soul." He had repeatedly "clasped his hands, and with uplifted eyes, [given] thanks to 'the Holy Virgin' who had led him out of his troubles." Benito Cereno similarly attributes his salvation to "God and his angels" (110)—another embellishment Melville added to his literary source.[15] Paralleling Benito Cereno's "many expressions of 'eternal gratitude' to the 'generous Captain Amasa Delano' " in his Deposition (111), Ruiz and Montez subsequently published a card in all the city papers, reiterating their "gratitude for their most unhoped for and providential rescue from the hands of a ruthless gang of African bucaniers" and "expressing . . . their thankfulness and obligation to Lieut. Com. T. R. Gedney, and the officers and crew of the U.S. surveying brig Washington, for their decision in seizing the Amistad, and their unremitting kindness and hospitality in providing for their comfort on board their vessel. . . ."[16]

Gedney himself, like the historical Amasa Delano, had ulterior motives for his vaunted generosity: he hoped to be awarded "prize or salvage money" for saving the *Amistad*, whose cargo had been valued at forty thousand dollars and its slaves at an additional "20 to 30 thousand dollars." Evidently he shared Delano's lack of scruples about taking his payment in money earned from the sale of slaves. That fine point also escaped the *New London Gazette*, which piously commented of Gedney and his officers: "[W]e hope they will get their just dues."[17]

The *Gazette* not only took its cue from Gedney, Ruiz, and Montez in its portrayal of them as heroes and martyrs and of the slaves as piratical cutthroats; it went on to conjure up further stereotypes of African savagery by depicting the scene of anarchy and neglect presented by the *Amistad*—a scene weirdly mirrored in "Benito Cereno," though Melville would purge it of many racist elements. On visiting the schooner, wrote the *Gazette* reporter, "we saw such a sight as we never saw before and never wish to see again." Due to protracted drifting without a crew to maintain the ship, the *Amistad*'s "bottom and sides," were "covered with barnacles and sea-grass," and her tattered sails and rigging recalled the "Flying Dutchman, after her fabled cruise." In yet another detail with no analogue in Delano's *Narrative*, Melville would describe the *San Dominick* as trailing "dark festoons of sea-grass" along its water-line, and dragging "a huge bunch of conglobated barnacles . . . below the water to the side like a wen" (49, 74).[18] Unlike the remarkably disciplined host of the *San Dominick*, the *Amistad*'s "Ethiop crew" had "pilfered" the cargo, according to the *Gazette*: "Over the deck were scattered in the most wanton and disorderly profusion, raisins, vermicelli, bread, rice, silk, and cotton goods," and the blacks had "decked" themselves "in the most fantastic manner, in silks and finery." One of them sported "a linen cambric shirt, whose bosom was worked by the hand of some dark-eyed daughter of Spain, while his nether proportions were enveloped in a shawl of gauze or Canton crape." In a curious reversal of the *Gazette*'s racist stereotyping, Melville would transform this *Amistad* African into a Spanish sailor, whose "soiled under garment of what seemed the finest linen, edged, about the neck, with a narrow blue ribbon," would lead Captain Delano to wonder: "But how come sailors . . . with silk-trimmed under-shirts . . . ? Has he been robbing the trunks of the dead cabin passengers?" (66–67). Another figure from the *Gazette* account of the *Amistad* who would reappear in altered guise aboard the *San Dominick* would be a "negro with white pantaloons, and the sable shirt which nature gave him, and a planter's broad brimmed hat upon his head, with a string of gewgaws about his neck." Melville would eliminate the stolen hat and savage "gewgaws"; instead he would highlight Babo's neatness in his improvised attire, consisting of "nothing but wide trowsers, apparently, from their coarseness and patches, made out of some old topsail; . . . clean, and confined at the waist by a bit of unstranded rope . . ." (57).[19]

Despite his patent biases, the *New London Gazette*'s reporter could not help feeling involuntary admiration for Cinquez, "the master spirit of this bloody tragedy," whom he saw "in irons" on the *Washington*, like Babo after his capture (116). "[Cinquez's] countenance, for a native African, is unusually intelligent, evincing uncommon decision and coolness, with a composure characteristic of true courage, and nothing to mark him as a malicious man," he noted bemusedly. True, Cinquez (unlike Babo) had "killed the Captain and crew with his own hand, by cutting their throats." Nevertheless, acknowledged the reporter, his physiognomy indicated a strong "claim to benevolence," and by phrenological criteria, "his moral sentiments and intellectual faculties predominate considerably over his animal propensities"—a perception Melville would convey by emphasizing that Babo's "brain, not body, had schemed and led the revolt" (116). Anticipating Melville's portrayal of Babo's dignity in defeat, the *Gazette*'s reporter ended with a tribute to Cinquez's valor: "He expects to be executed, but nevertheless manifests a *sang froid* worthy of a stoic under similar circumstances."[20]

The twenty-six-year-old Cinquez, said to be the "son of an African chief," combined the brilliance and leadership ability of Babo with the noble bearing and status of Babo's right-hand man Atufal, a "king in his own land" (62). His "powerful frame" and "erect," well-proportioned figure, appearing taller than his actual height of approximately five feet eight inches, drew widespread comment. He also impressed everyone who heard him speak as a consummate orator. Increasingly, journalists who came to ogle "savages" left questioning many of their original stereotypes and prejudices.[21]

By the time Melville could have begun reading accounts of the *Amistad* captives' trial, public sentiment had already shifted in their favor. He arrived home just in time for two dramatic breakthroughs in the case: the testimony of the British Commissioner for liberated Africans in Havana, identifying the *Amistad* slaves as having been recently kidnapped from Africa "in violation of the Spanish law" of 1820 prohibiting the importation of African slaves;

and the discovery of an African sailor who spoke the captives' language, Mendi, and could translate their testimony for the Court. That testimony included an acting out of the "passage from Africa to Havana," during which the captives had been "fastened together in couples by the wrists and legs" and frequently whipped.[22]

At issue in the trial were a series of complex legal problems that Melville would transmute into moral problems and develop as central themes in "Benito Cereno." First, did American courts have jurisdiction over a case involving the revolt of Spanish slaves on the high seas? Second, did the 1795 treaty between Spain and the United States, providing for the restoration to the proprietor of "ships and merchandise . . . rescued out of the hands of . . . pirates or robbers," apply to the Amistad?[23] Third, could the Amistad rebels be defined as pirates according to international law? Fourth, could they even be proved to be the legal property of Messrs. Ruiz and Montez? Fifth, did Gedney and his officers have a legitimate claim to salvage on the Amistad and its cargo, and if so, did the slaves constitute part of the "cargo"? And finally, what should the United States Government do with the Amistad rebels: return them to their masters or to the Spanish Government? sell them to pay off the salvage claim of the American officers who had rescued the Amistad? turn them loose to fend for themselves? or send them back to Africa?

Underlying the legal issues and sharpening the debate over the case was the controversy over American slavery that had been raging with unprecedented intensity since 1831. Southern advocates of slavery and their Northern allies wanted the Amistad case resolved in a manner that would not challenge the South's "peculiar institution" or imperil the Union between the two sections; antislavery partisans and their sympathizers, on the other hand, wanted to use the opportunity to combat racial prejudice and misconceptions about Africans and to increase public awareness of the threat that slavery represented to the security of slaveholders, the nation, and American democracy. Thus President John Tyler, a Virginia slaveholder, threw the weight of the United States Government behind the efforts of Ruiz and Montez to regain custody of the Amistad slaves, and actually despatched the U.S. schooner Grampus to New Haven with the purpose of transporting the captives back to Cuba as soon as the Court rendered its verdict—a verdict the government confidently expected to sustain the Spaniards' property rights. On their part abolitionists engaged eminent lawyers to defend the Amistad rebels and mobilized all available resources of press and pulpit to publicize their cause.

At the outset, everything seemed to militate against a fair trial for the Africans. Virulent racism held sway throughout the country, and during the 1830s, when abolitionists had begun calling for immediate emancipation and the extension of equal rights to people of color, the public had responded with bloody riots targeting blacks and abolitionists in many Northern cities and towns. As recently as the preceding year, the city of Philadelphia had been torn by racist violence that had destroyed black neighborhoods and a newly built abolitionist meeting hall. Moreover, the judge who was to preside over the *Amistad* trial, Andrew J. Judson of the U.S. District Court for Connecticut, where the ship had been towed, had himself led a particularly ugly campaign in 1833 against a school for young ladies of color that a Quaker woman had founded in his hometown of Canterbury.[24]

Contrary to all auguries, however, abolitionists succeeded in proving that the *Amistad* rebels had been kidnapped in Africa in 1839, "illegally carried to Cuba" in defiance of Spain's 1820 law against the African slave trade, and fraudulently purchased by Ruiz and Montez, who had fabricated Spanish names for the captives in order to pass them off as "ladinos," or "negroes long settled and acclimated in Cuba." In addition to the British Commissioner of liberated Africans, R. R. Madden, who had seen the *Amistad* captives in Havana shortly after they landed, two American witnesses testified that Ruiz himself had privately admitted the slaves to be fresh from Africa and totally unacquainted with the Spanish language. A linguist from Yale also determined with the help of the Mendi interpreter that the captives all had Mendi names with specific meanings in their own language.[25]

In the face of such overwhelming evidence, both Judson and the slaveholder-dominated Supreme Court, to which the U.S. Government appealed the case, were forced to rule that Ruiz and Montez had no legal claim to the *Amistad* slaves and that the 1795 treaty with Spain consequently did not apply. As John Quincy Adams argued in representing the captives at the Supreme Court level, the treaty stipulated that merchandise rescued from pirates or robbers should be returned to its owners, but "Who are the robbers, and what is the merchandise?" Melville would raise precisely this question in "Benito Cereno." By the Spaniards' own interpretation of the treaty, continued Adams, "the merchandise is the robbers and the robbers are the merchandise. . . . These Africans are themselves the robbers out of whose hands they themselves have been rescued"—an absurd contention. "We may lament the dreadful acts by which they asserted their liberty, and took possession of the Amistad, and endeavored to regain their native country," concurred the Supreme Court, but the Africans could not be "deemed pirates or robbers in the sense of the law of nations. . . ."[26]

Long before the Supreme Court reached its verdict in March 1841, two months after Melville's embarkation on the *Acushnet*, public sentiment had gone well beyond this position. As early as September 1839, the *Boston Courier* protested the injustice of trying the *Amistad* rebels for "*murder* or *piracy*." "In the language of humanity they have committed no crime at all," the *Courier* stressed. "They have attempted to regain the liberty, in which they were born, and which has been wrested from them by robbers, pirates, and murderers."[27] That is, the real pirates, according to the *Courier*, were not the slaves, but the masters, since both American and international law specifically branded the slave trade as piracy.[28] The *Portsmouth Journal* took an even more militant stand:

> Shall we, the sons of liberty, now attempt to appease our consciences by the miserable, the degrading, and the contemptible subterfuge or legal quibble, that . . . a certain Spanish Don, 'a gentleman,' to be sure, a SLAVE-DEALER, the VENDEE OF PIRATES, holds a certain manuscript under the hand and seal of a pirate, the murderer of one half the cargo on the middle passage, by virtue of which a portion of the survivors were instantly converted from being fairly human flesh into goods and merchandize! . . . Had these friendless Africans been Englishmen, can any person believe for a moment that such questions about *property* in *their* flesh would have been raised by astute lawyers and judges?[29]

Through an elaborate series of literary allusions and metaphors, Melville would invite readers of "Benito Cereno" to apply the same reasoning to the "Spanish Don" and African slaves of the *San Dominick*.

The public was no more sympathetic to the claim of the American Captain Gedney than to that of the "Spanish Don." The *Boston Atlas* opined that he would "fail altogether" to establish his entitlement to a portion of the cargo as "salvage" because the *Amistad* captives could not be considered "property" under either Spanish or Connecticut law. "In Connecticut they are free men, and as such they have all the rights of free men," proclaimed the *Atlas*. The *Portsmouth Journal* raised a more fundamental issue: "Many persons doubt whether we of the north have anything to do with slavery in our Southern States, *pro or con*. We can certainly be under no obligation to defend the Spanish slaveholder from being murdered by his own 'property.' " If so, Gedney had no authority to interfere in the *Amistad*'s concerns, let alone to seize the vessel, cargo, and slaves—a charge Adams also leveled in his address to the Supreme Court. Ultimately the Court compromised by awarding Gedney and his officers salvage on the ship and cargo, amounting to one third of their value, though not on the "negroes Cinquez and others."[30] Melville would similarly expose the contradictions between the humanitarian motives Delano professes and the mercenary aims he reveals when he instructs his sailors not to "kill or maim the negroes," but to take them alive "with the ship," and when he tells them "that the Spanish captain considered his ship as good as lost; that she and her cargo, including some gold and silver, were worth more than a thousand doubloons," and that if they succeed in taking her, "no small part should be theirs" (101).

Throughout the *Amistad* rebels' long ordeal, public pressure played a crucial role in influencing the Courts. The Africans inspired an extraordinary outpouring of popular fervor. Poems about them proliferated, a play titled *The Black Schooner or the Private Slaver "Amistad"* "ran . . . before packed houses at four theaters and took in over $5,000," a mezzotint engraving of the portrait the abolitionist Nathaniel Jocelyn painted of Cinquez sold widely, and a traveling wax exhibition of the Africans drew thousands of viewers.[31] Once the Supreme Court finally liberated the rebels, who had been awaiting the verdict in jail ever since their capture, it was the public that contributed funds to send them back to Mendi—a cost the U.S. Government refused to assume. To raise money for their repatriation, the Mendians toured New England and New York with their abolitionist and missionary benefactors, telling their story, describing the "manners and customs prevalent in their native country," singing English hymns and African songs, and demonstrating their progress in Christianity and civilization, at sessions attended by large crowds paying admission fees of fifty cents a head. These programs, which gave many Americans their first direct view of native Africans, helped dispel the myth of savagery and counteract the image of Africans as aliens. "They are perfectly black—but not without pleasing and striking impression," remarked one ingenuous observer. It was "impossible for any one to go away with the impression, that in native intellect these people were inferior to the whites," wrote another.[32]

In sum, the *Amistad* case marked a dramatic turning point in the struggle against slavery and a major advance in the American public's racial attitudes. Though the slaveowners' identity as Spaniards rather than Americans and the slaves' desire to return to Africa rather than strive for acceptance as equals in America undoubtedly contributed to defusing the hostility abolitionism had previously aroused, the awareness created by the agitation nevertheless helped prepare the public to take similar positions in later cases involving American slaves.[33]

III

For Melville, exposure to the publicity surrounding the *Amistad* revolt could hardly have come at a more formative moment in his development. His voyage to Liverpool as a "boy," or "green-hand," on the merchant ship *St. Lawrence* had stripped away the last shreds of the patrician identity bequeathed to him by his Melvill and Gansevoort ancestors, and confronted him personally with the meaning of slavery. The novel based on this experience— *Redburn: His First Voyage; Being the Sailor-boy Confessions and Reminiscences of the Son-of-a-Gentleman, in the Merchant Service* (1849)—represents it as an initiation in every sense. The scene in which young Redburn tries to pay a "social call" on the captain, naively believing that a man of his own class would "appreciate the difference between me and the rude sailors among whom I was thrown . . . and prove a kind friend and benefactor to me" is obviously fictional, yet it no doubt reflects the process of psychological reorientation Melville must have undergone as he came to realize that he would be subjected to the same brutal working conditions and social discrimination as other sailors.[34] Redburn's comment clearly indicates that at least in retrospect, if not during the actual voyage, Melville began to identify not only with his fellow sailors, but with their counterparts on southern plantations: "Miserable dog's life is this of the sea! commanded like a slave, and set to work like an ass! vulgar and brutal men lording it over me, as if I were an African in Alabama" (66). He also began to associate with the African Americans in his racially mixed crew on terms of greater social equality than he could ever have been able to at home.

In the novel, a shipmate named Jackson, who "had served in Portuguese slavers on the coast of Africa" (57), functionally reinforces the analogies Redburn has started to perceive between sailors and slaves and stimulates him to ponder the issue of slavery from a new perspective. As William H. Gilman has established, the St. Lawrence's crew included a Robert Jackson, whose age and birthplace correspond with the fictional Jackson's.[35] Hence the encounter may be autobiographical. Whether Melville sketched Jackson's portrait from life, fleshed out a skeleton of reality, or simply imagined him, the characterization certainly reveals the link in his mind between his voyage to Liverpool and his growing preoccupation with slavery and the slave trade. A petty tyrant reduced to the "foul lees and dregs of a man" (58), the fictional Jackson personifies the slave trade's dehumanization of both its perpetrators and its victims. He expatiates "with a diabolical relish" on the sufferings he has witnessed and inflicted, dwelling on how, during "the *middle-passage*, . . . the slaves were stowed, heel and point, like logs, and the suffocated and dead were unmanacled, and weeded out from the living every morning, before washing down the decks"; and he takes sadistic pleasure in recalling an occasion when British efforts to stop the slave trade by patrolling the African coast ended up killing the slaves: "he had been in a slaving schooner, which being chased by an English cruiser off Cape Verde, received three shots in her hull, which raked through and through a whole file of slaves, that were chained" (57).

Melville's six-week stay in Liverpool, the former capital of the slave trade, furthered the political education he received aboard the St. Lawrence in a variety of ways. Melville's father, like Redburn's, had actually met "the good and great [William] Roscoe, the intrepid enemy of the [slave] trade; who in every way exerted his fine talents toward its suppression" (156).[36] We do not know whether he, too, had "spoken to gentlemen visiting our house in New York, of the unhappiness that the discussion of the abolition of this trade had occasioned in Liverpool," as had Redburn's father, but we do know that the history of the long crusade against the slave trade and of the fierce opposition that the merchants of Liverpool mounted against abolition bulked large in Melville's consciousness as he reminisced about his visit to the city. Although Allan Melvill went to Liverpool in 1811 and met Roscoe in 1818, Melville dates Walter Redburn's visit to Liverpool in 1808, the year the slave trade officially ended.[37] In his account of Wellingborough Redburn's pilgrimage to his father's old haunts, Melville mentions Roscoe four times (144–45, 148, 156). The most climactic of these references occurs as Redburn contemplates "four naked figures in chains" adorning the pedestal of a monument commemorating Nelson's victories—figures whose "swarthy limbs and manacles" remind Redburn of "four African slaves in the market-place" (155). Meditating on these "woe-begone" sculptured captives, Redburn's thoughts "revert to Virginia and Carolina; and also to the historical fact, that the African slave-trade once constituted the principal commerce of Liverpool; and that the prosperity of the town was once supposed to have been indissolubly linked to its prosecution" (155). He then cites the role of Roscoe in turning the tide through a speech in Parliament which, "as coming from a member for Liverpool, was supposed to have . . . had no small share in the triumph of sound policy and humanity that ensued" (156).

Melville shared Redburn's fascination with the monument to Nelson, revisiting it "with peculiar emotion" in 1856.[38] Did he likewise share the experience of seeing a slaver at first hand? It seems unlikely, given the strict surveillance the British exercised. Yet Melville's description of the "little brig from the Coast of Guinea" (174) that Redburn sees anchored at Prince's dock once again suggests the extent to which his memories of Liverpool and of the *Amistad* case are intertwined. It also foreshadows the connections Melville establishes between slavery and piracy in "Benito Cereno." Echoing newspaper accounts of the "Long, Low, Black Schooner," with its "clipper-built" design, "disorderly" decks, and seemingly piratical character, he writes: "In appearance, she was the ideal of a slaver; low, black, clipper-built about the bows, and her decks in a state of most piratical disorder. . . . The crew were a bucaniering looking set . . ." (175).[39] The Guinea brig, Melville adds ironically, is moored alongside the "Floating Chapel, . . . the hull of an old sloop-of-war, which had been converted into a mariner's church" (175). He thereby introduces another chain of associations central to "Benito Cereno"—the equation of slavery with war and of both with the hypocritical religion of state that lends its sanction to crimes against humanity; for the *San Dominick*, as we have seen, is a former frigate of war that resembles a "white-washed monastery" (48).

Besides arousing his interest in the slave trade and sensitizing him to the issue of slavery, Melville's voyage to Liverpool challenged the racial prejudices he probably brought with him from America. In a key passage, Redburn comments on a phenomenon noticed by many American travelers in England, some with disgust, others with admiration: the striking absence there of anti-black prejudice and taboos against the social intermingling of blacks and whites.[40] "In Liverpool . . . the negro steps with a prouder pace, and lifts his head like a man," observes Redburn, since "no such exaggerated feeling exists in respect to him, as in America" (202). He drives home the point with an illustration that frequently recurs in the American abolitionist press: "Three or four times, I encountered our black steward, dressed very handsomely, and walking arm in arm with a good-looking English woman. In New York, such a couple would have been mobbed in three minutes; and the steward would have been lucky to escape with whole limbs" (202). Redburn proceeds to explain how his exposure to a new cultural environment has transformed his racial attitudes:

> Being so young and inexperienced then, and unconsciously swayed in some degree by those local and social prejudices, that are the marring of most men, and from which, for the mass, there seems no possible escape; at first I was surprised that a colored man should be treated as he is in this town; but a little reflection showed that, after all, it was but recognizing his claims to humanity and normal equality; so that, in some things, we Americans leave to other countries the carrying out of the principle that stands at the head of our Declaration of Independence. (202)[41]

Exactly a year after Melville's trip, an abolitionist who had attended the World Anti-Slavery Convention in London described scenes analogous to Redburn's encounter with the black steward and his English lady friend: "a mulatto woman walking arm in arm with a gentleman in Hyde Park"; "a black man with an elegantly dressed white lady leaning on his arm, and immediately following them, a white and black gentleman arm in arm." "What I noticed most particularly in all these cases," underscored the writer, "was, that not the least attention was attracted."[42]

This abolitionist witness also singled out a scene that helps explain the sequel of Redburn's reflections on the "local and social prejudices" he has learned to overcome. On attending Blackfriars church, our abolitionist saw "a head and face that marked the purest African descent"; the African in question was not "perched up in a corner," as in an American church, he emphasized, but occupying a prominent pew.[43] Redburn presents the lesson's obverse. His poverty-stricken appearance has repeatedly consigned him to the status of an outcast in England, he complains. Each time he has attended church, for example, the usher has relegated him to the equivalent of the American "Negro pew"—an "oaken bench in the . . . aisle" or a seat in an obscure corner with "some confounded pillar or obstinate angle of the wall in the way" (203–4). In short, Redburn comes to realize what it feels like to be a victim of prejudice when he faces the same kind of discrimination in England that blacks regularly meet with in the United States.

Melville may have acquired his own imaginative identification with social outcasts in a similar way. Sailors were not only treated as slaves on board their ships, but as pariahs on land. Friendless in Liverpool, with nothing to distinguish him from other members of the working class, Melville may well have experienced the mortification of being excluded from polite circles. He may not actually have found himself stuck in an out-of-the-way pew or turned away from a public reading room (as Redburn is in another incident [156]), but he evidently learned to put himself in the place of all who suffered such daily humiliations.

Thus Melville returned home from Liverpool in a frame of mind that would have made him particularly receptive to abolitionist principles, if he had not already developed an incipient abolitionist consciousness. And he returned home to a country abuzz with excitement about a group of African captives with whom he would now have been more prone to sympathize than at any previous time in his life.

IV

Ten years intervened, nevertheless, before Melville published the novel that allowed him to relive his initiation into the meaning of slavery and racism, and another six years before he wrote his 1855 story of a shipboard slave revolt, "Benito Cereno." During those years, the slave system strengthened its grip over the United States government, and Melville himself rejoined the ruling class from which he had been exiled as a sailor. Symbolizing the convergence of the personal and the political, Melville married the daughter of his father's best friend, Chief Justice Lemuel Shaw of the Massachusetts Supreme Court—a man committed to upholding the letter of the law in fugitive slave cases, "however disagreeable to our own natural sympathies and views of duty."[44]

In the Med case of 1836, Shaw had ruled that slaves brought to Massachusetts by their owners were entitled to claim their freedom—a ruling he broadened in the Lucas case of 1843, which liberated a slave on board the very ship that carried Melville back from the South Seas, the U.S.S. *United States*. Yet Shaw had carefully circumscribed these decisions to avoid setting precedents that would undermine the Fugitive Slave Law of 1793. In October 1842, eighteen months after the U.S. Supreme Court's liberation of the *Amistad* captives, Shaw judged his first fugitive slave case—that of George Latimer. As Garrison reported in the *Liberator*, Shaw seemed as "indifferent as though it were a case involving the ownership of an ox or an ass." While claiming to feel "as much sympathy" for the prisoner as the crowds demonstrating for Latimer's release, Shaw asserted that "an appeal to natural rights and to the paramount law of liberty was not pertinent," and that the Constitution and Fugitive Slave Law demanded absolute obedience under the compact between North and South. In language that reverberates through *Moby-Dick*, *Battle-Pieces*, and *Billy Budd*, Garrison pronounced Shaw's "remarks . . . as atheistical as were ever uttered by human lips" and fulminated:

Wo unto them that decree unrighteous decrees, and that write grievousness which they have prescribed; to turn aside the needy from judgment, and to take away the right from the poor of my people, that widows may be their prey, and that they may rob the fatherless![45]

Melville was in the Pacific during the uproar over the Latimer decision, but Shaw's two subsequent landmark verdicts—upholding racial segregation in the Roberts case of 1849, which laid the basis for the century-long ascendancy of the "separate but equal" doctrine, and remanding a fugitive slave in the notorious Sims case of 1851, the first to legitimate the reinforced Fugitive Slave Law of 1850—occurred as Melville was writing *Redburn* and *Moby-Dick*.

Shaw seems to have been in Melville's mind when he formulated his arguments against racial prejudice in *Redburn* and conceived Father Mapple's sermon in *Moby-Dick*, with its pregnant reference to plucking out sin "from under the robes of Senators and Judges."[46] Melville may also have been thinking of his father-in-law when he reworked the Deposition in "Benito Cereno" to highlight the travesty of justice by which a court representing slaveholders' interests sentenced slave rebels to death.[47] If so, we can perhaps guess why Melville chose not to use the *Amistad* case as his source when he finally wrote the story that had been simmering in his consciousness for so many years. Quite simply, the issues in the *Amistad* case were too clear-cut. Because the Africans' capture and rebellion had taken place after the passage of the law against the slave trade, their enslavement had been illegal and their freedom could be awarded on narrow legal grounds that did not challenge the basis of the slave system or invoke "natural rights and . . . the paramount law of liberty." Shaw, like Judson and the judges of the U.S. Supreme Court, would undoubtedly have ruled in favor of the captives, just as he had ruled in favor of Med and Lucas; conversely, he would have ruled against them had they staged their revolt thirty-odd years earlier, while the slave trade was still legal.

To raise the kinds of issues foreclosed in the *Amistad* case, Melville turned instead to a source that presented extraordinary parallels with it: Amasa Delano's *Narrative of Voyages and Travels*. Both involved the revolt of African slaves on a Spanish ship transporting them from one colonial port to another; the rescue of the Spaniards by a Yankee captain hoping to claim salvage rights on the vessel and cargo; and a court case that centered on determining the guilt of the slaves, the compensation due to the Yankee captain, and the applicability of the 1795 treaty between Spain and the United States, guaranteeing mutual aid in recovering hijacked ships.[48] The similitude even included hints of piracy. The historical Delano had actually served in his youth on a privateer called the *Mars* (a fact mentioned in the biographical sketch at the end of the book); moreover he complained in his account of the *Tryal* incident that his ungrateful Spanish beneficiary had tried to undermine his claim to salvage rights by summoning as witnesses several Botany Bay convicts in the crew, "who swore I was a pirate" (823).

Among the factors making Delano's account of the revolt on board the *Tryal* a more suitable vehicle for Melville's purposes than the *Amistad* case, however, were a number of significant differences. First, and perhaps most important, the *Tryal* revolt had occurred in 1804, four years before England and the United States declared the slave trade illegal, and sixteen years before Spain joined the international ban. It therefore resisted the easy legalistic solution the *Amistad* case permitted, and forced readers to take their stand on the riskier terrain of moral and ideological principle. As if to heighten the difficulty, Melville pushes the date further back to 1799, when crusaders against the slave trade were still fighting an uphill battle, and when the bloodiest slave uprising in history was raging on the island of San Domingo. Second, the Spanish tribunal that judged the slaves of the *Tryal*, unlike the American courts that judged those of the *Amistad*, had ended up convicting them of "insurrection and atrocities" and executing the ringleaders in a manner intended to strike terror into all potential rebels: dragging them to the gibbet at the tail of a mule, burning their corpses to ashes, and displaying their heads on poles in the plaza (841). This outcome made the *Tryal* case a much more effective illustration of the injustice at the heart of a slave society's legal system. Third, the *Tryal* revolt had taken a far more violent form, resulting in the killing of some twenty to twenty-five Spanish passengers and sailors, compared to two on the *Amistad*. Consequently, it prevented readers from taking refuge in comforting notions of the rebels' lenity toward their oppressors. Like the San Domingo and Nat Turner slave revolts, both of which had been cited by apologists of slavery as proof of African savagery, the *Tryal* revolt posed in its starkest possible terms the question of whether or not slaves had the right to fight for their freedom by any means necessary. Fourth, the *Tryal* numbered among its slaves a large contingent of mature women and nursing mothers—in contrast to the *Amistad*, which carried only three young girls. The women's presence and role in the revolt enabled Melville to expose an aspect of the slave trade generally veiled in silence— the routine raping of the captives—as well as to reveal the high status many African cultures conferred on women. Lastly, Delano lent himself much better than Captain Gedney of the *Washington* to an exploration of the issues that the happy resolution of the *Amistad* case had masked: the complicity of the United States in maintaining the international slave trade and the complicity of the North in buttressing Southern slavery. As he portrayed himself, the historical Delano embodied the contradictions of the Yankee character: convinced of his own benevolence, yet shrewd and grasping; full of good intentions, yet dangerously blind; spouting humanitarian ideals while massacring and enslaving people of color; mouthing republican doctrines while controlling his sailors by means of "good wholesome floggings" (814).[49] He thus provided Melville with a perfect exemplification of the American ideology Shaw codified in his verdicts.

Melville would adapt his narrative strategy primarily to an audience of men like his father-in-law, whose racial prejudices and legalistic reasoning he would attempt to undermine, and secondarily to the antislavery audience of *Putnam's Magazine*, whose founders had all actively espoused the abolitionist cause and could be expected to recall the *Amistad* case as they read "Benito Cereno."[50] He would challenge both groups to unlock the riddle of America's future, as symbolized not only by the slaves Delano finds on board the *San Dominick*, but by the unholy collusion between the American and Spanish captains in keeping them enchained.

V

Although Delano preens himself throughout the story on his superiority to the effete Don Benito, attributing that superiority to his Yankee energy and republican background, he ends up reenacting all of the Spaniard's fatal errors. He, too, regards Africans as born menials and "indisputable inferiors"; he, too, underestimates their intelligence, overestimates their "docility" and "unaspiring contentment" with their lot, and dismisses their capacity to mount a successful revolt—the assumptions that earlier put Benito Cereno and Aranda in the power of their slaves (83–84, 104). He, too, sets out in pursuit of slaves, just as Spanish slavetraders did in Africa. And he, too, intends to trade in them by exchanging them for cash—the purpose of the *San Dominick*'s voyage from Valparaiso to Callao (104).[51]

Melville reinforces these parallels through historical allusions that identify the two captains with the Spanish and English adventurers who seized the New World for their sovereigns and peopled it with slaves. "The image of Christopher Colon, the discoverer of the New World" (and the founder of slavery in the Spanish colony that became Santo Domingo) originally graced the *San Dominick*'s prow (107), and Benito Cereno resembles the "anchoritish" Charles V, successor to Columbus's patrons Ferdinand and Isabella, and initiator of the African slave trade in America (53).[52] Delano for his part, though obsessed with fears that the captain and crew of the *San Dominick* may be plotting piracy against him, ironically derives the name of his own vessel, the *Bachelor's Delight*, from the seventeenth-century buccaneers William Dampier and William Ambrose Cowley, who helped Britain to sap Spanish hegemony in the New World by preying on Spanish treasure-ships like the *San Dominick* in its prime, and by raiding Spanish ports.[53] Melville may have known that the buccaneers engaged in slave trading as well as piracy, and he certainly knew that their predecessor, the pirate John Hawkins, knighted by Queen Elizabeth for his depredations on Spanish shipping, enjoyed the dubious distinction of having launched England into the slave trade.[54]

In linking the activities of Benito Cereno and Delano with piracy, the slave trade, and the intertwined histories of the Spanish and Anglo-American slave empires, Melville is drawing attention to a facet of the *Amistad* case covered only in the abolitionist press: the connivance of Spanish and American officials in Havana with slave traders. The *Amistad*'s owners, Ruiz and Montez, had succeeded in landing their slaves in Havana and obtaining clearance for them from customs precisely because the Spanish officials whose job was to stamp out the trade enriched themselves by participating in it. Abolitionists accused the American Consul in Havana, Nicholas Trist, of doing the same thing. The illicit collaboration between Spanish and American slave traders had a long history. After the outlawing of the trade by the United States and Britain in 1808, American slavers, many of which had served as privateers during the War of 1812, had taken to running up the Spanish flag whenever they encountered patrollers, besides including a few Spaniards in their crews, one of whom could "pose as the captain while the real (American) captain would . . . pose as a passenger."[55] Once Spain joined the ban, the two countries' roles reversed. Because the United States refused to allow American vessels to be searched, even to "ascertain whether a suspected slaver displaying the American flag is, or is not, a bona fide *American* vessel," "Spanish, Portuguese, and Brazilian slave-traders, with outlaws and pirates of all nations, are now flocking under the cover of the American flag," charged abolitionists.[56] Hence nothing could have been more ironic than Delano's fears lest a ship that "showed no colors" prove a pirate craft—a detail Melville retained from his source (46–47, 816).

The *Amistad* case had centered on the question of whether or not the slave rebels could be condemned as pirates. A large segment of the Northern press and public had answered that question by pronouncing the real pirates to be the Spaniards who had illegally kidnapped them in Africa. In "Benito Cereno," Melville refocuses the debate around the American captain. At the end of the story, Delano, "with the scales dropped from his eyes, [sees] the negroes . . . with mask torn away, flourishing hatchets and knives, in ferocious piratical revolt" (99). Belying Delano's version of the truth, he himself plays the role of a pirate when he sends his chief mate—a former "privateer's-man, and, as his enemies whispered, a pirate"—in pursuit of the slaves, promising the sailors a share in the ship's booty if they capture her. The scene is straight out of a pirate narrative, as the sailors reply "with a shout" and board the ship "with a huzza" (101–2).

The court's verdict in the *Amistad* case had pivoted on the law defining the slave trade as piracy. One issue Melville raises in "Benito Cereno" is whether the absence of such a law makes any difference. To men like Shaw and Judson, it made all the difference in the world, as Shaw indicated by sending fugitive slaves back to their masters in deference to another law defining them as property. To abolitionists, slavery itself was piracy. As Garrison put it in the American Anti-Slavery Society's Declaration of Sentiments: "It is piracy to buy or steal a native African, and subject him to servitude. Surely, the sin is as great to enslave an American as an African. Therefore we believe and affirm—that there is no difference, in principle, between the African slave trade and American slavery."[57] Melville expresses this insight by symbolically identifying both Benito Cereno and Delano as pirates.

The freeing of the *Amistad*'s slaves seemed to confirm the justice and leniency of the American legal system. The Spanish tribunal in Lima that judged the slaves of the *San Dominick* showed itself to be far more ruthless. If Melville remembered the Nat Turner insurrection of 1831, however, he knew that American courts could be equally ruthless toward the slaves of their own citizens. He also knew that the historical Delano had not only turned the slaves over to the tribunal, but acted as a witness against them—another instance of Spanish-American collaboration in perpetuating the slave system. Although he indicted slaveholding "justice" through the Spanish court case he found in his source, Melville's critique of the court's procedures applies equally well to cases tried under the Fugitive Slave Law of 1850 and the slave codes of the South, both of which made a mockery of the democratic principles on which the American judicial system claimed to be founded.[58]

In incorporating the Deposition he found in Delano's *Narrative* into "Benito Cereno," Melville prefaces it with a statement that draws attention to the tribunal's glaring violations of due process (at least according to American judicial criteria for free white citizens):

> Some disclosures therein were, at the time, held dubious for both learned and natural reasons. The tribunal inclined to the opinion that the deponent, not undisturbed in his mind by recent events, raved of some things which could never have happened. But subsequent depositions of the surviving sailors, bearing out the revelations of their captain in *several* of the strangest particulars, *gave credence to the rest*. So that the tribunal, in its final decision, *rested its capital sentences upon statements which, had they lacked confirmation, it would have deemed it but duty to reject.* (103; italics added)

That is, the Spanish judges consider Benito Cereno's testimony incredible, evidently because their racist ideology pronounces Africans incapable, for "learned and natural reasons," of the intelligence the *San Dominick*'s slaves have manifested. Yet they accept that testimony because other witnesses have corroborated "*several* of the strangest particulars," which they argue gives "credence to the rest"—a clear violation of standard rules governing the evaluation of evidence. They then base their appalling "capital sentences" on allegations they themselves dispute and would normally have "deemed it but duty to reject," rationalizing their decision on the grounds that they have found (partial) "confirmation" for the dubious allegations.

Melville's preface invites readers to scrutinize the Deposition for further irregularities. If we follow his prompting, we will notice that the Spanish tribunal has relied heavily on the testimony of the slaves in "making record of their individual part in the past events, with a view to furnishing . . . the data whereon to found the criminal sentences to be pronounced." The refrain, "this is known and believed, because the negroes have said it" recurs repeatedly in this section of the Deposition (111–12). Yet a cardinal principle of American law, enshrined in the Fifth Amendment, holds that defendants should never be compelled to incriminate themselves.

American law also recognizes the importance of taking the defendant's motives into consideration when evaluating the seriousness of a crime. Depending on the motive and circumstances, a killing can be termed legitimate self-defense, involuntary manslaughter, or first- or second-degree murder, and the penalties differ accordingly. With these distinctions in mind, one journalist had denied that the *Amistad* rebels had committed mutiny or murder. "It is not every resistance of authority that constitutes mutiny. The authority exerted must be lawful," he had pointed out. Similarly, he had continued, "It is not every killing that is murder. Murder is the killing with malice aforethought. This was killing in self-defense, excusable or justifiable. These men were stolen, and were about to be made slaves for life; may they not lawfully resist?"[59] The same reasoning obviously pertains to the *San Dominick*'s slaves. Granted, Melville does not comment directly on the court's exclusion of the slaves' motives from its deliberations. In *Billy Budd*, however, he would drive home the harshness of a military tribunal by having Captain Vere argue that according to the Mutiny Act, "a martial court must . . . confine its attention to the . . . consequence" of an act, and that the "intent or non-intent" of a man the judges all recognize as morally innocent "is nothing to the purpose" (107–8, 111–12).

Melville also gives many indications of having read the Deposition between the lines with an eye to recovering the slaves' point of view. Even in his source, the slaves' motive for revolting, killing their master, and holding Benito Cereno hostage is easily discernible from the Spanish captain's explanation of his conduct. When Cereno tries to negotiate with the rebels by asking them what they want, they tell him they want to be taken either to a "negro" country in the vicinity, if any exists, or back to Senegal, and they agree to regulate their consumption of food and water conformably (829). Cereno then strings them along for nineteen days, steering toward ports where he hopes "to meet some Spanish or foreign vessel that would save" him, while pretending to comply with the demand that he stop to take in water before proceeding to Africa. Finally, the slaves decide to kill their master Aranda "because they said they could not otherwise obtain their liberty" (830). Melville preserves all this almost verbatim in his fictional

Deposition. But he additionally extrapolates throughout from the available slave testimony.[60]

For example, he highlights the motives behind the horrific detail he adds to his source—Babo's order that Aranda's corpse be divested of its flesh and that his skeleton be substituted for the figurehead of Columbus on the prow. Babo specifically tells Cereno that his purpose is "to prepare a warning" of the fate the Africans will mete out to the surviving Spanish seamen if they fail to "[k]eep faith with the blacks from here to Senegal" (106–7). The question Babo poses to Cereno and the other Spaniards as he confronts them one by one with the skeleton—"whether, from its whiteness, he should not think it a white's" (107)—strips racism literally down to its bare bones, revealing it as both deadly and senseless.

Nowhere does Melville display more insight into the slaves' viewpoint, more sensitivity in disclosing glimpses of their experience between the lines of the legal record, than in his treatment of the African women. The historical Deposition had specified that "the negresses of age, were knowing to the revolt, and influenced the death of their master," and that they "also used their influence to kill the deponent; that in the act of murder, and before that of the engagement of the ship, they began to sing, and were singing a very melancholy song during the action, to excite the courage of the negroes" (835). The Spaniards' reasons for recording this information were no doubt to provide warrant for inflicting a severe penalty, and to depict African women as irreclaimable savages. Melville, on the contrary, apparently deduced that the women's vengefulness arose from the sexual abuse to which they had been subjected, and that their militant ritual singing evidenced a complex culture in which women ranked high and played a vital role, in war as well as in peace.

He developed these insights in the many embellishments he introduced as he rewrote his source. His version of the Deposition accentuates the women's hatred of the Spaniards:

> the negresses, of age, . . . testified themselves satisfied at the death of their master, Don Alexandro; . . . had the negroes not restrained them, they would have tortured to death, instead of simply killing, the Spaniards slain by command of the negro Babo; . . . the negresses used their utmost influence to have the deponent made away with. . . . (112)

Given the familiarity Melville shows with the history of the African slave trade and with the protests against it by men like William Roscoe, he may have read the eyewitness account of the sexual license that prevailed on slave ships, furnished by Roscoe's colleague in the abolitionist movement, the repentant slave trader John Newton. Comparing the scene to "a town taken by storm, and given up to the ravages of an enraged and licentious army, of wild and unprincipled cossacks," Newton wrote:

When the women and girls are taken on board a ship, naked, trembling, terrified, perhaps almost exhausted with cold, fatigue, and hunger, they are often exposed to the wanton rudeness of white savages. The poor creatures cannot understand the language they hear, but the looks and manner of the speakers are sufficiently intelligible. In imagination, the prey is divided, upon the spot, and only reserved till opportunity offers. Where resistance, or refusal, would be utterly in vain, even the solicitation of consent is seldom thought of.[61]

Melville's ability to imagine what lay behind the African women's hatred certainly does not need to be ascribed to his reading, however, for he himself had seen sailors take comparable license with women of the Pacific islands.

Fleshing out his hints of the sexual debauchery on board slave ships, Melville has Delano himself ogle a "slumbering negress" he discerns "through the lace-work of some rigging" (73). The animal imagery into which Melville translates Delano's lust eloquently conveys his attitude toward African women and hints at how he may have behaved on occasions more propitious for satisfying his desires:

[She lay] with youthful limbs carelessly disposed, under the lee of the bulwarks, like a doe in the shade of a woodland rock. Sprawling at her lapped breasts was her wide-awake fawn, stark naked, its black little body half lifted from the deck, crosswise with its dam's; its hands, like two paws, clambering upon her; its mouth and nose ineffectually rooting to get at the mark. . . . (73)

Nevertheless, Melville does not portray the African women of the *San Dominick* as mere helpless victims of white men's lust. He reveals them to be full participants in Babo's plot, manipulating white men's predictable responses to blacks in order to ensure group survival and a life of dignity for their children. "[A]s if not at all concerned at the attitude in which she had been caught," the young mother uses her sexuality to distract Delano's attention from the sights and incidents that have been arousing his suspicions. Clasping her child "with maternal transports, covering it with kisses," she leads Delano to believe he is seeing nothing but "naked nature, . . . pure tenderness and love" (73). Delano accurately perceives that she and her sisters on board the *San Dominick* are "equally ready to die for their infants or fight for them," but he does not realize that what he is watching is part of an ongoing fight.[62]

Ironically, Delano's fantasies culminate in the reflection that "these perhaps are some of the very women whom Mungo Park saw in Africa, and gave such a noble account of" (73). Park had cited many occasions on which African women had "received me . . . into their cottages, when I was perishing of hunger[;] sympathized with me in my sufferings; relieved my distresses; and contributed to my safety."[63] Apparently it does not occur to

Delano that if these same women now find themselves on a slave ship, the "disinterested charity, and tender solicitude" they have displayed toward white men have been singularly ill requited. The publication date of Park's *Travels*—1799, the year of the *San Dominick*'s revolt—makes the possibility that Delano might be seeing some of the same women Park encountered more than an idle suggestion. In fact Melville's irony cuts against Park, too, for he traveled back to the coast in a slave coffle that included Africans who had befriended him before their capture, and returned to England via a slaver that stopped in the West Indies. While Park did not share Delano's habit of stereotyping Africans, he contradicted his own humanitarian professions in much the way the Yankee captain does; he even opined that in "the present unenlightened state of their minds," the abolition of the slave trade would not produce "so extensive or beneficial" an effect on the "manners of the natives . . . as many wise and worthy persons fondly expect."[64]

Park had visited the Senegambia region, where he evidently did not see women participating in battle. Thus Melville must have turned to other travel accounts to amplify the historical Benito Cereno's description of the slave women's militant role. "[I]n the various acts of murder, they sang songs and danced—not gaily, but solemnly," he elaborates; "and before the engagement with the boats, as well as during the action, they sang melancholy songs to the negroes, and . . . this melancholy tone was more inflaming than a different one would have been, and was so intended" (112). Delano's recollection that "Ashantee negresses . . . make . . . capital soldiers" (92), and Melville's inclusion of six Ashanti men and an unspecified number of Ashanti women among the *San Dominick*'s slaves—a departure from his source, which identified the *Tryal*'s slaves as "Senegal Negroes" (826)— suggests that he drew on accounts of that powerful West African kingdom, famous for its advanced civilization, warlike character, and fierce resistance to British attempts at conquest. The names he invented for two of the slaves he added to the list in the *Tryal* Deposition—Ghofan and Akim (104), both tributary peoples conquered by the Ashanti—also indicate more than a casual acquaintance with the available literature on African culture and history.[65] In sum, Melville's many interpolations add up to a consistent pattern: an unmistakable effort to reconstruct the slaves' side of the story and to accord it as much visibility as possible within the framework of a narrative faithful to the fact that the slaves' "tyrants have been their historians."[66]

VI

If the intricate web of historical allusion and the dense particularization of African culture in "Benito Cereno" reveal the influence of the *Amistad* case in teaching Melville how to read between the lines of such documents as Delano's *Narrative* and Benito Cereno's Deposition, the fictional text also bursts out of its sources' confines at the point where it comes closest to articulating the alternative reality the slaves are seeking to construct. The most haunting character in the story—Babo, "whose brain, not body ha[s] schemed and led the revolt, with the plot" (116)—owes almost nothing to records of the *Tryal* and *Amistad* cases. The historical Babo and his son Mure, whom Melville merged into one, remain shadowy figures in the original documents, and it is not they, but Benito Cereno himself, who suggests the idea of deceiving Delano with the masquerade of normality (831). Similarly, the *Amistad* rebel leader Cinquez, despite his oratorical charisma and leadership ability, shows no evidence of having possessed the extraordinary inventiveness Melville attributes to Babo.

In portraying Babo as the author of a "plot" that is also the plot of "Benito Cereno," Melville promotes his fictional character to the rank of co-author. As Joyce Adler has pointed out in one of the most astute analyses any critic has offered of Babo, Melville gives the slave leader "his own kind of poetic imagination," his own penchant for symbolism, his own sardonic humor.[67] (Once we begin reading the story from Babo's perspective, indeed, we see the black humor—in every sense—of many scenes that otherwise strike us as merely terrifying.) Melville credits to Babo nearly all the symbols he himself creates in the story. It is Babo who devises the stratagems that simultaneously disguise the rebels as traditional menials and represent their continued enslavement: stationing four elderly Africans, busily picking oakum, above the crowd, so that they can spy infractions of discipline and reimpose order; setting the six Ashantis, also strategically placed, at cleaning hatchets, which they can distribute to their fellow slaves in case of need; "presenting Atufal, his right-hand man, as chained, though in a moment the chains could be dropped" (109). It is Babo who suspends the key to the padlock ostensibly securing Atufal's chains on a "slender silken cord" around Don Benito's neck—"significant symbols, truly," as Delano observes (63), characteristically without understanding the invitation to unlock the problem of slavery. It is Babo who forces Benito Cereno to wear the inappropriately ornate garb and "artificially stiffened," but empty, scabbard that deceptively betoken his "despotic command" (116). And it is Babo who invents the most unforgettable and endlessly evocative symbol in the story: the skeleton replacing the figurehead of Columbus.

In an extraordinary fusion of his own artistry with Babo's Melville also allows us to observe Babo's creative intelligence in action when confronted with a new danger. While innumerable critics have commented on the famous shaving scene, few, if any, have noticed that Babo improvises it on the spot, just as Cereno is on the point of giving himself away by contradicting his story. With Delano emphatically asking for an explanation of the contradiction and Cereno "pausing an instant, as one about to make a plunging exchange of elements," Babo takes advantage of the coincidental arrival of a "messenger-boy . . . in the regular performance of his function" as time-keeper, and concocts an order he could never have received: "master told me never mind where he was, or how engaged, always to remind him, to a minute, when shaving-time comes" (81–82). The ploy, of course, ensures that "if master means to talk more to Don Amasa," a razor at his throat will swiftly deter him. And once again, the justly renowned symbolism of the ensuing scene is Babo's: the contemptuous use of the Spanish flag as a bib, the flaunting of the African's alleged love of "gay" colors (a trait the historical Delano had actually imputed to "natives"),[68] and the daring challenge to look reality in the face (84–85).

Through all of these symbols, Melville likewise challenges his readers to solve the life-and-death riddle of the nation's destiny. Can they, unlike Delano, recognize their African compatriots as fellow human beings, instead of reenacting the crimes of their Spanish predecessors? Can they, unlike Aranda and Cereno, escape the legacy of the past? Can they reverse the course of the history that has seen the explorer of a New World turn into a deadly destroyer, and a vessel of discovery into a death ship? Can they prevent a promised earthly paradise from turning into an irredeemable Valley of Dry Bones? Melville's final symbol suggests how little hope he apparently felt as he surveyed the future through Babo's eyes. The riddle he propounded for his nineteenth-century readers has yet to be solved. Looming over the society that has unavailingly tried to obliterate him from memory, Babo's impaled head still casts its shadow over America.

Notes

1. All page references will be to the standard edition of Herman Melville, "Benito Cereno" (1855), *The Piazza Tales and Other Prose Pieces, 1839–1860*, ed. Harrison Hayford, Alma MacDougall, G. Thomas Tanselle, and others (Evanston and Chicago: Northwestern University Press and Newberry Library, 1987), 46–117. Quotations in this paragraph are from 46–48. Subsequent page references will be given parenthetically in the text.

2. For analyses of the symbolic interrelationships Melville establishes among the rebels of the *San Dominick*, those of San Domingo, the Dominicans, and the Spanish Inquisition, see H. Bruce Franklin, *The Wake of the Gods: Melville's Mythology* (Stanford: Stanford University Press, 1963), 136–50; Laurie Lorant, "Herman Melville and Race: Themes and Imagery," Ph.D. dissertation, New York University, 1972, 125–40; John Bernstein, "*Benito Cereno* and the Spanish Inquisition," *Nineteenth-Century Fiction* 16 (March 1962): 345–50; Gloria Horsley-Meacham, "The Monastic Slaver: Images and Meaning in 'Benito Cereno,' " *New England Quarterly* 56 (June 1983): 261–66; and Eric J. Sundquist, "*Benito Cereno* and New World Slavery," *Reconstructing American Literary History*, ed. Sacvan Bercovitch (Cambridge, Mass.: Harvard University Press, 1986), 93–122.

3. For a different interpretation of Melville's allusion to Ezekiel's Valley of Dry Bones, drawing an analogy between ancient Israel and nineteenth-century America, rather than between Israelites and Africans, see Mario D'Avanzo, "Melville's 'San Dominick' and Ezekiel's Dry Bones," *College Literature* 8 (Spring 1981): 186–88. On the slaves' identification with

the ancient Israelites, as reflected in their spirituals, see Lawrence W. Levine, *Black Culture and Black Consciousness: Afro-American Folk Thought from Slavery to Freedom* (New York: Oxford University Press, 1977), 30–55; Eugene D. Genovese, *Roll, Jordan, Roll: The World the Slaves Made* (1974; reprint New York: Random House, Vintage Books, 1976), 248–55; and Albert J. Raboteau, *Slave Religion: The 'Invisible Institution' in the Antebellum South* (New York: Oxford University Press, 1978), 243–66. For a recent historical study of slave culture that cites Melville as a sympathetic observer of African American life, see Sterling Stuckey, *Slave Culture: Nationalist Theory and the Foundations of Black America* (New York: Oxford University Press, 1987), chapter 1; Melville is cited on 84–85.

    4. Mungo Park, *Travels in the Interior Districts of Africa: Performed under the Direction and Patronage of the African Association, in the Years 1795, 1796, and 1797* (1799; New York: Arno Press and New York *Times*, 1971), 198, 278–79. Sterling Stuckey and Joshua Leslie discuss Melville's reading of Mungo Park and its influence on "Benito Cereno" in "The Death of Benito Cereno: A Reading of Herman Melville on Slavery," *Journal of Negro History* 67 (December 1982): 287–301. The passage they quote (288–89), which Melville probably had in mind when he referred to the "women whom Mungo Park saw in Africa, and gave such a noble account of" (73), not only describes the kindness and hospitality shown toward Park by a woman, but tells of how her family "lightened their labour by songs, one of which was composed extempore; for I was myself the subject of it" (198). Park refers repeatedly to the *singing men*, explaining their function and providing many instances of how they used song to communicate (278–79, 324, 327–28). The abolitionist Lydia Maria Child quotes Park extensively in both her *Appeal in Favor of That Class of Americans Called Africans* (Boston: Allen and Ticknor, 1833) and her *History of the Condition of Women, in Various Ages and Nations* (Boston: John Allen, 1835), which contains an eighty-page section on African women in vol. 1.

    5. On the Egyptian origins of Greek civilization, see Martin Bernal, *Black Athena: The Afroasiatic Roots of Classical Civilization, Vol. 1: The Fabrication of Ancient Greece, 1785–1985* (New Brunswick: Rutgers University Press, 1987). Bernal discusses the evidence for the Egyptian origin of the Greek sphinx on 68–69. As Bernal shows, the racist campaign to deny the Egyptian origin of Greek civilization and to characterize the Egyptians themselves as Caucasians rather than Africans began at the end of the eighteenth century. The issue of the Egyptians' racial identity was hotly contested between abolitionists, who held to the earlier view of Egypt as an African civilization that had influenced the Greeks, and proslavery apologists, who played a major role in the racist campaign. See Child's *Appeal*, 156–58, for an excellent statement of the abolitionist argument. Child points out that according to many "ancient writers . . . Egypt derived all the arts and sciences from Ethiopia"; that "Herodotus, the earliest of the Greek historians," describes the Egyptians as having " 'black skin and frizzled hair' "; that "Egypt was the great school of knowledge in the ancient world"; that "[t]he wisest of the Grecian philosophers, among whom were Solon, Pythagoras and Plato, went there for instruction"; that "[a] large portion of Grecian mythology," as well as the concept of "one, invisible God," was derived from Egypt; and that "statues of the Sphinx have the usual characteristics of the negro race." She also quotes the American historian Alexander Everett as having asserted: " 'While Greece and Rome were yet barbarous, we find the light of learning and improvement emanating from the continent of Africa, (supposed to be so degraded and accursed,) out of the midst of this very woolly-haired, flat-nosed, thick-lipped, coal-black race, which some persons are tempted to station at a pretty low intermediate point between men and monkeys.' " Her quotation is taken from his *America: or a General Survey of the Political Situation of the Several Powers of the Western Continent, with Conjectures on their Future Prospects: by a Citizen of the United States* (1826; reprint New York: Garland, 1974), 213–14.

    6. These allusions include: the comparison of a Spanish sailor to "an Egyptian priest, making gordian knots for the temple of Ammon" (76) (an allusion that points toward the

Egyptian origin of European civilization and recalls Spain's five centuries of Moorish rule); the comparison of Don Benito's seeming tyranny over Atufal to a child trying to "lead a bull of the Nile by the ring in his nose" (78); the comparison of Babo to a "Nubian sculptor" (87); and the comparison of "the figure of Atufal, monumentally fixed at the threshold" with "one of those sculptured porters of black marble guarding the porches of Egyptian tombs" (92). In addition, Melville evokes the slave coffles traveling through the Sahara when he compares the longboat under which women and children have taken refuge to "a camel's skeleton in the desert" (81). For an exhaustive and illuminating study of the African allusions in "Benito Cereno," see Gloria Horsley-Meacham, "Bull of the Nile: Symbol, History, and Racial Myth in 'Benito Cereno,' " *New England Quarterly* 64 (June 1991): 225–42.

    7.   For an overview of American racist ideology and an analysis of its manifestations in Delano's observations about blacks, see Carolyn L. Karcher, *Shadow over the Promised Land: Slavery, Race, and Violence in Melville's America* (Baton Rouge: Louisiana State University Press, 1980), 19–27, 128–32.

    8.   Child, *Appeal in Favor of Americans Called Africans*, 180.

    9.   "The Slave Murders," unsigned editorial, *National Anti-Slavery Standard*, 23 June 1842, 11. The murders in question are described in an article titled "Horrible Events!," excerpted on the previous page from the *Natchez Free Trader*.

    10.   First identified as the main source for the story by Horace H. Scudder, "Melville's *Benito Cereno* and Captain Delano's Voyages," *PMLA* 43 (June 1928): 502–32, chapter 18 of Amasa Delano's *A Narrative of Voyages and Travels in the Northern and Southern Hemispheres . . .* (Boston, 1817) is reprinted as an appendix to the Northwestern-Newberry edition of *The Piazza Tales and Other Prose Pieces*, 810–47. All page references to chapter 18 will be to this appendix. References to other chapters will be to the facsimile reprint of the 1817 edition (Upper Saddle River, N.J.: Gregg Press, 1970).

    11.   Although a number of Melville scholars have noted the relevance of the *Amistad* case to "Benito Cereno," none has explored the parallels in depth or considered the impact it may have had on him at this formative stage of his development. See Sidney Kaplan, "Melville and the American National Sin: The Meaning of *Benito Cereno*," *Journal of Negro History* 42 (January 1957): 14–15; Jean Fagan Yellin, *The Intricate Knot: Black Figures in American Literature, 1776–1863* (New York: New York University Press, 1972), 216–17; Michael Paul Rogin, *Subversive Genealogy: The Politics and Art of Herman Melville* (New York: Alfred A. Knopf, 1983), 211–13; Brook Thomas, "The Legal Fictions of Herman Melville and Lemuel Shaw," *Critical Inquiry* 11 (September 1984): 29–30; and Sundquist, *"Benito Cereno* and New World Slavery," 113–15. For modern accounts of the *Amistad* case, see Christopher Martin, *The "Amistad" Affair* (New York: Abelard-Schuman, 1970); and Howard Jones, *Mutiny on the "Amistad": The Saga of a Slave Revolt and Its Impact on American Abolition, Law, and Diplomacy* (New York: Oxford University Press, 1987). For the chronology and details of Melville's voyage to Liverpool, see William H. Gilman, *Melville's Early Life and "Redburn"* (New York: New York University Press, 1951). According to Gilman, Melville signed up as a "boy," embarking for Liverpool on 4 June, leaving Liverpool on 13 August, and arriving back in New York on 1 October (128–45). On Melville's habit of likening sailors to slaves, see Karcher, *Shadow over the Promised Land*, chapter 2.

    12.   The *Amistad* case was so fascinating to the public that a member of the Connecticut Historical Society even compiled an account of it while it was still being tried in the Connecticut courts. See John W. Barber, *A History of the Amistad Captives: Being a Circumstantial Account of the Capture of the Spanish Schooner Amistad, by the Africans on Board; Their Voyage, and Capture near Long Island, New York; with Biographical Sketches of Each of the Surviving Africans{.} Also, an Account of the Trials had on Their Case, before the District and Circuit Courts of the United States, for the District of Connecticut. Compiled from Authentic Sources* (New Haven: E. L. and J. W. Barber, 1840). In addition to Barber, Martin, and Jones, I will also be relying heavily on contemporary newspaper accounts in the *Liberator* and the *National Anti-*

Slavery Standard. Nineteenth-century newspapers typically reprinted news reports from each other, since it was not yet current practice for newspapers to hire reporters of their own. Hence Melville could have seen the same accounts reprinted in almost any newspaper he read. The *Liberator* and the *Standard*, for example, reprinted the same newspaper accounts included in Barber's compilation and drew most of their reports from the *Journal of Commerce*, published in New York and representing the views of evangelical businessmen. Providing a gauge of the shift in public sentiment brought about by the *Amistad* case, the *Journal of Commerce* had been rabidly anti-abolitionist during the 1830s, yet became extremely sympathetic to the *Amistad* rebels.

13.   Reprinted in Barber, 3–5. All the quotations in the paragraphs that follow are taken from this widely reprinted *New London Gazette* article.

14.   A later article corrected this information: only the captain and cook were killed— the other two sailors escaped in a small boat; see Barber, 7.

15.   Compare Melville's version of the Deposition (110–11) to its original, as reprinted in the Northwestern-Newberry edition (833).

16.   Reprinted in Barber, 8.

17.   Barber, 5.

18.   The description in the *New York Sun* of 31 August 1839 of "The Long, Low, Black Schooner," quoted in Martin, *"Amistad" Affair*, 50–51, is even closer: "Her sides were covered with barnacles and long tentacles of seaweed streamed from her cable and her sides at the water line. Her jibs were torn and big rents and holes appeared in both foresail and mainsail as they flapped in the gentle breeze. . . . [Over] her rail . . . coal-black African faces, fixed with a mingled curiosity and fear, peered above forms clad in the most fantastic garb."

19.   Barber, 4.

20.   Barber, 4. Cinquez's actual name in his own language was Singbe, but I will follow the spelling most commonly used in the American press.

21.   Barber 4, 9. For an indication of the rapid evolution of public opinion, see the articles from the *Boston Courier, Dedham Patriot, Portsmouth Journal*, and *Boston Cultivator*, reprinted under the headline "Views of the Press," in the *Liberator*, 13 Sept. 1839, 146. It is the *Boston Cultivator* that (mistakenly) identifies Cinquez as the son of a chief. See also "The Long, Low, Black, Schooner," *New York Sun*, reprinted in *Liberator*, 6 Sept. 1839, 143. For comments on Cinquez's power as an orator, see Barber, 5; "Interesting Meeting of the Liberated Africans," *Evangelist*, reprinted in the *National Anti-Slavery Standard*, 13 May 1841, 195; "Africans of the Amistad," reprinted from *Journal of Commerce* and containing quotations from a New Haven newspaper, *National Anti-Slavery Standard*, 25 Mar. 1841, 167; Lydia Maria Child, "Letters from New-York," no. 12, *National Anti-Slavery Standard*, 2 Dec. 1841, 103.

22.   *Journal of Commerce*, 8 Oct. 1839, reprinted in Barber, 18–20.

23.   Article 9 of the 1795 treaty between the United States and Spain is quoted in full in "The Amistad Case," *Evening Post*, reprinted in *National Anti-Slavery Standard*, 21 Jan. 1841, 129. It is also paraphrased and partially cited in many other articles.

24.   For an eyewitness account of the Prudence Crandall case and Judson's role in it, see Samuel J. May, *Some Recollections of Our Antislavery Conflict* (Boston: Fields, Osgood, 1869), 40–71.

25.   Barber, 17–20; J. W. Gibbs, "On the Names of the Captured Africans," *New Haven Palladium*, reprinted in *Liberator*, 15 Nov. 1839, 184; Lewis Tappan, "Trial of the Amistad Africans," *Emancipator*, reprinted in *Liberator*, 17 Jan. 1840, 10; "The Amistad," reprinted from *Journal of Commerce*, *National Anti-Slavery Standard*, 28 Jan. 1841, 133.

26.   "The Captives of the Amistad," *Journal of Commerce*, reprinted in *National Anti-Slavery Standard*, 4 Mar. 1841, 153–54; "The Case of the Amistad. Supreme Court of the United States. January Term, 1841," *National Intelligencer*, reprinted in *National Anti-Slavery Standard*, 25 Mar. 1841, 165. Adams's full argument was published as a pamphlet: *Argument*

of John Quincy Adams, before the Supreme Court of the United States, in the Case of the United States, Appellants, vs. Cinque, and Others, Africans, Captured in the Schooner Amistad, by Lieut. Gedney, Delivered on the 24th of February and 1st of March, 1841. . . . (1841; reprint New York: Arno Press and New York *Times*, 1969).

27. Reprinted in *Liberator*, 13 Sept. 1839, 146.

28. Betty Fladeland, *Men and Brothers: Anglo-American Antislavery Cooperation* (Urbana: University of Illinois Press, 1972), 123, 134; Jones, *Mutiny on the "Amistad,"* 35.

29. "The Amistad," *Portsmouth Journal*, reprinted in *Liberator*, 11 Oct. 1839, 162.

30. "The African Captives," *Boston Atlas*, reprinted in *Liberator*, 27 Sept. 1839, 155; "Views of the Press," *Portsmouth Journal*, reprinted in *Liberator*, 13 Sept. 1839, 146; "The Captives of the *Amistad*," *Journal of Commerce*, reprinted in *National Anti-Slavery Standard*, 4 Mar. 1841, 153–54; "The Case of the Amistad. Supreme Court of the United States. January Term," *National Intelligencer*, reprinted in *National Anti-Slavery Standard*, 25 Mar. 1841, 165.

31. See the poems "Cinquez" and "Lines, Suggested on reading the capture of the schooner Amistad, and thirty-eight Africans, with their heroic leader, JOSEPH CINQUEZ," reprinted respectively from the *New Haven Record* and *Pennsylvania Freeman, Liberator* 11 and 25 Oct. 1839, 164, 172. William Cullen Bryant's "The African Chief" was also frequently reprinted. On the play see Jones, *Mutiny on the "Amistad,"* 156. The *Liberator* began advertising the mezzotint engraving of Cinquez on 19 Mar. 1841. On the wax exhibition, see Barber, 8; he reproduces profiles based on these wax figures on 9–15.

32. Barber, 25–29; "Interesting Meeting of the Liberated Africans," *Evangelist*, reprinted in *National Anti-Slavery Standard*, 13 May 1841, 195; Joseph Sturge, *A Visit to the United States in 1841*, quoted in Jones, 253n.5.

33. In December 1841, American slaves revolted aboard the Virginian brig *Creole*, which was transporting them to New Orleans, and forced the captain to take them to Nassau, where the British freed them. The *Creole* slaves were greeted as "heroes," and compared to the patriots of the American Revolution, a comparison invited by the name of their leader, Madison Washington. See "The Creole—Strike for Liberty!," *Journal of Commerce*, reprinted in *National Anti-Slavery Standard*, 30 Dec. 1841, 118. The abolitionist Lydia Maria Child, editor of the *Standard*, commented that the *Amistad* case had "prepared the way" for the public reaction to the *Creole* and marveled: "A few years ago, Madison Washington would have been dismissed by the American press as a 'base wretch,' 'a cut-throat,' &c. Now the press of the free States, with few exceptions, utters no condemnation, while very many pour forth expressions of sympathy, not unmingled with admiration." See her editorial, "The Iron Shroud," *National Anti-Slavery Standard*, 3 Mar. 1842, 154–55. Later that year, huge public meetings were held in Boston to protest the arrest of the fugitive slave George Latimer, remanded to his owner by Melville's father-in-law, Chief Justice Lemuel Shaw of the Massachusetts Supreme Court. The agitation resulted in the passage of Massachusetts' personal liberty law, which forbade State officials to cooperate in the detention and prosecution of fugitive slaves. The Latimer case will be briefly discussed below.

34. All references will be to the standard edition of *Redburn*, ed. Harrison Hayford, Hershel Parker, and G. Thomas Tanselle (Evanston and Chicago: Northwestern University Press and Newberry Library, 1969) and will be given parenthetically in the text. Quotations in this paragraph are from 60, 67.

35. See Gilman, *Melville's Early Life and "Redburn,"* 130–31 and 333n.35 on the actual crew of the *St. Lawrence* and how it compares to Melville's description in *Redburn*. Although no other information about Robert Jackson is available, Gilman has been able to substantiate Melville's descriptions of at least five other crew members. Hence it is not unreasonable to hypothesize that a core of fact underlies his characterization of Jackson.

36. According to Gilman, "Allan Melvill met Roscoe in 1818, through an introduction by William Lodge, a mutual friend" (189, 349n.31).

37. Gilman, 188–89, 349, notes 29 and 31; Fladeland, *Men and Brothers*, 69–74.

Considered a political milestone, even by the conservatives who opposed abolitionist agitation in the 1830s, the date of the slave trade's abolition was common knowledge.

38.   Gilman, 140; Herman Melville, *Journals*, ed. Howard C. Horsford with Lynn Horth (Evanston and Chicago: Northwestern University Press and Newberry Library, 1989), 50.

39.   See "The Long, Low, Black Schooner," *New York Sun*, reprinted in *Liberator*, 6 Sept. 1839, 143; and the *New London Gazette* of 26 Aug., reprinted in Barber, 3–5. The latter describes the *Amistad* as "clipper-built" and reports "the suspicion that she was a pirate." In an as yet unpublished article titled "Another Look at Melville's 'Nursery Tale,' " Laurie Robertson-Lorant has speculated that Melville may have written some of the early chapters of *Redburn* immediately upon his return from his 1839 voyage to Liverpool and then laid the manuscript aside, taking it up again in 1849. If so, this may account for the echoes of newspaper reports on the *Amistad* case in *Redburn*; it may also help explain the persistence of memories and associations that resurface both in *Redburn* and in "Benito Cereno."

40.   See note 42 below; also the anecdotes cited in Child, *Appeal in Favor of Americans Called Africans*, 141–42. All African Americans who visited England commented on the freedom from racial discrimination that they enjoyed there. See Frederick Douglass, *My Bondage and My Freedom* (1855; reprint New York: Dover, 1969), chapter 24; Harriet A. Jacobs, *Incidents in the Life of a Slave Girl*, ed. Jean Fagan Yellin (1861; reprint Cambridge, Mass.: Harvard University Press, 1987), chapter 37; and R. J. M. Blackett, *Building an Antislavery Wall: Black Americans in the Atlantic Abolitionist Movement, 1830–1860* (Baton Rouge: Louisiana State University Press, 1983), 39–41, 205–7.

41.   For a detailed analysis of this passage and how it refutes the claim that racial prejudice is a universal and ineradicable instinct, see Karcher, *Shadow over the Promised Land*, 31–32.

42.   "Treatment of Colored People in England," *Hartford Observer*, reprinted in *Liberator*, 3 July 1840, 107. In language very close to Melville's, Garrison commented on another such testimonial: "It really seems . . . that the aristocrats of England are much more *republican* in their feelings than the vaunting democrats of the U. States." See his editorial note at the end of an untitled article from the *Journal of Commerce*, reprinted in *Liberator*, 27 Sept. 1834, 155.

43.   "Treatment of Colored People in England," 107.

44.   "Legal Injustice," *Liberator*, 4 Nov. 1842, 175. On the bearing that family ties had on Melville's expression of his politics in his art, see Karcher, *Shadow over the Promised Land*, and Rogin, *Subversive Genealogy*. On the relationship between Melville's class consciousness and his narrative strategies, see H. Bruce Franklin, "From Outsider to Insider: Melville's Narrative Strategies," *Melville Society Extracts* 76 (February 1989): 3–6. Compare Shaw's argument that the law must be enforced, "however disagreeable to our own natural sympathies," to Vere's in *Billy Budd, Sailor (An Inside Narrative)*, ed. Harrison Hayford and Merton M. Sealts, Jr. (Chicago: University of Chicago Press, 1962), 111: "But let not warm hearts betray heads that should be cool. Ashore in a criminal case, will an upright judge allow himself off the bench to be waylaid by some tender kinswoman of the accused seeking to touch him with her tearful plea? Well, the heart here, sometimes the feminine in man, is as that piteous woman, and hard though it be, she must here be ruled out." Other relevant passages from *Billy Budd* will be cited below.

45.   "Legal Injustice," *Liberator*, 4 Nov. 1842, 175. On the moral and legal issues raised by the Latimer case, see William M. Wiecek, "Latimer: Lawyers, Abolitionists, and the Problem of Unjust Laws," *Antislavery Reconsidered: New Perspectives on the Abolitionists*, ed. Lewis Perry and Michael Fellman (Baton Rouge: Louisiana State University Press, 1979), 219–37. Wiecek notes the relevance of the case to *Billy Budd*, 235–37. For an analysis of Shaw's jurisprudence by a legal historian, see Leonard W. Levy, *The Law of the Commonwealth and Chief Justice Shaw* (Cambridge, Mass.: Harvard University Press, 1957). The cases I refer to are discussed in Chapters 5–7. For a brilliant analysis of the ideological assumptions on

which Shaw based his fugitive slave decisions, see Thomas, "Legal Fictions of Melville and Shaw," 24–50. In the prose Supplement to his volume of Civil War poems, *Battle-Pieces, and Aspects of the War* (1866; reprint Amherst: University of Massachusetts Press, 1972), Melville calls slavery an "atheistical iniquity" (268). On *Moby-Dick* see note 46 below.

46. See Charles H. Foster, "Something in Emblems: A Reinterpretation of *Moby-Dick*," *New England Quarterly* 34 (March 1961): 3–35; and Karcher, *Shadow over the Promised Land*, 31–32, 78. The quotation is from Herman Melville, *Moby-Dick or The Whale*, ed. Harrison Hayford, Hershel Parker, and G. Thomas Tanselle (Evanston and Chicago: Northwestern University Press and Newberry Library, 1988), 48.

47. Thomas, "Legal Fictions of Melville and Shaw," 26–31, also strongly implies this.

48. The 1795 treaty is not mentioned in Delano's *Narrative* proper, but in correspondence that Sterling Stuckey has uncovered, regarding the dispute between Cereno and Delano over Delano's claim. See Sterling Stuckey and Joshua Leslie, "Aftermath: Captain Delano's Claim Against Benito Cereno," *Modern Philology* 85 (February 1988): 276. It was Cereno who invoked the law against Delano.

49. These contradictions are apparent throughout Delano's *Narrative*, not only in chapter 18. Melville obviously based his characterization of Delano on a careful reading of the whole. In chapter 2, for example, Delano philosophizes about the need for a sea captain to treat his sailors humanely and to diversify "their employments, . . . appointing such as are adapted to their condition": "Many are the instances, in which generous and feeling minds have been ruined, and only relieved by death, when they were subject to the command of others, and during a period of depression were inhumanly treated without the means of redress. Sailors, and all men, even of the meanest education, have the essential qualities of high minds, and are exalted and improved, at the same time that they are won by generosity and kindness" (52). Yet several pages later he describes how he tries to bully a refractory sailor into submission by forcing him to "do his work over again according to my orders" (55); when this sailor leads an abortive mutiny against him, Delano has several of the participants flogged (57). In chapter 4, his humanitarian rhetoric attributing New Guinea natives' hatred of whites to "our own misconduct toward them" is similarly belied by his own behavior, as he reacts to the "treachery" of these same natives by killing "forty or fifty" of them in an encounter that could easily have been avoided (80, 94). This latter incident is also noted by Stuckey and Leslie, "Aftermath," 268–69.

50. On the antislavery character of *Putnam's*, see Yellin, *Intricate Knot*, 216; and Karcher, *Shadow over the Promised Land*, 13–14. In two provocative articles, Charles Swann suggests that Melville was simultaneously targeting an audience of southern paternalists who embraced the plantation myth and an audience of northern liberals who opposed slavery, but still held many racist or romantic racialist ideas about Africans. See his "*Benito Cereno*: Melville's De(con)struction of the Southern Reader," *Literature and History* 12 (Spring 1986): 3–15; and "Whodunnit? Or, Who Did What? *Benito Cereno* and the Politics of Narrative Structure," *American Studies in Transition*, ed. David E. Nye and Christen Kold Thomsen (Odense: Odense University Press, 1985), 204–6, 228–29. See also Franklin, "Past, Present, and Future Seemed One," in this volume, on Hawthorne as a representative of the audience Melville is targeting.

51. For fine analyses of the many similarities between Delano and Cereno, see Sandra A. Zagarell, "Reenvisioning America: Melville's 'Benito Cereno,' " *ESQ: Journal of the American Renaissance* 30 (4th Quarter 1984): 245–59, especially 245 and 249; and Swann, "Whodunnit?," 221–23. For analyses of another historical fact symbolized by this relationship between the two captains—the United States' recent attempts to take over the remnants of Spain's New World slave empire—see Allan Moore Emery, " 'Benito Cereno' and Manifest Destiny," *Nineteenth-Century Fiction* 39 (June 1984): 48–68; Sundquist, "*Benito Cereno* and New World Slavery," 107–10, 116–22; and Franklin, "Past, Present, and Future Seemed One," in this volume.

52. See Franklin, *Wake of the Gods*, 136–50, and "Past, Present, and Future Seemed One," in this volume; Horsley-Meacham, "Monastic Slaver," 261–66; and Sundquist, *"Benito Cereno* and New World Slavery," 99–101.

53. Harold Beaver, ed. *Billy Budd, Sailor, and Other Stories* (Middlesex and New York: Penguin Books, 1970), 435, 449, was the first to point out the derivation of the name Melville substituted for Delano's ship (actually called the *Perseverance*). See also Zagarell, "Reenvisioning America," 256; and especially Franklin, "Past, Present, and Future Seemed One," in this volume. Christopher Lloyd, *William Dampier* (Hamden, Conn.: Archon Books, 1966), 43–44, identifies the *Bachelor's Delight* as a Danish ship; he comments: "How [the bucaneers] disposed of . . . the sixty black girls they found on board their prize, we do not know: probably she was a Danish slaver and her cargo was sold to one of the numerous slave traders who ranged this coast at a time when the trade was a perfectly legal and respectable business." Lloyd does not give a source for this information, however, and I have not succeeded in identifying one to which Melville might have had access. Although Melville clearly read Dampier's and Cowley's narratives, neither mentions "sixty black girls" among the other cargo they found on their prize, and which they disposed of in the slavetrading port of Sherborough, on the Guinea Coast; nor does either mention the rechristening of their "prize" as the *Bachelor's Delight*. Melville may have read the narrative by their companion Lionel Wafer, who does mention the *Bachelor's Delight* (though not the "sixty black girls"); he refers to Wafer along with Dampier and Cowley in Sketch Sixth of "The Encantadas," *Piazza Tales*, 145. See Wafer's *A New Voyage & Description of the Isthmus of America*, ed. L. E. Elliott Joyce (1699; reprint Nendeln/Liechtenstein: Kraus Reprint, 1967), 112, and Joyce's excellent introduction and notes.

54. Hawkins's slavetrading activities were common knowledge; see Child, *Appeal in Favor of Americans Called Africans*, 2.

55. Fladeland, *Men and Brothers*, 111–12.

56. Jones, 18–20; "Right of Search," excerpted from "Judge Jay's recent work on 'War and Peace,' " *National Anti-Slavery Standard*, 31 Mar. 1842, 169–70; [Ellis Gray Loring], "Consul Trist's Correspondence," *National Anti-Slavery Standard*, 8 July 1841, 17.

57. William Lloyd Garrison, *Selections from the Speeches and Writings of William Lloyd Garrison* (1852; reprint, New York: Negro Universities Press, 1968), 68.

58. Vincent Harding, *There Is a River: The Black Struggle for Freedom in America* (1981; reprint New York: Vintage Books, 1983), 157, succinctly summarizes the provisions of the 1850 Fugitive Slave Law: "Only a sworn affidavit would be necessary to claim a black man, woman, or child as someone's escaped slave, to seize them from streets and houses and hiding places, and haul them before a federal commissioner. The apprehended individual had no right to a trial by jury, nor could his or her testimony be admitted in any legal proceedings which challenged the capture. The commissioners were to receive ten dollars for each case in which a black person was sent into slavery, and five dollars for each release. Moreover, federal marshalls were empowered to summon any citizen to aid in the capture of a fugitive, and the penalties for interference with this legal kidnapping process were to be maximum fines of a thousand dollars and imprisonment for up to six months." On the slave codes of the South, see George Stroud, *Sketch of the Laws Relating to Slavery in the Several States of the United States of America* (1827; reprint Philadelphia: n.p., 1856); and Child, *Appeal in Favor of Americans Called Africans*, chapter 2.

59. "The Amistad," *Journal of Commerce*, reprinted in *National Anti-Slavery Standard*, 28 Jan. 1841, 133. For a similar statement, see "The Amistad Case," *Evening Post*, reprinted in *National Anti-Slavery Standard*, 21 Jan. 1841, 129.

60. The attention Melville pays to the slaves' motives and to their African heritage is what most clearly distinguishes "Benito Cereno" from Poe's incontrovertibly racist *Narrative of Arthur Gordon Pym*, to which Sidney Kaplan, for example, has likened it. See Kaplan, "Melville and the American National Sin," 42.(1957): 26.

Past, Present, and Future Seemed One

H. Bruce Franklin

work by Melville is more thoroughly and dynamically fused with history
"Benito Cereno." Historical time and narrative time in the tale are
:twined in convolutions as devious as those of the "double-bowline-knot,
e-crown-knot, back-handed-well-knot, knot-in-and-out-knot, and jam-
g-knot" tied as a furtive symbol by an aged Spanish sailor.[1] In fact,
ito Cereno" is made up of at least three overlaid stories, each serving as
tricate interpretation and extension of the others.

The surface layer consists of a mysterious tableau of enslavement and
ery presented to Captain Amasa Delano and the readers, Delano's misin-
etations of this drama, his eventual discovery that the roles of master
lave have been reversed, his violent restoration of the proper relations
ack slaves to white masters, the official version of the events which
ded and set up the scenes of the action, retrospective views by Delano
Cereno inserted in the narrative after the official documents but occurring
e them, and a concluding description of the deaths of Babo and Cereno.
second story, that of the slaves' revolt and ingenious masquerade, is
ted in the ponderous documents of the official deposition but is also
led more deeply—at least on rereading—in the events that Delano
aterprets. The third layer of story is a great sweep of history, presenting
ontext and matrix of the other stories, while they in turn explicitly
, dramatize, probe, and project this history into the future. "With
involutions," it is no surprise that "past, present, and future seemed
(98).

Since Melville's concerns here are so intensely historical, and since the
s of the past few decades have led twentieth-century readers to an
ising appreciation of *Benito Cereno*'s profound insights into our history,
y prove instructive to explore the snarled knots of its stories by tracing
historical, rather than just their narrative, chronology. This may lead
t only back to the past, which the novella incorporates, and through
lle's present, which shaped it, but also into the future it extrapolates,
determines meanings we now find in "Benito Cereno."

say was written specifically for this volume and is published here for the first time by permission
uthor.

61.   John Newton, *Thoughts upon the African Slave Trade*, c
Rev. John Newton . . . (London: Samuel Whiting; New-York: 1
519–46. Quotations are from 532. Newton's works went through
well known both in his own right and as the friend of the poet V
inspired to write his abolitionist poems. For another description of
aboard slave trading ships, see Olaudah Equiano, *The Interesting Na
Equiano, or Gustavus Vassa, the African*, chapter 5.

62.   For a superb reading of this passage, which overlaps v
Franklin, "Past, Present, and Future Seemed One," in this volume
of gender as an aspect of "the construction of power," both in th
the story, see Dana D. Nelson, *The Word in Black and White:*
Literature, 1638–1867 (New York: Oxford University Press, 199

63.   Park, *Travels in the Interior of Africa*, 263; see also 69-
Leslie, "Death of Benito Cereno," 289, likewise cite these passag
gentle black female described by Mungo Park to have become, in
advocate that all whites be destroyed suggests that some inhuman
that she . . . had cohabited with evil."

64.   Park, 298, and chapters 24–25. Zagarell, "Reenvisi
also sees Melville's irony as cutting against Park, but for somew

65.   I have been unable to identify Melville's source on the
on the Ashanti confirms the picture Melville sketches of the w
"Ashanti women are as brave and daring as the men. But for the
that keeps them at the home-front they might even have outshon
wars. For the situation changes when villages are attacked. The v
war-cries and supply them with stones and sticks for offence or c
sudden and caught the men unprepared the women, especially tho
filled in quite adequately by bringing out all accessible defer
Tufuo and C. E. Donkor, *Ashantis of Ghana: People with a Soul (
Publications, 1969), 60. Neither of the nineteenth-century v
Ashanti women's role in war, though both contain other inform
See John Beecham, *Ashantee and the Gold Coast: Being a Sketch of
Superstitions of the Inhabitants of Those Countries: with a Notice of the St
among Them* (1841; reprint New York: Johnson Reprint Corp
Dupuis, *Journal of a Residence in Ashantee* (1824; London: Frank
Ghofan and Akim are mentioned in both: Beecham, chapter 1;
mentions an incident similar to Babo's mutilation of Aranda's
Denkerans, caused by their king's having seduced the wife of tl
disinterred the body of the Denkeran king, separated the flesh
to serpents, and preserved the skull and thigh-bones as trophies
the six Ashantees as Babo's "bravoes" (109) seems to indicate son
discussed in Beacham, 111–12.

66.   Child, *Appeal in Favor of Americans Called Africans*,

67.   Joyce Sparer Adler, *War in Melville's Imagination* (Nev
Press, 1981), 109. Nelson, *The Word in Black and White*, 128
'plot' has, in effect, been the narrator's plot," but reads the cl
the terms of [Babo's] sentence, and . . . *represen*[ing] its produ
and thus implicating both the narrator and the reader in the I
Babo.

68.   See Delano, *Narrative of Voyages and Travels*, 100,
"Every thing should be coarse and cheap, and *the colours should*
trade with the natives of New Guinea and other islands (italic

N
tha
int
trel
mi
"Be
an

mas
ter
and
of
pre
and
bef
The
narr
reve
mis
the
evol
such
one

ever
incr
it m
thei
us n
Mel
whic

Let us then begin with the earliest historical event twisted explicitly into the temporal labyrinth of "Benito Cereno": Christopher Columbus's "discovery" of what was soon to be called "the New World."[2] Indeed, all the action on the San Dominick literally follows that leader, who had been the ship's original figurehead, and his replacement, the shrouded bones of the slaves' owner, "a skeleton, which had been substituted for the ship's proper figure-head, the image of Christopher Colon, the discoverer of the New World" (107). At the climax of the action, this new leader is exposed as an emblem of death itself: "But by this time the cable of the San Dominick had been cut; and the fag-end, in lashing out, whipped away the canvas shroud about the beak, suddenly revealing, as the bleached hull swung round towards the open ocean, death for the figure-head, in a human skeleton; chalky comment on the chalked words below, *Follow your leader*" (99). It is Babo who explains that the San Dominick's figurehead literally leads its crew, and who suggests a far deeper meaning in this leadership:

"Keep faith with the blacks from here to Senegal, or you shall in spirit, as now in body, 'follow your leader,' pointing to the prow." (107)

The final event of the narrative is Benito Cereno's death in the monastery to which he has retired. The very last words of "Benito Cereno" are "Benito Cereno, borne on the bier, did, indeed, follow his leader." But to which leader does this refer? Christopher Columbus? The slaves' original owner, Alexandro Aranda, who had been transformed by Babo into the white skeletal embodiment of death? Babo, whose commands Cereno was forced to obey? The divine head of the church to which Cereno is led by "the monk Infelez" (114)? Or the leader of the decaying slave empire that Cereno had served?

Columbus's voyages and claims of discovery led directly to the metamorphosis of Spain into the first truly global empire, one based on ruthless colonization, slave labor wrung from millions of kidnapped Africans, and a transcendent belief in the empire's Christian mission. The earliest ruler of this vast empire was Charles V, the last Holy Roman Emperor to be crowned by a pope. The ship's name, *San Dominick*, evokes the island of San Domingo, also known as Hispaniola, which, not long after its discovery by Columbus, became the seat of Spanish power in the New World. After the Spaniards had exterminated most of the natives of San Domingo, the island became the site of the first large-scale importation of African slaves into the Western Hemisphere, as authorized in a 1517 decree issued by Charles.

Charles, like Alexandro Aranda and Benito Cereno, as well as Amasa Delano, evidently convinced himself that he was motivated by the very best intentions when he thus initiated the Atlantic slave trade. After all, he was responding to the pleas of the priest Bartolomé de Las Casas, who argued to Charles that it would be far more humane to kidnap blacks from Africa and enslave them in the New World than to continue working the "Indians" to death in the Spanish mines and plantations.[3]

Cereno's retirement to a monastery and his death there constitute the only change that Melville made in the basic plot of his primary source, the actual Amaso Delano's narrative. Shortly after Cereno is introduced, his ultimate fate is foreshadowed by comparing him to his imperial predecessor: "His manner upon such occasions was, in its degree, not unlike that which might be supposed to have been his imperial countryman's, Charles V, just previous to the anchoritish retirement of that monarch from the throne" (53). Charles V, who in name held absolute rule over more of the earth's surface than any other person in the history of the planet, who saw himself as the incarnation of a divine and global union between church and state, ended his life as an almost spectral emblem of impotence and futility, a captive and prisoner of the church and faith he sought to impose upon the world.[4]

Thus in his passage to monastic retirement and death, Benito Cereno is a true follower—if not the actual ghost—of his imperial leader. Yet this is not only the end of his story but also its beginning. For even before the Spanish captain appears, his ship gives off an eerie image redolent of the monastery in Spain to which Charles had retreated:

> Upon gaining a less remote view, the ship . . . appeared like a white-washed monastery after a thunder-storm, seen perched upon some dun cliff among the Pyrenees. But it was no purely fanciful resemblance which now, for a moment, almost led Captain Delano to think that nothing less than a shipload of monks was before him. Peering over the bulwarks were what really seemed, in the hazy distance, throngs of dark cowls; while, fitfully revealed through the port-holes, other dark moving figures were dimly descried, as of Black Friars pacing the cloisters. (48)

The Black Friars were the Dominicans, who, operating directly under the orders of Charles V, became the principal executors of the Spanish Inquisition, a crucial instrument of imperialism and racism. In an involuted snarl of ironies, the Black Friars of "Benito Cereno" are the mutinous African slaves who now command the ship that Melville has rechristened the *San Dominick*, patron saint of the Dominican order, while the enslaved captain of this monastic ship sleeps in a cuddy where the table holds a "thumbed missal," the bulkhead bears a "meager crucifix," some "melancholy old rigging" lies like "a heap of poor friars' girdles," the washstand looks like a "font," and the settees are as "uncomfortable to look at as inquisitors' racks" (82–83).

It is here, amid these emblems of monasticism and the Inquisition, that Babo carries out his most audacious reversal of imperial power, forcing Cereno to be shaved, sitting in a "large, misshapen armchair" which "seemed some grotesque, middle-age engine of torment" (82–83) and sporting as a barber's apron the flag of the Spanish empire. The bizarre, ironic inversions of church and state, master and slave, glory and debasement, past and present are underlined by Delano's obtuse commentary: " 'why, Don Benito, this is the flag of Spain you use here. It's well it's only I, and not the King, that sees this' " (85).

By the time that the story opens, of course Spanish imperial power was becoming a mere ghost of its former self, and Melville's tale is pervaded by the theme of rotting imperialism. Penetrating beyond the hallucinatory image of the monastery, the original viewer sees "the true character" of the *San Dominick*:

> Upon a still nigher approach, this appearance was modified, and the true character of the vessel was plain—a Spanish merchantman of the first class, carrying negro slaves, amongst other valuable freight, from one colonial port to another. A very large, and, in its time, a very fine vessel, such as in those days were at intervals encountered along that main; sometimes superseded Acapulco treasure-ships, or retired frigates of the Spanish king's navy, which, like superannuated Italian palaces, still, under a decline of masters, preserved signs of former state. (48)

"Those days" refer to the period into which Melville resets Delano's narrative, the closing year of the eighteenth century.

By then, it was the New World that threatened the stability of the Old as the antimonarchist, anticolonial, republican, and, in some aspects, democratic revolution of thirteen of Britain's American colonies brought European visions of rationalism and liberty home with a vengeance. Waves of revolution seemed to swell as they swept back and forth across the Atlantic. The French Revolution openly proclaimed the egalitarianism that had been subordinated by the triumphant merchants and planters of the American Revolution. And San Domingo, that original site of New World slavery, now became the vanguard of world revolution as the black slaves interpreted the message of the American and French revolutions precisely in the way most dreaded by the plantation owners of the South and the French Caribbean colonies. Acting upon the belief that the Rights of Man, the declaration that "all men are created equal," and the slogan "liberté, egalité, et fraternité" all applied to them also, the slaves of San Domingo rose in a rebellion that was to haunt slave owners for decades to come. Melville chooses 1799 as the date for "Benito Cereno," thus making the rebellion on the *San Dominick* contemporaneous with the extension of Toussaint L'Ouverture's revolution over the entire island of San Domingo.

The contradictions central to the new American republic in 1799, which had announced its independence from the decaying monarchies of Europe with the declaration "We hold these truths to be self-evident, that all men are created equal, that they are endowed with their Creator with certain unalienable rights, that among these are life, liberty, and the pursuit of happiness," are acted out on the decks of the *San Dominick* by that good Massachusetts Yankee, Amasa Delano. (A year before the appearance of "Benito Cereno," Melville published *Israel Potter*, his meditation on the American Revolution and how a new elite had used it to establish their own class rule over the very people who had fought to win liberty for the nation.) Delano demonstrates how America's republican ideals operated in practice as he doles out the water and food brought from his ship for the emiserated sailors and slaves of the *San Dominick*. First "with republican impartiality" he distributes the water, "this republican element, which always seeks one level," "serving the oldest white no better than the youngest black"—except for his fellow captain, Don Benito, to whom he gives an entire pitcher, since his "condition, if not rank, demanded an extra allowance" (80). (Delano's lavish dispensation of water costs him nothing, since his ship was anchored at a source of water [46].) As soon as this egalitarian show is over, Delano dishes out the food:

> Two of the less wilted pumpkins being reserved for the cabin table, the residue were minced up on the spot for the general regalement. But the soft bread, sugar, and bottled cider, Captain Delano would have given the whites alone, and in chief Don Benito. . . . (80)

Delano fails to see the blatant disparity between his "republican" behavior with the water and racist, hierarchical performance with the food, for precisely the same reason that the founding fathers could proclaim that all men are created equal and possess the inalienable right to liberty while institutionalizing black chattel slavery in the very Constitution of their new republic.

And when Amaso Delano learns that the blacks on the *San Dominick* have in fact rebelled against slavery, his horrified response represents the main reaction of that new republic's white citizens to the rebellion of the slaves of San Domingo. Indeed, from the late eighteenth century through the publication of *Benito Cereno* in 1855, the San Domingo revolt terrorized the imagination of slave-owning America. This nightmare of black insurrection was transformed into powerful propaganda for the expansion into the Caribbean of U.S. slavery, which was presented as a force of order and stability capable of replacing impotent, decadent, and downright sinister Spanish rule. As James Buchanan wrote in the Ostend Manifesto of 1854, the official U.S. State Department document which was to help make him the victorious Democratic presidential candidate of 1856, the United States had the moral duty to seize Cuba from the incompetent Spain, if Spain would not sell us the island, for otherwise Cuba might "be Africanized and become a second St. Domingo, with all its attendant horrors to the white race."[5]

When Delano considers "withdrawing the command" from Benito Cereno "on some benevolent plea" because the "dark Spaniard" "was not fit to be trusted with the ship" (69), he serves as a representative American of his own time, of Melville's time, and of the time on the eve of our own century when the United States would achieve its "manifest destiny" by seizing what was left of the collapsing Spanish empire and thus itself becoming a global empire.[6]

At the time of the publication of "Benito Cereno", the crusade to seize Cuba and other Caribbean lands was part of a larger strategy to expand U.S. slavery and make it politically and economically dominant within the nation at large. With the inspiring slogan "Manifest Destiny," the forces of slavery and its allies turned both west and south.

Texas, which had been torn away from Mexico by American colonists, enriched and empowered by the cotton and slave plantation economy they imported from the Southern states, was annexed as a slave state in 1845. Supporters of slavery had then instigated war with Mexico, which allowed the United States to annex what amounted to the northern half of Mexico in 1848. The possibility of turning this vast area into slave states, thus ending the balance between slave and free states arranged by the Missouri Compromise of 1820, was confirmed by the so-called Compromise of 1850. This fateful series of acts established the principle that Congress had no authority to prohibit slavery in any part of the territory seized from Mexico or in any state formed from that territory, gave full U.S. government legitimacy to slavery within the District of Columbia and to slave trading in and between every other slaveholding state and territory, and made the recapture and reenslavement of fugitive slaves the legal duty of all citizens of the United States and of all governments and courts of states, territories, and the District of Columbia. A new land of opportunity now lay open for slavery.

The path to it was widened by the 1852 landslide election of expansionist and anti-abolitionist Franklin Pierce, whose influential campaign biography by Nathaniel Hawthorne denounced all antislavery "agitation" as threatening "the ruin of two races which now dwelt together in greater peace and affection . . . than had ever elsewhere existed between the taskmaster and the serf."[7] In 1854, Pierce signed the Kansas-Nebraska Act, which explicitly repealed the Missouri Compromise and established "the principle of non-intervention by Congress with slavery in the States and Territories."[8] Several months before the publication of "Benito Cereno," the Kansas legislature (elected by gangs of proslavery men who swarmed across the border from Missouri to stuff the ballot boxes of Kansas) enacted legislation making it a capital offense to aid a fugitive slave and a felony even to question the legality of owning slaves.

To the south, Cuba, with its thriving sugar and tobacco fields worked by slaves, beckoned as a potential bastion from which the entire Caribbean could be transformed into a U.S. slave plantation. This American dream of annexing Cuba had begun as early as Delano's revolutionary, slave-owning contemporary Thomas Jefferson, who called it essential to extending our "empire for liberty."[9] It was at the very heart of the campaign for Manifest Destiny from 1848 through 1855, and was a prominent feature of Pierce's Inaugural Address, which declared that American imperial expansion was "essential for the preservation of the rights of commerce and the peace of the world."[10]

This bleak scene for all those who were, like Melville, horrified by "Benito Cereno"'s slavery[11] that was the context of "Benito Cereno," and it informs the story from beginning to end. Just as the voters of America had evidently ratified Hawthorne's view that the millions of black slaves felt great "affection" for their masters, Delano sees "affection" in Babo's view of his master Cereno (51), believes that "the negro" serves his master with "affectionate zeal" (52), and even exclaims, " 'Don Benito, I envy you such a friend; slave I cannot call him' " (57). Like Hawthorne and the other Americans who chose to ignore the messages for the future being communicated by slave rebellions, abolitionism, and the internecine conflict already emerging in Kansas, Delano suppresses his growing sense of alarm by reminding himself that "the blacks" were "too stupid" to be plotting against him and by asking himself the reassuring question, "Besides, who ever heard of a white so far a renegade as to apostatize from his very species almost, by leaguing in against it with negroes?" (75). Later, in authorizing the use of brutal force to recapture and reenslave every man, woman, and child among the rebellious Africans, Delano is doing no more than what the Fugitive Slave Act of 1850 required of all law-abiding American citizens.

Indeed, Delano is presented by the narrator as a model of justice and legality, sharply contrasted to the aura of piracy associated with the Spanish ship. Though appropriate to the story's 1799 setting, the theme of piracy which permeates the story might seem at first glance rather remote from the context of its 1855 publication. But piracy, at least in the discourse of the mid–nineteenth century, was inextricably interwoven with *Benito Cereno*'s principal themes of slavery and imperialism.

Through Captain Delano's telescope we get our first view of the Spanish ship, sailing without colors on seas then frequented by pirates, and entering a harbor noted for "lawlessness and loneliness" (46–47). Only its evident lack of familiarity with the harbor shows that it "could be no wonted freebooter" (47). Delano, trying to convince himself later that the apparent helplessness of the *San Dominick* proves that she could not "at present, be of a piratical character," then remembers tales of "Malay pirates" who only feign helplessness in order to ambush other vessels (68). But the paragraph which thus insinuates that the tale may explode with a revelation of the "piratical character" of the Spanish captain and his ship opens and closes with even more devious hints of the piratical character of the American captain and his ship.

This paragraph opens with a sentence that parenthetically calls attention to the name of "his ship (the Bachelor's Delight)." The *Bachelor's Delight* was in fact one of the most infamous of all pirate vessels. Commanded by William Ambrose Cowley and William Dampier, and carrying "the choicest batch of cutthroats on the Main,"[12] the namesake of Delano's ship terrorized the very area where he now prowls. In case readers might be unacquainted with the original *Bachelor's Delight*, Melville associates Delano with a synonym for pirate familiar to all his contemporaneous readers: "rover." Indeed, Delano's suspicions about Cereno's piracy are punctuated by his continual eager views of his approaching boat, "Rover by name" (77). In the concluding sentence of the paragraph in which he speculates that the innocent appearance of the Spanish ship merely conceals its treacherous potential, Delano conjures up a fantasy that when the two vessels end up next to each other in the harbor, the *San Dominick*, might "like a slumbering volcano, suddenly let loose energies now hid" and overwhelm his own ship. But this image reverses the actual events, for it is the supposedly innocent, helpless, and peaceful *Bachelor's Delight* that will unleash hidden energies and overwhelm the *San Dominick*.

When he decides to seize the Spanish ship, reenslave the blacks, and thus add to his profits on the voyage, Delano chooses his chief mate, "who had been a privateer's-man, and, as his enemies whispered, a pirate— to head the party" (101). The nature of this "party" is spelled out in the next words:

> The more to encourage the sailors, they were told, that the Spanish captain considered his ship as good as lost; that she and her cargo, including some gold and silver, were worth more than a thousand doubloons. Take her, and no small part would be theirs. The sailors replied with a shout.

To incite the greed of his men for booty, Delano concocts this gold and silver, which are included in neither of the two inventories of the *San Dominick*.[13] So Delano's projection of the *San Dominick* as a "haunted pirate-ship" (77) seems far more accurate as a vision of the true nature of his own vessel, a strange reincarnation of the original *Bachelor's Delight*.

In fact, the actual Amasa Delano precisely matched Melville's description of his mate: he certainly "had been a privateer's-man, and, as his enemies whispered, a pirate."[14] His adventure with Benito Cereno ended with the Spanish captain alleging in court that Delano was indeed a pirate, an argument he substantiated with depositions from five of the Yankee captain's former crewmen, who swore that he was a "pirate."[15]

Melville's story about a slave ship, a mutiny by its human cargo, and its bloody recapture by an apparently well-intentioned, innocent Yankee obliquely raises the question, "Who are the real pirates?" For Melville and his contemporaries, this question would certainly invoke the most recent case of a successful black uprising on a Spanish slave ship, the *Amistad* revolt of 1839. Carolyn Karcher has indicated how the theme of piracy connects *Benito Cereno* to the *Amistad* case:

> The American brig of war *Washington*, whose officers hoped to claim the *Amistad*'s cargo as salvage, took the rebels into custody, and the Africans remained in jail for two years until the Supreme Court freed them in 1841. Charges of piracy were central to the trial. The press had repeatedly described the *Amistad* as a pirate ship when it was sighted off the East coast, but the Africans' defense team, headed by former President John Quincy Adams, successfully argued that it was not piracy for persons to rise up against those who illegally held them captive. . . .[16]

But as Melville was writing *Benito Cereno*, there were also real pirates in operation. These were the "filibusters," those American adventurers who were attempting to "rescue" Cuba, Haiti, and Central America by organizing war parties similar to those Delano dispatched to capture the Spanish ship. The term *filibuster* was the Anglicized form of a Spanish corruption of the Dutch word *vrijbuiter*, whose more direct English version was "freebooter," the very term used to introduce the theme of piracy (47). Just as Delano projects onto Cereno piratical schemes that he himself will blithely—and with the best intentions—actually perpetrate, so the United States in the mid–nineteenth century was projecting onto the decaying Spanish empire images that would legitimize its own piratical—but of course well-intentioned—expansionism.

Focusing on the theme of piracy provides a clear view of Melville's authorial strategy in "Benito Cereno" and of what—or at least how—the story "means." The question of whether Amasa Delano is a pirate is raised openly in his own narrative, where he defends himself against the charge. Why would Melville eliminate the explicit statement of the theme, electing instead to secrete it in the names of Delano's ship and boat, the Yankee captain's fantasies, and suggestive details of description and dialogue? Because this maneuver is part of his transformation of the story into a cryptic show of symbols staged to confront, perplex, hoodwink, and even pillory at least some of its readers.

To comprehend its oblique, allusive, involuted meanings, one must contextualize *Benito Cereno* not only in the history it probes, but also in the development of Melville's narrative art, which was forced upon him by this history. For it was not a mere coincidence that Melville's strange and estranged relationship with his audience evolved in the early 1850s, along with his rhetorical strategy "directly calculated to deceive—egregiously deceive, the superficial skimmer of pages" (*PT*, 251).

Herman Melville's greatest creative period, the years between 1846 and 1857, when he produced all nine novels and all the short stories to be published in his lifetime, was a period when the hopes for liberty and equality aroused by the American revolution and the revolutions inspired by it seemed about to be swamped by a global tidal wave of reaction. While American slavery, imperialism, and industrial capitalism were surging in the Mexican War and its aftermath, the European revolutions of 1848 were being crushed all across the continent. "After 1848," as Melville puts it in the introductory sketch to *The Piazza Tales*, "all round the world, these kings, they had the casting vote, and voted for themselves" (*PT*, 3). Or as he says in the opening words of the 1853 story "Cock-a-Doodle-Doo!," "In all parts of the world many high-spirited revolts from rascally despotisms had of late been knocked on the head" (*PT*, 268).

Drawing ever-increasing military and economic powers from industrial capitalism, the European empires were now able to execute the most enormous expansion in history. In 1799, at the time of the action of "Benito Cereno," about one-third of the earth's surface was ruled by Europeans and their descendants. By 1875, white nations would rule over two-thirds of the globe. Having seen firsthand the operations of white imperial power, Melville in 1846 branded "the white civilized man" as "the most ferocious animal on the face of the earth."[17]

From his first book in 1846 through *Billy Budd*, which he was finishing at the time of his death in 1891, Herman Melville's moral vision centered on the oppressed, the exploited, the victims of American, British, and European society. This vision, which was shaped by his own labor amid some of the most oppressed people of his age, was in stark contradiction to the values dominant among those in the nineteenth century who had the education and leisure to read serious fiction—that is, the affluent gentlemen and ladies who constituted his audience.[18]

At first, Melville chose to address his bourgeois readers as a lowly worker, a common sailor whose experiences, quite alien from their own, they might find entertaining and instructive. His first five novels, published between 1846 and 1850, are not only narrated by this sailor who had fallen from the readers' social ranks, but contain long narrative and polemic sections openly denouncing imperialism, militarism, capital and corporal punishment, prisons, slavery, racism, and even capitalism itself.

Melville's forthright pleas for liberty and equality found few receptive ears in a class whose imperial ambitions were burgeoning so spectacularly in this very period. Indeed, the anti-imperialist core of *Typee* (1846) was censored out of the American edition, and *Mardi* (1849) was reviled for its intellectual and moral pretensions. In 1850, Melville published "Hawthorne and His Mosses," containing his manifesto of the author as fugitive, trickster, marginalized Jeremiah or Ishmael.

In *Moby-Dick* (1851), which contains the last of his extended first-person sailor narratives, Melville began to switch his narrative strategy. In *Pierre*, his first book without any first-person narrator, the author appears—à la

Alfred Hitchcock—only as a "gamesome sailor" who slyly warns our hero as they pass in the street (349). The novel was savaged by the critics, who charged that Melville "strikes with an impious, though, happily, weak hand, at the very foundations of society," and called upon readers, "as representatives of our own race," to "freeze him into silence."[19] Almost as if responding to this injunction, Melville now makes silence the hallmark of both his authorial voice and principal characters in his fiction, until finally, less than two years after "Benito Cereno," he is indeed silenced, his career as a fiction writer ended.

Between 1853 and 1856, Melville shifted almost entirely to short stories, many published in magazines anonymously or pseudonymously. In this short fiction, except for reminiscences in "The Encantadas," Melville no longer speaks as one who has experienced oppression. Instead of addressing his affluent readers from below, Melville creates narrators who assume their point of view. The oppressed, the exploited, the victims are now the objects perceived, with little or no comprehension, by observers from the readers' own social class. A Wall Street lawyer gabs about a woebegone and enigmatic white collar worker formerly in his employ. A gentleman in the "seedsman's business" depicts the emiserated women he encounters on a tour of a factory that makes paper for him, contrasting this to cozy experiences he shared in England with leisured gentleman of his own class. A landed gentleman witnesses the miserable death of a poor family and its imperial rooster. Another gentleman describes his visit to America's rural poor and his brush with England's urban poor forty years earlier. In "Benito Cereno," we see the action through the eyes of a third-person narrator who takes the Yankee captain's point of view and through legalistic documents submitted to a Spanish imperial court.

In these stories, the people whose misery is the concomitant of the comforts of Melville's readers have very little to say for themselves. Bartleby says to the narrator, "I know you . . . and I want nothing to say to you" (PT, 43). The "native American poor," remarks the gentleman-narrator of "Poor Man's Pudding and Rich Man's Crumbs," "never lose their delicacy or pride" (PT, 296). The women who work in the factory in "The Tartarus of Maids" are not allowed to talk on the job: "Nothing was heard but the low, steady overruling hum" of the machines because "[t]he human voice was banished" (PT, 328). In "The Bell-Tower," workers are replaced altogether by metal images of women whose only function is to be clubbed by the manacled arms of a slave automaton; this robot works with such uncanny silence that his first blow crushes the brain of his creator. After the reenslavement of the Africans, Babo "uttered no sound, and could not be forced to" (116).

At the core of these stories is a terrifying revelation of the society that Melville sees developing, a society based on the enslavement of human beings, who are imprisoned in factories, ships, plantations, and offices, forced to expend their human creativity to enrich those who convert everything of human value into money. And the beneficiary of this ruthless oppression is the social class that includes his polite audience.

The relations among Melville, his narrator, and his readers are epitomized in "The Paradise of Bachelors and The Tartarus of Maids," published anonymously on April Fool's Day, 1855, a few months before the appearance of "Benito Cereno." We now realize that the hidden meanings of this pair of trick sketches were intended to expose, not to enlighten, most of Melville's genteel readers, who would have had him instantly silenced if they had understood what he was doing. His strategy here depends on a narrator who cannot comprehend what he sees, but who unwittingly reveals its significance to a few perceptive readers.

First the narrator tells of his pleasant visit to "The Paradise of Bachelors," a retreat of bourgeois professional gentlemen who, like many of the tale's readers, scoff at the very notion of the existence of human misery. As a member of this class, and as a bizarre instrument of Melville's narrative strategy, this gentleman could not possibly understand that the entrance to this retreat is an anus, that the alimentary pleasures of this "Paradise" are loveless perversions occurring within a giant digestive tract, or that the price of the bachelors' revelry is the pain and suffering that he witnesses in the paper mill he visits in "The Tartarus of Maids." Though he is dimly aware that the women enslaved to machines in the factory embody a grotesque perversion of human creativity, as a businessman he cannot recognize that he profits from their exploitation, that their enslavement to machinery is fundamental to the profits he derives from the commodity they produce, paper he uses as envelopes for his seeds. Thus of course he cannot possibly know that he himself embodies a perverted male sexuality entering a woman's genitals in the quest for dollars, or that, on another level, his business as a seedsman represents the expansion of industrial capitalism and wage slavery in the America of the mid-1850s.[20]

In "Benito Cereno," Amasa Delano plays a role similar to the obtuse observer-narrator of "The Paradise of Bachelors and the Tartarus of Maids" and to the narrator of "Bartleby," who is both myopic observer and principal character. But faced with the existence of an autobiographical narrative by the actual Amasa Delano, Melville could not very well make Delano the narrator of a fictionalized tale so closely parallel to the captain's own published version. So Melville devises a gentlemanly narrator whose consciousness approximates Delano's while also providing another angle of misinterpretation.

For example, as Babo prepares to fashion Benito Cereno into a living display of the fate of empire by draping him in the flag of Spain, forcing him to sit in one of the malacca chairs "uncomfortable to look at as inquisitors' racks," and plying a finely honed razor on his throat, the narrator expatiates on what this reveals about "the negro":

There is something in the negro which, in a peculiar way, fits him for avocations about one's person. Most negroes are natural valets and hairdressers; taking to the comb and brush congenially as to the castinets, and flourishing them with almost equal satisfaction. There is, too, a smooth tact about them in this employment, with a marvelous, noiseless, gliding briskness, not ungraceful in its way, singularly pleasing to behold, and still more so to be the manipulated subject of. And above all is the great gift of good humor. Not the mere grin or laugh is here meant. Those were unsuitable. But a certain easy cheerfulness, harmonious in every glance and gesture; as though God had set the whole negro to some pleasant tune. (83)

It is essential to recognize that this profoundly racist misreading of Babo's actions and their significance comes not from Delano but directly from the narrator, who next goes on to explain that the negro's suitability for personal servitude is enhanced by "the docility arising from the unaspiring contentment of a limited mind" (84). Because of this trait and the negro's "susceptibility of blind attachment sometimes inhering in indisputable inferiors, one readily perceives why those hypochondriacs, Johnson and Byron," he expounds, "took to their hearts, almost to the exclusion of the white race, their serving men, the negroes" (84). The narrator is as blandly racist as Delano, who, "like most men of a good, blithe heart," "took to negroes, not philanthropically, but genially, just as other men to Newfoundland dogs" (84). But he is more literary and more intellectual than Delano, even closer than the sea captain to the class outlook of the typical mid–nineteenth-century American reader of belletristic literature. The narrator entices the reader into sharing Delano's amusement "with an odd instance of the African love of bright colors and fine shows, in the black's informally taking from the flag-locker a great piece of bunting of all hues, and lavishly tucking it under his master's chin for an apron" (84). When this bunting loosens enough to reveal its true identity, unwary readers are lured into joining with Delano in his response, while insightful readers (especially those who are rereading the story) have the opportunity to share Babo's amusement:

"The castle and the lion," exclaimed Captain Delano—"why, Don Benito, this is the flag of Spain you use here. It's well it's only I, and not the King, that sees this," he added with a smile, "but"—turning towards the black,— "it's all one, I suppose, so the colors be gay"; which playful remark did not fail somewhat to tickle the negro. (85)

Readers who identify with either Delano or the narrator here become objects of Babo's brilliantly ironic show—which is of course also Melville's show. For neither showman is motivated primarily by a desire to entertain the audience.

Readers of "Benito Cereno" have two surrogates: Amasa Delano, who attempts to penetrate the meaning of the spectacle being staged for him, and the narrator, who bridges between the responses of the sea captain and those of the readers, for whom the spectacle is also being staged. But neither Delano nor the narrator is the surrogate of the author, who understands full well what the show means, for of course he has staged it. In fact, most of the scenes and spectacles that Melville adds to Delano's narrative—including the shaving scene, the skeleton figurehead, the giant slave in chains, Cereno's costume, the oakum pickers, the hatchet polishers, the display of "naked nature" by the young slave woman—are scenes and spectacles created by the slaves as parts of their show. Thus the surrogates of the author are Babo and the other blacks, fellow artists and dramatists, designers of shows intended "to deceive—egregiously deceive" those members of the audience who think like Delano and the narrator.[21] Indeed, Melville never expressed a more intriguing self-image than when, at the end of the story, he refers to Babo's impaled head as "that hive of subtlety" (116).[22]

The dramatist-audience relationship structures all the action witnessed by Delano on the *San Dominick*. The "theatrical aspect of Don Benito in his harlequin ensign" makes Delano briefly wonder if the shaving scene could be some mere "play of the barber" (87). Delano's reaction to the spectacle of the giant in chains is typical: " '. . . this scene surprises me; what means it, pray?' " (62). But the captain cannot fathom the meaning of the show, for, unlike both Babo and Melville, he is "incapable of satire or irony" (63).

He is also a prisoner of his own racist, imperialist, authoritarian, and even sexist consciousness. Unlike Melville, who must constantly put himself in the position of the slaves in order to jointly conjure with them their deceptive shows, Delano can view all other people only from the vantage point of his own privileged class, race, and sex. All this is illustrated most revealingly in the sideshow arranged by one of the slave women.

Just as his suspicions are aroused by an abortive interrogation of one of the Spanish sailors, Delano's "attention" is "drawn to a slumbering negress, partly disclosed through the lace-work of some rigging, lying, with youthful limbs carelessly disposed" (73). Whatever her spread legs permit the captain to see makes him quickly forget the previous suspicious scene. He continues to ogle her exposed body through the suggestively revealing "lace-work":

Sprawling at her lapped breasts was her wide-awake fawn, stark naked, its black little body half lifted from the deck, crosswise with its dam's; its hands, like two paws, clambering upon her; its mouth and nose ineffectually rooting to get at the mark; and meantime giving a vexatious half-grunt, blending with the composed snore of the negress. (73)

Like all those twentieth-century readers who have been given license to gawk at the bare breasts of non-European women fortuitously displayed in *National Geographic* (usually in one article per issue), Delano's primitivist fantasy allows him to savor a spectacle that he would be obliged to censor if this were a woman of his own race and class. Of course, he has no inkling that the woman's snore may be "composed" in a more sophisticated sense. When she seems to wake, "as if not at all concerned at the attitude in which she had been caught, delightedly she caught the child up, with maternal transports, covering it with kisses." Delano's response indicates how well the show has worked—and why: "There's naked nature, now; pure tenderness and love, thought Captain Delano, well pleased." Utterly incapable of comprehending that this African woman may have been consciously manipulating his own racism and sexism to deceive him, the good American captain can only believe that her show was merely an unconscious opportunity for his delight and entertainment. After all, isn't he the master of the *Bachelor's Delight*?

The namesake of Delano's vessel was originally a Danish slave ship. The pirates who seized it and turned it into their own predatory craft left no record of what they did with "the sixty black girls they found on board their prize."[23] But the gang rapes customarily perpetrated on slave ships suggest an unpleasant source for the ship's name. They also suggest the source of the special rage of the slave women on the *San Dominick*, whose consciousness remains alien to all those who cannot fathom the horrors of slavery and imperialism.[24]

Both Delano and the narrator epitomize all those good, respectable, prosperous nineteenth-century Americans who remained oblivious not only to the human price paid by others for their own comfort and power, but also to the future implicit in the exploitation and oppression to which the American republic had become deeply committed. By conquering the vessel of the decaying Spanish empire and inheriting its cargo of slaves, Delano—that representative American—embodies the message scrawled above the skeleton figurehead: "Follow Your Leader." As William Graham Sumner explained in his 1898 essay, "The Conquest of the United States by Spain," by taking over what was left of Spanish imperialism, America doomed itself to experience the same fate: "war, debt, taxation, diplomacy, a grand governmental system, pomp, glory, a big army and navy, lavish expenditures, political jobbery—in a word, imperialism."[25] It took the explosive urban rebellions of 1964–1968, the Vietnam War, and the subsequent economic and moral decay of America during the period of its apparent global triumph to create an audience capable of comprehending the deadliness of the future foreshadowed by the past and present in "Benito Cereno."

Notes

1. Herman Melville, "Benito Cereno," in *The Piazza Tales and Other Prose Pieces, 1839–1860*, ed. Harrison Hayford, Alma A. MacDougall, G. Thomas Tanselle, et al (Chicago and Evanston: Northwestern University Press and the Newberry Library, 1987), p. 76. Subsequent citations will be simply parenthetical references to this edition. References to other writings in this volume will be indicated by parenthetical "*PT*" and page number.

2.   For Melville's possible use of Washington Irving's *The Life and Voyages of Christopher Columbus* as a source, see Mary Y. Hallab, "Victims of 'Malign Machinations': Irving's *Christopher Columbus* and Melville's 'Benito Cereno,' " *Journal of Narrative Technique* 9 (1979); 199–206. My argument about the role of Columbus is closer to that developed by Gloria Horsley-Meacham, "The Monastic Slaver: Images and Meaning in 'Benito Cereno,' " *New England Quarterly* 66 (1983); 261–66.

3.   For a detailed and perceptive discussion of the role of Las Casas, as well as Melville's contemporaneous sources, see Horsley-Meacham, "The Monastic Slaver," 262–64, 266.

4.   Melville, who refers to Charles's abdication and "dotage" in other works (see for example, *Mardi*, chapter 97, *White-Jacket*, chapter 46, and "I and My Chimney"), seems in "Benito Cereno" to have drawn on a source that was frequently reprinted in the early 1850s, William Stirling's *The Cloister Life of the Emperor Charles the Fifth*. In *The Wake of the Gods: Melville's Mythology* (Stanford: Stanford University Press, 1963, 1982), 136–50, a slightly revised version of " 'Apparent Symbol of Despotic Command': Melville's *Benito Cereno*," *New England Quarterly* 34 (1961); 462–77, I offer a detailed account of Melville's possible use of Stirling to create the strange monastic surroundings of Benito Cereno on the *San Dominick*, suggest the demonic powers of the Church, and dramatize the theme of rotting empires.

5.   "Ostend Manifesto," in Henry Steele Commager, ed., *Documents of American History*, 6th edition (New York: Appleton-Century-Crofts, 1958), 335.

6.   Allan Moore Emery, " 'Benito Cereno' and Manifest Destiny," *Nineteenth-Century Fiction* 39 (1984); 48–68, provides a very useful discussion of Manifest Destiny as context for "Benito Cereno," though he tends to understate the role of slavery in both the imperialist movement and the novella. My own historical contextualization of Melville's tale owes much to the splendid essays of Sandra A. Zagarell, "Reenvisioning America: Melville's 'Benito Cereno,' " *ESQ* 30 (1984); 245–59; and Eric J. Sundquist, "*Benito Cereno* and New World Slavery," in Sacvan Bercovitch, ed., *Reconstructing American Literary History* (Cambridge: Harvard University Press, 1986), 93–122.

7.   Nathaniel Hawthorne, *The Life of Franklin Pierce*, in *The Complete Writings of Nathaniel Hawthorne*, 22 vols. (Boston: Houghton, Mifflin, 1900), 17:164.

8.   "Kansas-Nebraska Act," in Commager, ed., *Documents of American History*, 332.

9.   In 1809, Jefferson wrote "I candidly confess that I have ever looked upon Cuba as the most interesting addition that can be made to our system of States" and argued that "We should then have only to include the North [Canada] in our confederacy, which should be, of course, in the first war, and we should have such an empire for liberty as she has never surveyed since the creation . . ." (*The Writings of Thomas Jefferson*, 20 vols., ed. Andrew A. Lipscomb and Albert E. Bergh [Washington, D.C.: Thomas Jefferson Memorial Association, 1904], 12:277).

10.   Basil Rauch, *American Interest in Cuba*: 1848–1855 (New York: Columbia University Press, 1948), 254, and passim.

11.   In the last few decades, there has been much fine work on Melville's vision of slavery in his fiction and specifically in "Benito Cereno," including Edward S. Grejda, *The Common Continent of Men: Racial Equality in the Writings of Herman Melville* (Port Washington, N.Y.: Kennikat Press, 1974); Marvin Fisher, *Going Under: Melville's Short Fiction and the American 1850s* (Baton Rouge: Louisiana State University Press, 1977); and the leading authority on the subject, Carolyn L. Karcher, *Shadow Over the Promised Land: Slavery, Race, and Violence in Melville's America* (Baton Rouge: Louisiana State University Press, 1980).

12.   Victor Wolfgang Von Hagen, ed., *The Encantadas, Or, Enchanted Isles, by Herman Melville* (Burlingame, Cal.: William P. Wreden, 1940), xxi.

13.   James Kavanaugh, " 'That Hive of Subtlety': 'Benito Cereno' as Critique of Ideology," *Bucknell Review* 29 (1984); 156–57; this essay presents an invaluable analysis of Delano's thinking as a dramatization of bourgeois ideology, including its self-deceptions. Since Melville

carefully revised one of the inventories for the *Piazza Tales* edition, it seems unlikely that the omission of the gold and silver was his oversight.

14. Writing without any reference to "Benito Cereno," Samuel Eliot Morison in 1941 indicated that Delano was a privateersman by the age of sixteen, and that he and his brother later "sailed as far as Tasmania, where they matched rascalities and exchanged brutalities with one of the British convict colonies (*The Maritime History of Massachusetts, 1783–1860* [Boston: Houghton Mifflin, 1941], 62; originally cited in Max Putzel, "The Source and Symbols of Melville's 'Benito Cereno,' " *American Literature* 34 [1962]: 194).

15. Like most of Delano's crew, these men were former Botany Bay convicts; these five he had forced ashore just before the appearance of the Spanish ship (Delano, *A Narrative of Voyages and Travels.* . . . [Boston: E. G. House, 1817], 819–20, 823).

16. Karcher, Notes to "Benito Cereno," in *The Heath Anthology of American Literature*, 2 vols. (Lexington, Mass.: D. C. Heath, 1990), 1:2464–2522.

17. Herman Melville, *Typee: A Peep at Polynesian Life* (Chicago and Evanston: Northwestern University Press and the Newberry Library, 1968), 125.

18. My argument about relations among Melville's work experience, his moral vision, and the form and content of his fiction is made in more detail in my "Redburn's Wicked End," *Nineteenth-Century Fiction* 20 (1965); 190–94; *Prison Literature in America: The Victim as Criminal and Artist*, expanded edition (New York: Oxford University Press, 1989); and "From Outsider to Insider: Melville's Narrative Strategies," *Melville Society Extracts* 76 (1989); 3–6.

19. [George Washington Peck?], Review of *Pierre, American Whig Review* 16 (1852); 446–54; reprinted in Watson G. Branch, ed., *Melville: The Critical Heritage* (London: Routledge & Kegan Paul, 1974), 314–29. The quotation is from Branch, 316–17.

20. The digestive and anal landscape of "The Paradise of Bachelors" was first explored in my "Herman Melville: Artist of the Worker's World," in Norman Rudich, ed., *Weapons of Criticism* (Palo Alto, Cal.: Ramparts Press, 1976) and revised in *Prison Literature in America*, ch. 2; the comments on "The Tartarus of Maids" are also drawn from the analyses in these sources.

21. Joyce Adler indicates that Babo "has the qualities of mind of a master psychologist, strategist, general, playwright, impresario, and poet," notes that "Melville endows him with his own poetic insight," and argues that Melville is "doing in this tale what he has Babo do, create a work of great imagination with a surface appearance and a hidden reality" (*War in Melville's Imagination* [New York: New York University Press, 1981], 104, 109).

22. Babo's role as trickster-showman also foreshadows that of Black Guinea, who entertains the passengers and the readers of *The Confidence Man* with an exhibition of possibly apocalyptic disguises. Black Guinea first appears in the place of the mute lamblike man, just as Babo immediately follows Bartleby in Melville's arrangement of *The Piazza Tales*.

23. Christopher Lloyd, *William Dampier* (Hamden, Conn.: Archon, 1966), 44.

24. The research about the original *Bachelor's Delight* was done by Carolyn Karcher, who explores the background of shipboard rape of slave women in her essay in the present volume. The suggestion that the pirates may have named the ship in celebration of acts they perpetrated on the slave women they captured was made by Jane Franklin. The most powerful section of Melville's *The Encantadas*, Sketch Eighth, "Norfolk Isle and the Chola Widow," centers on gang rapes carried out by sailors against a defenseless woman.

25. Sumner, "The Conquest of the United States by Spain," in *War and Other Essays* (New York: Yale University Press, 1911), 325.

Index

♦

"Abolition of Negro Slavery" (Dew), 157
"About Niggers," 154
Achilli, Giacinto, 114n26
Adams, Henry, 147
Adams, John Quincy, 160, 204–5, 238
Adler, Joyce Sparer, 11, 220
Adrian VI, Pope, 95
Alexander the Great, 108
Alighieri, Dante, 44
Althusser, Louis, 117
American Antislavery Society, 157
American Party, 127
American Renaissance (Matthiessen), 6
Amistad, The, 38–39, 121, 149, 159,
    199, 201, 203–5, 216, 238
Amistad case, The, 13, 38–39, 121–22,
    160, 196, 200–01, 203–6, 208,
    211–15, 219–20, 223n11, 225n33,
    226n39, 238; as a source for "Benito
    Cereno," 200–1, 203, 205, 211–12,
    214, 219
Anderson, Charles Robert, 95
"Apparition, The" (Melville), 78
Aptheker, Herbert, 36n21, 46n1
Arvin, Newton, 7–8, 58, 63n2

Baines, Barbara J., 13, 183
Balzac, Honoré de, 117,
Bancroft, George, 95–96, 150
Baraka, Amiri, 137
Barber, John W., 223n12
Bartholomew, St., 72, 74
"Bartleby, the Scrivener" (Melville), 42,
    240; structure, 58

Bates, Joshua, 39
Battle-Pieces (Melville), 78, 83, 86, 89,
    178, 210
Baym, Nina, 135
Beecher, Lyman, 155
"Bell-Tower, The" (Melville), 12, 240
"Benito Cereno":
    allusions to piracy, 102, 113n19, 131,
        141, 143n14, 213–215, 228n53,
        236–38, 246n14
    ambiguity in, 8, 45, 47n9, 59, 60–61,
        65, 69, 74, 106, 115n30, 116, 124,
        136
    animal imagery in, 43, 85, 127, 157,
        182, 218
    as artistic failure, 7, 26–28, 58–60
    as artistic success, 7–9, 21, 34n1, 63,
        63n2
    Babo's evil, 7, 27, 30–31, 40, 42, 45,
        88–89, 183
    Babo's moral victory, 36n23, 45
    cannibalism in, 43, 142n4, 149, 175,
        182–83, 191–93
    characterization of Africans, 42–43,
        218–219
    characterization of Babo, 27, 40, 66–67,
        76, 88, 124–25, 136–37, 156–57,
        160, 183, 220–21, 243, 246n22
    characterization of Cereno, 27, 41–42,
        73–74, 76, 86–87, 133, 156
    characterization of Delano, 27, 33,
        40–41, 68–69, 76, 84–86, 91,
        105–8, 120, 128–32, 140–41,
        151–52, 156, 197–99, 213–14,
        234, 241–44

"Benito Cereno" (*cont.*)
color symbolism, 43–45, 76–77,
82–84, 92
composition of, 2
Delano's attitude toward blacks, 35,
36n21, 40–41, 73, 82, 84–86, 107,
120, 127, 129, 196, 198–99, 213,
218–19, 236, 242
departures from Delano's *Narrative*, 4,
27, 42, 50, 102–2, 104–5, 107,
113n19, 113n23, 129, 140–41, 147,
155, 186, 200–201, 211–12, 217,
219, 220, 232, 238, 243
figurehead of the *San Dominic*, 80, 84,
90, 101, 121, 141, 149, 150–51,
175, 183–85, 197, 217, 220, 231,
243, 244
fluidity of meaning in, 135–36
gender relationships in, 134–35
moral structure, 27
narrative strategy, 199, 226n44,
242–43
as a political tale, 12, 100, 122
point of view, 4–5, 33, 84, 87–88,
120, 123–24, 240
relationship of Cereno and Babo, 81–84,
134
reviews of, 3
rhetorical strategy, 238
significance of the name Babo, 32, 42,
46n4
sources for Babo's character, 42, 149,
220
stern-piece of the *San Dominic*, 42, 55,
69–70, 78, 90–91, 96, 101, 122,
138
structure of, 4, 58–61, 63n2, 67, 84;
style, 3, 22, 26–27, 61–63, 64n2,
67, 92, 113n17
symbolism, 7, 32, 35n20, 43, 76,
82–83, 92, 101, 106, 112n14, 150,
220–21
tableaux, 82–84
treatment of slave women, 218–19,
243–44
treatment of slavery, 9, 12, 24–25, 30,
34, 35n9, 37, 49, 66–68, 76,
81–84, 88–90, 92, 94, 112n7,
124–25, 134, 136, 138, 150,
218–19, 222n6
Bernal, Martin, 222n5
Berthoff, Warner, 8
Bigelow, John, 161

Billy Budd (Melville), 7, 31, 63, 77, 210,
216, 239; mutiny in, 159
Black Athena (Bernal), 222n5
*Black Diamonds Gathered in the Darkey
Homes of the South* (Pollard), 162
*Black Schooner or the Private Slaver
"Amistad,"* 39, 205
Bloom, Harold, 2
Bonaparte, Charles Louis Napoleon. *See*
Louis Napoleon
Bonaparte, Napoleon, 147–48
Bosman, Willem, 191–92
Boston Atlas, 205
Boston Courier, 204
Bounty, H.M.S., 159
Bowdich, T. Edward, 187–88, 191–92
Briggs, Charles F., 178
Brooks, Van Wyck, 34n5
Brown, Charles Brockden, 3
Brown, John, 37–38, 89
Brown, Sterling, 9, 10, 36n23, 39, 47n9
Brown, William Wells, 148
Buchanan, James, 234
Bushnell, Horace, 45

Calhoun, John C., 37, 171
"Cannibalism in Melville's 'Benito
Cereno' " (McElroy), 183
Catholic Church. *See* Roman Catholic
Church
Cavalier and Yankee, 172
Cenci, The (Shelley), 177
"Change the Joke and Slip the Yoke"
(Ellison), 178
Channing, William Ellery, 39
Charles V, 50–56, 73–74, 94–97, 104,
109, 150, 213, 231–32
Chase, Richard, 63n2
Chesnut, Mary, 172–75
Child, Francis J., 65
Child, Lydia Maria, 199, 222n4, 222n5,
225n33
Choate, Rufus, 38
Christian Freeman and Family Visiter, 3
Cinquez, Joseph, 39, 149, 159–60, 202,
205–6, 220
Citizen (New York), 3
Civil War, The, 76, 99, 146, 152
Clarel (Melville): slavery in, 86
Clark, Benjamin C., 154
Clay, Henry, 119
Clemens, Samuel L. (Mark Twain), 28, 44

Cloister Life of the Emperor Charles the Fifth (Stirling), 13, 50, 52

"Cloister Life of the Emperor Charles V, The" (Stirling), 50

Clough, Arthur Hugh, 65

"Cock-a-Doodle-Do" (Melville), 239–40; parody of Wordsworth's "Resolution and Independence" and Transcendentalism, 130–31

Columbus, Christopher, 56, 72, 89–90, 94–95, 139, 141, 149, 151, 163, 164n3, 213, 217, 220, 231

Compromise of 1850, 99, 118, 152, 156, 235

Confessions (Turner), 151

Confidence Man, The, 246n22

"Conquest of the United States by Spain, The" (W. G. Sumner), 244

Conrad, Joseph, 35n5, 64n2

Cooper, James Fenimore, 131, 143n14

Cosas de España (Mackie), 107, 115n35

Cowley, William Ambrose, 113n19, 141, 213, 228n53, 237

Creole, The, 38, 152, 160, 225n3

Creole case, The, 39, 159

Curtis, George William, 2, 5–6, 60

Daily Times (New York), 3

Daily Tribune (New York), 3

Dampier, William, 213, 228n53, 237

Dana, Richard Henry, 122

Davis, Charles W., 162

Davis, David Brion, 149

Dealings with the Inquistion (Achilli), 114n26

DeBow's Review, 154, 156, 163–64

Democratic Review. See United States Magazine and Democratic Review

Dessalines, Jean Jacques, 148–49, 160

Dew, Thomas, 157

Dimock, Wai-Chee, 10, 12

Dispatch (New York), 3

Dix, J. A., 5

Dix and Edwards (publishers), 2, 5

Dominican order, 51, 73–74, 96, 104, 150, 196, 232

"Donelson" (Melville), 83

Douglass, Frederick, 37–38, 157, 161

Duban, James, 99

Edinburgh Review, 50

Edwards, Bryan, 149

Eliot, T. S., 6, 45

Elizabeth I, 213

Elkins, Stanley, 174

Ellison, Ralph, 67, 178

Emerson, Ralph Waldo, 37, 45, 65, 68, 131

Emery, Alan Moore, 12, 128

"Encantadas, The" (Melville), 6, 19, 22, 27–28, 63, 113n19, 115n35, 240; slavery in, 81; structure, 27

English in America (Ohmann), 5

Equiano, Olaudah, 180, 229n61

"Ethan Brand" (Hawthorne), 67

"Ethnogenesis" (Timrod), 162

Everett, Alexander, 222n5

Ezekiel, 54, 197

"Fall of the House of Usher, The" (Poe), 44

Faulkner, William, 67

Faust (Goethe), 46n4

Fawkes, Guy, 107

Feltenstein, Rosalie, 29–31, 34n5, 47n9

Ferdinand V of Castile, 94, 97n3, 213

Fiedler, Leslie, 7

Fillmore, Millard, 119

Fisher, Marvin, 11, 169–70

Fiske, John, 36n21

Fogle, Richard Harter, 8

Forgie, George B., 139

Franklin, Benjamin, 139

Franklin, H. Bruce, 13, 74, 94, 126n9

Fraser's Magazine, 50

Freeman, John, 4, 35n5, 64n2

Freemasonry, 114n27

Fugitive Slave Act of 1793, 118, 122, 210

Fugitive Slave Act of 1850, 118–19, 122–24, 211, 228n58, 236

Garnett, Henry Highland, 150, 160

Garrison, William Lloyd, 39, 174, 210, 215

Gedney, T. R., 200, 203, 205, 212

Genovese, Eugene, 148

George III, 56

"Gerontion" (Eliot), 45

Gide, André, 64n3

Gilman, William H., 207

Glicksberg, Charles I., 9–10, 37, 39, 47n9

Godey's Lady's Book and Magazine, 3

Goethe, Johann Wolfgang von, 46n4

Going Under (Fisher), 169

"Gold-Bug, The" (Poe), 59

Gray, Thomas, 151
Guillén, Nicolás, 89
Gunn, Giles, 6
Gunpowder Plot, 107
Guttmann, Allen, 15n25, 93n2, 126n5
Guzman, St. Domingo de, 104

Hamlet (Shakespeare), 73
Harper's New Monthly Magazine, 2, 113
Harris, Dennis J., 163
Hassal, Mary, 148–49
Hawkins, John, 38, 213
"Hawthorne and His Mosses" (Melville),
    169, 239
Hawthorne, Nathaniel, 3, 6, 37, 44,
    63n2, 169, 176, 178, 181n15;
    defense of slavery, 12, 235–36
Heimert, Alan, 99
"Herman Melville and the American
    National Sin" (Kaplan), 9–10,
    168–69
"Heroic Slave, The" (Douglass), 159
Herrera, Antonio de, 150
Higgins, Brian, 2–3
Higginson, Thomas Wentworth, 157–58,
    180
History of the Amistad Captives (Barber),
    223n12
History of the United States (Bancroft), 95,
    150
Holly, John T., 163
Horsley-Meacham, Gloria, 12
House of Seven Gables, The (Hawthorne),
    178, 181n15

"I and My Chimney" (Melville), 50; as a
    political tale, 99–100
Inquistion, The, 51, 73–74, 104–5,
    108–9, 137, 154–55, 158, 232
Invisible Man (Ellison), 178
Irving, Washington, 3, 95–96, 150
Isabella of Castile, 94, 97n3, 213
Israel Potter, 2, 115n35, 128, 138, 234

Jackson, Robert, 207, 225n35
James I, 56, 108
James, Henry, 64n3
Jameson, Fredric, 116, 124
Jefferson, Thomas, 152, 236
Jeronymite Fathers, 94–95, 97n3
Jocelyn, Nathaniel, 206
Jones, John Paul, 139

Journal of a Residence on A Georgia Plantation
    (Kemble), 181n10
Judson, Andrew J., 204, 211, 214

Kansas-Nebraska Act, 161, 235
"Kansas Question, The," 161
Kaplan, Sidney, 9–10, 124, 168–69, 170,
    172, 178–79, 183
Karcher, Carolyn L., 11–13, 126n9, 134,
    169–70, 172, 182, 238
Kavanaugh, James, 12
Kemble, Frances Anne, 175, 181n10
Knights of the Golden Circle, 163
Know-Nothing Party, 104, 114n27, 127
Kossuth, Louis, 163

"Lady or the Tiger, The?" (Stockton), 47
Langer, Suzanne K., 35n20
La Casas, Bartolomew de, 95–97, 97n6,
    98n12, 150, 231
Latimer case, The, 210–11, 225n33
Lawson, John Howard, 47n9
Leclerc, Charles Victor Emmanuel, 147
Ledyard, John, 144n29, 186
Leslie, Joshua, 13, 159
Liberator, 37, 210
Life and Voyages of Christopher Columbus, The
    (Irving), 95, 150
Lincoln, Abraham, 42, 162, 164
Louis Napoleon, 160
L'Ouverture, Toussaint, 56, 94, 147–49,
    154, 160, 196, 233
Lowell, James Russell, 66
Lucas case, The, 210–11

McDowell, James, 157
McElroy, John Harmon, 13, 183
Mackie, John Milton, 115n35
Madden, R. R., 204
Manifest Destiny, 100, 103, 108, 111–12,
    127, 153, 155, 162, 235–36, 245
Mankowitz, Wolf, 45
Mardi (Melville), 46, 50, 87, 100, 111,
    115n41, 170–71, 239; anticipates
    Civil War, 89; treatment of slavery,
    30, 86, 92, 113n22
Matlack, James, 11
Matthiessen, F. O., 6–8, 46, 47n8
Med case, The, 210–11
Melvill, Allan (father), 116–17, 207
Melville, Herman: admiration for "Young
    Goodman Brown," 73; anticipates
    Civil War, 89; attitude toward

slavery, 9–10, 24, 30, 33, 35n16,
46, 49, 65, 89, 91, 124, 168,
207–11, 213, 217, 219, 239; effect
of the death of his father, 116–17;
fascination with mutiny, 159; his
topicality, 99, 112; letters to
Hawthorne, 181n15; on success, 177;
opinion of rebellion, 31; relationship
with audience, 241; Timonism, 21;
views on American expansionism,
100, 102–3; 111; views on Spain,
113n25
Merk, Frederick, 146
Middleton family, 65–66
Miranda, Francisco, 153
Mission from Cape Coast Castle to Ashantee
(Bowdich), 187–89
Missouri Compromise, 118, 235
Moby-Dick (Melville), 2, 22, 32, 45, 47n5,
58, 99–100, 138, 177–78, 210;
color symbolism, 31–32, 43–44, 67;
Father Mapple's sermon, 211;
portrayal of Islamic-Christian strife,
96; style, 3, 62; treatment of black
characters, 10, 30, 44, 124; "The
Town Ho's Story," 41
Montez, Pedro, 200–01, 203–4
Morison, Samuel Eliot, 246n14
Mumford, Lewis, 4, 34n5, 42
My Bondage and My Freedom (Douglass),
157

Narrative of Arthur Gordon Pym (Poe), 45,
228n60
Narrative of Voyages and Travels (Delano), 4,
13, 21, 26, 29, 32, 37–38, 42, 50,
59, 66, 76, 113n19, 129, 136–41,
151, 155, 159, 186, 190–92,
200–01, 211–12, 219, 227n49
National Geographic, 243
"Nebraska Question, The" (Parker),
155–56, 161
Neider, Charles, 46
Nelson, Horatio, 208
Nevius, Henry Martin, 118
New Criticism, The, 5–6
New London Gazette, 200–02
Newton, John, 217–18, 229n61
Nietzsche, Friedrich, 67
Norton, Andrews, 65
Norton, Charles Eliot, 65–68

O'Brien, Edward J., 34n1
Oedipus, 198

Ohmann, Richard, 5
Omoo (Melville), 3, 22; similarity of Bembo
and Babo, 42
Ostend Manifesto, 162, 234
Othello (Shakespeare): similarity of Iago and
Babo, 42, 45, 46n3, 73, 124

"Paradise of Bachelors and The Tartarus of
Maids, The" (Melville), 6, 12, 26,
240–41
Park, Mungo, 144n29, 186, 198, 218–19,
222n4, 229n63
Parker, Theodore, 155–56, 161
Philip II, 54, 104
Philip IV, 54
Phillips, Ulrich B., 36n21
"Piazza, The" (Melville), 2, 239
Piazza Tales, The (Melville), 2–3, 26, 29,
38, 44, 170, 239; notices of, 19–20
Pierce, Franklin, 12, 160–61, 235–36
Pierre, 2, 6–7, 177, 239–40; attack on
American values and institutions, 128;
critical reception of, 2, 176–77; effect
of reviews on reception of "Benito
Cereno," 2–3
Plea for the West, The (Beecher), 155
Poe, Edgar Allan, 3, 6–7, 37, 44, 49, 59
Political Unconscious, The (Jameson), 116,
124
Pollard, Edward, 162
"Poor Man's Pudding and Rich Man's
Crumbs" (Melville), 240
Portsmouth Journal, 205
Potter, David, 161
Pound, Roscoe, 116
Prigg v. *The State of Pennsylvania*, 122
Prosser, Gabriel, 38, 155
Putnam's Monthly Magazine, 2–3, 21, 29,
44, 46n4, 60, 66, 100–01, 103,
107, 115n35, 161, 170, 213;
antislavery tone of, 154

Quinn, Arthur Hobson, 35n16, 169

Randolph, John, 171
Rattray, R. S., 192
Red Rover, The (Cooper), 131
Redburn (Melville), 177, 206, 210;
characterization of blacks, 30;
characterization of Jackson, 207;
echoes reports of the *Amistad* case,
208, 226n39; treatment of slavery,
207–09

Reising, Russell, 6
Religion and Art in Ashanti (Rattray), 192
"Resolution and Independence"
    (Wordsworth), 130
*Review of the Debate in the Virginia
    Legislature of 1831–32* (Dew), 157
Roberts v. The City of Boston, 123
Robertson-Lorant, Laurie, 226n39
Rogin, Michael Paul, 12, 99, 128, 132,
    157
Roman Catholic Church, 12, 35n20, 66,
    94, 104–5, 108–9, 150, 156, 158
Roosevelt, Franklin Delano, 132
Roscoe, William, 207–8, 217
Ruiz, Jose, 200–01, 203–4
Russell, William Howard, 171

Scarlet Letter, The (Hawthorne), 67
Schiffman, Joseph, 9–10, 37, 39, 45,
    47n9
Schouler, James, 36n21
Scudder, Harold H., 4, 13
Secret History; or, The Horrors of St. Domingo
    (Hassal), 148–49
Sedgwick, Ellery, 29–30
Shadow Over the Promised Land (Karcher),
    169
Shadrach, 118–19, 122
Shaw, Lemuel, 12, 116–20, 122–24, 177,
    210–11, 213–14; attitude toward
    slavery, 118, 210; decision in the
    Latimer case, 210–11, 225n33;
    decision in the *Lucas* case, 210;
    decision in the *Med* case, 210;
    decision in the *Roberts* case, 211;
    decision in the *Sims* case, 119, 211;
    influence on Melville, 117; stand on
    the Fugitive Slave Act, 123
Shelley, Percy Bysshe, 47n9, 177
Shulman, Robert, 6
Simms, William Gilmore, 37, 170; praise
    for *Mardi*, 170–71; response to *White-
    Jacket*, 171
Sims, Thomas, 118–19, 121–22
Sims case, The, 118–19, 121, 211
"Slave Ship" (Baraka), 137
Somers, U.S.S., 99
Soulouque, Faustin Élie, 154, 160, 163
Southern Literary Messenger, 3, 29
Stirling, James, 172, 179
Story, Joseph, 29, 121–22
Stowe, Harriet Beecher, 37, 65, 67, 124,
    152

Stuckey, Sterling, 13, 159
Styron, William, 67
Subversive Genealogy (Rogin), 128
Sumner, Charles, 39, 122, 150, 161
Sumner, William Graham, 244
Sundquist, Eric J., 12
"Supplement" to *Battle-Pieces* (Melville),
    86, 178
Supreme Judicial Court of Massachusetts,
    116, 210, 225n33
Swann, Charles, 12
Swedenborg, Emanuel, 45

Taine, Hippolyte, 30
Taylor, William R., 172
Thomas, Brook, 12
Thompson, Lawrence, 8
Thorp, Willard, 35n16
Times, The (London), 171
Timrod, Henry, 162
Tocqueville, Alexis de, 171
Transcendentalism, 131
Travels in the Interior Districts of Africa
    (Park), 198, 219, 222n4, 229n63
Trist, Nicholas, 214
Truth, Sojourner, 37
Turner, Nat, 38, 42, 134, 147, 149, 156,
    159–60, 212, 215
Twain, Mark. *See* Clemens, Samuel L.
"Two Temples, The" (Melville), 177
Tyler, John, 203
Typee (Melville), 3, 22, 88, 239; treatment
    of black characters, 10

Uncle Tom's Cabin (Stowe), 33, 169
*United States Magazine and Democratic
    Review*, 29, 160
United States Supreme Court, 39, 121,
    160, 204, 206

Van Buren, Martin, 160
Vanderbilt, Kermit, 11
Van Doren, Carl, 35n5
Van Vechten, Carl, 34n5
Vesey, Denmark, 38, 46n2, 156
Vietnam War, 11, 244

Walker, William, 162–63
War in Nicaragua, The (Walker), 162
Warren, Robert Penn, 67
Washington, George, 148, 176

Washington, Madison, 39, 159, 225n33
Webster, Daniel, 39, 118–19, 152, 159–60
White Slavery in the Barbary States (C. Sumner), 150
White-Jacket (Melville), 10, 45–46, 50, 77, 88, 115n41, 171, 177, 179; mutiny in, 159
Wieland (Brown), 149
Williams, Stanley T., 29–30, 32
Winters, Yvor, 35n9, 64n2, 87

Wish, Harvey, 38
Wordsworth, William, 130

Ximenes de Cisneros, Francisco, 95, 97n3

Yellin, Jean Fagin, 11, 151
Young America movement, 127
"Young Goodman Brown" (Hawthorne), 73

Zagarell, Sandra A., 12